Communication in Face to Face Interaction

Selected Readings

Edited by John Laver and Sandy Hutcheson

Penguin Books

Penguin Books Ltd, Harmondsworth,
Middlesex, England
Penguin Books Inc, 7110 Ambassador Road,
Baltimore, Md 21207, USA
Penguin Books Australia Ltd,
Ringwood, Victoria, Australia

First published 1972
This selection copyright © John Laver and Sandy Hutcheson, 1972
Introduction and notes copyright © John Laver and Sandy Hutcheson, 1972
Copyright acknowledgement for items in this volume
will be found on page 407

Made and printed in Great Britain by
Hazell Watson & Viney Ltd,
Aylesbury, Bucks
Set in Monotype Times

Contents

Preface

This book is a collection of articles about how people communicate with each other in face-to-face interaction. We have tried to choose Readings which are sufficiently self-contained and non-technical to appeal to interested non-specialists, and which are yet detailed enough to give students and specialists a comprehensive basis for further work in the subject.

The Readings are all as they originally appeared, with the exception that we have made minor editorial adjustments where necessary for consistency, especially to footnotes, and have standardized the bibliographical references. Where journal titles have been abbreviated, we have followed the conventions of the fourth edition of the *World List of Scientific Periodicals 1900–1960*, and of the *Linguistic Bibliography* of the Permanent International Committee of Linguists (Spectrum; Utrecht and Antwerp).

We would like to express our gratitude for advice and comment on the book to David Abercrombie, David Crystal and John Lyons; for bibliographical research to Halina Rentoul; and for typing parts of the manuscript to Jeanie Yamane and Valerie Chuter.

Introduction

Conversational interaction is remarkably skilled social behaviour, and we have all spent all our lives learning the appropriate skills. Speech occupies a preeminent place amongst these, but it is far from being the only behavioural skill involved. As the editors of this book, we follow Abercrombie (pp. 64–70 in this book) in thinking of conversation as relying on *all* channels of communication through which information is exchanged by individuals during face-to-face interactions. As Abercrombie puts it 'We speak with our vocal organs, but we converse with our entire bodies; conversation consists of much more than a simple interchange of spoken words'. Other strands of communication interwoven with speech to form the fabric of conversation thus include such factors as facial expressions; eye-contacts, gestures and posture; and body orientation, proximity and physical contacts. We view conversation, then, as the total system of communication employed by participants in face-to-face interaction.

Defined in as broad a sense as this, conversation is a topic of interest to many different disciplines in the social sciences. In bringing together a number of articles from the fields of linguistics, anthropology, sociology, psychology and psychiatry, our aim has been to reflect this multidisciplinary interest and to show that their different viewpoints can offer valuable insights into the variety of intricate behavioural codes used in conversation.

The book addresses itself to two basic questions. Firstly, what sort of information is exchanged between participants in a conversation? And secondly, what are the behavioural means for achieving this exchange? All the Readings chosen suggest some answers to these two questions.

If we look first at the *information* exchanged between the participants, it is useful to distinguish between at least three different kinds. The first is what is sometimes referred to as *cognitive information*; this is the propositional or purely factual content of the linguistic signals exchanged. There is a large body of linguistic literature which deals with the semantic structure of language (Ullmann, 1957, 1962; Lyons, 1968), and it is not part of the objective of this book to explore this area of conversation in any detail.

The second kind of information is what has been called *indexical information* (Abercrombie, 1967, p. 6). This is information about the speaker himself. The listener uses it to draw inferences about the speaker's identity, attributes, attitudes and mood. It thus includes any behavioural information which serves as evidence for a speaker's biological, psychological or social characteristics. Most of the Readings are implicitly concerned with the communication of indexical information. A tacit theme running through the book is that a participant uses *all* the communicative strands of conversation for a variety of indexical purposes. He uses them not only to announce his individual identity and personal characteristics, but also to state his view of the social and psychological structuring of the interaction. In brief, a participant projects indexical information in order to define and control the role he plays during the conversation.

Thirdly, there is the information that the participants exchange in order to collaborate with each other in organizing the temporal progress of the interaction. This kind of information might be called *interaction–management information*. It allows the participants to initiate and terminate the interaction in a conventional, mutually acceptable way; it also allows them to indicate the transitions within the interaction from one stage to another. Finally, it enables the participants to control the time-sharing of the interaction, in terms of who should occupy the role of speaker, and when he should yield it to the other participant. Thus conversational interaction involves the exchange of cognitive, indexical and interaction–management information.

The behavioural *means* for communicating this information can be broadly classified within two descriptive divisions: *vocal* versus *non-vocal* behaviour, and *verbal* versus *non-verbal* behaviour.

Vocal behaviour consists of all the actions involved in producing speech. Non-vocal behaviour is made up of all communicative activities other than speech, and therefore includes such factors as gesture, posture and so forth. The terms 'verbal' and 'non-verbal' have had, and continue to be given, many different meanings. However, in this introduction, verbal elements in conversation are taken to mean the actual words used (considered as units in language, and distinct from all vocal considerations of how they might be pronounced). Non-verbal behaviour is then all vocal and non-vocal conversational behaviour which is not verbal in the sense given above. To exemplify the classification of behavioural features using this four-way division, vocal verbal features are spoken words as linguistic units; vocal non-verbal features include intonation, spoken emphasis and voice quality; non-vocal verbal features (not considered in this book) would be written or printed words as linguistic units; and non-vocal non-verbal features would consist, for example, of elements such as facial expression, gesture and posture.

Together with the four-way classification outlined above, the means by which participants exchange information in conversation can also be divided into *linguistic*, *paralinguistic* and *extralinguistic* features.

The question of which communicative features are linguistic is relatively uncontroversial: it is much more difficult to find widespread agreement about the nature of paralinguistic features, and this conceptual disagreement (characteristic of any subject as young as 'paralinguistics') is reflected in the articles concerned with 'paralanguage' in this book. We personally favour a view that paralinguistic features are comprised of all those non-linguistic, non-verbal features (both vocal and non-vocal), which participants manipulate in conversation. The interpretation of such paralinguistic features, like that of linguistic features, is subject to conventions which are shared with other members of one's culture. In this view, vocal paralinguistic features would include all activities which are usually loosely referred to as contributing to 'tone of voice'. Non-vocal paralinguistic features would consist of such communicative actions as gestures, body-orientations, postures, facial expressions, eye-contacts, manipulations of proximity and physical contacts.

The major part of the book deals in one way or another with the role of linguistic and paralinguistic features in conversational interaction, mostly in terms of the communication of indexical information. Extralinguistic features also communicate indexical information, but, unlike linguistic and paralinguistic features, they are not subject to manipulation by the speaker within the course of a single interaction. They are by definition non-verbal, non-linguistic and non-paralinguistic, but they can be either vocal or non-vocal. One vocal extralinguistic feature would be voice quality, the personal vocal background to an individual speaker's speech-articulations. Voice quality as such is not voluntarily manipulable during an interaction, but it does signal a good deal of indexical information to the listener about biological, psychological and social characteristics of the speaker (see Laver, pp. 189–203 in this book). An example of a non-vocal extralinguistic feature which also conveys indexical information would be a participant's style of dress.

Having drawn a distinction between the information exchanged in conversation and the means for effecting that exchange, it is now possible to offer suggestions about which of the different types of communicative behaviour, in terms of linguistic, paralinguistic and extralinguistic features, serve to convey the cognitive, indexical and interaction–management information.

Cognitive information is conveyed chiefly by linguistic means. Occasionally, paralinguistic means are used; those gestures which are substitutable for verbal elements could be said to have semantic correlates equivalent to the verbal elements they replace.

Interaction–management is achieved mostly by paralinguistic and partly by linguistic means. Signals for yielding the role of speaker to the other participant are given by eye-contact behaviour, particular intonation patterns and body movements, for instance. Transitions from the main business phase of an interaction to the terminal, parting phase (Argyle and Kendon, p. 19 in this book) are indicated by the use of certain ritual phrases of farewell, and other linguistic indications of cordiality and solidarity, together with characteristic visual, postural and facial behaviour.

Indexical information of different sorts is transmitted by all the features – linguistic, paralinguistic and extralinguistic. In speech, biological details are conveyed by the extralinguistic features; psychological and social information is inferred from the linguistic and paralinguistic features. Evidence from the three types of features allows the listener to construct a profile of the speaker's characteristics in terms of his membership of particular social groups, his individual identity within such groups, and his psychological and physical state at any given moment (cf. Abercrombie, 1967, p. 7; Laver, pp. 189–203 in this book).

The intricate nature of conversational skills is particularly apparent when one considers not only that there is a continual interchange of several different kinds of information, but also that this information is communicated by means of the simultaneous manipulation of many behavioural features. Since these skills have had to be learned, it is hardly surprising that some people are less expert than others at controlling them. For conversational interaction to be harmonious, the two participants have to be able to mesh their performances together to their mutual satisfaction; if one participant is less skilled than the other at transmitting or interpreting the signals of a particular behavioural code, then awkwardness, misunderstanding and even offence may ensue. When the interactants do not share the same codes, but operate instead with radically different ones, then the situation can cause even more difficulty; the most striking instance of such a discrepancy occurs when they are members of different cultures. Individuals are normally expert at interaction only within the context of their own culture, because the conventions which guide and constrain their behaviour are not 'natural' and absolute, but arbitrary and culturally relative (La Barre, pp. 207–24 in this book). Few individuals ever acquire a completely native-like understanding and control of the whole range of the behavioural conventions of face-to-face interaction in another culture. Consequently, communication between members of different cultures is usually less than perfect.

Incongruous conversational behaviour can thus lead to embarrassment and distress: nevertheless, it remains true that much of the reward we experience in our social relations derives directly from our expertise in the complex skills of conversation. The Readings reprinted in this volume each attempt to illuminate some facets of this expertise.

References

ABERCROMBIE, D. (1967), *Elements of General Phonetics*,
  Edinburgh University Press.
LYONS, J. (1968), *Introduction to Theoretical Linguistics*,
  Cambridge University Press.
ULLMAN, S. (1957), *The Principles of Semantics*, Blackwell.
ULLMAN, S. (1962), *Semantics*, Blackwell.

Part One
The Analysis of Conversational Interaction

The four Readings in this first section each offer a general theoretical framework within which the analysis of conversation as a multi-stranded system of communication can be conducted.

Argyle and Kendon (1) report on a wide range of literature in experimental and social psychology, and in sociology. They propose an analysis of the patterns of activity in interactions, identifying the various components that participants exploit, and emphasize the skilled nature of this behaviour. In commenting on the indexical function that interaction has of allowing the individual to project a particular image, they show how aspects of certain mental illnesses can be seen as 'breakdowns in social skill'.

Sapir (3), as an anthropologist and linguist, has been particularly influential in the development of research into paralinguistic features. In this Reading, he discusses various extralinguistic, paralinguistic and linguistic sources of indexical conclusions about personality which can be drawn from vocal behaviour.

A constant theme in Sapir's article is the need to contrast a speaker's behaviour with the social norms from which it varies, before one can either assess the communicative force of his actions, or see him as an individual against the background of his social group.

Birdwhistell (4) traces the progress of paralinguistic study from Sapir to the work in the 1950s of Trager and his colleagues (itself rather too technical to be included in this book), and then extends the approach of Sapir and Trager to his own outline of *kinesic* analysis of bodily movements.

For Birdwhistell, as an anthropologist, the study of paralinguistic features is an example of 'micro-culture analysis', which he sees as a valuable preliminary to general cross-cultural analysis.

Abercrombie (2), as a linguist, looks at paralinguistic features in terms of their relation to language. He states that 'Paralinguistic phenomena are non-linguistic elements in conversation. They occur alongside spoken language, interact with it, and produce together with it a total system of communication.' He also maintains that 'the conversational use of spoken language cannot be properly understood unless paralinguistic elements are taken into account'.

His Reading concludes with the statement of a hypothesis which has profound implications for the study of universal factors in human communication. Abercrombie suggests that 'in all cultures, conversation communicates more or less the same total of "meaning" of all kinds, . . . referential and emotive. . . . Where cultural groups differ, however, is in the way the total information is distributed over the linguistic and paralinguistic elements of the conversation.'

1 M. Argyle and A. Kendon

The Experimental Analysis of Social Performance

M. Argyle and A. Kendon, 'The experimental analysis of social performance', in
L. Berkowitz (ed.), *Advances in Experimental Social Psychology*, Academic Press
1967, pp. 55–98.

Introduction

This article deals with what people do when they openly cooperate in one
another's presence to sustain some joint form of activity. Such occasions,
termed by Goffman (1963) *focused interaction*, are exemplified by card
games, musical performances, fist fights, cooperative tasks such as sawing
down a large tree, dancing, and by conversation, interviews, lectures, and
other social occasions when people talk together. Occasions of talk have,
of course, been the main concern of those interested in this field, and are
our main concern also.

We shall here suggest that it is fruitful to look upon the behavior of
people engaged in focused interaction as an organized, skilled performance, analogous to skills such as car driving. First, an outline will be presented of the model that has been developed in the last fifteen years for the
analysis of sensorimotor skills, but with specific reference to the interaction situation. Studies of the patterns of activity involved in interaction
will then be reviewed; here we shall consider all aspects of a person's
behavior that have been found to affect the other in interaction, including
physical proximity, posture, orientation, language and speech, patterns of
looking at the other, bodily movements and facial expression. Where
possible, we shall indicate the way these different aspects of behavior are
interrelated. The final section will be concerned with the presentation of the
self-image, the breakdown of the social performance, and the question of
training in specific social skills.

Theoretical framework
The sensorimotor skill model and interaction

A skill may be defined as an organized, coordinated activity, in relation to
an object or a situation, that involves a chain of sensory, central and motor
mechanisms. One of its main characteristics is that the performance, or
stream of action, is continuously under the control of the sensory input.
This input derives in part from the object or situation at which the performance may be said to be directed, and it controls the performance in the

sense that the outcomes of actions are continuously matched against some criterion of achievement or degree of approach to a goal, according to which the performance is corrected. Thus skilled performance is performance that is nicely adapted to its occasion (Bartlett, 1958; Welford, 1958).

We suggest that an individual engaged in interaction is engaged in a more or less skilled performance. His behavior here, as when he is driving a car, is directed, adaptive, and far from automatic, though it may be seen to be built of elements that are automatized. Here, too, we have an individual carrying out a series of actions that are related to consequences that he has in mind to bring about; in order to do this, he has to match his output with the input available to him and must correct his output in the light of this matching process. Thus he may be discussing current affairs with an acquaintance, and be concerned perhaps merely to sustain a pleasant flow of talk. He must be on the watch, then, for signs of emotional disturbance in his acquaintance, which might signal that he had said something that might provoke an argument. At another level, he must be on the lookout for signals that his acquaintance is ready for him to talk or for him to listen. He must make sure his tone of voice and choice of words, his gestures, and the level of involvement in what he is saying, are appropriate for the kind of occasion of the encounter (cf. Goffman, 1957).

In the treatment of human performance as developed by such workers as Welford (1958) and Crossman (1964) distinctions are drawn between the perceptual input, the central translation processes by which this input is integrated into a plan of action that is governed by the goal the individual has set for himself, and the motor output, or performance. These three stages of the process are interrelated as shown in Figure 1.

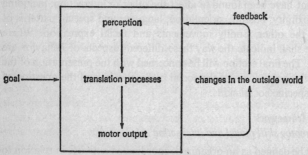

Figure 1 The sensorimotor skill model

Perception. Students of perceptual processes in human performance have stressed its selective nature, and that the aspects of the input that are selected are determined by the aim of the performer (Welford, 1958;

Broadbent, 1958). It is, indeed, a mark of a highly skilled performer that he has learned what input he can ignore (Annett and Kay, 1956). Similar considerations probably apply in social interaction. Thus, as Jones and Thibaut (1958) suggested, an interactor's main requirement is for information relative to the adequate maintenance of a particular performance. They suggested that the type of cues an individual will be on the lookout for in interaction and the use he makes of these cues will vary according to his aim in the situation. A few studies that lend support to this idea have been reported: Lundy (1956) showed that a subject's conception of the person with whom he has interacted differs according to whether the subject was attending mostly to the other person or to himself; Rosenbaum (1959) demonstrated that the perception of others varies according to whether the interaction with them is cooperative or competitive; and Steiner (1955) has reviewed a number of studies which show that effectiveness in social performance is related to the accurate perception of relevant features of the situation rather than to the accuracy of perception of others in general. There is room for much more work here, however, especially on the information selected and made use of within the ongoing activity of interaction.

Translation processes. When the input has been selected and interpreted, it must be put to use. Welford (1958) distinguished as *translation processes* the way in which items perceived are acted upon; *translation* is the term used to refer to the rule by which a particular signal is interpreted as requiring particular action. A great deal of what occurs while a skill is built up consists in the development of translations which, once established, are 'ready to hand', so that action taken in regard to incoming signals is usually immediate. Where a new translation has to be set up, a great deal of hesitancy and halting can be observed in the subject's performance.

Little in current studies on the social performance is concerned with the acquisition and development of translations. Yet it is clear that anyone who can interact competently must have a large repertoire of translations with which he deals with input that distinguishes one kind of encounter from another and that enables him to adapt his style of handling another person as an encounter progresses. There are also the whole set of translations that are involved in processing language and other communicative systems. A great deal of training in specific social skills consists of training people to deal with particular kinds of persons or interaction situations. Much that is involved in the acquisition of these skills consists in building up new translations or in developing already existing ones.

Effector processes. Effector processes are the actions the person takes, or the performance itself. Welford (1958) noted that the effector processes are to be seen as organized on a number of levels, hierarchically arranged. He suggested that it is useful to distinguish a general orientation, or plan, which determines in broad outline what is to be done. This plan may be seen as composed of a number of general methods, or subplans, that are in turn composed of 'particular knacks and dexterities which in turn bring into play detailed muscular movements' (Welford, 1958, p. 26). Thus, we may describe an activity, such as typing, at the level of general orientation, which will include how the typist will sit before her typewriter and sustain a particular posture. At the level of general methods, we divide the task as a whole into several subtasks, such as changing the sheets of paper and typing. The activity of typing may itself be further subdivided into producing a line of words and moving the carriage back at the end of each line. At the level of knacks and dexterities, we describe how the finger movements are grouped into complex units by which the phrases, words and letter combinations within the words are put onto the paper.

The social performance can probably be analysed in a similar way. Thus we distinguish at the level of *general orientation* how individuals may adopt a distinctive pattern of activities appropriate for, say, an interview, a cocktail party, or a stroll on the beach with a friend. At the level of *general method*, or subplans, we note that, for instance, an interview may have several phases: an opening 'greeting' phase; a phase in which rapport is established; one in which the main business of the interview may be accomplished; and a terminating phase. At the level of *knacks and dexterities*, we deal with such things as sequencing of acts of communication. Below this level, we must analyse the actual muscular movements – the motor structure of utterance and movement patterns, for instance. In the third part of this article (p. 44) an attempt will be made to suggest how some studies of patterns of activity in interaction might be fitted into a scheme of this sort.

In considering a performance in this way, we note how it may be said to be made up of a combination of elements, though what we refer to as an element will depend on the level in the hierarchy we are discussing. Elements may often be recombined in a fairly flexible way, and this makes a skill very adaptive. On the other hand, once a particular combination of elements achieves, for the performer, an acceptable level of success, and provided the sequence of sensory input is stable when the skill is used on subsequent occasions, it is found that many sequences of actions in the performance become 'automatized', that is, freed from continuous sensory control. Though we shall not give it much consideration here, it seems likely that a similar phenomenon of automatization occurs with social skills. Lecturers and interviewers, for instance, who use a fairly standard social technique on repeated occasions, may be able to run off long sequences of actions automatically. Museum guides offer a notorious example of automatization that has gone too far. Lecturers have occasionally reported on this process in themselves. Thus Lashley (1951) mentioned a colleague who reported to him that 'he had reached a stage where he could arise before an audience, turn his mouth loose, and go to sleep' (p. 184).

The interrelating of performances

In any consideration of the social performance we cannot ignore the fact that it takes place within an encounter, and is thus interrelated with the performance of another individual who can take initiatives of his own and is not, like the machine, entirely dependent on the operator. Indeed, the existence of an encounter presupposes that the participants can interrelate their performances. They must do this in several ways at once. They must be able to agree as to what the encounter is about, who is dominant, who submissive; they must agree upon the level of intimacy; and there must be coordination in terms of emotionality and the patterning of actions in time. All these are aspects of what Goffman (1959) called the *working consensus* of an encounter. The following are some of the conditions that bring it about.

In some encounters, where the form is highly structured and the participants all know their 'parts' in advance, the working consensus is, as it were, ready-made. This is often the case in the early stages of many encounters where stereotyped patterns of interaction are adopted. If, however, there is no ready-made formula to provide the working consensus, the participants have to work out some accommodation between themselves. Usually they proceed by edging rather cautiously forward from stereotyped patterns of response, trying out different social techniques to see how the other responds.

An important factor that sets limits upon people's ability to work out such an accommodation is the character of the individual's style of handling encounters. This factor has been investigated at several different levels. Chapple, for example, whose work is discussed later, showed how individuals differ in their styles of interaction, assessed in terms of the patterning of actions in time. For many years he has stressed that successful, stabilized relations between people will depend on their ability to bring their action patterns into an appropriate relation with one another (Chapple, 1940a; 1940b; 1962; Chapple and Coon, 1942). At other levels of description, there are studies such as those summarized by Tharp (1963), which stress the importance of compatibility of role expectation for marital relations. Related to this is the notion of 'interpersonal orientation' as

M. Argyle and A. Kendon 23

developed by Schutz (1958). No studies have been made of the behavioral styles or social performance strategies manifested by people with different interpersonal orientations, but Schutz (1955) was able to show that groups vary, in their productiveness and in the degree of satisfaction they afford members, in relation to the kinds of interpersonal orientation the group members have as determined from his FIRO questionnaire, which assesses desires for affection, inclusion and control on the part of self and others.

Breer (1960) showed that by combining measures of the personality and social characteristics of individuals in a group, a better prediction could be made of a given individual's dominance in subsequent interaction than if these characteristics of the individual were taken on their own. Carment, Miles and Cervin (1965) similarly were able to predict who in a dyad would speak more, and dominate, from a consideration of the relative extraversion and intelligence of the interactants. Studies of friendship pairs or groupings in relation to the characteristics of the individuals involved are also relevant here. Work such as that of Jennings (1950) and Northway and Wigdor (1947) has emphasized importance of compatibility in interaction; studies such as those of Triandis (1960) illustrated the limiting effect of differences in cognitive style; and Newcomb's (1961) work illustrated the importance of compatibility of values. This area has been fully reviewed by Lott and Lott (1965).

The characteristics of interaction in pairs or groups of people who have stable relationships have been described by several workers, and some studies have traced the way the patterns of interaction change with time toward a stable state (for example, Heinicke and Bales, 1953; Lennard and Bernstein, 1960). This stable state has been described by some investigators as an equilibrium. Chapple and Coon (1942) made explicit use of the idea that the pattern of interaction in a group was a stable equilibrium in the sense that anything tending to change the pattern would produce compensating changes. This idea has been taken up by Homans (1950), Simon (1952), and in a rather different form by Bales (1953). An equilibrium model has also been used by Goffman (1955). Explicit evidence for the appropriateness of this notion is, however, rather scant; Lennard and Bernstein (1960), in their longitudinal study of psychotherapeutic dyads, provided the most relevant data. They found that after two months of daily sessions the proportion of time occupied in speech by the therapist had become highly stable, not deviating by more than 6·5 per cent from his average. But in comparing one session with the next it was found that if the therapist had spoken rather less than usual on one occasion, he would make up for it by talking more on the next.

An attempt at a detailed theoretical analysis of this problem was put forward by Thibaut and Kelley (1959) in terms of games theory. They posited that each interactor, A and B, has a repertoire of alternative social responses. For each combination of responses there will be rewards or costs for each interactor. A stable relationship will be formed if each gains rewards that are better than those obtainable in alternative situations or relationships that are available to him. At initial meetings the interactor will explore the situation to see if this is likely to be the case. It is generally supposed that people will select styles of behavior that offer the maximum rewards, or the minimum costs, or some combination of these.

It should be noted that during unstable periods of interaction there can be the very reverse of equilibrium, that is positive feedback cycles. If A is very nice to B, this elicits similar behavior from B, and so on. Such increasing intimacy develops until it is halted by anxiety about excessive intimacy, increased difficulties of meshing, and other demands on time: the result is an equilibrium point. Such an equilibrium point can also be looked at as the result of a balance between approach and avoidance forces, as described by Miller (1944). This idea has been explicitly developed in a study of the role of distance and eye-contact in interaction by Argyle and Dean (1965).

Structure of the social performance

In this section we shall review a selection of studies dealing with the analysis of patterns of activity in focused encounters. That is, we shall concentrate on the performance itself. Some attempt will be made to follow the descriptive model proposed by Welford (1958). Thus certain components of the performance can be distinguished, such as posture, distance and orientation, which change little throughout a given encounter; these can perhaps be seen as functioning at the level of general orientation. They are called the *standing features* of the performance. There are, on the other hand, *dynamic features* – the utterances, movements and patterns of looking that each participant in any focused interaction is likely to engage in. The latter activities may be ordered into a hierarchical set of units, much as was indicated earlier for typing. Where possible we shall show how this might be done.

Standing features

In focused interaction participants tend to group themselves into huddles in which they make each other available to mutual visual inspection (Goffman, 1963). This positioning in space and orientation appears to be a distinctive behavioral mark of focused interaction, setting it off from other kinds of activity. Focused interactions themselves are varied in type, however, and within a given culture or subculture only a certain range of types will be found. For instance, dons at Oxford many encounter students in about five ways – at a tutorial, seminar, lecture, private consultation or sherry. The rules of behavior differ in each of these occasions, and one way to classify them might be in terms of the different sets of rules prevailing. One dimension of a rule classification is that of formality, for example, the amount of variation of behavior permitted – compare taking Communion with a party. An example of an attempt at encounter classification from this point of view may be found in Barker and Wright (1955).

Encounters can also be classified by the motivation of those taking part. Thus we can show how people seek different sorts of satisfaction in social interaction, and that encounters may differ in type according to the satisfactions they may more readily or typically give rise to. Besides this, in encounters such as psychotherapy sessions or tutorials, the therapist or tutor may be aiming at a particular goal that is defined by his job. Watson and Potter (1962) and Jones and Thibaut (1958), in rather different ways, provided examples of classifications from this functional point of view. In each case the motivation can be looked at as a need for certain types of response on the part of others or for the establishment of certain kinds of relationship.

Such differences are partly marked by their settings and by the type of equipment present and how it is used. However, there are also differences in postures, spacings and orientations, and in styles of behavior that vary systematically with the type of interaction and that may also indicate the type of encounter each participant takes it to be. This section presents some of the static features of the performance, which appear to function in this way.

The static aspects of the social performance have been systematically treated by Hall (1963). He distinguished seven such components: posture, orientation, the physical distance between interactants, the presence or absence of physical contact, the form physical contact takes, whether (and if so, how) the interactants are looking at one another, and whether thermal and olfactory sensory channels could be operative in the encounter. He pointed out how each of these components may form different combinations, and that different participants may employ different combinations so that the system may be highly flexible. More recently Hall (1964) attempted to show how these components may be coordinated into a system to define four different 'distance sets', which he termed (following Joos, 1962) *Intimate*, *Casual-Personal*, *Social-Consultative* and *Public*, after the type of interaction with which each is associated. Each of these distance sets is distinguishable from the others partly, at least, in terms of the different sets of senses that can operate. For example, at the Intimate distance, physical contact, olfaction, and the thermal senses all play a part, but vision plays a rather minor role. Compared with this, at the limit of the

Casual-Personal distance, where interactants are about five feet apart, only vision and hearing are employed.

From this analysis of what the senses are capable of at different distances, we would expect, as Hall suggested, systematic differences in their use, and this would have consequences for the type of interaction that is possible. Variations in posture and orientation at different distances might also be expected. A number of interesting questions are generated by this framework, but few have been investigated yet. For instance, how invariable are the interrelations Hall has described? If there are variations, what are their consequences? Some studies dealing with some of these components follow.

Distance. Sommer (1959) pioneered in the experimental study of the use of distance in interaction; he found that for conversation subjects tend to choose a nose-to-nose distance of roughly five feet. Little (1965) approached this question perceptually. His subjects positioned either cardboard cutout silhouettes or actual people for different types of interaction in different settings. He found that Americans tend to think of friends as standing closer to one another than acquaintances or strangers, and he also found that distances tend to be less when the setting was impersonal, such as a public street, than when it was an intimate setting, such as a living room. Congruent with this, Sommer (1965) noted that chairs are placed at much greater distances in living rooms than they are when people gather together in a larger room. Presumably, merely to be present in a living room is to be in a social gathering, so proximity is not necessary to indicate that such is the case; in a public street, however, it is only through spatial positioning that people can signal, to each other and to others, the boundaries of a gathering.

Argyle and Dean (1965) investigated how visual orientation may vary with the distance separating interactors; they found that when subjects were placed only two feet from one another, they looked into the other's line of regard very much less than they did when they were six to ten feet apart. They proposed, as does Hall, that both closer distances and increased amounts of looking at the other mark higher degrees of intimacy. Here the level of intimacy between the subjects was constant and the changes in amount of looking were seen as compensating for the changes in distance.

As will be noted later, changes of distance during an encounter have definite significance and may function to signal changes in the relationship. The movements of A when he enters B's office vary considerably with the intimacy and relative status of the two people; observers of silent films of such an occurrence had no difficulty in deducing the relations between them (Burns, 1964).

It should be borne in mind that all these studies were carried out in Anglo-American cultures. As Hall (1959, 1963) has emphasized, physical distance, as well as the other components to be dealt with, is used in rather different ways in other cultures.

Distance is also of significance among animals. Thus, in several primate species, social relationships may be indicated by distance; for instance, the position of the male langur in the dominance hierarchy in his group is reflected in the distance others in the group sit from him (Jay, 1965). Hediger (1955) showed that animals adopt distances between one another that are characteristic of their species; they also seek to maintain a certain population density, and instinctive biological mechanisms have evolved for doing this (Wynne-Edwards, 1962). Hutt and Vaizey (1966) found a similar process operating in children in an experiment in which they varied the density of children in a playroom. Whereas normal and brain-damaged children became more aggressive as the density increased, this was not the case with autistic children.

Orientation. Besides the distances interactors place between one another, the manner of their orientation to one another may also be important. Hall (1963) classified orientation by angle, ranging from face-to-face to back-to-back, and noted that positions from face-to-face to side-to-side are used for various kinds of interaction. Spiegel (summarized in Machotka, 1965) proposed a similar scheme. Sommer (1959) found that people who are sitting at a table for conversation frequently sit diagonally across the corner from one another rather than directly opposite or side by side. In another study Sommer (1965) found that different seating patterns are adopted by pairs of people according to the type of interaction they are engaged in. Where this interaction is unfocused, as when two students are studying together at the same table, a distance seating pattern is chosen: the interactors sit so that they are distant but not facing one another. Where the pair is cooperating on some task, such as going through a problem together, they choose the 'corner' arrangement or they sit side by side (though this is much rarer). In competitive dyads Sommer found an overwhelming tendency for the people to sit directly opposite one another. To account for these findings he suggested that a major determinant of seating pattern is the way in which it facilitates or inhibits visual contact between people.

In groups larger than two there is some evidence that people tend to position themselves opposite those in the group with whom they talk most; where the seating arrangements limit the freedom of movement of the group members, this determines to some extent the communication structure of the group. Thus Steinzor (1950) observed that in a discussion group of ten, most interaction took place between those who were sitting opposite each other, and not between neighbors; similar observations were reported by Bass and Klubeck (1952). Hare and Bales (1963) found that where a group of five is arranged around three sides of a long rectangular table, those occupying the two end positions and the person in the middle of the long side interacted with each other more than they did with those at the corners of the table.

Where there are differences in role or status between the group members, this is often expressed in the pattern of positions the members take up in space. A chairman or a lecturer usually faces as many of the others as he can (Sommer, 1961). Furniture is arranged accordingly; Hazard (1962) noted, for instance, how the arrangement of furniture in a courtroom reflects the role relationships of the various functionaries. Blood and Livant (1957) observed how, within a cabin at a boys' summer camp, the beds were arranged in a way that was related to who was friends with whom, and also to who was trying to protect himself from whom.

Posture. Hall (1963) distinguished three types of posture: standing, sitting and lying; but there are clearly many more possibilities. Scheflen (1964), for instance, drew attention to the way participants in focused gatherings may vary the way in which they are sitting or standing to be congruent with or noncongruent with others present – for example, by having their legs crossed or arms folded. Goffman (1961a) noted how, at the staff meetings of a psychiatric hospital, those with high status, such as the psychiatrists, would sit in relaxed postures putting their feet on the table, whereas those junior to them would assume more formal ways of sitting. Few other authors have reported on this topic. Hewes (1955) examined the variety of typical postures in different societies, but his work has only marginal relevance to social interaction. Sarbin and Hardyck (1955) asked subjects to make judgements of stick figure drawings in various postures; they found considerable consistency in judgement, and suggested that this be used as a test of social perceptiveness. The work of Machotka and Spiegel (Machotka, 1965), in which drawings of groups of people in various positions were judged by subjects, showed that posture and orientation are compelling indicators of social relationships. It is clear that posture is an important feature of the social performance, but a great deal more needs to be done before we can say much about how it functions.

Physical contact. Physical contact is a static component where, for instance, walking arm-in-arm or holding hands occurs. This kind of physical contact usually signals extreme intimacy. Mention may also be made of the way physical contact may play its part, in a more momentary fashion, in the communicative system. Thus, shaking hands, kissing, steering by the elbow and patting on the back all have particular significance and a particular place within the interaction sequence. Physical contact as a communicative system has received systematic treatment by Frank (1957). Jourard (1966) also reported a study in which he asked subjects to report where they had been touched and by whom. He found students were touched most by their mothers and by friends of the opposite sex; for many of them, their fathers touched no more than their hands. This study illustrated how amount and type of physical contact may be one of the defining features of a relationship. Physical contact is far more widely used in some cultures than in others. Mediterranean peoples, for instance, use touch considerably, whereas it is used relatively little in north-west Europe and the United States.

Besides the components we have discussed, Hall (1963, 1964) distinguished amount and type of visual contact, loudness of voice, and linguistic style. We shall deal with these components as part of the set of dynamic features of the performance. So far as thermal and olfactory sensory channels are concerned, Hall (1963) gives a few examples of their use, but no systematic studies of them have been reported.

Dynamic features

Posture, orientation and distance may be said to form the backdrop for a particular flow of events, just as sitting in a particular posture at the typewriter may be said to form a backdrop to the actions in typing. We have suggested that these static aspects of the performance function partly as continuous indications of how and with whom a particular individual is 'in play'. We must now look at the things a person is doing while he is in play. This includes movements of the body, changes in facial expression, changes in the direction of gaze and bursts of speech. This flow of events has structure, but in spite of the considerable work that has been done on interaction, our understanding of this structure is remarkably sketchy.

An attempt to describe this structure was initiated by Scheflen (1964, 1965, 1965b), who analysed in detail sound film records of psychotherapy encounters. He aimed at a full analysis of the elements of the social performance, and he attempted to show how changes in posture, smaller bodily movements, utterances, and so on, are integrated into units of communication, which are organized into a hierarchy quite analogous to the hierarchical models of behavior proposed by Lashley (1951), Welford (1958), and Miller, Galanter and Pribram (1960), and employed also for the description of language structure (Gleason, 1961). He proposed that the total performance of an individual in a given encounter be termed a *presentation*; that this unit be seen as being composed of one or more *positions*; and that these positions in turn be seen as comprising one or more *points*. For instance, at a seminar, an individual's presentation can be seen as made up of a series of positions – that of listener, arguer, challenger, questioner, and so on. Each of these units is then said to be composed of one or more points; for instance, when a question is asked, there may be several parts to it or it may be iterated several times.

Scheflen showed how each of these units of communication is marked by changes in posture, visual orientation, the semantic and syntactic features of the language employed, and the stress patterns, intonation patterns and patterns of pausing in the units of speech. Reference will be made to Scheflen's work again in the discussion of bodily movement and patterns of looking, since he put forward several suggestions in regard to their functions. However, his analytic framework will not be used in the review that follows, since it is as yet insufficiently developed. Instead, some of the different components of the performance that have been studied will each be dealt with in turn.

The patterning of action in time. A participant in focused interaction may be observed to alternate between periods when he is actively sending messages to the other – usually by speech and gesture – and periods when he is not. These periods may be called *actions* and *silences*, respectively. Measurement of their occurrence, length, patterning in time and interrelation with those of the others in the encounter, was first developed by Chapple (1940a), and has since been taken up by a number of others. Chapple suggested that the patterning of action in time and the interrelation of actions are dimensions of social interaction of major significance, and that the degree and manner of coordination of actions in an encounter may have important consequences for its outcome. He compared (1940b) frequency distributions by length of actions and silences for several individuals in several conversations, and found that these frequency distributions and the way they change from one conversation to the next are characteristic of the individuals concerned. This finding has since been confirmed by Goldman-Eisler (1951), among others. Subsequently Chapple (1953) developed a 'standard interview' in which the length and timing of the interviewer's actions and silences are governed by fixed rules. In this way direct comparisons between the interaction patterns of different individuals are possible. Using this interview, Chapple (1949) and Matarazzo and his colleagues (Saslow and Matarazzo, 1959) have shown that on a number of indices of the temporal patterning of action and silences people are highly stable. Some attention has been paid to the relationship between differences in interaction pattern and other measures of personality; in particular, it has been shown that this technique of analysis can discriminate between categories of psychiatric patient (Chapple and Lindemann, 1942; Matarazzo and Saslow, 1961). Chronic schizophrenics, for instance, in comparison to normals, have highly irregular action lengths, and they do not coordinate their actions with those of the interviewer (Chapple *et al.*, 1960). Chapple and Donald (1947) have shown that an analysis of individual interaction patterns is useful in personnel selection, at least where the jobs to be done, as in selling, involve interaction.

Here our interest is in how the performance of one individual is affected by that of his interlocutor. A few studies pertinent to this question will be reviewed. A number of investigators have compared the performance of individuals in several different encounters. Borgatta and Bales (1953) measured the act-rates (that is, number of acts per unit of time) of individuals as they took part in several different three-person discussion groups. They found that the lower the act-rates of the other participants, the higher the individual's act-rate. However, each individual appeared to have a maximum act-rate which was characteristic of him. Thus it was possible to predict a given individual's act-rate in a group provided his own maximum and that of the other participants was known. Similar findings were reported by Leik (1965).

Goldman-Eisler (1952) compared the performance of three psychiatrists, each of whom interviewed five depressed and five active patients. She measured act-rate, amount of action and patterns of silence. She found that over the ten interviews each psychiatrist remained relatively stable and characteristic in his rate of action, but the amount he spoke varied inversely with the amount the patient spoke. However, the psychiatrists always retained the same rank order in amount of action relative to one another. The patients, on the other hand, always spoke the same amount, regardless of which psychiatrist interviewed them, but the occasions on which they spoke, and hence their rate of action, depended on the psychiatrist. Similar findings were reported by Saslow, Goodrich and Stein (1956). They illustrate how different aspects of an individual's performance are differently affected, according to his position in the role system of the encounter.

Kendon (1963) reported a study of twenty-two individuals who each took part in three to five conversations with different partners. He measured act-rate, lengths of actions and silences, the total amount of action, and the amount of time the interactors spent in waiting before replying or in simultaneous action. He confirmed that individuals were characteristic in their patterning of action from one conversation to the next and that their behavior in the conversations was related to their behavior in Chapple's Standard Interview. He found that the mean length of an individual's actions was strongly and positively related to the mean length of his partner's silences, but was inversely related to his partner's action lengths. His rate of action changed relatively less from conversation to conversation, however. It seemed that the subjects varied the total amount of time spent in action by altering the length of their actions and silences rather than by altering their rate of action. It was also found that subjects were highly characteristic in their tendency to pause before replying and in their tendency to interrupt, though each individual would interrupt the other more in proportion to the amount that he was interrupted.

Kendon, as just mentioned, found that the lengths of a subject's actions were inversely related to the lengths of those of his partners. Here the partners were initially unacquainted and were merely instructed to get to know one another. Where partners are closely acquainted, however, the relationship between lengths of actions appears to be positive. This was found by Chapple (1940a) for a pair of close friends, by B. W. Lundy (1955) in a psychotherapy pair, and by Kendon (1963) for twelve pairs of spouses. A similarly positive relationship has been found in situations where, presumably, there is no competition for available time. Thus the relationship between the action lengths of astronauts and their ground communicators has been found to be positive (Matarazzo et al., 1964b); in interviews where the interviewer systematically lengthens and shortens his actions in different periods, the interviewee shows concomitant variations (Matarazzo, et al., 1963; Matarazzo, Wiens and Saslow 1965).

Variations in the timing of actions of one person have been found to have dramatic effects on the lengths of the actions of the other. This has been studied in the Chapple Standard Interview, where the lengths of the interviewer's actions are held constant at five seconds throughout, but in which, according to the period of the interview, he either inserts his actions immediately after those of the interviewee, inserts an action only if the interviewee has been silent for fifteen seconds, or persistently interrupts the interviewee. Where the interviewer does not pause before replying, the interviewee tends to become stable in the lengths of his actions, though there are marked individual differences in their actual values (Guze and Mensch, 1959; Tuason et al., 1961; Matarazzo, Wiens and Saslow 1965). Where the interviewer fails to respond, however, there is a dramatic drop in the subject's action length and a tendency for his rate to increase. Usually the subject will stop acting altogether after a while, and will sit and wait until the interviewer speaks again. When he does so, the subject's reply tends to be of greatly increased length. There, are however, very large individual differences in the subject's reponse to the 'silence' behavior of the interviewer, and general statements are difficult. Interruption by the interviewer more often produces marked shortening of utterances, and it induces the subject to interrupt the interviewer. The foregoing findings were reported by Kendon (1963), who made a detailed study of the patterning of action in Chapple's Standard Interview of thirty-nine professional and student employees at a large New York psychiatric hospital. Data on the behavior of schizophrenics, neurotics and various normal groups in this interview have also been reported, though in less detail, by Matarazzo and his colleagues (Saslow and Matarazzo, 1959; Matarazzo and Saslow, 1961; Matarazzo, 1962).

A few studies have investigated changes in behavior over a series of encounters between the same pair of individuals. Lennard and Bernstein (1960), in a longitudinal study of eight psychotherapeutic dyads, found that after two months the psychotherapists' utterances had decreased in frequency but increased in length, as had the utterances of the patient. Further, the utterance lengths of both patient and therapist tended to approach a stable value, the particular value depending on the dyad. Similarly, Jaffe (1964) reported that, over a series of psychotherapy sessions, variations in the length of sentences became positively correlated between interviewer and interviewee. A positive correlation also developed between the frequency of ratio of '*I*' to '*you*' for patient and therapist, and there was an increase in similarity of vocabulary.

Some studies have varied other aspects of an interviewer's behavior. Kanfer *et al.* (1960) found that, during a period in an interview when the interviewer changed from open-ended to interpretative utterances, the lengths of subjects' actions were much reduced. Likewise, Pope and Siegman (1962, 1965) and Siegman and Pope (1962, 1965) reported several studies of the effects of the specificity of the interviewer's utterances. It was found that both decreasing the specificity of the question and increasing the anxiety-provoking potential of the topic were associated with more talk from the subjects, but that these effects were independent of one another. An analysis of certain features of utterance structure showed that where the topic was anxiety-arousing the subjects showed more speech disturbances, and that where the questions were less specific the subjects showed greater hesitancy in their speech (Pope and Siegman, 1965; Siegman and Pope, 1965).

Matarazzo *et al.* (1964a) reported a study in which the interview included a fifteen-minute period during which the interviewer supplied 'head-nods'. This led to an increase in the lengths of the subjects' action. A similar result was obtained by Matarazzo and Wiens (1965) with '*un-hums*'.

By way of conclusion to this section, it may be said that although sufficient work along these lines has been done to show that interesting results can be gathered by this method of analysis, a properly developed theoretical framework is still much needed. In particular, a definition of Chapple's units is needed which specifies their relationship to other possible units of behavior into which the social performance may be analysed.

Language and speech. It will be clear from our review of the work of Kanfer *et al.* (1960), Pope and Siegman (1962, 1965), and Matarazzo *et al.* (1964a), that what is said may often have important consequences for the structuring of the performance. However, there is as yet little systematic understanding of the functioning of language in social interaction. Anthropologists such as Sapir (1921) and Malinowski (1928), and linguists such as Bloomfield (1933) and, more recently, Pike (1954) have recognized the importance of this question, yet it is only quite recently that any relevant studies have been reported. No systematic treatment of the results of these studies seems possible at this time, and here we shall merely cite a few examples.

Soskin and John (1963) have made one of the most direct attacks on this question. By means of portable radio transmitters, they recorded all the verbal output of two married couples over a period of two weeks, and their results clearly illustrate the diversity of functions language has for people. Other studies have been concerned with more limited questions. Ferguson (1964) has studied baby talk in a variety of languages, and he has discussed its appearance in situations where the role relationships of the interactants are that of an adult and small child, either actually, symbolically or playfully. Joos (1962) has pointed out that for different types of encounters a different linguistic style is adopted. He distinguished Intimate, Casual-Personal, Social-Consultative, Formal and Frozen styles, and he provided some description of their differences. For instance, Casual style contrasts with Consultative style in that ellipses in grammatical construction and jargon or slang are common, and no attempt is made, as in Consultative style, to supply background information on what is being talked of. Both of these differ from intimate style, where there is no reference to public information at all, but where speakers only use language as a means of regulating their relationship. A related idea has been developed by Bernstein (1964), who drew a distinction between 'elaborated' and 'restricted' linguistic codes. He suggested that a restricted code, in which the range of grammatical forms is small and the actual words are restricted in number and highly predictable, may be used to regulate more or less formalized or conventionalized encounters, whereas an elaborated code is made use of in situations where new material is being dealt with or new relationships are being developed.

Moscovici and Plon (1966) have shown experimentally how the physical arrangements of interactants may affect the style of language that is used. They compared the linguistic styles used by pairs of subjects seated face-to-face; facing, but screened; side-by-side; and back-to-back. They found that in the first two conditions, the subjects spoke more, used more verbs and more redundancy, and the conversation was less abstract; in the other two conditions, regarded as more formal, the speech was more like writing.

Also relevant to this line of inquiry are those studies that have been concerned with the use of different languages in different social situations. Ferguson (1959) examined a number of communities in which two languages are in common use, and has shown how their use is systematically related to the social situation. A similar type of study has been reported by Herman (1961). Ervin-Tripp (1964) made an experimental study of the circumstances in which Japanese-speaking Japanese Americans make use of English and Japanese, and what sort of consequences this may have for the social relationships involved and the sort of things talked about.

So far as the study of speech is concerned, some attempts have been made to analyse the communicative functions of variations in tones of voice, speed of utterance, patterns of intonation, and so forth. Many such studies adopted a method analogous to the one most widely used in the study of facial expression, in which subjects are presented with samples of speech varied in a number of ways. It has been found that people are able to judge what emotion is being expressed through variations of this sort. This work was recently reviewed by Kramer (1963), and a representative and illuminating set of studies was presented by Davitz (1964). There has been little research on these variations as they actually occur in interaction, however, and much useful work would be possible. Thus, many observers have noted that there are appropriate voice levels, tones of voice, speeds of communication, and so on, which particularly suit either funerals, wedding receptions or formal interviews. Although descriptive systems for dealing with these aspects of speech have now been developed (Trager, 1958; Crystal and Quirk, 1964), very little appears to have been done with them. Pittenger, Hockett and Danehy (1960; Pittenger, 1958; Pittenger and Smith, 1957); Dittman and Wynne (1961), and Eldred and Price (1958) have applied Trager's descriptive system to interaction sequences in psychotherapeutic sessions, but their work is only suggestive of the sort of findings this may yield.

A more fully developed line of research into speech has been the analysis of patterns of hesitations and of disturbances in the production of words or sequences of words. The focus of interest here, however, has been on the light these phenomena may throw upon the processes of linguistic encoding (Maclay and Osgood, 1959; Goldman-Eisler, 1958), or on the possibility that such variations in speech performance are associated with variations in the speaker's emotional state (see, for example, Mahl, 1963). It seems fairly clear that there are more hesitation pauses and a faster rate of speech when subjects are anxious. This whole area of research was very fully reviewed by Mahl and Schulze (1964), who reported that they found no studies in which the place of these phemomena in interaction had been considered.

Visual orientation. It is widely acknowledged that where a person is looking or where he is likely to look is a matter of considerable social significance. Recent studies, such as those of Goffman (1963) and Sommer (1965) have, as we have seen, drawn attention to the way interactants tend to arrange themselves so that they may readily look at one another. Gibson and Pick (1963) have shown that people are able to discriminate when another is looking at them with a high degree of efficiency. A study to be reported by Exline, in which a Mackworth eye-marker camera was used, suggests however that the efficiency of these judgements is much affected by the subject's response set, and by where in his face the other is looking. A survey by Tomkins (1963) testified to the very ancient social traditions concerning the significance of the look. In this section we shall survey recent experimental studies that throw light on this.

We may distinguish three ways in which visual orientation functions in interactions:

1. To look at another is a social act in itself.
2. To meet the gaze of another is a significant event, and may often be an important part of the goal sought in interaction.
3. In seeing another, much important information about him may be gathered in addition to his direction of gaze.

First, we consider the act of looking, and how it is interpreted. Focused interaction is often started by a period of eye-contact, which seems to signal that each is ready to interact with the other (Goffman, 1963). Once under way, each person looks at the other in the region of the eyes intermittently, in glances of varying length, usually between one and seven seconds. The proportion of time each person looks at the other may vary from 0 per cent to 100 per cent. The proportion of time spent in eye-contact is, however, always much less than the proportion of time spent looking by either subject. The person listening gives longer glances than the one talking, and tends to look considerably more, at least in dyads (Nielsen, 1962; Kendon, 1967; Exline and Winters, 1965). Use is also made of peripheral vision, and waiters and chairmen are able to avoid having their eye caught in this way.

There are a few studies that throw light on how being looked at is interpreted. Weisbrod (1965) studied looking patterns in a seven-member seminar and found that who looked at whom during the discussion was most strongly related to the power coalitions that were formed in the group. Thus, those individuals in the group who looked most at a speaker were rated by the speaker as instrumental to his goals and as valuing him more. Further, the more looks an individual received while he was speaking, the more powerful he felt himself to be. Those individuals who were looked at most by speakers in the group saw themselves, and were seen by other group members, as being more powerful in the group than those who were looked at less. Weisbrod concluded that to look at someone while he is speaking is to signal a request to be included by him in discussion, and that to receive looks back from the speaker is seen as a signal from the speaker that he is including the other.

Another study on the perception of being looked at is that of Mehrabian (Winer and Mehrabian, no date), where the experimenter interviewed two subjects simultaneously, but spent more time looking at one subject than at the other. The subjects were then asked to rate the attitude of the interviewer toward them, and it was found that the subject who received the most looking judged the experimenter to be more positive toward her than the subject who was looked at less. Kendon (1966, unpublished data) found that subjects thought that an interviewer who did not look at them for part of the interview had lost interest in what they were saying. Exline and Kendon, in an unpublished study, found that individuals are judged as more 'potent' where they do not look while the subject is speaking, as compared to a condition in which they do look while he is speaking. Exline and Eldridge, also in an unpublished study, showed that subjects judge a speaker as more sincere if he looks at them when he speaks than if he does not.

Studies complementary to these have investigated some of the factors associated with how much an individual looks at another. Exline and Winters (1965) had subjects interviewed simultaneously by two interviewers both of whom looked at the subject continuously throughout the interview. It was found that subjects showed a clear tendency to look more at the interviewer they preferred. In another experiment reported in the same paper, participants were subjected to either positive or negative treatment by an interviewer: this produced feelings of dislike in the negatively treated subjects, and these subjects looked less at the interviewer than did those in the positive condition.

Other studies reported by Exline and his colleagues (Exline, 1963; Exline, Gray and Schuette 1965) lend further support to the notion that the general level of looking is related to the subject's orientation to the others. They showed that, in non-competitive discussion and in an interview, people who score high on a measure of 'affiliativeness' (measured by French's sentence-completion test and by Schutz's FIRO) look more than do those who score lower on this dimension. Where the discussion is competitive, however, people who are low on affiliativeness look more and high 'affiliates' look less.

There is some evidence that the recognition of the look in another is instinctive, and that to see a pair of eyes looking at one acts as a releaser for specifically social action. Thus Ambrose (1963) argued that the eyes of another may be the first figural entity consistently perceived by the infant. Furthermore, as Ahrens has shown (cited by Ambrose, 1963), the pair of eyes is the first visual stimulus to elicit a smiling response. Ambrose suggested that this may be likened to the following response in birds. The infant's smile and his fixation of the eyes of the person looking at him may be seen as component instinctual responses of the infant, which themselves may elicit further approach and caring behavior in the mother (Bowlby, 1958; Wolff, 1963). This may be one of the bases for the affiliative function of eye contact that was suggested by some of the studies by Exline already cited.

The look also plays a part in sexual behavior, though the systematic evidence here is less direct. Tomkins (1963) showed that taboos on mutual looking are very widespread and are associated with the sexually arousing properties of eye-contact, which he also discusses. Finally, the widespread belief in the evil eye (Elworthy, 1895) and the use of the look as a gesture of threat both in man and in monkeys and apes (see DeVore, 1965, for example), suggests a further motivational function, that of arousing fight-flight reactions.

Variations in the look associated with the elicitation of affiliative, sexual or fight-flight reaction is little understood, though recent work of Hess (1965) suggested that enlarged pupil size in a woman is sexually arousing to a man, and the narrowed pupils of the aggressive look are proverbial. The associated facial expression is doubtless of great importance as well.

Taken together, these considerations suggest that in the mutual look the participants express their involvement with one another. The longer the periods of eye contact, the greater the level of this mutual involvement, other things being equal. But in any situation there is a limit to the amount of mutual involvement that may be tolerated, and too much mutual looking may arouse anxiety. Argyle and Dean (1965) put forward the theory that there is an approach-avoidance balance, following the N. E. Miller (1944) model, resulting in an equilibrium level of both eye contact, physical proximity, and other components of intimacy. It was suggested that a shift along one dimension would lead to compensating shifts along the others.

This received some support in the experiment described earlier where it was found that eye contact fell off rapidly with physical proximity.

Some work has been done on factors associated with the avoidance of eye contact, though more is needed. Exline and his colleagues (1961, 1965) showed that subjects look away when they are asked personally embarrassing questions and, with the exception of those who score high on Christie's Machiavellianism scale, when they are lying. These authors suggested that this may be a result of either an attempt at self-concealment or an attempt to avoid the unwelcome responses of the other person. It could also reflect an attempt to escape the relationship with the other. A further possibility is that it is more difficult to answer personal questions or to lie during mutual gaze. In addition, the turning away of the gaze is probably an attempt to reduce the intake of information. In another study Exline and Winters (1965) showed that when subjects have to talk about cognitively more difficult material they look less at the other. Kendon (1967) reported that during passages of hesitant speech subjects look away, but during fluent speech they look back. These findings suggest that it is during the formulation of thought, when subjects might want to reduce information intake, that they look away. They look back as they speak only when their sentence is fully formed.

Emotional processes undoubtedly contribute to the aversion of the gaze. Laing (1960) reported on a series of adult patients who characteristically averted their gaze: they were 'overwhelmed by a feeling of rejection' and did not wish to be seen. Riemer (1955) described a number of different types of abnormal gaze, all of which, according to him, serve to 'wall off' the individual from the world, and arise as a result of unexpressed hostility. Hutt and Ounsted (1966) reported extreme aversion of gaze in autistic children, which may reflect an extreme fear of being rejected by others. These authors also suggested that autistic children are chronically overaroused, and their averted gaze is interpreted as a device whereby the arousal is kept at manageable levels.

Finally, as we mentioned, when A looks at B he can pick up information about him. He can see whether or not B is looking at him; he can also observe B's facial expression, posture, movements, and so on. The face is, of course, a peculiarly expressive instrument, and the eyes may be its most expressive part. The mere fact that it is an area of such high information value may be sufficient to explain why people look there, more than at other parts of their co-interactants. Argyle *et al.* (1967) found that as B was progressively concealed from A (by dark glasses, mask, no vision), A found interaction increasingly uncomfortable, though it is noteworthy that they found a greater increase in difficulty when the face, rather than just the eyes was concealed.

Bodily movement, facial expression and looking patterns. Studies in which the functioning of posture and bodily movement has been examined in interaction have only recently appeared. Scheflen (1964, 1965a) has begun to report the results of his detailed analyses of psychotherapy encounters; while here he aims at a full analysis of the elements of the social performance, his main work so far has been concerned with the functions of postural change.

He found that each of the units of communication into which he suggests that social performance may be analysed are marked by changes in posture and patterns of movement. He suggested that the presentation is marked by gross changes in space. At the end of a conversation the participants may leave the room, for instance, or perhaps, at a party, they may turn to talk with other people. As we have seen, any given presentation may be seen to be signaled by a particular general orientation and position in space. The *positions* that ocur within a given presentation are marked by particular postures, their boundaries being indicated by changes in posture. In Scheflen's (1965a) analysis of the performance of a psychotherapist, for instance, the latter was found to lean forward toward the patient when he was engaged in 'active interpretation', and he would then lean back in his chair when the patient was 'free associating'.

The *points* of which positions may be composed are marked, Scheflen suggested, by shifts in head position and in visual orientation. He reported (1964) that interactants in psychotherapy show three to five head positions which occur repeatedly and which appear in contrasting sequences as the successive points appear. He gave an example of two head positions a therapist was observed to use repeatedly during an interpreting position. While listening to the patient, the therapist's head was slightly lowered and cocked to the right, so that her eyes were averted from the patient. With the onset of making an interpretative remark, she would raise her head, hold it erect, look directly at the patient, and then speak. At the end, she would turn her head to the right, away from the patient, and then resume the listening head position. Studies by Kendon (1967) of visual orientation in fourteen subjects filmed in conversation showed associated patterns of looking, with the individual looking directly at his interlocutor at the ends of grammatically complete phrases. These patterns are clearly similar to those reported by Scheflen.

There is as yet no clear evidence of the functions of these changes in posture, head position and visual orientation, though it seems probable that they have a regulatory function for the recipients. The distinctive postures of the different positions, for instance, may serve as continuous signals to the other and assist in keeping him in step. Scheflen (1965a, 1965b) suggested that encounters follow characteristic programs that may be described in terms of the sequences of positions, and if positions are marked by distinctive postures, this may help to keep people together as the program proceeds. Scheflen (1965a) described the progression of positions of two closely collaborating psychotherapists as they attempted to establish a particular pattern of relationships with the patient, and he indicated how each therapist waited for the postural signal from the other before shifting into the next position in the sequence.

Rather similar considerations may apply to the changes in head position and visual orientation, which are closely associated with this and which appear to mark the succession of points. Thus Kendon (1967) reported that the ends of utterances where there is a change of speaker are often marked by a sustained gaze at the other combined with a characteristic head position. Where such kinesic accompaniments to utterance endings did not appear, as was the case in several instances, the response of the other person was less immediate. This suggested that the look and the associated head position functioned in part as change-over signals and assisted in the smooth progression of the interaction. Kendon also reported that the speaker looks up at his interlocutor intermittently while he is speaking, and that this occurs at the ends of sentences or completed phrases, and it is here that the listener most often supplies his attention signals. During hesitations, on the other hand, the speaker characteristically turns his head away, and Kendon suggested that this may partly function as an inhibitory signal to the other. Certainly during periods of hesitation associated with averted head and gaze, responses of the listener were found to be very rare.

Besides these shifts in posture and head and eye positions, an individual may be observed to make a variety of other complex movements as he is talking. He may move his hands, nod his head up and down, move his eyebrows, and vary the positions of his eyelids. Some of these movements do not appear to be integrated into the total flow of behavior. Such extraneous movements were studied recently by Dittman (1962) and were found to be associated with hesitation pauses. Birdwhistell (1964) recently reported some of his observations on the close relation between speech and body movement. He described how nods or sweeps of the head, eye blinks or brow movements, and movements of the hands or fingers appear in association with points of linguistic stress. He also reported observations of units of movement, variable in the actual body part involved, that appear to be associated with particular kinds of utterance. In references to the self, he noted a consistent tendency for the speaker to make a proximal movement, whereas in references to others the movement is distal. When the pronoun is plural, the movement normally associated with it is modified with a slight sweep. *Area markers* refer to movements made with prepositions or prepositional phrases and include, for instance, a backward jerk of the head over *behind*, as in *Put that behind the stove*, or a forward jerk of the head over *to* as in *I am going to London*. *Manner markers* are movements that mark adverbs and adverbial phrases, such as *roughly*, *quickly*, and so on (Birdwhistell, 1966).

These observations have yet to be fully reported, and again we can only speculate as to what the functions of these movements might be. From the point of view of the recipient, however, they may serve to reduce the ambiguity of what the speaker is saying, and in dividing up the discourse into relatively small chunks, they may keep his attention. It is fairly easy to observe that when a person is speaking loudly and with emphasis the kinesic accompaniments to his speech become much more pronounced. One or two studies have been reported which show that comprehension of speech is better if the speaker can be seen (Sumby and Pollack, 1954), and it is possible that the speech-related movements Birdwhistell described play a part in this. On the other hand, these movements may have some functional significance for the speaker rather than the listener. Recent work (Condon and Ogston, 1966) has indicated that people in interaction closely coordinate one another's movement. In a study reported by Argyle *et al.* (1967), interaction took place with one subject progressively concealed from the other; the one who was not concealed found the encounter increasingly uncomfortable, but only if he could still be seen by the other person. Perhaps it is of particular value for A to be able to see B only when B can also see A, because in these circumstances A must coordinate his movements with those of B, which he need not do if B cannot see him.

The work just described has been primarily concerned with the functions of postural changes, bodily movements, and changes in visual orientation as regulators of the interaction process. Besides this there is a considerable body of work concerned with the function of movement, particularly of facial expressions as expressive of emotion. Schlosberg (1954) and Osgood (1966), among others, studied the dimensions along which people distribute their judgements of facial expressions, and they showed that there is considerable consistency in this. Sarbin and Hardyck (1955), Ekman (1965) and Machotka (1965) have begun to make analogous explorations with posture. Ekman suggested, for instance, that whereas affective information of various kinds is conveyed by the face, posture is judged predominantly along a dimension of tension relaxation. None of the work in this tradition has, however, concerned itself with the question of the functions of, for example, facial expression within an interaction sequence. Although we may now place a photograph of a smiling face fairly precisely on Schlosberg's Oval, thus placing it within a set of 'dimensions of emotional expression', even a cursory consideration of where smiles actually occur in interaction sequences should be enough to show that their meaning is not to be exclusively defined in terms of their position on these judgemental dimensions. For instance, smiles may be used to reassure another or to appease him: they are an integral part of greetings, and they may be used as a device for establishing the range of expressiveness that is to be permitted within a given encounter. It does not seem particularly helpful to say, in each of these cases, that a particular emotion is being expressed. It seems far more likely that smiles are, as often as not, employed as part of a more or less ritualized code that serves to handle particular aspects of the interaction process. A large field of research awaits cultivation here.

Self-presentation and competence

We turn now from the study of the behavioral details of the social performance to certain higher order features of it. In all encounters, since each person's performance is built upon his conception of the kind of other he is dealing with, so one of the main functions of the social performance must be to convey this conception. This is the problem of self-presentation, which we shall discuss first. Second, in many encounters, those taking part are aiming at fairly specific outcomes, the achievement of which depends on the participants' success in keeping the encounter going and steering it in appropriate directions. Some people are better at this than others; we say they have greater social competence, or better social skills. We shall outline some studies that deal with this question and with methods of training people in social skills. Next we will comment on research into specific social skills, and finally, we will briefly consider mental illness and will indicate how much of it may be seen as a failure of social skill or competence.

The presentation of self in social encounters

One of the special features of social interaction is that interactors are open to observation by the others present and are concerned about the perceptions and attitudes that the others have of them. This can be regarded as a special case of the processes that have already been described – the goal here is to bring about certain perceptions and attitudes on the part of the others, and a repertoire of social techniques is used for doing so; the equilibrium includes certain stabilized appraisals of one another by the participants. This is a very important aspect of interaction, however, as it is intimately bound up with the establishment of social relationships and with their breakdown. Information about this aspect of social behavior has been derived mainly from observational studies (Goffman, 1955, 1956, 1961a) and clinical studies (Erikson, 1956), though there have also been a few experimental studies. This field has been reviewed by D. R. Miller (1963) and Stagner (1961).

The motivation for self-presentation. Perhaps the most basic motivation for self-presentation by A is that interaction is impossible for B unless he knows enough about A to know how to respond to him appropriately. Similarly B wants A to react to him appropriately. There are at least two further sources of motivation for self-presentation:

1. People who are unsure of their self-image need continual confirmation that they really are what they half-believe themselves to be and would like to be. Similarly, they may need confirmation of their uncertain self-esteem. Maslow *et al.* (1945) called this condition *insecurity*, and showed how people in the various combinations of high and low security and high and low self-esteem characteristically behave. Adolescents are particularly insecure; they have not crystallized a stable self-image, so that reactions from others may have a more disturbing effect on them than on older people. Hysterics are another insecure group and are constantly trying to project their self-image on others: this reaches an extreme in impostors and people in fugue states.

2. Others may want to project a self-image primarily for professional reasons. Teachers, psychotherapists and other social skill performers are more successful if they can project an image of professional competence and thereby win the confidence of their clients. Goffman (1956) has described some of the professional techniques that are used to do this.

The self-image is the descriptive part of the self, including such things as body image, age, sex, occupation and social class, and it can be assessed by the Semantic Differential or a *Q* sort. Self-esteem is evaluative and can be assessed by attitude scales, as was done by Rosenberg (1965). Both seem to be associated with motivational forces in the personality. Clinical writers are widely agreed that there are 'pressures toward consistency', toward the establishment of a unitary ego identity (D. R. Miller, 1963, pp. 696 ff.). According to Erikson (1956), these pressures become heightened during late adolescence in Western society. There are also pressures to maximize self-esteem, though this may be due to an effort to obtain self-reactions and other reactions that are consistent with earlier reactions to the self of parents (Secord and Backman, 1964). This drive is constantly in conflict with evidence from current performance and reactions of others in the present; if reality loses, a state of paranoia ensues. Self-image and self-esteem probably have three main origins: (1) introjection of the reactions of others (Argyle, 1964); (2) comparison of self with siblings and other peers; and (3) the playing of roles. The individual has to select which of these items to emphasize and which to de-emphasize in order to construct a prestigeful and unitary identity.

The social techniques used for self-presentation. To create perceptions of and attitudes toward the self on the part of others present is a subtle social skill, though one that is usually practised quite unconsciously. How is it done? A can simply tell B about himself, but this is not socially acceptable, except in the most modest and indirect form. The same is true of hints, name-dropping, and the various techniques of one-upmanship described by Stephen Potter (1952). Another method of projecting an identity is by means of clothes and general appearance, which are in fact excellent clues to a person's self-image. Third, a person's style of behavior can indicate, by gesture, manner of speech, and general demeanor, the kind of person he thinks he is and the way he is used to being treated. Finally, the most effective way is by aspects of behavior that are relevant to the self-image; these can prove, as words cannot, that a person really is what he claims to be. Generally speaking, people present a somewhat idealized, or at least edited, version of themselves for public inspection. Thus they conceal a great deal about themselves; they reveal most to those whom they can trust not to reject them, and reveal least about topics such as sex and money (Jourard, 1964).

What happens when a self-image is presented but is not accepted by the others present? As will be shown later, this is one of the main sources of embarrassment. If a person is able to retain his poise, various strategies are open to him. He may adopt alternative techniques for establishing the same image, though these often involve more overt claims and may make the speaker look ridiculous. He may have to alter the image he is presenting, perhaps temporarily accepting the group's evaluation of him. Finally, he may engage in defensive behavior, categorizing the others negatively and preserving his self-image, as salesgirls do for customers who won't buy (Lombard, 1955); or simply failing to perceive the responses of others accurately.

Embarrassment and stage fright. Both embarrassment and stage fright are conditions in which the social performance is disrupted because of anxiety about the reactions of others toward the self.

When a person becomes embarrassed, he blushes, sweats, stutters, and in extreme cases flees from the situation or commits suicide. He loses control of his social behavior and is temporarily incapable of interacting; his state is liable to spread to the others present. Gross and Stone (1964) collected a thousand descriptions of instances of embarrassment from students and others. They classified the causes into three main types: (1) failure to be able to confirm the self-image that was presented; (2) loss of poise through failing to control self or physical objects in the situation; (3) disturbance of assumptions about other people or about the situation.

Goffman (1955) emphasized the first of these causes – the inability to sustain an identity. He also mentioned (Goffman, 1957) some other sources of embarrassment – when one person is underinvolved in the encounter; when he is overinvolved; and when he talks about this interaction itself. The common element behind most of these causes is the sudden breakdown of the smooth course of interaction for one or another reason. Garfinkel (1963) experimented with various ways of disturbing interaction: (1) treating the other in an inappropriate role, such as treating a customer in a shop as a salesman; (2) behaving in an inappropriate role, such as a student behaving like a lodger in his own family; (3) breaking the rules of a game, such as moving the opponent's pieces. All of these kinds of behavior created embarrassment and in some cases anger. It follows from the first process mentioned that some people – those who are presenting a false front or concealing large areas of their true selves (Jourard, 1964) – will be more easily embarrassed than others. When a person has become embarrassed he needs time to recover his poise, and may need to be helped back into the pattern of interaction. Goffman (1955) described how the others present may help: they may try to avoid its happening by being 'tactful'; they may pretend that nothing has happened; they may make excuses for A's lapse of behavior; and they may help to provide him with a new image and thus to rehabilitate him in the group.

While self-presentation can be looked at as an example of social skill, embarrassment can best be seen as a failure to establish or maintain equilibrium. The social system includes patterns of interaction with the other, and perceptions and attitudes toward him; the two parts are intimately bound up together. If the perceptions are suddenly changed, a breakdown of interaction follows, and a new one must be established if a relationship is to be resumed.

Audience anxiety may be experienced in some degree whenever a person can be perceived by another, because the former is concerned about how the latter will react. Experiments comparing performance with an audience, without an audience, and with audiences of different sizes, showed that speech errors increase (Levin *et al.*, 1960), and that there are more mistakes and greater rigidity at tasks when an audience is present. Probably the Yerkes–Dodson principle operates, so that performance at first improves, but deteriorates with larger and more critical or important audiences. Paivio, Baldwin and Berger (1961) found that readiness to volunteer to speak was positively correlated with a questionnaire measure of exhibitionism and negatively with self-consciousness. Levin *et al.* suggested that an approach–avoidance conflict is produced by these opposing forces; this is confirmed by their finding that speech errors were highest for subjects high in both exhibitionism and self-consciousness. Subjects both seek positive responses and fear negative ones from those who can see them; the strength of these two expectations presumably depends on past experience.

Argyle *et al.* (1967) varied the conditions of vision between a speaker and his audience. Subjective ratings of discomfort and speech errors were lowest when the speaker was behind the audience; next lowest was when he was in front but some distance away, and greatest when he was wearing dark glasses. It looks as if cutting down feedback from the audience, or perhaps simply reducing eye contact, reduces audience anxiety. Unfortunately this also reduces useful aspects of the feedback, so that the performance is likely to be worse under these conditions. It is commonly found that adolescents suffer from this kind of anxiety – they do not like being looked at, and are very concerned about their personal appearance. This is probably because their ego identity is not yet stabilized, so that the reactions of others are very important to them.

Social competence; training in social skills

1. Measures of competence. Competence in the performance of non-social motor skills can be measured by the speed and quality of performance; competence in social skills is more difficult to assess. In the case of professional social skills, competence clearly involves the successful attainment of some combination of goals. The good salesman, for example, both sells a lot of goods *and* satisfies the customer, so that the latter is likely to go to that shop again. In the case of non-professional social skills the criteria are less clear, though they might include such things as establishing and maintaining friendly relationships, being cooperative and helpful in everyday encounters, being able to communicate clearly and to persuade other people to do things. Negatively, many mental patients are deficient in social skills: they cannot sustain friendly, cooperative behavior with others, and they annoy people. Attempts have been made to assess 'social intelligence' and competence at particular skills, such as foremanship, by means of questionnaires. There appears to be a high correlation between such measures and IQ (Thorndike and Stein, 1937), although their relation to actual behavior is less certain. Somewhat better results have recently been obtained with the Chapin Social Insight Test (Gough, 1965). It is not known how far there is a general factor of social skill. People vary in their capacity to perform different social tasks, such as teaching, psychotherapy and interviewing, mainly as a result of special training and experience. Although special social techniques must be mastered for each of these skills, there may be a number of common elements as well, such as perceptual sensitivity, warmth, flexibility, energy and a large repertoire of social techniques.

2. Learning by repetition. Whereas manual workers are often given carefully designed training courses, those who have to deal with people are often given none at all, and have to pick it up as they go along. Experiments with small groups by Mohanna and Argyle (1960) and Crossman and Everstine (1965) showed that groups can increase in their speed and efficiency of communicating and solving problems: time fell to one-sixth and errors to one-third in the former experiment, and new methods of coding messages were observed to be evolved in the latter. Other studies have been concerned with one subject dealing with a succession of 'clients'. Experiments by Argyle, Lalljee and Lydall (cf. Argyle, 1967) showed that sheer repetition of teaching another the slide rule or how to play Scrabble produced fewer speech errors, more fluency and longer speeches. The performance also became more stereotyped. Studies of salesgirls by the same investigators found an over-all average increase of 60 per cent to 100 per cent over twelve months in different shops, but some individuals did not improve at all, while some actually got worse.

Whether sheer repetition will lead to improvement probably depends on the amount of feedback and the motivation of the learners.

3. Role-playing with feedback. In this method of training, the trainees role-play a series of typical situations encountered in interviewing, selling and similar situations. They are then given feedback, which may be verbal commentary from the trainer, the other trainees, a tape recording, or a video tape recording, or by earphones during the actual performance. It seems probable that the immediate playback of a video tape recording is one of the most effective methods of feedback. Haines and Eachus (1965) found that there was better learning of the behavior appropriate in an imaginary other country when a video tape was used in addition to verbal commentary.

A number of studies have found that role-playing with verbal feedback is effective in training for supervision. The feedback is not enjoyed, but is essential for learning (cf. Argyle, Smith and Kirton, 1962, for a review of these studies), and several sets of suitable situations for role-playing have been prepared (Corsini, Shaw and Blake, 1961; Maier, Solem and Maier, 1957). Several variations on this theme can be used; for example, the same trainee confronts a variety of programmed others, or roles are reversed in a second session. The main practical difficulty with role playing is in giving the feedback in a way that is not disturbing and is acceptable. It is also essential to have a good set of situations.

4. T-group training. This method has gained rapidly in popularity since it was first developed at Bethel, Maine, in 1947. The procedure is for a trainer to meet with about twelve trainees for a series of two-hour sessions, during which the only task of the group is to study itself. The trainer does not direct the group's activities, but may intervene to interpret what is happening, or to show how to give feedback on a member's behavior. There have now been a number of fairly well-controlled follow-up studies, using before and after measure and control groups (cf. Stock, 1964). The most satisfactory is that by Bunker (1965) of 200 people who attended the Bethel laboratories. The conclusion of these studies is that 60 per cent to 75 per cent benefit, whereas a small percentage become emotionally disturbed and some have nervous breakdowns. The benefits are mainly greater sensitivity to inter-personal phenomena and clearer self-perception.

Various criticisms can be made of T-group methods:

1. They are emotionally disturbing for a minority of participants. This could be avoided by reducing the emotional violence of feedback, but it is recognized that this might reduce the positive effects – 'It depends on what you are prepared to pay for psychically,' as one trainer put it. Another alternative would be to screen out those who are likely to be upset by these procedures.

2. T-group methods increase sensitivity and insight, but may not improve job *performance*. Furthermore, each job has its own special problems and social techniques that must be dealt with; T-group courses usually include some relevant role-playing in addition to the T-group sessions. An earlier report by Lippitt (1949) showed that good follow-up results were obtained from a laboratory course that included role-playing and some of the other ingredients, but no actual T-groups: it would be interesting to know which part of the T-group procedures is responsible for the positive effects.

3. T-groups are unlike any real groups, since the latter have real jobs to do, and contain leaders wielding real power, often undemocratically. In other words, the social techniques learned in T-groups could be used in other T-groups but may be ineffective in many real-life situations.

5. *Other methods of training*. Sensitivity can be increased by other methods than T-groups. For example, Jecker *et al.* (1964) succeeded in training teachers to perceive more accurately whether pupils had understood what they were being taught. The measure consisted of a series of one-minute films of a child; the training consisted in studying films and drawing attention to the cues for comprehension.

The imitation of models, for example of experts observed through a one-way screen or filmed, can be useful. This is valuable when rather unfamiliar social skills are being taught, and can be used to draw attention to the variety of social techniques needed to deal with particular problems.

Lectures, discussion, reading and case studies are all used regularly for human-relations training. There is evidence from follow-up studies that the combination of lectures and group methods can be successful here (Sorenson, 1958). On the other hand, cognitive methods alone, such as lectures and reading, probably do not have much effect on social performance (Argyle, Smith and Kirton, 1962).

Research into specific social skills

There has been a considerable amount of research into specific social skills, such as the survey, assessment and personnel interview, psychotherapy, teaching and lecturing, the supervision of groups, and so on. Research has been concerned with which techniques are most effective under particular conditions and what happens during the encounters. One kind of research consists in the comparison of good and bad performers where this can be assessed in some fairly objective way. There have been a number of such studies comparing supervisors of high- and low-output work groups that were similar in other respects (for example, Argyle, Gardner and Cioffi, 1958). Such studies have not usually analysed behavior in terms of the kind of variables that we have been considering in this chapter, and research of this kind could be greatly extended by so doing. One of the most interesting questions in this field could be solved in this way: Fiedler (1953) and others have shown that effective psychotherapists establish a similar kind of relationship with their patients: they are warm, permissive, interested in the patient and able to empathize with him, and they treat him as a co-worker on a common problem; but they do not share any therapeutic techniques. To this it has been replied, however, that this common element must consist of certain shared social (or therapeutic) techniques (Gardner, 1964).

Nor do these comparative studies allow for the possibility of superior methods of skill performance not used by anybody – yet manual skills are commonly improved by method study. An example of such a suggested set of superior social techniques was put forward by McGregor (1960) for supervision. He suggested that supervisors should lead subordinates to set their own goals and assess their own progress, and that they try to align the needs of individuals and the aims of the organization by showing individuals how to meet their needs in an acceptable manner. A social skill that is urgently in need of new techniques at present is the handling of adolescent children by parents. McPhail (1966) found some of the things that are ineffective – emotional tirades, unreasonable restriction and pointless punishments – but which techniques *are* effective must still be discovered.

The social techniques that are evolved by experienced performers are often very complex and may involve a carefully planned sequence of moves, or a 'strategy'. The personnel interview, for instance, may include the following steps:

1. The supervisor (S) obtains background information about the worker (W).
2. S meets W and establishes rapport.
3. S explains objectively that there is a problem.
4. S sympathetically invites W to give his side of the story.
5. S and W engage in joint problem-solving.
6. If W is uncooperative, S uses persuasion, appealing to relevant needs in W.
7. If W is still uncooperative, the possibility of stronger sanctions is mentioned.
8. S reviews what has been decided, when they shall meet again, and so on (Sidney and Brown, 1961; Maier, 1952).

It may be necessary to vary the social techniques used with the personality of the other or with the situation. Although democratic supervisors usually get better results with their work groups, this is not the case if the group members are themselves authoritarian (Haythorn, 1956), if the task must be carried out with meticulous accuracy and timing (Fiedler, 1964), or in times of crisis (Hamblin, 1958).

Further discussion of research into problems connected with specific social skills is given in Argyle (1967).

Mental disorders as failures of social skill

If social interaction is regarded as a social skill, it should be instructive to examine the ways in which failures of skill may occur – the equivalents of breakdowns of motor skill under stress of fatigue, including accidents. Some of the most interesting kinds of failure in social performance occur in mental disorders; study of such failures may, therefore, throw light on social interaction and may be important for the study of mental disorders. There are two main ways in which failure of social performance may be causally related to other aspects of disorder. (1) Social failure may be primary, leading to social rejection and failure to cope, which lead to anxiety and other symptoms. (2) Social failure may be a secondary result of other personality disturbances, but may lead to social rejection and incompetence and hence to an exacerbation of stress.

It is not necessary to repeat the more familiar aspects of the social incompetence of mental patients; the general features of the social behavior of schizophrenics, hysterics and psychopaths, etc., are described in textbooks of psychiatry. What can be added to such descriptions are the results of using special test situations of special measuring instruments. A brief list of some examples of these studies follows.

1. Voice quality. Ostwald (1965) made frequency analyses of the speech of different kinds of patients, showing that, for example, the speech of depressives is flat, low-pitched and monotonous, whereas that of manics has a robust, resonant quality.

2. *Timing of speech*. Chapple's Standard Interview (1953) has been used in a number of studies of patients: Matarazzo and Saslow (1961), for example, found that schizophrenics had longer silences than normals before replying, often failed to respond at all, and at other times interrupted; their meshing is poor.

3. *Person perception*. This factor was studied in patients by laboratory tests for accuracy of recognizing emotion from characteristics such as speech and facial expression. Davitz (1964) found that schizophrenics were poor at recognizing emotions from speech quality. McDavid and Schroder (1957) found that delinquents were poor at discriminating approval and disapproval as presented in a series of situational descriptions.

4. *Gaze direction*. Hutt and Ounsted (1966) found that autistic children suffered from avoidance of gaze; furthermore, in a test room they took no interest in masks of human faces, but were interested in animal faces and the furniture. The present authors observed a series of schizophrenics interacting with a continuously staring confederate: the patients showed almost no eye contact and their glances were extremely short.

5. *Physical appearance*. A person's clothes and posture are an important clue to his concern with projecting a self-image. The drab, ill-kept appearance of many mental patients suggests that they do not care; this is far from true, however, of manics, hysterics and paranoids. Manics wear smart, striking, but loud, clothes; hysterics are greatly concerned with their appearance; paranoids dress to fit their fantasies.

We will now consider the different ways in which the social performance of mental patients may fail. It is possible to classify these failures in terms of the model for social skill presented earlier.

1. *Failures of perception*. All kinds of patients who have been studied showed failures of perception. In schizophrenia, failures seem to result from a deliberate misattention to social stimuli, though schizophrenics are least aware of emotional elements – they can, for example, follow instructions quite well. Paranoids fail to receive messages that contain any criticism of themselves. Manics and depressives fail to perceive *themselves* realistically.

2. *Disturbances of motivation*. There may be general overarousal or underarousal, as in the affective psychoses. There may be undue strength of particular drives, such as aggression. Schizophrenics appear to be lacking in affiliative motivation, but there is recent evidence that in childhood schizophrenia there is physiological *over*arousal producing frozen inactivity

(Hutt *et al.*, 1964); this does not, however, explain why there should be social inactivity in particular. Psychopaths also appear to have low affiliative needs, but they continue to seek out social situations in order to disrupt them.

3. Disturbances of translation, social techniques and meshing. Schizophrenics cannot interact at all because of an inability to mesh and establish any kind of interaction system. Delinquents and many other adolescents can interact within the peer group, but not with any one else. Most mental patients apart from schizophrenics can interact, but cannot form social relationships because they are so unrewarding to be with. This could be due to a failure to correct social techniques in the light of feedback, or failure of perception, or lack of alternative social techniques. Berne (1966) described the games used by his neurotic patients. These games are destructive and aggressive social strategies motivated by the desire to humiliate others or by complex dynamic processes, such as avoiding the recognition of personal inadequacies.

4. Disturbance of self-image. Such failures occur in most disorders. Hysterics are much concerned with getting confirmation of their self-image; this is particularly true of impostors and pretenders who half-believe the parts they are playing (Deutsch, 1955). Paranoids, on the other hand, have no doubt about their self-image, but are upset because no one else will accept it. Another type of failure occurs in adolescents and schizophrenics – a failure to integrate the elements of self-perception into a stable ego identity (ego diffusion).

Summary and conclusion

In this article it has been suggested that the model developed by Welford (1958) and Broadbent (1958) for the analysis of sensorimotor performance may be usefully applied in the analysis of the behavior of people engaged in social interaction. Since we deal with *interaction*, however, the interrelationship of performances cannot be ignored, and the notion of equilibrium was put forward as a useful one for dealing with this.

A wide variety of studies have been reviewed, in an attempt to show how the social performance may be analysed into a number of components, each differing in function. Thus a distinction was drawn between features of the performance that remain relatively constant throughout the interaction, such as relative spatial position and orientation, and posture, and aspects of the performance that are more dynamic. The constant or standing features of the performance appear to function to 'set the stage' of a given encounter. The dynamic features, which include speech, and patterns of movement, have a variety of functions according to the kind of encounter considered. It was noted, for instance, how movement may serve to clarify or emphasize aspects of messages transmitted through speech; how patterns of looking and movement may serve to regulate the pacing of action in the encounter; and how the emotional relationships between the participants may be regulated, particularly through facial expression and levels of eye contact. This analysis remains sketchy. Much yet remains to be learned. The structure and function of movements significant for interaction is only beginning to be understood. The place of facial and other kinds of expression awaits systematic formulation. And, perhaps surprisingly, remarkably little is known about the role of language and speech.

There is no doubt of the value of studies such as these. As we have tried to make clear in the discussion of self-presentation and competence in social skill, the more we know about how the social performance is organized, what its components are, the better we shall be able to understand the nature of interpersonal processes. We have stressed the idea that there are a number of different social skills, each specific in function, and a detailed understanding of their organization opens up the possibility of social skills training, analogous to training in industrial skills which has followed so fruitfully upon the analysis of sensorimotor performance. This may have an important application in dealing with mental illness, in so far as these may be seen as breakdowns in social skill.

References

AMBROSE, J. A. (1963), 'The concept of a critical period for the development of social responsiveness in early human infancy', in B. M. Foss (ed.), *Determinants o Infant Behaviour*, vol. II, Methuen.

ANNETT, J., and KAY, H. (1956), 'Skilled performance', *Occup. Psychol.*, vol. 30, pp. 112–17.

ARGYLE, M. (1964), 'Introjection: a form of social learning', *Brit. J. Psychol.*, vol. 55, pp. 391–402.

ARGYLE, M. (1967), *The Psychology of Interpersonal Behaviour*, Penguin.

ARGYLE, M., and DEAN, J. (1965), 'Eye-contact, distance and affiliation' *Sociometry*, vol. 28, pp. 289–304. [Reprinted in this book, pp. 301–16.]

ARGYLE, M., GARDNER, G., and CIOFFI, F. (1958), 'Supervisory methods related to productivity, absenteeism and labour turnover', *Hum. Relat.*, vol. II, pp. 23–45.

ARGYLE, M., SMITH, T., and KIRTON, M. (1962), *Training Managers*, Acton Society Trust.

ARGYLE, M., LALLJEE, M., COOK, M., and LATANÉ, J. (1967), 'Effects of the visibility of the other in social interactions', unpublished paper.

BALES, R. F. (1953), 'The equilibrium problem in small groups', in T. Parsons R. F. Bales and C. A. Shils (eds.), *Working Papers in the Theory of Action*, Free Press.

BARKER, R. G., and WRIGHT, H. (1955), *Midwest and Its Children*, Harper & Row.

BARTLETT, F. C. (1958), *Thinking: An Experimental and Social Study*, Basic Books.

BASS, B. M., and KLUBECK, S. (1952), 'Effects of seating arrangements in leaderless group discussions', *J. abnorm. soc. Psychol.*, vol. 47, pp. 724–7.

BERNE, E. (1966), *Games People Play*, Grove Press; Penguin.

BERNSTEIN, B. (1964), 'Elaborated and restricted codes: their social origin and some consequences', *Amer. Anthrop.*, vol. 66, part 2, pp. 55–69.

BIRDWHISTELL, R. L. (1964), 'Communication without words', in P. Alexandre (ed.), *L'Aventure Humaine* (forthcoming).

BIRDWHISTELL, R. L. (1966), 'Some relations between kinesics and spoken American English', in A. G. Smith (ed.), *Communication and Culture: Readings in the Codes of Human Interaction*, Holt, Rinehart & Winston.

BLOOD, R. O., and LIVANT, W. P. (1957), 'The use of space within the cabin group', *J. Social Issues*, vol. 13, pp. 47–53.

BLOOMFIELD, L. (1933), *Language*, Henry Holt.

BORGATTA, E. F., and BALES, R. F. (1953), 'Interaction of individuals in reconstituted groups', *Sociometry*, vol. 16, pp. 302–20.

BOWLBY, J. (1958), 'The nature of the child's tie to his mother', *Int. J. Psycho-Analysis*, vol. 39, pp. 350–73.

BREER, P. E. (1960), 'Predicting interpersonal behavior from personality and role', unpublished doctoral dissertation, Harvard.

BROADBENT, D. E. (1958), *Perception and Communication*, Macmillan; Pergamon.

BUNKER, D. (1965), 'The effect of laboratory education on individual behavior' in E. H. Schein and W. G. Bennis (eds.), *Personal and Organizational Change Through Group Methods*, Wiley.

BURNS, T. (1964), 'Non-verbal communication', *Discovery*, no. 10, vol. 25, pp. 30–37.

CARMENT, D. W., MILES, C. G., and CERVIN, V. B. (1965), 'Persuasiveness and persuasibility as related to intelligence and extraversion', *Brit. J. Social and Clinical Psychology*, vol. 4, pp. 1–7.

CHAPPLE, E. D. (1940a), 'Measuring human relations', *Genet. Psychol. Monogr.*, vol. 22, pp. 3–147.

CHAPPLE, E. D. (1940b), ' "Personality" differences as described by invariant properties of individuals in interaction', *Proc. natn. Acad. Sci. USA*, vol. 26, pp. 10–16.

CHAPPLE, E. D. (1949), 'The interaction chronograph: its evolution and present application', *Personnel*, vol. 25, pp. 295–307.

CHAPPLE, E. D. (1953), 'The standard interview as used in interaction chronograph investigations', *Hum. Org.*, vol. 12, no. 2, pp. 23–32.

CHAPPLE, E. D. (1962), 'Quantitative analysis of complex organizational systems', *Hum. Org.*, vol. 21, pp. 67–80.

CHAPPLE, E. D., and COON, C. S. (1942), *Principles of Anthropology*, Holt, Rinehart & Winston.

CHAPPLE, E. D., and DONALD, G., Jr (1947), 'An evaluation of department store sales people by the interaction chronograph', *J. Marketing*, vol. 12, pp. 173–85.

CHAPPLE, E. D., and LINDEMANN, E. (1942), 'Clinical implications of measurements on interaction rates in psychiatric interviews', *Applied Anthropology*, vol. 1, pp. 1–11.

CHAPPLE, E. D., CHAPPLE, M. F., WOOD, L. A., MIKLOWITZ, A., KLINE, N. S., and SAUNDERS, J. C. (1960), 'Interaction chronograph method for analysis of differences between schizophrenics and controls', *AMA Archs. gen. Psychiat.*, vol. 3, pp. 160–67.

CONDON, W., and OGSTON, W. D. (1966), 'Sound film analysis of normal and pathological behavior patterns', *J. nerv. ment. Dis.*, vol. 143, pp. 338–47.

CORSINI, R. J., SHAW, M. C., and BLAKE, R. R. (1961), *Role Playing in Business and Industry*, Free Press.

CROSSMAN, E. R. F. W. (1964), 'Information processes in human skill', *Brit. med. Bull.*, vol. 20, pp. 32–7.

CROSSMAN, E. R. F. W., and EVERSTINE, L. (1965), 'Information transfer, feeddback, and the coding of communications within task-oriented groups', unpublished paper.

CRYSTAL, D., and QUIRK, R. (1964), 'Systems of prosodic and paralinguistic features in English', *Janua linguarum* (ser. minor), no. 34, Mouton.

DAVITZ, J. R. (1964), *The Communication of Emotional Meaning*, McGraw-Hill.

DEUTSCH, H. (1955), 'The impostor: contribution to ego psychology of a type of psychopath', *Psychoanal. Q.*, vol. 24, pp. 483–505.

DEVORE, I. (ed.) (1965), *Primate Behavior: Field Studies of Monkeys and Apes*, Holt, Rinehart & Winston.

DITTMAN, A. T. (1962), 'The relationship between body movements and moods in interviews', *J. consult. Psychol.*, vol. 26, p. 480.

DITTMAN, A. T., and WYNNE, L. C. (1961), 'Linguistic techniques and the analysis of emotionality in interviews', *J. abnorm. soc. Psychol.*, vol. 63, pp. 201–4.

EKMAN, P. (1965), 'Communication through non-verbal behavior: a source of information about an interpersonal relationship', in S. S. Tomkins and C. E. Izzard (eds.), *Affect, Cognition and Personality*, Springer.

ELDRED, S. H., and PRICE, D. B. (1958), 'A linguistic evaluation of feeling states in psychotherapy', *Psychiatry*, vol. 21, pp. 115–21.

ELWORTHY, F. T. (1895), *The Evil Eye: The Origins and Practices of Superstition*, John Murray.

ERIKSON, E. H. (1956), 'The problem of ego identity', *J. Amer. psychoanal. Ass.*, vol. 4, pp. 56–111.

ERVIN-TRIPP, S. (1964), 'An analysis of the interaction of language, topic and listener', *Amer. Anthrop.*, vol. 66, no. 6, part. 2, pp. 82–102.

EXLINE, R. V. (1963), 'Explorations in the process of person perception: visual interaction in relation to competition, sex and need for affiliation', *J. Personality* vol. 31, pp. 1–20.

EXLINE, R. V., and WINTERS, L. C. (1965), 'Affective relations and mutual glances in dyads', in S. S. Tomkins and C. E. Izzard (eds.), *Affect, Cognition and Personality*, Springer.

EXLINE, R. V., GRAY, D., and SCHUETTE, D. (1965), 'Visual behaviour in a dyad as affected by interview content, and sex of respondent', *J. Personality and Social Psychology*, vol. 1, pp. 201–9.

EXLINE, R. V., THIBAUT, J., BRANNON, C., and GUMPERT, P. (1961), 'Visual interaction in relation to Machiavellianism and an unethical act', *Amer Psychol.*, vol. 16, p. 396.

FERGUSON, C. (1959), 'Diglossia', *Word*, vol. 15, pp. 325–40.

FERGUSON, C. (1964), 'Baby talk in six languages', *Amer. Anthrop.*, vol. 66, no. 6, part 2, pp. 103–14.

FIEDLER, F. E. (1953), 'Quantitative studies on the role of therapists' feelings towards their patients', in O. H. Mowrer (ed.), *Psychotherapy, Theory and Research*, Ronald.

FIEDLER, F. E. (1964), 'A contingency model of leadership effectiveness', *Advance in Experimental Social Psychology*, vol. 1, pp. 150–90.

FRANK, L. K. (1957), 'Tactile communication', *Genet. Psychol. Monogr.*, vol. 56, pp. 209–25.

GARDNER, G. (1964), 'The psychotherapeutic relationship', *Psychol. Bull.*, vol. 61, pp. 426–37.

GARFINKEL, H. (1963), 'Trust and stable actions', in O. J. Harvey (ed.), *Motivation and Social Interaction*, Ronald.

GIBSON, J. J., and PICK, A. D. (1963), 'Perception of another person's looking behavior', *Amer. J. Psychol.*, vol. 76, pp. 386–94.

GLEASON, H. A. Jr (1961), *An Introduction to Descriptive Linguistics* (2nd edn), Holt, Rinehart & Winston.

GOFFMAN, E. (1955), 'On face-work: an analysis of ritual elements in social interaction', *Psychiatry*, vol. 18, pp. 213–31. [Reprinted in this book, pp. 319–46.]

GOFFMAN, E. (1956), 'Embarrassment and social organization', *Amer. J. Sociol.*, vol. 62, pp. 264–71.

GOFFMAN, E. (1957), 'Alienation from interaction', *Hum. Relat.*, vol. 10, pp. 47–60. [Reprinted in this book, pp. 347–63.]

GOFFMAN, E. (1959), *Presentation of Self in Everyday Life*, Doubleday.

GOFFMAN, E. (1961a), *Asylums*, Aldine.

GOFFMAN, E. (1961b), *Encounters*, Bobbs-Merrill.

GOFFMAN, E. (1963), *Behavior in Public Places*, Free Press.

GOLDMAN-EISLER, F. (1951), 'The measurement of time sequences in conversational behavior', *Brit. J. Psychol.*, Vol. 42, pp. 355–62.

GOLDMAN-EISLER, F. (1952), 'Individual differences between interviewers and their effect on interviewees' conversational behavior', *J. ment. Sci.*, vol. 98, pp. 660–71.

GOLDMAN-EISLER, F. (1958), 'Speech analysis and mental processes', *L & S*, vol. 1, pp. 59–75.

GOUGH, H. G. (1965), 'A validational study of the Chapin Social Insight Test', *Psychol. Rep.*, vol. 17, pp. 355–68.

GROSS, E., and STONE, C. P. (1964), 'Embarrassment and the analysis of role requirements', *Amer. J. Sociol.*, vol. 70, pp. 1–15.

GUZE, S. B., and MENSCH, I. N. (1959), 'An analysis of some features of the interview with the interaction chronograph', *J. abnorm. soc. Psychol.*, vol. 58, pp. 269–71.

HAINES, D. B., and EACHUS, H. T. (1965), 'A preliminary study of acquiring cross-cultural interaction skills through self-confrontation', Aerospace Medical Research Laboratory, Wright-Patterson Air Force Base, Ohio.

HALL, E. T. (1959), *The Silent Language*, Doubleday.

HALL, E. T. (1963), 'A system for the notation of proxemic behavior', *Amer. Anthrop.*, vol. 65, pp. 1003–26. [Reprinted in this book, pp. 247–73.]

HALL, E. T. (1964), 'Silent assumptions in social communication', *Res. Publs. Ass. Res. nerv. ment. Dis.*, vol. 42, pp. 41–55, [Reprinted in this book, pp. 274–88.]

HAMBLIN, R. L. (1958), 'Leadership and crises', *Sociometry*, vol. 21, pp. 322–35.

HARE, A. P., and BALES, R. F. (1963), 'Seating position and small group interaction', *Sociometry*, vol. 26, pp. 480–86.

HAYTHORN, W. (1956), 'The effects of varying combinations of authoritarian and equalitarian leaders and followers', *J. abnorm. soc. Psychol.*, vol. 52, pp. 210–19.

HAZARD, J. (1962), 'Furniture arrangement and judicial roles', *ETC.*, vol. 19, pp. 181–8.

HEDIGER, H. (1955), *Studies of the Psychology and Behaviour of Captive Animals in Zoos and Circuses*, Butterworth.

HEINICKE, C., and BALES, R. F. (1953), 'Developmental trends in the structure of small groups', *Sociometry*, vol. 16, pp. 7–38.
HERMAN, S. N. (1961), 'Explorations in the social psychology of language choice', *Hum. Relat.*, vol. 14, pp. 149–64.
HESS, E. H. (1965), 'Attitude and pupil size', *Scient. Amer.*, vol. 212, no. 4, pp. 46–54.
HEWES, G. W. (1955), 'World distribution of certain postural habits', *Amer. Anthrop.*, vol. 57, pp. 231–44.
HOMANS G. C. (1950), *The Human Group*, Harcourt, Brace & World.
HUTT, C., and OUNSTED, C. (1966), 'The biological significance of gaze aversion: with special reference to childhood autism', *Behavl. Sci.*, vol. 11, pp. 346–56.
HUTT, C., and VAIZEY, M. J. (1966), 'Differential effects of group density on social behaviour', *Nature*, vol. 209, pp. 1371–2.
HUTT, C., HUTT, S. J., LEE, D., and OUNSTED, C. (1964), 'Arousal and childhood autism', *Nature*, vol. 204, p. 908.
JAFFE, J. (1964), 'Verbal behavior analysis in psychiatric interviews with the aid of digital computers', *Res. Publs. Ass. nerv. ment. Dis.*, vol. 42, pp. 389–99.
JAY, P. (1965), 'The common langur of North India', in I. DeVore (ed.), *Primate Behavior: Field Studies of Monkeys and Apes*, Holt, Rinehart & Winston.
JECKER, J. D., MACCOBY, H., BREITROSE, H. S., and ROSE, E. D. (1964), 'Teacher accuracy in assessing cognitive visual feedback', *J. appl. Psychol.*, vol. 48, pp. 393–7.
JENNINGS, H. S. (1950), *Leadership and Isolation* (2nd edn), McKay.
JONES, E. E., and THIBAUT, J. W. (1958), 'Interaction goals as bases of inference in interpersonal perception', in R.Tagiuri and L. Petrullo (eds.), *Person Perception and Interpersonal Behavior*, Stanford University Press.
JOOS, M. (1962), 'The five clocks', *IJAL*, vol. 28, no. 2, part 5.
JOURARD, S. M. (1964), *The Transparent Self*, Van Nostrand.
JOURARD, S. M. (1966), 'An exploratory study of body-accessibility', *Brit. J. Soc. clin. Psychol.*
KANFER, F. H., PHILLIPS, J. S., MATARAZZO, J. D., and SASLOW, G. (1960), 'The experimental modification of interviewer content in standardized interviews', *J. consult. Psychol.*, vol. 24, pp. 528–36.
KENDON, A. (1963), 'Temporal aspects of the social performance in two-person encounters', unpublished doctoral dissertation, Oxford.
KENDON, A. (1967), 'Some functions of gaze direction in social interaction', *Acta psychol.*, vol. 26, pp. 22–63.
KRAMER, E. (1963), 'Judgment of personal characteristics and emotions from non-verbal properties of speech', *Psychol. Bull.*, vol. 60, pp. 408–20. [Reprinted in this book, pp. 172–88.]
LAING, R. (1960), *The Divided Self*, Quadrangle.
LASHLEY, K. S. (1951), 'The problem of serial order in behavior', in L. A. Jeffress (ed.), *Cerebral Mechanisms in Behavior*, Wiley.
LEIK, R. K. (1965), 'Type of group and probability of initiating acts', *Sociometry*, vol. 28, pp. 57–65.
LENNARD, H. L., and BERNSTEIN, A. (1960), *The Anatomy of Psychotherapy*, Columbia University Press.
LEVIN, H., BALDWIN, A. L. GALLWEY, M., and PAIVIO, A. (1960), 'Audience stress, personality and speech', *J. abnorm. soc. Psychol.*, vol. 61, pp. 469–73.
LIPPITT, R. (1949), *Training in Community Relations*, Harper & Row.
LITTLE, K. B. (1965), 'Personal space', *Journal of Experimental and Social Psychology*, vol. 1, pp. 237–47.

LOMBARD, G. G. F. (1955), *Behaviour in a Selling Group*, Harvard University Press.

LOTT, A. J., and LOTT, B. E. (1965), 'Group cohesiveness as interpersonal attraction: a review of relationships with antecedent and consequent variables', *Psychol. Bull.*, vol. 64, pp. 239–309.

LUNDY, B. W. (1955), 'Temporal factors of interaction in psychotherapy', unpublished doctoral dissertation, University of Chicago.

LUNDY, R. M. (1956), 'Assimilative projection and accuracy of prediction in interpersonal perceptions', *J. abnorm. soc. Psychol.*, vol. 52, pp. 33–8.

MCDAVID, J., Jr and SCHRODER, H. M. (1957), 'The interpretation of approval and disapproval by delinquent and non-delinquent adolescents', *J. Personality*, vol. 25, pp. 539–49.

MCGREGOR, D. (1960), *The Human Side of Enterprise*, McGraw-Hill.

MACHOTKA, P. (1965), 'Body movement as communication', *Dialogue: Behavioral Science Research*, Western Interstate Commission for Higher Education, Boulder, Colorado.

MACLAY, H. and OSGOOD C. E. (1959), 'Hesitation phenomena in English', *Word*, vol. 15, pp. 19–44.

MCPHAIL, P. (1966), 'Adolescent problems of adjustment', in G. N. P. Howat (ed.), *Essays to a Young Teacher*, Macmillan; Pergamon.

MAHL, G. F. (1963), 'The lexical and linguistic levels in the expression of the emotions', in H. Knapp (ed.), *Expressions of Emotion in Man*, International University Press.

MAHL, G. F., and SCHULZE, G. (1964), 'Psychological research in the extralinguistic area', in T. A. Sebeok, A. S. Hayes and M. C. Bateson (eds.), *Approaches to Semiotics*, Mouton.

MAIER, N. R. F. (1952), *Principles of Human Relations*, Wiley.

MAIER, N. R. F., SOLEM, A. R., and MAIER, A. A. (1957), *Supervising and Executive Development*, Wiley.

MALINOWSKI, B. (1928), 'The problem of meaning in primitive languages', supplement I to C. K. Ogden and I. A. Richards, *The Meaning of Meaning* (rev. edn), Harcourt, Brace & World, 1966. [Excerpt reprinted in this book, pp. 146–52.]

MASLOW, A. H., HIRSH, E., STEIN, M., and HONIGMANN, I. (1945), 'A clinically derived test for measuring psychological security-insecurity', *J. genet. Psychol.*, vol. 33, pp. 24–41.

MATARAZZO, J. D. (1962), 'Prescribed behavior therapy. Suggestions from noncontent interview research', in A. Bachrach (ed.), *Experimental Foundations of Clinical Psychology*, Basic Books.

MATARAZZO, J. D., and SASLOW, G. (1961), 'Difference in interview interaction behavior among normal and deviant groups', in I. A. Berg and B. M. Bass (eds.), *Conformity and Deviation*, Harper & Row.

MATARAZZO, J. D., WIENS, A. N., and SASLOW, G. (1965), 'Studies of interview speech behavior', in L. Krasner and L. P. Ullman (eds.), *Research in Behavior Modification: New Developments and Their Clinical Implications*, Holt, Rinehart & Winston.

MATARAZZO, J. D., WEITMAN, M., SASLOW, G., and WIENS, A. N. (1963), 'Interviewer influence on duration of interviewee speech', *J VL V B*, vol. 1, pp. 451–8.

MATARAZZO, J. D., SASLOW, G., WIENS, A. N., WEITMAN, M., and ALLEN, B.V. (1964a), 'Interviewer headnodding and interviewee speech durations', *Psychotherapy, Theory, Research and Practice*, vol. 1, pp. 54–63.

MATARAZZO, J. D., WIENS, A. N., SASLOW, G., DUNHAM, R. M., and VOAS, R. B. (1964b), 'Speech duration of astronaut and ground communicator', *Science*, vol. 143, pp. 148-50.

MILLER, D. R. (1963), 'The study of social relationships: situation, identity and social interaction', *Psychology: A Study of a Science*, vol. 5, pp. 639-737.

MILLER, G. A., GALANTER, E., and PRIBRAM, K. H. (1960), *Plans and the Structure of Behavior*, Holt, Rinehart & Winston.

MILLER, N. E. (1944), 'Experimental studies of conflict', in J. McV. Hunt (ed.), *Personality and the Behaviour Disorders*, Ronald.

MOHANNA, A. I., and ARGYLE, M. (1960), 'A cross-cultural study of structured groups with unpopular central members', *J. abnorm. soc. Psychol.*, vol. 60, pp. 139-40.

MOSCOVICI, S., and PLON, M. (1966), 'Les situations collogues: observations théoriques et expérimentales', *Bull. Psychol.*, vol. 247, pp. 702-22.

NEWCOMB, T. M. (1961), *The Acquaintance Process*, Holt, Rinehart & Winston.

NIELSEN, G. (1962), *Studies in Self Confrontation*, Munksgaard.

NORTHWAY, M. L., and WIGDOR, B. T. (1947), 'Rorschach patterns as related to the sociometric status of school children', *Sociometry*, vol. 10, pp. 186-99.

OSGOOD, C. E. (1966), 'Dimensionality of the semantic space for communication via facial expressions', *Scand. J. Psychol.*, vol. 7, pp. 1-30.

OSTWALD, P. F. (1965), 'Acoustic methods in psychiatry', *Scient. Amer.*, vol. 212, no. 3, pp. 82-91.

PAIVIO, A., BALDWIN, A. L., and BERGER, S. M. (1961), 'Measurement of children's sensitivity to audiences', *Child Dev.*, vol. 32, pp. 721-30.

PIKE, K. L. (1954), *Language in Relation to a Unified Theory of the Structure of Human Behavior*, Summer Institute of Linguistics, vol. 1.

PITTENGER, R. E. (1958), 'Linguistic analysis of tone of voice in communication of affect', *Psychiat. Res. Rep.*, vol. 8, pp. 41-54.

PITTENGER, R. E., and SMITH, H. L. (1957), 'A basis for some contributions of linguistics to psychiatry', *Psychiatry*, vol. 20, pp. 61-78.

PITTENGER, R. E., HOCKETT, C. F., and DANEHY, J. J. (1960), *The First Five Minutes: A Sample of Microscopic Interview Analysis*, Martineau.

POPE, B., and SIEGMAN, A. W. (1962), 'The effect of therapist activity level and specificity on patient productivity and speech disturbances in the initial interview' *J. consult. Psychol.*, vol. 26, p. 489.

POPE, B., and SIEGMAN, A. W. (1965), 'Interviewer specificity and topical focus in relation to interviewee productivity', *JVLVB*, vol. 4, pp. 188-92.

POTTER, S. (1952), *One-upmanship*, Hart-Davis.

RIEMER, M. D. (1955), 'Abnormalities of the gaze - a classification', *Psychiat. Q.*, vol. 29, pp. 659-72.

ROSENBAUM, M. E. (1959), 'Social perception and the motivational structure of interpersonal relations', *J. abnorm. soc. Psychol.*, vol. 59, pp. 130-33.

ROSENBERG, M. (1965), *Society and the Adolescent Self-image*, Princeton University Press.

SAPIR, E. (1921), *Language: An Introduction to the Study of Speech*, Harcourt, Brace & World.

SARBIN, T. R., and HARDYCK, C. R. (1955), 'Conformance in role perception as a personality variable', *J. consult. Psychol.*, vol. 19, pp. 109-11.

SASLOW, G., and MATARAZZO, J. D. (1959), 'A technique for studying changes in interview behavior', in E. A. Rubinstein and M. B. Parloff (eds.), *Research in Psychotherapy*, American Psychological Association.

SASLOW, G., GOODRICH, D. W., and STEIN, M. (1956) 'Study of therapist behavior in diagnostic interviews by means of the interaction chronograph', *J. clin. Psychol.*, vol. 12, pp. 133–9.

SCHEFLEN, A. E. (1964), 'The significance of posture in communication systems', *Psychiatry*, vol. 27, pp. 316–21. [Reprinted in this book, pp. 225–46.]

SCHEFLEN, A. E. (1965a), *Stream and Structure of Communicational Behavior*, Eastern Pennsylvania Psychiatric Institute.

SCHEFLEN, A. E. (1965b), 'Natural history method in psychotherapy: communicational research', in L. Gottschalk and A. H. Auerbach (eds.), *Methods of Research in Psychotherapy*, Appleton-Century-Crofts.

SCHLOSBERG, H. (1954), 'Three dimensions of emotion', *Psychol. Rev.*, vol. 61, pp. 81–8.

SCHUTZ, W. C. (1955) 'What makes groups productive?', *Hum. Relat.*, vol. 8, pp. 429–65.

SCHUTZ, W. C. (1958), *FIRO: A Three Dimensional Theory of Interpersonal Behavior*, Holt, Rinehart & Winston.

SECORD, P. F. and BACKMAN, C. W. (1964), *Social Psychology*, McGraw-Hill.

SIDNEY, C., and BROWN, M. (1961), *The Skills of Interviewing*, Tavistock.

SIEGMAN, A. W., and POPE, B. (1962), 'An empirical scale for the measurement of therapist specificity in the initial psychiatric interview', *Psychol. Rep.*, vol. 11, pp. 515–20.

SIEGMAN, A. W., and POPE, B. (1965), 'Effects of question specificity and anxiety producing messages on verbal fluency in the initial interview', *Journal of Personality and Social Psychology*, vol. 2, pp. 522–30.

SIMON, H. A. (1952), 'A formal theory of interaction in social groups', *Amer. Sociol. Rev.*, vol. 17, pp. 202–11.

SOMMER, R. (1959), 'Studies in personal space', *Sociometry*, vol. 22, pp. 247–60.

SOMMER, R. (1961), 'Leadership and group geography', *Sociometry*, vol. 24, pp. 99–109.

SOMMER, R. (1962), 'The distance for comfortable conversation', *Sociometry*, vol. 25, pp. 111–16.

SOMMER, R. (1965), 'Further studies of small group ecology', *Sociometry*, vol. 28, pp. 337–48. [Reprinted in this book, pp. 289–300.]

SORENSEN, O. (1958), 'The observed changes enquiry', General Electric Company.

SOSKIN, W. F., and JOHN, V. P. (1963), 'The study of spontaneous talk', in R. G. Barker (ed.), *The Stream of Behavior: Exploration of Its Structure and Content*, Appleton-Century-Crofts.

STAGNER, R. (1961), *Psychology of Personality*, McGraw-Hill.

STEINER, I. D. (1955), 'Interpersonal behaviour as influenced by accuracy of social perception', *Psychol. Rev.*, vol. 62, pp. 268–74.

STEINZOR, B. (1950), 'The spatial factor in face to face discussion groups', *J. abnorm. soc. Psychol.*, vol. 45, pp. 552–5.

STOCK, D. (1964), 'A survey of research on T-group', in L. P. Bradford, J. R. Gibb and K. D. Benns (eds.), *T-Group Theory and Laboratory Method*, Wiley.

SUMBY, W. H., and POLLACK, I. (1954), 'Visual contribution to speech intelligibility in noise', *J. acoust. Soc. Amer.*, vol. 26, pp. 212–15.

THARP, R. G. (1963), 'Psychological patterning in marriage', *Psychol. Bull.*, vol. 60, pp. 97–117.

THIBAUT, J. W., and KELLEY, H. H. (1959), *The Social Psychology of Groups*, Wiley.

THORNDIKE, R. L., and STEIN, S. (1937), 'An evaluation of the attempts to measure social intelligence', *Psychol. Bull.*, vol. 34, pp. 275–85.

TOMKINS, S. S. (1963), *Affect, Imagery, Consciousness.* Vol. II. *The Negative Effects*, Springer.

TRAGER, G. L. (1958), 'Paralanguage: a first approximation', *SIL*, vol. 13, pp. 1–12.

TRIANDIS, H. C. (1960), 'Cognitive similarity and communication in a dyad', *Hum. Relat.*, vol. 13, pp. 175–83.

TUASON, V. B., GUZE, S. B., McCLURE, J., and BEGNELIN, J. (1961), 'A further study of some features of the interview with the interaction chronograph', *Amer. J. Psychiat.*, vol. 118, pp. 438–46.

WATSON, J. and POTTER, R. J. (1962), 'An analytic unit for the study of interaction', *Hum. Relat.*, vol. 15, pp. 245–63.

WEISBROD, R. M. (1965), 'Looking behavior in a discussion group', term paper submitted for Psychology 546, under the direction of Prof. Longabaugh, Cornell University, Ithaca, New York.

WELFORD, A. T. (1958), *Ageing and Human Skill*, Oxford University Press.

WINER, M. and MEHRABIAN, A. 'Beyond meaning: a communication channel in verbal behavior', unpublished manuscript.

WOLFF, P. H. (1963), 'Observations on the early development of smiling', in B. M. Foss (ed.), *Determinants of Infant Behaviour*, vol. 2, Methuen.

WYNNE-EDWARDS, V. C. (1962), *Animal Dispersion in Relation to Social Behavior*, Harcourt, Brace & World.

2 D. Abercrombie

Paralanguage

D. Abercrombie, 'Paralanguage', *British Journal of Disorders of Communication*, vol. 3, 1968, pp. 55–9.

We speak with our vocal organs, but we converse with our entire bodies; conversation consists of much more than a simple interchange of spoken words. The term *paralanguage* is increasingly commonly used to refer to non-verbal communicating activities which accompany verbal behaviour in conversation. Anyone with a professional interest in spoken language is likely, sooner or later, to have to take an interest in paralanguage too.

I do not, all the same, like the term paralanguage very much, although I have used it for my title, and although it has been widely adopted. It seems to me potentially misleading: it can give the impression that, because there exists a (more or less) homogeneous entity called *language*, there must be, existing beside it, a comparably homogeneous entity called *paralanguage*. I believe this is not so. (The word *paralinguistics*, I regret to say, has already emerged as a name for a new subject, the study of para-language; and we may be sure that *paralinguist*, or *paralinguistician*, will not be far behind to designate the person who practises it.) These non-verbal, though conversational, activities to which the word paralanguage refers are far too diverse, too little codified, too uninvestigated, and too insufficiently understood, to be given the air of unity which a noun confers on them; so, having used 'Paralanguage' for the title of my paper, I shall, as far as I can, from now on avoid it. The adjective *paralinguistic* (which was the first of all these terms to be coined) seems to me, however, much more innocuous, with less power to mislead; and I shall therefore prefer to speak of paralinguistic phenomena, or behaviour, or activities, rather than of paralanguage.

Paralinguistic phenomena are neither idiosyncratic and personal, on the one hand, nor generally human, on the other. They must, therefore, be culturally determined, and so, as one would expect, they differ from social group to social group. They differ a great deal, and the differences go with language differences, even with dialect differences within languages, though they sometimes cut across linguistic boundaries. These aspects of human behaviour are bound therefore to interest language teachers, psychiatrists, anthropologists, speech therapists, and of course linguists and phoneticians too. Their systematic investigation started comparatively recently, though a desultory interest in them is of long standing. However, a great deal has been done during the last few years – particularly, interestingly enough, by, or in collaboration with, psychiatrists; and I would like here to summarize, sometimes critically, what has so far been accomplished in this area.

Paralinguistic phenomena are non-linguistic elements in conversation. They occur alongside spoken language, interact with it, and produce together with it a total system of communication. They are not necessarily continuously simultaneous with spoken words. They may also be interspersed among them, or precede them, or follow them; but they are always integrated into a conversation considered as a complete linguistic interaction. The study of paralinguistic behaviour is part of the study of conversation: the conversational use of spoken language cannot be properly understood unless paralinguistic elements are taken into account.

All animals communicate with each other by means of noises, bodily movements and postures, and human beings are no exception; they too communicate by acts which are not different in kind. But human beings have language as well, and these more primitive communicative acts have often become entangled with spoken language when used in conversation, and hence become paralinguistic. Of course, plenty of other 'animal-like' communicative acts are used in various circumstances by human beings, but not as part of conversation: they are then not paralinguistic. This is perhaps a good point to try to delimit the application of 'paralinguistic' rather more strictly than some writers have done. Paralinguistic activities must (a) communicate, and (b) be part of a conversational interaction. These two requirements rule out several sorts of activity which have at times been put together with paralinguistic activities. They rule out, for example, a nervous twitch of the eyelid which some people have while talking, since it does not communicate, and many personal mannerisms and tics, since they do not either; and they rule out, for example, the act of taking one's hat off, or a 'wolf whistle', which communicate but do not enter into conversation. (They may initiate one.) Moreover to be accounted paralinguistic an element in conversation must, at least potentially, be consciously controllable: hoarseness may communicate the fact that one has a cold, but it is not a paralinguistic element in conversation.

We see then that paralinguistic behaviour is non-verbal communication, but not all non-verbal communication is paralinguistic. I have just limited the application of the word, compared to the way it is used by some other writers; I should now like to widen its current application in an important respect. This is connected with a second reason why I do not like the noun *paralanguage* being used in this field. It inevitably runs the risk of being brought into association with that rather special meaning given to the word *language* by certain linguists today who, following Bloomfield, say it can only be 'the noise you make with your face'. If language is this, then – it will be said – paralanguage too must be facial noises. And in fact this is the way the word paralanguage is used by most people nowadays. When systematic investigation of the field first started, in America, the word *metalinguistic* was (not very happily) chosen for these non-linguistic elements in conversation (Smith, 1950), and they were divided into two classes, called *kinesics* and *vocalizations* (another rather unhappy term) – roughly, elements due to movements and elements due to sounds. When the term *paralanguage* was introduced (see Trager, 1958, for the early history of these studies) it was applied only to what earlier had been called vocalizations, and kinesics pursued a largely independent existence. This has been a pity. Parallels between the two have been obscured, and kinesics has expanded to include the study of all human bodily movement and posture, whether paralinguistic or not.

I would therefore go back to the early days, and apply the word paralinguistic to both movements and sounds. It is convenient for descriptive purposes to have this dichotomy of paralinguistic elements into *visible movements and postures* and *audible movements and postures* (as many have pointed out, there is a strong gestural aspect about sounds produced by the vocal organs), but it should not be taken to imply difference of function between them in conversation. I do not think there is any. (I would suggest it might be an advantage to restrict the word *kinesics* to the study of non-conversational bodily movements of all kinds.)

If we start examining visible paralinguistic elements, we find another dichotomy, a functional one, useful here, which I suggested some years ago (Abercombie, 1954). This dichotomy is into those elements which *can* be *independent* of the verbal elements of conversation, and those which *must* be *dependent* on them. A participant in a conversation may nod his head, for example, at the same time as he says the word '*yes*'; or he may nod but say nothing – the nod will still communicate. This, therefore, is an *independent* paralinguistic element – it *can* occur alone, though it does not have to. Manual gestures of emphasis, on the other hand, must always accompany spoken words, and communicate nothing without them. These therefore are *dependent* paralinguistic elements.

Much of dependent visible paralinguistic behaviour comes under the heading of posture – the general way in which the whole body is disposed, either when sitting or standing during conversation. Posture goes through a series of changes while people converse (Scheflen, 1964): legs are crossed or uncrossed, participants lean forward or back, elbows are placed on tables, and so on. These changes in posture have a punctuative role in conversation: they indicate the beginnings and endings of contributions to the interaction, show when a point has been made, make clear the relations of participants to each other at any given moment. They are not, as might be supposed, random. The number of postures used in any given culture appears to be limited, and their configurations are determined culturally: Englishmen, we are told by Scheflen, cross their legs differently from Americans. (The study of posture already has its own name in some quarters: 'body semantics'.)

Conversations take place most commonly in the world, perhaps, while the participants are standing up. The distance at which they stand from each other is then of paralinguistic importance, and moreover may vary greatly from culture to culture. Each person unconsciously adopts the conversational proximity appropriate to situations in his own culture; the use of the wrong distance – whether too close or too far away – can give offence (Hall, 1964). (The study of the proximity of conversationalists also already has a name: 'proxemics'.)

It is probably necessary to distinguish at least three more dependent ingredients in visible paralinguistic communication, each making its own contribution to the interaction: gesture, facial expression and eye contacts between the participants. Gesture is superimposed on posture, involves less of the body at any one time, and changes more rapidly. The amount of gesture that accompanies the verbal elements of conversation varies very much between cultures, as has often been pointed out, and so do the gesture movements themselves. Much of facial expression is probably idiosyncratic and not to be accounted paralinguistic, though some of it undoubtedly is in some cultures. It is characteristic of other cultures that changes in facial expression are absent in conversation ('dead-pan'). The role of eye contacts in conversation is only recently beginning to be understood (Argyle, 1967).

Gesture and facial expression supply the independent visible elements in paralinguistic communication: shrugs, nods, winks, and so on. ('Gesture languages' or 'sign languages', whether of the deaf or of American Indians, are, as their name indicates, linguistic and not paralinguistic; they are systems of communication which are structured as language.)

The same dichotomy, into independent and dependent elements, is useful for handling audible elements of paralinguistic behaviour also. Independent elements are what are usually called *interjections*, and examples are easy to find in all languages. They are characterized by the fact that they do not follow the normal phonological rules of the language. In English we have recognized ways of spelling many of them – *tut tut*, *whew*, *uh-huh*, *ahem*, *humph*, *sh*, *ugh* – though one could not pronounce them from the spelling unless one already knew what the interjection was.

Dependent audible elements, which are extremely varied, might all be put together under another popular term, *tones of voice*. They are produced by variations from the social *linguistic* norm in features of voice dynamics (Abercrombie, 1967, p. 95) – loudness, tempo, register, tessitura and others; and also by 'talking through' sobs, yawning, laughter, and so on. A large number of categories have been developed by some writers (Trager, 1958; Crystal and Quirk, 1964) for dealing with them.

I have simply tried here to indicate briefly the state of our knowledge of paralinguistic phenomena at the present time. Their investigation has perhaps not made the progress it should in some directions, and this is for diverse reasons: because of the initial unfortunate separation of the visible and the audible components; because of over-categorization – too much taxonomy without enough to classify; and because linguists have left too much of the work to others. There is an urgent need for the comparative study, over as much of the world as possible, of the full range of paralinguistic phenomena – the kind of thing for which the linguistic field-worker is best fitted. Fact-finding, not theorizing, is what is wanted at this present juncture. True, fact-finding needs a theoretical framework within which to be conducted, but at this stage categories should be kept flexible, not allowed to proliferate, and regarded mainly as heuristic rather than explanatory. The difficulties – and the expense – of investigation should not, of course, be underrated. Talking films seem essential for obtaining data, and they would probably have to be clandestinely taken, 'candid camera' fashion, to be of real value, which raises difficult moral problems about invasion of privacy. There is also the problem of devising a notation adequate for a paralinguistic text parallel with the linguistic one. The most ambitious attempt at this so far is probably Pittenger, Hockett and Danehy (1960); other examples of notations and texts can be found in Birdwhistell (1952), Crystal and Quirk (1964), Austin (1965), and others. Sybille Bedford (1958) accompanied her account of the trial of Dr Adams by well-observed notes on the paralinguistic behaviour of the participants, though they are hardly adequate for scientific analysis. A good example of reporting on paralinguistic facts from a linguistic field-worker is Revill (1966) – though here one meets a new danger in this field, the use of the 'amateur actor'. The investigator asks a subject to demonstrate how he would show distaste, or anger, or fear, and so on; but most people, unfortunately, are bad amateur actors, and information so obtained must often be unreliable.

At this point it is appropriate to ask, what sort of things are all these paralinguistic elements communicating in a conversational exchange? The answer sometimes given is that they are communicating attitudes and emotions, the linguistic side of the interchange being more 'referential'.

But this is not really satisfactory. Paralinguistic elements are often clearly referential – many independent gestures, for instance, which can even be translated directly into words such as 'tomorrow', or 'money'. And on the other hand linguistic elements in a conversation may often communicate attitudes or emotions.

It seems to me a possible hypothesis, in the present state of our knowledge, that in all cultures conversation communicates more or less the same total of 'meaning' of all kinds – sense, feeling, tone, intention; or however one wants to divide up referential and emotive components. Where cultural groups differ, however, is in the way the total information is distributed over the linguistic and the paralinguistic elements of the conversation. For instance, Jules Henry (1936) reports that among the Kaingang of Brazil concepts of degree and intensity are communicated by such things as changes in pitch, facial expression and bodily posture, though we communicate these things by formal linguistic devices. On the other hand in Dakota, an American Indian language, an emotional state such as annoyance, which with us would be communicated in conversation by facial expression or tone of voice, has formal linguistic expression by means of a particle added at the end of the sentence (of normal phonological structure, and therefore not an interjection).

Almost anything can be communicated linguistically, and almost anything paralinguistically. What is to be regarded as linguistic and what as paralinguistic depends not on the nature of what is communicated, but on how it is communicated – whether by formal systems and structures, in which case it is linguistic, or not, in which case it is paralinguistic.

References

ABERCROMBIE, D. (1954), 'Gesture', *ELT*, vol 9. (Reprinted in *Problems and Principles in Language Study*, Longmans, 1956.)

ARGYLE, M. (1967), *The Psychology of Interpersonal Behaviour*, Penguin.

AUSTIN, W. M. (1965), 'Some social aspects of paralanguage', *CJL*, vol. 11, pp. 31–9.

BEDFORD, S. (1958), *The Best We Can Do*, Penguin.

BIRDWHISTELL, R. L. (1952), *Introduction to Kinesics*, University of Louisville Press.

CRYSTAL, D. and QUIRK, R. (1964), *Systems of Prosodic and Paralinguistic Features in English*, Mouton.

HALL, E. T. (1964), 'Silent assumptions in social communication', in D. M. Rioch and E. A. Weinstein (eds.), *Disorders of Communication*, The Williams & Wilkins Co. [Reprinted in this book, pp. 247–73.]

HENRY, J. (1936), 'The linguistic expression of emotion', *Amer. Anthrop.*, vol. 38, pp. 250–56.

PITTENGER, R. E., HOCKETT, C. F., and DANEHY, J. J. (1960), *The First Five Minutes*, Paul Martineau.

REVILL, P. M. (1966), 'Preliminary report on para-linguistics in Mbembe', appendix viii in K. L. Pike, *Tagmemic and Matrix Linguistics Applied to Selected African Languages*, University of Michigan Center for Research on Language and Language Behavior.

SCHEFLEN, A. E. (1964), 'The significance of posture in communication systems', *Psychiatry*, vol. 27, pp. 316–21. [Reprinted in this book, pp. 225–46.]

SMITH, H. L. (1950), *The Communication Situation*, Foreign Service Institute, Department of State, Washington (mimeographed).

TRAGER, G. L. (1958), 'Paralanguage: a first approximation', *SIL*, vol. 13, pp. 1–12.

3 E. Sapir

Speech as a Personality Trait

E. Sapir, 'Speech as a personality trait', *American Journal of Sociology*, vol. 32, 1927, pp. 892–905.

If one is at all given to analysis, one is impressed with the extreme complexity of the various types of human behavior, and it may be assumed that the things that we take for granted in our ordinary, everyday life are as strange and as unexplainable as anything one might find. Thus one comes to feel that the matter of speech is very far from being the self-evident or simple thing that we think it to be; that it is capable of a very great deal of refined analysis from the standpoint of human behavior; and that one might, in the process of making such an analysis, accumulate certain ideas for the research of personality problems.

There is one thing that strikes us as interesting about speech: on the one hand, we find it difficult to analyse; on the other hand, we are very much guided by it in our actual experience. That is perhaps something of a paradox, yet both the simple mind and the keenest of scientists know very well that we do not react to the suggestions of the environment in accordance with our specific knowledge alone. Some of us are more intuitive than others, it is true, but none is entirely lacking in the ability to gather and be guided by speech impressions in the intuitive exploration of personality. We are taught that when a man speaks he says something that he wishes to communicate. That, of course, is not necessarily so. He intends to say something, as a rule, yet what he actually communicates may be measurably different from what he started out to convey. We often form a judgement of what he is by what he does not say, and we may be very wise to refuse to limit the evidence for judgement to the overt content of speech. One must read between the lines, even when they are not written on a sheet of paper.

In thinking over this matter of the analysis of speech from the point of view of personality study, the writer has come to feel that we might have two quite distinct approaches; two quite distinct analyses might be undertaken that would intercross in a very intricate fashion. In the first place, the analysis might differentiate the individual and society, in so far as society speaks through the individual. The second kind of analysis would take up the different levels of speech, starting from the lowest level, which is the voice itself, clear up to the formation of complete sentences. In ordinary life we say that a man conveys certain impressions by his speech, but we rarely stop to analyse this apparent unit of behavior into its super-imposed levels. We might give him credit for brilliant ideas when he merely possesses a smooth voice. We are often led into misunderstandings of this sort, though we are not generally so easily fooled. We can go over the entire speech situation without being able to put our finger on the precise spot in the speech complex that leads to our making this or that personality judgement. Just as the dog knows whether to turn to the right or to the left, so we know that we must make certain judgements, but we might well be mistaken if we tried to give the reason for making them.

Let us look for a moment at the justification for the first kind of analysis, the differentation between the social and the purely individual point of view. It requires no laboured argument to prove that this distinction is a necessary one. We human beings do not exist out of society. If you put a man in a cell, he is still in society because he carries his thoughts with him and these thoughts, pathologic though they be, were formed with the help of society. On the other hand, we can never have experience of social patterns as such, however greatly we may be interested in them. Take so simple a social pattern as the word *horse*. A horse is an animal with four legs, a mane and a neigh; but, as a matter of fact, the social pattern of reference to this animal does not exist in its purity. All that exists is my saying *horse* today, *horse* yesterday, *horse* tomorrow. Each of the events is different. There is something peculiar about each of them. The voice, for one thing, is never quite the same. There is a different quality of emotion in each articulation, and the intensity of the emotion too is different. It is not difficult to see why it is necessary to distinguish the social point of view from the individual, for society has its patterns, its set ways of doing things, its distinctive 'theories' of behavior, while the individual has his method of handling those particular patterns of society, giving them just enough of a twist to make them 'his' and no one else's. We are so interested in ourselves as individuals and in others who differ, however slightly, from us that we are always on the alert to mark the variations from the nuclear pattern of behavior. To one who is not accustomed to the pattern, these variations would appear so slight as to be all but unobserved. Yet they are of maximum importance to us as individuals; so much so that we are liable to forget that there is a general social pattern to vary from. We are often under the impression that we are original or otherwise aberrant when, as a matter of fact, we are merely repeating a social pattern with the very slightest accent of individuality.

To proceed to the second point of view, the analysis of speech on its different levels. If we were to make a critical survey of how people react to voice and what the voice carries, we would find them relatively naïve about the different elements involved in speech. A man talks and makes certain impressions, but, as we have seen, we are not clear as to whether it is his voice which most powerfully contributes to the impression or the ideas which are conveyed. There are several distinct levels in speech behavior, which to linguists and psychologists are, each of them, sets of real phenomena, and we must now look at these in order to obtain some idea of the complexity of normal human speech. I will take up these various levels in order, making a few remarks about each of them as I proceed.

The lowest or most fundamental speech level is the voice. It is closest to the hereditary endowment of the individual, considered out of relation to society, 'low' in the sense of constituting a level that starts with the psychophysical organism given at birth. The voice is a complicated bundle of reactions and, so far as the writer knows, no one has succeeded in giving a comprehensive account of what the voice is and what changes it may undergo. There seems to be no book or essay that classifies the many different types of voice, nor is there a nomenclature that is capable of doing justice to the bewildering range of voice phenomena. And yet it is by delicate nuances of voice quality that we are so often confirmed in our judgement of people. From a more general point of view, voice may be considered a form of gesture. If we are swayed by a certain thought or emotion, we may express ourselves with our hands or some other type of gesturing and the voice takes part in the total play of gesture. From our present point of view, however, it is possible to isolate the voice as a functional unit.

Voice is generally thought of as a purely individual matter, yet is it quite correct to say that the voice is given us at birth and maintained unmodified throughout life? Or has the voice a social quality as well as an individual one? I think we all feel, as a matter of fact, that we imitate each other's voices to a not inconsiderable extent. We know very well that if, for some reason or other, the timbre of the voice that we are heir to has been criticized, we try to modify it, so that it may not be a socially unpleasant instrument of speech. There is always something about the voice that must be ascribed to the social background, precisely as in the case of gesture. Gestures are not the simple, individual things they seem to be. They are largely peculiar to this or that society. In the same way, in spite of the personal and relatively fixed character of the voice, we make involuntary adjustments in the larynx that bring about significant modifications in the voice. Therefore, in deducing fundamental traits of personality from the voice we must try to disentangle the social element from the purely personal one. If we are not careful to do this, we may make a serious error of judgement. A man has a strained or raucous voice, let us say, and we might infer that he is basically 'coarse-grained'. Such a judgement might be entirely wide of the mark if the particular society in which he lives is an out-of-doors society that indulges in a good deal of swearing and rather rough handling of the voice. He may have had a very soft voice to begin with, symptomatic of a delicate psychic organization, which gradually toughened under the influence of social suggestion. The personality which we are trying to disentangle lies hidden under its overt manifestations, and it is our task to develop scientific methods to get at the 'natural', theoretically unmodified voice. In order to interpret the voice as to its personality value, one needs to have a good idea of how much of it is purely individual, due to the natural formation of the larynx, to peculiarities of breathing, to a thousand and one factors that biologists may be able to define for us. One might ask at this point: why attach importance to the quality of the voice? What has that to do with personality? After all is said and done, a man's voice is primarily formed by natural agencies, it is what God has blessed him with. Yes, but is that not essentially true of the whole of personality? Inasmuch as the psychophysical organism is very much of a unit, we can be quite sure on general principles that in looking for the thing we call personality we have the right to attach importance to the thing we call voice. Whether personality is expressed as adequately in the voice as in gesture or in carriage, we do not know. Perhaps it is even more adequately expressed in the voice than in these. In any event, it is clear that the nervous processes that control voice production must share in the individual traits of the nervous organization that condition the personality.

The essential quality of the voice is an amazingly interesting thing to puzzle over. Unfortunately we have no adequate vocabulary for its endless varieties. We speak of a high-pitched voice. We say a voice is 'thick', or it is 'thin'; we say it is 'nasal', if there is something wrong with the nasal part of the breathing apparatus. If we were to make an inventory of voices, we would find that no two of them are quite alike. And all the time we feel that there is something about the individual's voice that is indicative of his personality. We may even go so far as to surmise that the voice is in some way a symbolic index of the total personality. Some day, when we know more about the physiology and psychology of the voice, it will be possible to line up our intuitive judgements as to voice quality with a scientific analysis of voice formation. We do not know what it is precisely that makes the voice sound 'thick' or 'vibrant' or 'flat' or what not. What is it that arouses us in one man's voice, where another's stirs us not at all? I remember listening many years ago to an address by a college president and deciding on the spur of the moment that what he said could be of no interest to me. What I meant was that no matter how interesting or pertinent his remarks were in themselves, his personality could not touch mine because there was something about his voice that did not appeal to me, something revealing as to personality. There was indicated – so one gathered intuitively – a certain quality of personality, a certain force, that I knew could not easily integrate with my own apprehension of things. I did not listen to what he said, I listened only to the quality of his voice. One might object that that was a perfectly idiotic thing to do. Perhaps it was, but I believe that we are all in the habit of doing just such things and that we are essentially justified in so doing – not intellectually, but intuitively. It therefore becomes the task of an intellectual analysis to justify for us on reasoned grounds what we have knowledge of in pre-scientific fashion.

There is little purpose in trying to list the different types of voice. Suffice it to say that on the basis of his voice one might decide many things about a man. One might decide that he is sentimental; that he is extraordinarily sympathetic without being sentimental; that he is cruel – one hears voices that impress one as being intensely cruel. One might decide on the basis of his voice that a person who uses a very brusque vocabulary is nevertheless kind-hearted. This sort of comment is part of the practical experience of every man and woman. The point is that we are not in the habit of attaching scientific value to such judgements.

We have seen that the voice is a social as well as an individual phenomenon. If one were to make a profound enough analysis, one might, at least in theory, carve out the social part of the voice and discard it – a difficult thing to do. One finds people, for example, who have very pleasant voices, but it is society that has made them pleasant. One may then try to go back to what the voice would have been without its specific social development. This nuclear or primary quality of voice has in many, perhaps in all, cases a symbolic value. These unconscious symbolisms are of course not limited to the voice. If you wrinkle your brow, that is a symbol of a certain attitude. If you act expansively by stretching out your arms, that is a symbol of a changed attitude to your immediate environment. In the same manner the voice is to a large extent an unconscious symbolization of one's general attitude.

Now all sorts of accidents may happen to the voice and deprive it, apparently, of its 'predestined form'. In spite of such accidents, however, the voice will be there for our discovery. These factors that spoil the basic picture are found in all forms of human behavior and we must make allowances for them here as everywhere else in behavior. The primary voice structure is something that we cannot get at right away but must uncover by hacking away the various superimposed structures, social and individual.

E. Sapir 75

What is the next level of speech? What we ordinarily call voice is voice proper plus a great many variations of behavior that are intertwined with voice and give it its dynamic quality. This is the level of voice dynamics. Two speakers may have very much the same basic quality of voice yet their 'voices', as that term is ordinarily understood, may be very different. In ordinary usage we are not always careful to distinguish the voice proper from voice dynamics. One of the most important aspects of voice dynamics is intonation, a very interesting field of investigation for both linguist and psychologist. Intonation is a much more complicated matter than is generally believed. It may be divided into three distinct levels, which intertwine into the unit pattern of behavior which we may call 'individual intonation'. In the first place, there is a very important social element in intonation which has to be kept apart from the individual variation; in the second place, this social element of intonation has a twofold determination. We have certain intonations which are a necessary part of our speech. If I say, for example, *Is he coming?* I raise the pitch of the voice on the last word. There is no sufficient reason in nature why I should elevate the voice in sentences of this type. We are apt to assume that this habit is natural, even self-evident, but a comparative study of the dynamic habits of many diverse languages convinces one that this assumption is on the whole unwarranted. The interrogative attitude may be expressed in other ways, such as the use of particular interrogative words or specific grammatical forms. It is one of the significant patterns of our English language to elevate the voice in interrogative sentences of a certain type, hence such elevation is not expressive in the properly individual sense of the word, though we sometimes feel it to be so.

But more than that, there is a second level of socially determined variation in intonation – the musical handling of the voice generally, quite aside from the properly linguistic patterns of intonation. It is understood in a given society that we are not to have too great an individual range of intonation. We are not to rise to too great a height in our cadences; we are to pitch the voice at such and such an average height. In other words, society tells us to limit ourselves to a certain range of intonation and to certain characteristic cadences, that is, to adopt certain melody patterns peculiar to itself. If we were to compare the speech of an English country gentleman with that of a Kentucky farmer, we would find the intonational habits of the two to be notably different, though there are certain important resemblances due to the fact that the language they speak is essentially the same. Neither dares to depart too widely from his respective social standard of intonation. Yet we know no two individuals who speak exactly alike so far as intonation is concerned. We are interested in the individual as the representative of a social type when he comes from some far place. The

Southerner, the New Englander, the Middle Westerner, each has a characteristic intonation. But we are interested in the individual as an individual when he is merged in, and is a representative of, our own group. If we are dealing with people who have the same social habits, we are interested in the slight intonational differences which the individuals exhibit, for we know enough of their common social background to evaluate these slight differences. We are wrong to make any inferences about personality on the basis of intonation without considering the intonational habit of one's speech community or that which has been carried over from a foreign language. We do not really know what a man's speech is until we have evaluated his social background. If a Japanese talks in a monotonous voice, we have not the right to assume that he is illustrating the same type of personality that one of us would be if we talked with his sentence melody. Furthermore, if we hear an Italian running through his whole possible gamut of tone, we are apt to say that he is temperamental or that he has an interesting personality. Yet we do not know whether he is in the least temperamental until we know what are the normal Italian habits of speech, what Italian society allows its members in the way of melodic play. Hence a major intonation curve, objectively considered, may be of but minor importance from the standpoint of individual expressiveness.

Intonation is only one of the many phases of voice dynamics. Rhythm, too, has to be considered. Here again there are several layers that are to be distinguished. First of all, the primary rhythms of speech are furnished by the language one is brought up in and are not due to our individual personality. We have certain very definite peculiarities of rhythm in English. Thus, we tend to accent certain syllables strongly and to minimize others. That is not due to the fact that we wish to be emphatic. It is merely that our language is so constructed that we must follow its characteristic rhythm, accenting one syllable in a word or phrase at the expense of the others. There are languages that do not follow this habit. If a Frenchman accented his words in our English fashion, we might be justified in making certain inferences as to his nervous condition. Furthermore, there are rhythmic forms which are due to the socialized habits of particular groups – rhythms which are over and above the basic rhythms of the language. Some sections of our society will not allow emphatic stresses, others allow or demand a greater emphasis. Polite society will allow far less play in stress and intonation than a society that is constituted by attendance at a baseball or football game. We have, in brief, two sorts of socialized rhythm – the rhythms of language and the rhythms of social expressiveness. And, once more, we have individual rhythmic factors. Some of us tend to be more tense in our rhythms, to accent certain syllables more definitely, to lengthen more vowels, to shorten unaccented vowels more freely. There are, in other words, individual rhythmic variations in addition to the social ones.

There are still other dynamic factors than intonation and rhythm. There is the relative continuity of speech. A great many people speak brokenly, in uneasy splashes of word groups, others speak continuously, whether they have anything to say or not. With the latter type it is not a question of having the necessary words at one's disposal, it is a question of mere continuity of linguistic expression. There are social speeds and continuities and individual speeds and continuities. We can be said to be slow or rapid in our utterances only in the sense that we speak above or below certain socialized speeds. Here again, in the matter of speed, the individual habit and its diagnostic value for the study of personality can only be measured against accepted social norms.

To summarize the second level of language behavior, we have a number of factors, such as intonation, rhythm, relative continuity and speed, which have to be analysed, each of them, into two distinct levels, the social and the individual; the social level, moreover, has generally to be divided into two levels, the level of that social pattern which is language and the level of the linguistically irrelevant habits of speech manipulation that are characteristic of a particular group.

The third level of speech analysis is pronunciation. Here again one often speaks of the 'voice' when what is really meant is an individually nuanced pronunciation. A man pronounces certain consonants or vowels, say, with a distinctive timbre or in an otherwise peculiar manner and we tend to ascribe such variations of pronunciation to his voice, yet they may have nothing at all to do with the quality of his voice. In pronunciation we again have to distinguish the social from the individual patterns. Society decrees that we pronounce certain selected consonants and vowels, which have been set aside as the bricks and mortar, as it were, for the construction of a given language. We cannot depart very widely from this decree. We know that the foreigner who learns our language does not at once take over the sounds that are peculiar to us. He used the nearest proncunciation that he can find in his own language. It would manifestly be wrong to make inferences of a personal nature from such mispronunciations. But all the time there are also *individual* variations of sound which are highly important and which in many cases have a symptomatic value for the study of personality.

One of the most interesting chapters in linguistic behavior, a chapter which has not yet been written, is the expressively symbolic character of sounds quite aside from what the words in which they occur mean in a referential sense. On the properly linguistic plane sounds have no meaning, yet if we are to interpret them psychologically we would find that there is a subtle, though fleeting, relation between the 'real' value of words and the unconscious symbolic value of sounds as actually pronounced by individuals. Poets know this in their own intuitive way. But what the poets are doing rather consciously by means of artistic devices we are doing unconsciously all of the time on a vast, if humble, scale. It has been pointed out, for instance, that there are certain expressive tendencies toward diminutive forms of pronunciation. If you are talking to a child, you change your 'level of pronunciation' without knowing it. The word *tiny* may become *teeny*. There is no rule of English grammar that justifies the change of vowel, but the word *teeny* seems to have a more directly symbolic character than *tiny*, and a glance at the symbolism of phonetics gives us the reason for this. When we pronounce the *ee* of *teeny*, there is very little space between the tongue and the roof of the mouth; in the first part of the *i* of *tiny* there is a great deal of space. In other words the *ee* variation has the value of a gesture which emphasizes the notion, or rather feeling, of smallness. In this particular case the tendency to symbolize diminutiveness is striking because it has caused one word to pass over to an entirely new word, but we are constantly making similar symbolic adjustments in a less overt way without being aware of the process.

Some people are much more symbolic in their use of sounds than others. A man may lisp, for instance, because he is unconsciously symbolizing certain traits, which lead those who know him to speak of him as a 'sissy'. His pronunciation is not due to the fact that he cannot pronounce the sound of *s* properly, it is due to the fact that he is driven to reveal himself. He has no speech defect, though there is of course also a type of lisping that is a speech defect and that has to be kept apart from the symbolic lisp. There are a great many other unconsciously symbolic habits of articulation for which we have no current terminology. But we cannot discuss such variation fruitfully until we have established the social norm of pronunciation and have a just notion of what are the allowable departures within this social norm. If one goes to England or France or any other foreign country and sets down impressions on the interpretative significance of the voices and pronunciation perceived, what one says is not likely to be of value unless one has first made a painstaking study of the social norms of which the individual phenomena are variants. The lisp that you note may be what a given society happens to require, hence it is no psychological lisp in our sense. You cannot draw up an absolute psychological scale for voice, intonation, rhythm, speed or pronunciation of vowels and consonants without in every case ascertaining the social background of speech habit. It is always the variation that matters, never the objective behavior as such.

The fourth speech level, that of vocabulary, is a very important one.

We do not all speak alike. There are certain words which some of us never use. There are other, favorite, words which we are always using. Personality is largely reflected in the choice of words, but here too we must distinguish carefully the social vocabulary norm from the more significantly personal choice of words. Certain words and locutions are not used in certain circles; others are the hall-mark of locale, status or occupation. We listen to a man who belongs to a particular social group and are intrigued, perhaps attracted, by his vocabulary. Unless we are keen analysts, we are likely to read personality out of what is merely the current diction of his society. Individual variation exists, but it can be properly appraised only with reference to the social norm. Sometimes we choose words because we like them; sometimes we slight words because they bore or annoy or terrify us. We are not going to be caught by them. All in all, there is room for much subtle analysis in the determination of the social and individual significance of words.

Finally, we have style as a fifth speech level. Many people have an illusion that style is something that belongs to literature. Style is an everyday facet of speech that characterizes both the social group and the individual. We all have our individual styles in conversation and considered address, and they are never the arbitrary and casual things we think them to be. There is always an individual method, however poorly developed, of arranging words into groups and of working these up into larger units. It would be a very complicated problem to disentangle the social and individual determinants of style, but it is a theoretically possible one.

To summarize, we have the following materials to deal with in our attempt to get at the personality of an individual, in so far as it can be gathered from his speech. We have his voice. We have the dynamics of his voice, exemplified by such factors as intonation, rhythm, continuity and speed. We have pronunciation, vocabulary and style. Let us look at these materials as constituting so and so many levels on which expressive patterns are built. One may get a sense of individual patterning on one of these levels and use this sense to interpret the other levels. Objectively, however, two or more levels of a given speech act may produce either a similarity of expressive effect or a contrast. We may illustrate from a theoretical case. We know that many of us, handicapped by nature or habit, work out compensatory reactions. In the case of the man with a lisp whom we termed a 'sissy', the essentially feminine type of articulation is likely to remain, but other aspects of his speech, including his voice, may show something of his effort to compensate. He may affect a masculine type of intonation or, above all, consciously or unconsciously he may choose words that are intended to show that he is really a man. In this case we have a very interesting conflict, objectified within the realm of speech behavior. It is here as in all other types of behavior. One may express on one level of patterning what one will not or cannot express on another. One may inhibit on one level what one does not know how to inhibit on another, whence results a 'dissociation', which is probably, at last analysis, nothing but a notable divergence in expressive content of functionally related patterns.

Quite aside from specific inferences which we may make from speech phenomena on any one of its levels, there is a great deal of interesting work to be done with the psychology of speech woven out of its different levels. Perhaps certain elusive phenomena of voice are the result of the interweaving of distinct patterns of expression. We sometimes get the feeling that there are two things being communicated by the voice, which may then be felt as splitting itself into an 'upper' and a 'lower' level.

It should be fairly clear from our hasty review that, if we make a level-to-level analysis of the speech of an individual and if we carefully see each of these in its social perspective, we obtain a valuable lever for psychiatric work. It is possible that the kind of analysis which has here been suggested, if carried far enough, may enable us to arrive at certain very pertinent conclusions regarding personality. Intuitively we attach an enormous importance to the voice and to the speech behavior that is carried by the voice. We have not much to say about it as a rule, not much more than an 'I like that man's voice' or 'I do not like the way he talks'. Individual speech analysis is difficult to make, partly because of the peculiarly fleeting character of speech, partly because it is especially difficult to eliminate the social determinants of speech. In view of these difficulties there is not as much significant speech analysis being made by students of behavior as we might wish, but they do not relieve us of the responsibility for making such researches.

4 R. L. Birdwhistell

Paralanguage Twenty-five Years after Sapir

R. L. Birdwhistell, 'Paralanguage twenty-five years after Sapir', in H. G. Brosin (ed.), *Lectures in Experimental Psychiatry*, Pittsburgh University Press, 1961, pp. 43–63.

The history of science could probably be written in terms of recurring and interdependent cycles of concern with theory and methodology. Ideally, new procedures test all but the most sacred of old hypotheses and make public hitherto hidden data which demand appraisal and arrangement. And, unless workers bog down in concern with the particular, new developments in theory, reorganization and generalization expose the need for relevant testing devices. This is no less true for the applied sciences than for those devoted to so-called pure research. The arena of application, dramatic and public, often contributes to a climate which speeds the cyclical process. On the other hand, the very visibility of applied research may make it particularly subject to hidden and traditionally maintained impediments to change and development.

Even the briefest survey of those sciences dealing with man and his behavior, whether concerned with description or manipulation, is convincing as to the cyclicity of the theory-research emphasis. Out of the great advances of the last half of the nineteenth century have come conceptions which have outstripped the research methodologies requisite for their testing. In a sense we are only now recovering from a half century which has seen all too many researchers waste their patrimony: some in a merry-go-round search of data to support nineteenth-century dogma, others at grindstones designed to sharpen tools already made archaic by theory which they ignored.

During the past seventy-five years those concerned with the relationship between the individual and society have become increasingly aware of the need for more definitive tools relevant to research in human behavior; individual or interactional, normal or pathological. Unfortunately, the recognition that man and society could be studied, that psychological and social behavior were lawful, and that this lawfulness could be abstracted by methods as rigorous as those employed in other areas of science is a nineteenth-century legacy that did not carry it methodologies which could test the implications of these recognitions. However, it did provide an environment which encouraged such developments. For those who sought to avoid being enlisted on either side of the philosophical heredity *v.* environment or individual *v.* society controversies, it became increasingly evident that we needed to know how man behaves and how society behaves. Only then could we hope to assess the dynamic process by which the individual becomes a member of society and by which he makes his own unique contribution to its shape. No simple circular model could suffice to explain such a complex involvement of systems, and a number of students became devoted to the proposition that this was a problem which demanded a new kind of research to provide a new order of data – not data supplied by speculation, but data from rigorously explicit methods developed in the full awareness that not only is man natural but that society is his natural habitat, that not only his actions but his interactions are lawful and comprehensible. Out of these recognitions came studies of the family, of government, of religion, even of art and of science itself as systematically institutionalized regularities. But the old atomism maintained itself in the area of the interpersonal. Communication between human beings continued to be described as though one human being sent out signals which were registered and reacted to in some on-going action-reaction series. Sender and receiver models dominated all discussion of the transmission of information from one human being to another. Traditional conceptions of language, of its structure and function, precluded the development of a theory of communication and supported the essential atomism of the action-reaction approach. Communication, in the sense that the term is used below remained obscure and inapproachable. It was not until the descriptive linguists turned to the observation of language in operation that the developments discussed below could take place.

While many of the techniques used in the abstraction and analysis of communication systems are relatively new, the insights on which the approach is based have been around for some time. A popular beginning point for those concerned with the history of modern communication theory is Darwin's *Expression of the Emotions in Man and Animals* (1872). In this work, the great biologist attempted to organize an extensive body of observations into some kind of ordered theory about the audible and visible behavior of mammals and the emotional states which induce such behavior. A rigorous observer, Darwin set a model for behavioral description which can be read with profit today. However, his concern with certain kinds of psychological problems, many of which remain unsolved, vitiated his attempt to regulate his data. In his role as synthesist he was hampered by preconceptions which even the sternest materialists of his day could not avoid.

Inheritance, as Darwin used it, seems at times a genetic, and at other times a social phenomenon. Perhaps it makes little difference to his major thesis which aspects of human behavior are biologically inherited as long as he demonstrates the continuity of the species and the society. However, for certain problems with which the human sciences are concerned today, it makes a great deal of difference whether or not vocal and body motion systems ultimately derive their order from the biological base or are exclusively a production of social experience. Careful reading of Darwin leads one to believe that if he had had some knowledge about social systems or even about the systematic quality of language and its cultural inheritance, he might have unravelled or at least loosened some of these knots himself. Clearly, his work does set the stage for many of the problems with which some anthropologists, the modern ethnologists and the comparative psychologists are now concerned:

1. Are certain kinds of social behavior, particularly gestures, facial expression and certain sounds somehow closer to the biological base than others?

2. Are such behaviors biologically inherited and thus specially revealing as descriptions of the emotional life of certain groups or members within the group?

3. Are there particular sounds and expressions and gestures which can be studied *in isolation* and which are evidence of particular, predisposing psychological states regardless of the cultural context of their appearance?

Cross-cultural research suggests that the answer to all of these questions are negative. How can we, then, comprehend and rephrase the evident regularities which we observe within particular social groups? And how can we assess the variations within these regularities? Scholars for over a hundred years have been concerned with analysing the relationship between language and body motion and the personalities which express them. Insightful and even brilliantly intuitive though many of them are, most are directed toward a different order of data than we are developing here. They were concerned primarily with isolated examples of vocalic variation or gesture and posture as expressional behavior; their patent ethnocentrism, atomism or biologism has precluded rather than encouraged cross-cultural study. With few exceptions most of the work is not of direct concern to this presentation.

The development of microcultural analysis owes much to the work of Boas,[1]

1. The influence of Boas is expressed in the work of his students, particularly Mead, Sapir and Efron. Professor Boas was amongst the first scholars to utilize the movie camera as a field-research instrument.

Efron (1941), Bateson,[2] Devereux,[3] La Barre (1947) and Margaret Mead, among others. Mead's work especially has been stimulating to the development of kinesic analysis. Her reappraisal of the Gesellian position on development (1956), her work with Bateson which dramatized the usefulness of the camera as a research tool (1942; Mead and MacGregor, 1951), and her consistent stress on careful problem arrangement in the analysis of culture and personality data were important contributions to the analytic procedures outlined below. Several psychologists have also provided hypotheses, the analyses of which have led to the clarification of the linguistic-kinesic approach. Among these are Dunlap (1927), Krout (1933), Klineberg (1927), Murphy (1947), Carroll (1953), and, especially, Osgood (Osgood and Sebeok, 1954). This is by no means an exhaustive review of the influences contributing to the development of the linguistic-kinesic approach to microcultural analysis. From every discipline making up the behavioral sciences have come insights which lead to the perspective best put by Bateson:

Our new recognition of the complexity and patterning of human behaviour has forced us to go back and go through the natural history phase of the study of man which earlier scholars skipped in their haste to get to laboratory experimentation.[4]

The most direct contribution to the development of a microculture approach to the relationship between communication systems and personality structure comes from the linguists. Language is probably the only cultural system sufficiently analysed to permit separation of socially from individually patterned behavior. The exhaustive description of language as a system provides a source of data and a model for the investigation of other systems contributing to the communicative process.

The primary figure in the background of the microcultural analysis of communication is Edward Sapir. Stimulated by Boas and by association with a number of psychiatrists and students concerned with the relationship between culture and personality, he realized early that linguistics, his central professional interest, had implications for culture and personality research. In his articles, 'Speech as a personality trait' (1927a) and in 'The unconscious patterning of behavior in society' (1927b), he anticipates

2. Bateson has been a consistent pioneer in both theoretical and methodological approaches to communication analysis. See particularly Bateson and Mead (1942); Ruesch and Bateson (1951). His films, made with the assistance of the Josiah Macy Jr Foundation, laid the groundwork for the study of family interaction by microcultural techniques.

3. Devereux has shown a consistent interest in the analysis of communication, particularly in the clinical context. For his interest in cross-culturally measured paralanguage, see Devereux (1949).

4. Personal communication in research seminar, CASBS, Palo Alto, 1956.

much of the discussion below. In the former paper he says that two distinct but ultimately intermeshing approaches to the analysis of speech should be taken from the point of view of personality study. Initially he says:

It is not difficult to see why it is necessary to distinguish the social point of view from the individual, for society has its patterns, its set ways of doing things, its distinctive 'theories' of behavior, while the individual has his method of handling those particular patterns of society, giving them just enough of a twist to make them 'his' and no one else's (1927a, in Mandelbaum, 1949, p. 534).

There is nothing very startling about this directive. Basic to all cross-cultural research on personality structure or development, its statement is almost commonplace among students of culture and personality. However, Sapir's genius is revealed when he does not content himself with this as a piety, but directs attention to the behavior, which must be examined if we are to convert this ideal into reality. He goes on to point out that speech should be regarded as having a series of 'levels' which should be analysed separately. Only by such an analysis, which he admitted had not been done, can we 'put our finger on the precise spot in the speech complex that leads to our making this or that personality judgement' (1927a, in Mandelbaum, 1949, p. 534).

Beyond the linguistically discrete phenomena, he develops five different levels of speech behavior, which he finds particularly telling in the description of personality. I shall present these in outline below as points of departure for the discussion of recent advances in microculture analysis.

Voice

'We do not know what it is precisely that makes a voice sound "thick" or "vibrant" or "flat" or what not.' 'If one were to make a profound enough analysis, one might, at least in theory, carve out the social part of the voice and discard it . . .' 'These unconscious symbolisms are . . . not limited to the voice. If you wrinkle your brow, that is a symbol of a certain attitude. If you act expansively by stretching out your arms, that is a symbol of a changed attitude to your immediate environment.'

Voice dynamics
Intonation

'. . . society tells us to limit ourselves to a certain range of intonation and to certain characteristic cadences. . . . Yet we know no two individuals who speak exactly alike so far as intonation is concerned.' 'We are wrong to make any inferences about personality on the basis of intonation without considering the intonational habit of one's speech community or that which has been carried over from a foreign language . . . until we have evaluated his social background.'

Rhythm

We first distinguish – 'the primary rhythms of speech . . . furnished by the language one is brought up in . . .' Further, 'Some sections of our society will not allow emphatic stresses, others allow or demand a great emphasis.' But, as individuals, 'some of us tend to be more tense in our rhythms, to accent certain syllables more definitely, to lengthen more vowels, to shorten unaccented vowels more freely'.

Relative continuity of speech

'A great many people speak brokenly, in uneasy splashes of word groups, others speak continuously . . .' 'We can be said to be slow or rapid in our utterances only in the sense that we speak

Speed of speech

above or below certain socialized speeds . . . the individual habit and its diagnostic value for the study of personality can only be measured against accepted social norms.'

Pronunciation

'Society decrees that we pronounce certain selected consonants and vowels, which have been set aside as the bricks and mortar, as it were, for the construction of a given language. We cannot depart very widely from this decree. . . . But . . . there are also *individual* variations of sound which are highly important.'

Vocabulary

'Personality is largely reflected in the choice of words, but here too we must distinguish carefully the social vocabulary norm from the more significantly personal choice of words.'

Style

'There is always an individual method, however poorly developed, of arranging words into groups and of working these up into larger units. It would be a very complicated problem to disentangle the social and individual determinants of style, but it is a theoretically possible one.'

Summary. 'It is always the variation that matters never the objective behavior as such' (1927a, in Mandelbaum, 1949, pp. 535–43).

Sapir recognized the importance of body movement in the communication context.

I have quoted before his challenging statement . . .

In spite of . . . difficulties of conscious analysis, we respond to gestures with an extreme alertness and, one might almost say, in accordance with an elaborate code that is written nowhere, known by none, and understood by all (1927b, in Mandelbaum, 1949, p. 556).

He understood fully that there is an intimate relationship between certain levels of speech and body motion behavior. He left no doubt in his writings about his convictions that these learned and patterned systems had to be comprehended as wholes before items from either could be reliably measured in the interactional or personality context. This, plus his conviction that man is aware of only a small part of what is internalized, makes it possible to avoid the particularistic explanations and the atomism which characterize the work of his predecessors and many of his contemporaries.

It would be gratifying to report that the past thirty years brought Sapir's vision to reality. However, before these ambitions for behavioral research in communication could be realized, a tremendous amount of basic research had to be conceptualized, tested and weighed. Probably the fairest estimate of the progress to date is that we have begun to clarify the nature of the problem, have gained at least programmatic control of the levels of speech and kinesic behavior, and have engaged in some preliminary tests which make us optimistic about research in the future.

This discussion is primarily concerned with the first three of Sapir's levels: we have most clearly isolated the relationship between these phenomena and the structure of body motion. However, exciting work is proceeding on the implications which emphasize vocabulary usage and style. Very promising work is being done by Zelig Harris (1951), whose discourse analysis opens the way for the investigation of large stretches of interactional behavior. His recognition of the structure of discourse (particularly when combined with the suggestive research of Eliot Chapple (personal communication), using the interaction chronograph), makes it possible for us to go beyond the sentence-sized data of the traditional linguist. Even larger shapes and stretches of linguistic material are being considered by the psycholinguists. Following the leads suggested by Whorf (Carroll, 1956), these scholars from a variety of fields have been investigating the role of language as a shaper of thought and action (Osgood and Sebeok, 1954). There can be little doubt that as research proceeds in microanalysis, in discourse analysis, and in psycholinguistics, that these fields, now following separate research paths, will converge on the central problem of the relationships between communication and the other cultural systems as shapers of cultural character and personality.

It is unfair, perhaps, to put this much stress on the work of Sapir. Bloomfield (1933), a contemporary of Sapir's, far less concerned with the broader implications of linguistic research, had probably as much or even more influence on the technical development of linguistic science than did Sapir. But, whoever it was that ushered in the emergence of linguistics as a leader among the social sciences left his followers with no easy task. Before individual behavior could be measured against the social patterns within which it appears, these patterns had to be abstracted and analysed.

Unfortunately, only one language, American English, has been sufficiently described to allow differentiation at the analytic levels in human speech behavior. Similarly, only the American body motion system has been sufficiently examined to give perspective on comparable material from this area. There is no reason to believe that all language and body motion systems will function as this one. However, if our experience in general linguistics is any guide, this patterning should provide a working model and a stimulant to similar exhaustive analyses of communication behavior in other societies.

A series of writings contributed to the initial establishment of the difference between what we now call microlinguistic and paralinguistic behavior. As will be seen below, it is the paralinguistic behavior referred to by Sapir which seems to show the greatest promise for microcultural analysis, but until separated from its linguistic matrix, it cannot be properly fixed or analysed. Bloch and Trager, in 1942, demonstrated that American English is a four-stress language and that stress is systematic, permitting us to assign phonemic value to it. That is, the recognition of the four stresses, or degrees of loudness (primary, secondary, tertiary and weak), makes it possible to be explicit about the differences we hear in the children's joke *I scream for ice cream*. In this utterance *I* is under primary stress; *scream* is under secondary stress; *ice* has primary; and *cream* has tertiary stress. This joke also demonstrated Bloch and Trager's second contribution: the role of the internal juncture. Once we understand how stress is customarily patterned by speakers of American English, we are also in a position to measure objectively any variation from this expectancy. The research of the past two years, and particularly, that for the *Natural History of an Interview* demonstrates the value of this contribution (Bateson *et al.*, forthcoming). Further, the discovery of the structure of phonemic stress permitted more adequate and systematic description of longer stretches of loudness and softness on other language levels. As any parent knows a child gains early control of this part of the communicational system. Long before he has words or sentences the child uses loudness to effect the parent–child interaction.

In the same way, the analysis of phonemic intonation put varying degrees of pitch into paralinguistic perspective. Rulon Wells in 1945 recognized the phonemic significance of intonation in American English.

Shortly thereafter, from independent research, Kenneth Pike (1946) published what is undoubtedly the most extensive examination of the role of tone in the American speech pattern. In 1951, Trager and Smith, in *An Outline of English Structure* put intonation into structural relationship with stress and the terminal junctures. They agreed completely with the conclusions of Pike and Wells concerning the four pitch patterns of American English. Careful analysis of superfix patterns revealed that Americans have three terminal junctures, 'double bar' (where the voice rises at the end of a sentence); 'double cross' (where the voice drops at the end of a sentence); and 'single bar' (where the pitch is held). These have proved invaluable in the location of symptomatic features in psychiatric interviews, for they help to measure the interaction sequence.

While Smith and Trager were at the Foreign Service Institute, (1948–53) they began work on what they were later at the suggestion of A. A. Hill to call 'paralanguage'. But it was 1958 before control of the data permitted a tentative summary of this level for American English (Trager, 1958). Earlier, Trager had sharply distinguished prelinguistic data from that to be included under language. 'Prelinguistics is concerned with the study of the physical and biological events which enter into the act of speech (and hearing)' (1949). Events of this order are sharply differentiated from those which occur in language. In language proper 'There are three main fields of interest: the analysis of the sounds of language, the analysis of the grammatical forms, and the analysis of the reference of these forms (their meaning).'

Voice qualities

Quality	Description
Pitch range	Spread upward or downward or narrowed
Vocalic control	Heavy rasp or hoarseness to openness
Glottis control	Over and under voicing and breathiness
Pitch control	Sharp or smooth pitch transitions
Articulation control	Forceful (precise) to relaxed (slurred)
Rhythm control	Smooth to jerky stretches
Resonance	Resonant to thin
Tempo	Increased or decreased from a norm

This does not exhaust the significant phenomena of speech. Found in systematic association with language are *vocal qualifiers, the voice qualities* and *vocalizations* (Trager, 1958). These paralanguage behaviors, which Sapir had foreseen as so important for personality research, are phenomena patterned and responded to within the first few months of a person's life. Thus they have special significance for those attempting a behavioral description of the socialization process. Patterned in particular interactions as is language, they provide us with easily accessible, objective data for the description of the idiosyncratic pattern, *once we have described the norm patterning for the particular society*.

While all of these seem to occur in pairs, this pairing is partially a function of their isolation and abstraction and, apparently, is partially derived from their special role in the American speech system. At present it seems unnecessary to record more than the extremes of such behavior from the actor's (and the group's) baseline, but as we look at other societies, a more refined system may be necessary. The important thing to remember is that while these have a definite role in determining the function of an utterance in the social setting, they are not phonemic in weight and may extend over varying stretches of linguistic behavior. As Trager puts it, these are background characteristics of the voice.

Vocalizations

The vocalizations are divided into three categories, the *vocal characterizers*, the *vocal qualifiers* and the *vocal segregates*. These are composed of distinguishable sounds or aspects of sounds which clearly differ from the straight linguistic material. These may be over or between stretches of speech behavior. They are learned, patterned and functional communicationally.

Vocal characterizers

Laughing and crying	Similar structurally – may be extremes of a continuum.
Yelling and whispering	Clearly different from overloud and oversoft.
	Discussed below under the qualifiers.
Moaning and groaning	Among the most difficult vocal behaviors to classify.
Whining and breaking	(Some disagree as to their composition.)
Belching and yawning	

There are probably others of this nature within the American vocalic system. There seems no doubt but that we will find that this area is highly complex when other societies are exhaustively studied.

Vocal qualifiers

The vocal qualifiers deal with three conditioning phenomena: *intensity*, *pitch height* and *extent*. Originally seen as being polar points or extremes of variation from a norm pattern, research by Trager, Dittman and Wynne at the National Institute of Mental Health, by Smith, Trager and Pittenger at the Upstate Medical Center of the State University of New York, and by Hockett and McQuown on the NIH study has forced a revision of this position (Pittenger and Smith, 1957). It now looks as though each of these is more usefully described by a six-point system of variation from the baseline. The descriptions of this range of variation remain somewhat unsatisfactory. And, while almost any trained ear can detect the extremes within each range, only practice makes possible the detection of the other testably significant degrees of variation.

Qualifier	Degree	Qualitative description
Intensity	Third	Very much overloud
	Second	Considerably overloud
	First	Somewhat overloud
	First	Somewhat oversoft
	Second	Considerably oversoft
	Third	Very much oversoft
Pitch height	Third	Greatly overhigh
	Second	Appreciably overhigh
	First	Slightly overhigh
	First	Slightly overlow
	Second	Appreciably overlow
	Third	Greatly overlow
Extent	Third	Extreme drawl
	Second	Noticeable drawl
	First	Slight drawl
	First	Slight clipping
	Second	Noticeable clipping
	Third	Extreme clipping

The last grouping of the vocalizations occurs over a number of items which, while quite similar to the sounds basic to the language, did not appear in sequences of phonations which behaved like 'words'. Originally thought to be only such behavior as appears in the forms *uh-hunh* and *unh-unh*, in shapes like the Japanese (sh) or hiss, or in non-phonemic clicking, the microanalysis of long stretches of interaction sequences reveals that this is a much more complex category whose components can be diagrammed in a manner comparable to the conventional phonetic articulation chart.

While other languages have not been analysed as exhaustively as American English, linguists have long recognized that comparable levels of speech activity probably occur in every society. It is probable, however, that the categories developed for English cannot be transferred directly to other speech systems. Even preliminary investigation reveals that each language system uses speech noises in its own fashion. However, the present research provides a model which should accelerate the collection and analysis of speech behavior in other societies. We may even within the foreseeable future, be able to begin cross-cultural analysis on how children learn to talk. In linguistics and kinesics we have a tool which enables us go do more detailed and objective description of the socialization process.

Kinesics and parakinesics

Since the *Natural History of an Interview* (Bateson *et al.*, forthcoming) contains an extensive description of the theoretical and technical aspects of kinesics, a brief summary of the structure of kinesics proper may suffice here. Kinesics, as a methodology, is concerned with the communicational aspects of learned, patterned body motion behavior. When, in 1951, it was experimentally determined that body motion could be abstracted and analysed in a manner analogous to speech behavior, it was clear that systematization of such behavior necessitated a clear distinction between that behavior which was prekinesic and that which was subject to kinesic analysis (Birdwhistell, 1952). It is necessary to separate those aspects of behavior which are biological from those which are systematically adapted to the communication needs of the particular society. Only then can we hope to measure the particular interaction or personality system.

This paper, in a sense, completes a preliminary research cycle. Exhaustive analysis of certain American movement patterns was necessary in order to distinguish the *kines* or at least classes of significant movement. Once isolated from non-significant articulations, it was possible to formulate the rules for their dependent association in the complex forms of the *kinemorph* and the *kinemorphic construction*. Then microkinesic and parakinesic distinctions were established. When this distinction is clearly delineated, it is possible to return to the particular mover and examine this particular movement pattern for his symptomatic idiosyncratic elements.

What we popularly call 'gestures' whether of the shape of a 'thumbed nose', a 'head shake' or 'nod', a 'snoot' or a 'clenched fist' are revealed by analysis to be specially bound kinemorphs which cannot appear in isolation as a complete action. That is, 'gestures' are like stem forms in language in that they are always bound up in a more complex package, the analysis of which must be completed before the 'social meaning' of the complex can be assessed. Just as we have built dictionaries of the 'meanings' of words, we have heretofore acted as though a gesture had a meaning in and of itself. Such preconceptions as these have interfered with our understanding of the communication process.

While kinesic and linguistic systems are analogous and mutually supportive in communication, there are some outstanding differences between them. We have, thus far, been unable to isolate a grammar or syntax in the kinesic system. There are, however, complex arrangements of individual kines and kinemorphs, the variation of which changes the significance of the activity in the interactional scene. Kinesic junctures of various kinds mark internally meaningful stretches of behavior as clearly as does morpheme construction in linguistics. Similarly, there are junctures which delineate longer stretches of material and tie together the kinemorphic constructions within them.

In other words, body motion can be studied as a patterned system which must be learned by every individual if he is to participate fully as a member of his society. Complex and ordered, its internalization is integral to both enculturation and socialization. Learned largely out of awareness, its patterning is probably every bit as coercive as is that of language and once abstracted may be even more revealing of basic character and personality complexes. The future of personality research from the point of view of linguistics and kinesics proper, depends entirely on the development of researcher training programs with such an orientation.

I presume that as we come to understand the structure of the dynamic relationship between the linguistic and the kinesic system we may find (in the context of semological, psycholinguistic and conversation analysis) that stylistic variations as well as choice of vocabulary and action items will contribute to the organization of character profiles for the measurement of particular personalities. I prefer, for the purposes of this paper, to stress the parakinesic material. As in the case of language, this material appears in perspective only when the microkinesic system has been abstracted, leaving revealed that material which cross-references, modifies and gives special emphasis to the kinesic stream. Once isolated, this material is particularly useful in the determination of idiosyncratic patterns. Like the paralinguistic material, it is learned early and is especially revealing when measured against the content of a given interaction.

Parakinesics

The parakinesic material includes the *motion qualifiers* which serve to modify small stretches of kinic or kinemorphic phenomena, the *activity modifiers*, which are descriptive of an entire body in motion or of the structure of the motion of the participants in an interaction, and, finally, the *set-quality* activity which will be discussed in the summary of this article.

As far as I have been able to see, this five-point patterning appears in the body-motion system of all American movers. Concentration within scales seems to be characteristic of the idiokinesic system. Thus, while the range is characteristic of the movement system, measurement of the baseline of a given mover against this range provides the objective structure to the idiosyncratic system. In the NIH research, the qualifiers, when examined in the context of the linguistic and paralinguistic material, clearly pointed up critical moments in the interaction which proved useful in the spotlighting of special personality factors. Also, the careful analysis of the qualifier behavior was extremely useful in delineating 'flattened' or 'fattened' effect, which seems to be made up of incongruities in the parakinesic and paralinguistic behaviour as measured against the verbal content.

Motion qualifiers		
Type	Degree	General description
Intensity	Overtense Tense Normal Lax Overlax	Concerned with the degree of muscular tension in production of kine, kinemorph or kinemorphics construction.
Duration	Overshort Shortened Normal Lengthened Overlong	Length in time of given kine, kinemorph or construction
Range	Narrow Limited Normal Widened Broad	Extent of movement involved in production of kine, kinemorph or construction.

Probably the most currently accessible and important behavior for personality description is that included under the *action modifiers*. The action modifiers have a primary identification function in the communicational sequence. At the same time they are intimately related to the idiosyncratic complex which operates within the social frame. It is important to remember that the modifiers describe the movement, not the mover. It is the tendency to stress one or more of these movement patterns rather than others which is recorded as baseline or idiosyncratic behavior.

The modifiers operate very close to awareness, at least in so far as the viewer is concerned. The novelist and playwright often include references to these in their descriptions of action and many informants volunteer descriptions of variation in such communicational distortion when subjects from differing class or ethnic backgrounds attempt to interact.

Action modifiers type	Behavioral description
Unilateral–Bilateral	Not to be confused with handedness. Mover favours one side of the body. Contrasts with sustained inclusion of both sides.
Specific–Generalized	Mover tends to concentrate on (or consistently avoid) one body area. Contrasts with constant variation in area usage.
Rhythmic–Disrhythmic	Not just non-rhythmic. Mover tends to adopt rhythms of others. Contrasts with mover's tendency to disrupt rhythms.
Graceful–Awkward	Mover has minimum of searching movements. Contrasts with a concentration of these. (It is important to realize that the descriptive term 'graceful' denotes a recognized variation from the norm just as does 'awkward'.)
Fast–Slow	Mover tends to high velocity of production of kinesic elements. Contrasts with markedly decreased overall velocity.
Integrated–Detached	Mover tends toward general integration of body parts as against body part loss, apparently contradictory usage, and body splitting.
Intertensive–Intratensive	The intertensive mover tends to be extraordinarily responsive, even to the point of completing the movements of others. The Intratensive seems to set up a circular system within his own behavior *with minimal-rejection behavior*.
Self-possession–Self-containment	(A difficult category which may later prove to be a complex grouping.) Self-possession seems to be signalled by congruent movement in and out of the context accompanied by maximal control. Self-containment is marked by restraint and apparent avoidance of stimuli.

The norms between groups vary sufficiently that expectable patterns in one group may well be taken as evidence of serious disorder in another. No better illustration of this exists than in the difficulties apparent in the interaction between a middle majority coastal southerner and a Piedmont southerner or a New England mover. One of my own central interests is the search for some kind of developmental pattern for such varying groups. Even preliminary investigation suggests that such phenomena are going to be important in assessing some of the differences between four to six years olds, eight to eleven year olds and adolescents. Cross-cultural investigation should give us some interesting data with which to make a clearer statement concerning the relationship between somatic and social factors in growth and development.

I shall not here attempt to present the suggestive but still amorphous material which is accumulating concerning either voice set or body set and quality. This is to be presented in outline elsewhere (Birdwhistell, 1957). Still analysed insufficiently, the material is not immediately applicable to the task at hand. Suffice it to say that from all levels of speech and body-motion behavior is derived material which is patterned to identify special roles and reciprocals in the interaction situation. Covering complete interactional sequences, this pattern of internal activity cross-references and maintains the interaction sequence and provides a final check on the congruity or incongruity of the particular pieces of behavior appearing within the sequence. Apparently basic to all social behavior, animal or human, these complexes of behavior indicating age, sex, state of health, rhythm phase, mood, toxic state, position, and others, will, when standardized probably give sharp definitions of the socialization process. Again patterned by the subgroup, these should provide special tools for the examination of personality and temperament studies.

Summary

We can summarize these most recent developments in linguistics and kinesics by saying that work during the past thirty and particularly the past ten years now makes possible a series of methodological approaches (many of which Sapir specifically anticipated), to the description of individual behavior.

The systematic derivation and description of those units, complexes and constructions which make up the linguistic and kinesic system makes possible a description of the socially prescribed elements of the individual's expressional system.

This provides us with tools for the more adequate measurement of the personal characteristics expressed in communication behavior. When combined with the carefully analysed paralinguistic and parakinesic material we can assess problems relating to the analysis of individual and model personality. We should, as cross-cultural data accumulates, systematically contribute to studies aimed at separating temperament and character generalizations. These, in term, should provide clearly stated behaviorally described models for the objectification of individual personality studies.

To the reader unacquainted with linguistic and/or kinesic research, the analytic procedures outlined above may seem overelaborate and labored.

Certainly, if the thirty years of work described for the leveling and analysis of American English had to be repeated for every society with which we might be concerned, the microanalytic procedure offers little of immediate value to cross-cultural research. This is hardly the case. The analysis of American English provides us with a model which should make it possible for skilled analysts to order the communicational behavior in a much shorter time than seemed possible before. And, once analysed, the control of patterned communication sharply increases both the acuity and the reliability of the observer.

If the experience gained within the past three years is a guide, one of the most important questions raised by microanalytic studies is related to the amount of data required for the description of personality. All students of personality, particularly when people in exotic societies are being considered, are plagued by the question of how long should they stay in the field, how much material and what orders of materials should be collected. This is an absolute parallel to the task confronting the clinical researcher. How much tape does he need? How many hours must he analyse? How much reliance can he put on his own sensitized intuition to tell him what aspects of an interview to stress? Like other students of personality we have been impressed with the sheer repetitiousness of human behavior. We have observed the same pattern of behavior repeated hundreds of times within a twenty-minute period. A stretch of sound film twenty seconds in duration will often, when adequately analysed, reveal patterns so basic to the baseline of an actor that intensive descriptions of these twenty seconds will often prove more productive than hours of interviewing. Without longer stretches of film, say an hour, and without perspective on the social and cultural matrix in which the activity occurs, such a record provides little more than an extended set of candid close-ups or, at best, a piece of ethnographic curiosae. But in familiar context even very brief pieces of behavior provide us with extensive generalizations *which can be systematically tested.*

Another methodological implication of this work relates to the use of linguistics and kinesics as a coordinate tool for the analyst using projective techniques. We have done no *systematic* investigation in this area, but even our preliminary tests reveal that microanalysis of the non-content aspects of the interaction involved in testing, multiplies the emergent data and provides reliability checks on it. This is particularly important for those working with non-literate peoples. Our present guess is that in pseudostatistics probably no more than 30 to 35 per cent of the social meaning of a conversation or an interaction is carried by the words. Microcultural analysis offers objective measures of at least a portion of the remainder.

Finally, and this is for the future, the microculture approach should as research proceeds, make it possible for us to use the derived systems, jokes, games, folklore, dances and drama as controlled laboratories for the measurement of the participants. We do not as yet have control of these derived systems – we do not have the research necessary to understand what special structuring these systems exert on language and body motion. But it is clear from even our most limited investigation that the sound camera and the tape recorder can now be regarded as necessary field tools. With carefully planned filming and taping, the field worker or the clinical researcher can come back with a record for extended laboratory analysis. It may take some time for schools to decide to include courses in sound photography in their curricula; an even longer period of demonstration may be required before foundations and other fund-granting institutions recognize the necessity for these tools, but such research can now be justified for those with sufficient training to do the analysis.

References

BATESON, G., and MEAD, M. (1942), *Balinese Character: A Photographic Analysis* Special Publications of the New York Academy of Sciences, Vol. 11.

BATESON, G., BIRDWHISTELL, R. L., BROSIN, H. W., HOCKETT, C. F., and McQUOWN, N. (forthcoming), *The Natural History of an Interview*, Grune & Stratton.

BIRDWHISTELL, R. L. (1952), *Introduction to Kinesics*, University of Louisville Press.

BIRDWHISTELL, R. L. (1957), 'Kinesics in the context of motor habits', paper read at the Annual Meeting, American Anthropological Association, Chicago.

BLOCH, B., and TRAGER, G. L. (1942), *Outline of Linguistic Analysis*, Linguistic Society of America.

BLOOMFIELD, L. (1933), *Language*, Holt, Rinehart & Winston.

CARROLL, J. (1953), *The Study of Language*, Harvard University Press.

CARROLL, J. (ed.) (1956), *Language, Thought, and Reality: Selected Writings o Benjamin Lee Whorf*, MIT Press.

DARWIN, C. (1872), *The Expression of the Emotions in Man and Animals*, Murray.

DEVEREUX, G. (1949), 'Mohave voice and speech mannerisms', *Word*, vol. 5, pp. 268–72.

DUNLAP, K. A. (1927), 'A project for investigating the facial signs of personality' *Amer. J. Psychol.*, vol. 39, pp. 156–61.

EFRON, D. (1941), *Gesture and Environment*, King's Crown Press.

HARRIS, Z. (1951), *Methods in Structural Linguistics*, University of Chicago Press.

KLINEBERG, O. (1927), 'Racial differences in speed and accuracy', *J. abnorm. soc. Psychol.*, vol. 22, pp. 273–7.

KROUT, M. H. (1933), 'The social and psychological significance of gestures (a differential analysis)'. *J. genet. Psychol.*, vol. 47, pp. 385–412.

LA BARRE, W. (1947), 'The cultural basis of emotions and gestures', *J. Personality*, vol. 16, pp. 49–68. [Reprinted in this book, pp. 207–24.]

MEAD, M. (1956), 'On the implications for anthropology of the Gesell-Ilg approach to maturation', in D. Haring (ed.), *Personal Character and the Cultural Milieu* (3rd revised edn), Syracuse University Press.

MEAD, M., and MACGREGOR, F. C. (1951), *Growth and Culture*, Putman.

MURPHY, G. (1947), *Personality*, Harpers.

OSGOOD, C. E. and SEBEOK, T. A. (eds.) (1954). *Psycholinguistics: A Survey of Theory and Research Problems*, Report of the 1953 Summer Seminar sponsored by the Committee on Linguistics and Psychology of the Social Science Research Council, Waverly Press.

PIKE, K. L. (1946), *The Intonation of American English*, University of Michigan Publications in Linguistics, 1, University of Michigan Press.

PITTENGER, R. E. and SMITH, H. L., Jr (1957), 'A basis for some contributions of linguistics to psychiatry', *Psychiatry*, vol. 20, pp. 61–78.

RUESCH, J. and BATESON, G. (1951), *Communication: The Social Matrix of Psychiatry*, Norton.

SAPIR, E. (1927a), 'Speech as a personality trait', *Amer. J. Sociol.*, vol. 32, pp. 892–905. Reprinted in D. G. Mandelbaum (ed.), *Selected Writings of Edward Sapir in Language, Culture, and Personality*, University of California Press, 1949. [Reprinted in this book pp. 71–81.]

SAPIR, E. (1927b), 'The unconscious patterning of behavior in society', in E. S. Dummer (ed.), *The Unconscious: A Symposium*, Knopf. Reprinted in D. G. Mandelbaum (ed.), *Selected Writings of Edward Sapir in Language, Culture and Personality*, University of California Press, 1949.

TRAGER, G. L. (1949), 'The field of linguistics', *SIL*, Occasional Papers, 1, Battenburg Press.

TRAGER, G. L. (1958), 'Paralanguage: a first approximation', *SIL*, vol. 13, pp. 1–12.

TRAGER, G. L. and SMITH, H. L., Jr. (1951), *An Outline of English Structure*, *SIL*, Occasional Papers, 3, Battenburg Press.

Part Two
Language, Status and Solidarity

These three Readings are concerned with the communication of indexical information by means of particular verbal behaviour.

Brown and Gilman (5) and Brown and Ford (6) show how a speaker can signal his perception of his social and psychological relationship with a listener by the words he chooses to address him. Brown and Gilman discuss the use of pronouns of direct address in various European languages, and Brown and Ford look at the variety of titles of address and other naming devices in English. In both Readings, the two factors which constrain the speaker's verbal choice are relative social status ('power'), and the degree of intimacy or shared social characteristics ('solidarity').

The Reading by Malinowski (7) is concerned with the same principle, the use of language to reflect psychological and social relationships, but at a very much more general level. As an anthropologist, Malinowski was interested in the different functions that language fulfils. In this Reading, he isolates a particular use of language which does not serve as 'an instrument of reflection' but as a 'mode of action' (p. 148). (In our terms, he is discussing its indexical as opposed to its cognitive function.) His notion of *phatic communion*, as a use of language to imply and reinforce social solidarity between speaker and listener, has been widely adopted.

While it is probably true that nearly all spoken interaction fulfils this purpose to some degree, social solidarity is probably primarily reinforced by the verbal activity which characterizes the initial stage of a conversation. It is in this stage that we typically utter the ritual, stereotyped phrases of greeting, and the 'small talk' which 'breaks the ice'. Similar demonstrations of social solidarity also occur during the terminal stage of a conversation, in the use of ritual phrases of farewell.

5 R. Brown and A. Gilman

The Pronouns of Power and Solidarity

R. Brown and A. Gilman, 'The pronouns of power and solidarity', in
T. A. Sebeok (ed.), *Style in Language*, MIT Press, 1960, pp. 253–76.

Most of us in speaking and writing English use only one pronoun of
address; we say *you* to many persons and *you* to one person. The pronoun
thou is reserved, nowadays, to prayer and naïve poetry, but in the past it
was the form of familiar address to a single person. At that time *you*
was the singular of reverence and of polite distance and, also, the invariable plural. In French, German, Italian, Spanish and the other languages
most nearly related to English there are still active two singular pronouns
of address. The interesting thing about such pronouns is their close association with two dimensions fundamental to the analysis of all social life –
the dimensions of power and solidarity. Semantic and stylistic analysis of
these forms takes us well into psychology and sociology as well as into
linguistics and the study of literature.

This paper is divided into five major sections. The first three of these are
concerned with the semantics of the pronouns of address. By semantics
we mean covariation between the pronoun used and the objective relationship existing between speaker and addressee. The first section offers a
general description of the semantic evolution of the pronouns of address
in certain European languages. The second section describes semantic
differences existing today among the pronouns of French, German and
Italian. The third section proposes a connection between social structure,
group ideology and the semantics of the pronoun. The final two sections
of the paper are concerned with expressive style by which we mean covariation between the pronoun used and characteristics of the person speaking.
The first of these sections shows that a man's consistent pronoun style
gives away his class status and his political views. The last section describes
the ways in which a man may vary his pronoun style from time to time so as
to express transient moods and attitudes. In this section it is also proposed
that the major expressive meanings are derived from the major semantic
rules.

In each section the evidence most important to the thesis of that section
is described in detail. However, the various generalizations we shall offer
have developed as an interdependent set from continuing study of our

whole assemblage of facts, and so it may be well to indicate here the sort of motley assemblage this is. Among secondary sources the general language histories (Baugh, 1935; Brunot, 1937; Diez, 1876; Grimm, 1898; Jespersen, 1905; Meyer-Lübke, 1900) have been of little use because their central concern is always phonetic rather than semantic change. However, there are a small number of monographs and doctoral dissertations describing the detailed pronoun semantics for one or another language – sometimes throughout its history (Gedike, 1794; Grand, 1930; Johnston, 1904; Schliebitz, 1886), sometimes for only a century of so (Kennedy, 1915; Stidston, 1917), and sometimes for the works of a particular author (Byrne, 1936; Fay, 1920). As primary evidence for the usage of the past we have drawn on plays, on legal proceedings (Jardine, 1832–5) and on letters (Devereux, 1853; Harrison, 1935). We have also learned about contemporary usage from literature but, more importantly, from long conversations with native speakers of French, Italian, German and Spanish both here and in Europe. Our best information about the pronouns of today comes from a questionnaire concerning usage which is described in the second section of this paper. The questionnaire has thus far been answered by the following numbers of students from abroad who were visiting in Boston in 1957–8: fifty Frenchmen, twenty Germans, eleven Italians and two informants each from Spain, Argentina, Chile, Denmark, Norway, Sweden, Israel, South Africa, India, Switzerland, Holland, Austria and Yugoslavia.

We have far more information concerning English, French, Italian, Spanish and German than for any other languages. Informants and documents concerning the other Indo-European languages are not easily accessible to us. What we have to say is then largely founded on information about these five closely related languages. These first conclusions will eventually be tested by us against other Indo-European languages and, in a more generalized form, against unrelated languages.

The European development of two singular pronouns of address begins with the Latin *tu* and *vos*. In Italian they became *tu* and *voi* (with *Lei* eventually largely displacing *voi*); in French *tu* and *vous*; in Spanish *tu* and *vos* (later *usted*). In German the distinction began with *du* and *Ihr* but *Ihr* gave way to *er* and later to *Sie*. English speakers first used *thou* and *ye* and later replaced *ye* with *you*. As a convenience we propose to use the symbols T and V (from the Latin *tu* and *vos*) as generic designators for a familiar and a polite pronoun in any language.

The general semantic evolution of T and V

In the Latin of antiquity there was only *tu* in the singular. The plural *vos* as a form of address to one person was first directed to the emperor and there are several theories (Byrne, 1936; Châtelain, 1880) about how this may have come about. The use of the plural to the emperor began in the fourth century. By that time there were actually two emperors; the ruler of the eastern empire had his seat in Constantinople and the ruler of the west sat in Rome. Because of Diocletian's reforms the imperial office, although vested in two men, was administratively unified. Words addressed to one man were, by implication, addressed to both. The choice of *vos* as a form of address may have been in response to this implicit plurality. An emperor is also plural in another sense; he is the summation of his people and can speak as their representative. Royal persons sometimes say *we* where an ordinary man would say *I*. The Roman emperor sometimes spoke of himself as *nos*, and the reverential *vos* is the simple reciprocal of this.

The usage need not have been mediated by a prosaic association with actual plurality, for plurality is a very old and ubiquitous metaphor for power. Consider only the several senses of such English words as *great* and *grand*. The reverential *vos* could have been directly inspired by the power of an emperor.

Eventually the Latin plural was extended from the emperor to other power figures. However, this semantic pattern was not unequivocally established for many centuries. There was much inexplicable fluctuation between T and V in Old French, Spanish, Italian and Portuguese (Schliebitz, 1886), and in Middle English (Kennedy, 1915; Stidston, 1917). In verse, at least, the choice seems often to have depended on assonance, rhyme or syllable count. However, some time between the twelfth and fourteenth centuries (Gedike, 1794; Grand, 1930; Kennedy, 1915; Schliebitz, 1886), varying with the language, a set of norms crystallized which we call the non-reciprocal power semantic.

The power semantic

One person may be said to have power over another in the degree that he is able to control the behavior of the other. Power is a relationship between at least two persons, and it is non-reciprocal in the sense that both cannot have power in the same area of behavior. The power semantic is similarly non-reciprocal; the superior says T and receives V.

There are many bases of power – physical strength, wealth, age, sex, institutionalized role in the church, the state, the army or within the family. The character of the power semantic can be made clear with a set of examples from various languages. In his letters, Pope Gregory I (590–604) used T to his subordinates in the ecclesiastical hierarchy and they invariably said V to him (Muller, 1914). In medieval Europe, generally, the nobility said T to the common people and received V; the master of a household said T to his slave, his servant, his squire, and received V. Within the family, of whatever social level, parents gave T to children and were given V. In Italy in the fifteenth century penitents said V to the priest and were told T (Grand, 1930). In Froissart (late fourteenth century) God says T to His angels and they say V; all celestial beings say T to man and receive V. In French of the twelfth and thirteenth century man says T to the animals (Schliebitz, 1886). In fifteenth-century Italian literature Christians say T to Turks and Jews and receive V (Grand, 1930). In the plays of Corneille and Racine (Schliebitz, 1886) and Shakespeare (Byrne, 1936), the noble principals say T to their subordinates and are given V in return.

The V of reverence entered European speech as a form of address to the principal power in the state and eventually generalized to the powers within that microcosm of the state – the nuclear family. In the history of language, then, parents are emperor figures. It is interesting to note in passing that Freud reversed this terminology and spoke of kings, as well as generals, employers and priests, as father figures. The propriety of Freud's designation for his psychological purposes derives from the fact that an individual learning a European language reverses the historical order of semantic generalization. The individual's first experience of subordination to power and of the reverential V comes in his relation to his parents. In later years similar asymmetrical power relations and similar norms of address develop between employer and employee, soldier and officer, subject and monarch. We can see how it might happen, as Freud believed, that the later social relationships would remind the individual of the familial prototype and would revive emotions and responses from childhood. In a man's personal history recipients of the non-reciprocal V are parent figures.

Since the non-recriprocal power semantic only prescribes usage between superior and inferior, it calls for a social structure in which there are unique power ranks for every individual. Medieval European societies were not so finely structured as that, and so the power semantic was never the only rule for the use of T and V. There were also norms of address for persons of roughly equivalent power, that is, for members of a common class. Between equals, pronominal address was reciprocal; an individual gave and received the same form. During the medieval period, and for varying times beyond, equals of the upper classes exchanged the mutual V and equals of the lower classes exchanged T.

The difference in class practice derives from the fact that the reverential V was always introduced into a society at the top. In the Roman Empire only the highest ranking persons had any occasion to address the emperor, and so at first only they made use of V in the singular. In its later history in other parts of Europe the reverential V was usually adopted by one court in imitation of another. The practice slowly disseminated downward in a society. In this way the use of V in the singular incidentally came to connote a speaker of high status. In later centuries Europeans became very conscious of the extensive use of V as a mark of elegance. In the drama of seventeenth-century France the nobility and bourgeoisie almost always address one another as V. This is true even of husband and wife, of lovers, and of parent and child if the child is adult. Madame de Sévigné in her correspondence never uses T, not even to her daughter the Comtesse de Grignan (Schliebitz, 1886). Servants and peasantry, however, regularly used T among themselves.

For many centuries French, English, Italian, Spanish and German pronoun usage followed the rule of non-reciprocal T–V between persons of unequal power and the rule of mutual V or T (according to social-class membership) between persons of roughly equivalent power. There was at first no rule differentiating address among equals but, very gradually, a distinction developed which is sometimes called the T of intimacy and the V of formality. We name this second dimension *solidarity*, and here is our guess as to how it developed.

The solidarity semantic

The original singular pronoun was T. The use of V in the singular developed as a form of address to a person of superior power. There are many personal attributes that convey power. The recipient of V may differ from the recipient of T in strength, age, wealth, birth, sex or profession. As two people move apart on these power-laden dimensions, one of them begins to say V. In general terms, the V form is linked with differences between persons. Not all differences between persons imply a difference of power. Men are born in different cities, belong to different families of the same status, may attend different but equally prominent schools, may practice different but equally respected professions. A rule for making distinctive use of T and V among equals can be formulated by generalizing the power semantic. Differences of power cause V to emerge in one direction of address; differences not concerned with power cause V to emerge in both directions.

The relations called *older than*, *parent of*, *employer of*, *richer than*, *stronger than* and *nobler than* are all asymmetrical. If A is older than B, B is not older than A. The relation called 'more powerful than', which is abstracted from these more specific relations, is also conceived to be asymmetrical. The pronoun usage expressing this power relation is also asymmetrical or non-reciprocal, with the greater receiving V and the lesser T. Now we are concerned with a new set of relations which are symmetrical;

for example, *attended the same school* or *have the same parents* or *practise the same profession.* If A has the same parents as B, B has the same parents as A. Solidarity is the name we give to the general relationship and solidarity is symmetrical. The corresponding norms of address are symmetrical or reciprocal with V becoming more probable as solidarity declines. The solidary T reaches a peak of probability in address between twin brothers or in a man's soliloquizing address to himself.

Not every personal attribute counts in determining whether two people are solidary enough to use the mutual T. Eye color does not ordinarily matter nor does shoe size. The similarities that matter seem to be those that make for like-mindedness or similar behavior dispositions. These will ordinarily be such things as political membership, family, religion, profession, sex and birthplace. However, extreme distinctive values on almost any dimension may become significant. Height ought to make for solidarity among giants and midgets. The T of solidarity can be produced by frequency of contact as well as by objective similarities. However, frequent contact does not necessarily lead to the mutual T. It depends on whether contact results in the discovery or creation of the like-mindedness that seems to be the core of the solidarity semantic.

Solidarity comes into the European pronouns as a means of differentiating address among power equals. It introduces a second dimension into the semantic system on the level of power equivalents. So long as solidarity was confined to this level, the two-dimensional system was in equilibrium (see Figure 1a), and it seems to have remained here for a considerable time in all our languages. It is from the long reign of the two-dimensional semantic that T derives its common definition as the pronoun of either condescension or intimacy and V its definition as the pronoun of reverence or formality. These definitions are still current but usage has, in fact, gone somewhat beyond them.

The dimension of solidarity is potentially applicable to all persons addressed. Power superiors may be solidary (parents, elder siblings) or not solidary (officials whom one seldom sees). Power inferiors, similarly, may be as solidary as the old family retainer and as remote as the waiter in a strange restaurant. Extension of the solidarity dimension along the dotted lines of Figure 1b creates six categories of persons defined by their relations to a speaker. Rules of address are in conflict for persons in the upper left and lower right categories. For the upper left, power indicates V and solidarity T. For the lower right, power indicates T and solidarity V.

The abstract conflict described in Figure 1b is particularized in Figure 2a with a sample of the social dyads in which the conflict would be felt. In each case usage in one direction is unequivocal but, in the other direction, the two semantic forces are opposed. The first three dyads in Figure

2a involve conflict in address to inferiors who are not solidary (the lower right category of Figure 1b, and the second three dyads involve conflict in address to superiors who are solidary (the upper left category in Figure 1b).

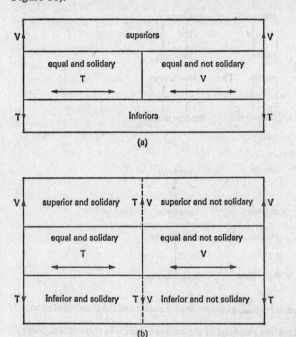

Figure 1 The two-dimensional semantic (a) in equilibrium and (b) under tension

Well into the nineteenth century the power semantic prevailed and waiters, common soldiers and employees were called T while parents, masters and elder brothers were called V. However, all our evidence consistently indicates that in the past century the solidarity semantic has gained supremacy. Dyads of the type shown in Figure 2a now reciprocate the pronoun of solidarity or the pronoun of non-solidarity. The conflicted address has been resolved so as to match the unequivocal address. The abstract result is a simple one-dimensional system with the reciprocal T for the solidary and the reciprocal V for the non-solidary.

It is the present practice to reinterpret power-laden attributes so as to turn them into symmetrical solidarity attributes. Relationships like *older than*, *father of*, *nobler than* and *richer than* are now reinterpreted for purposes of T and V as relations of *the same age as, the same family as, the same kind of ancestry as* and *the same income as.* In the degree that these relationships hold, the probability of a mutual T increases and, in the degree that they do not hold, the probability of a mutual V increases.

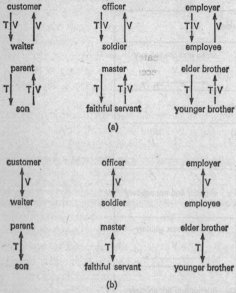

Figure 2 Social dyads involving (a) semantic conflict and (b) their resolution

There is an interesting residual of the power relation in the contemporary notion that the right to initiate the reciprocal T belongs to the member of the dyad having the better power-based claim to say T without reciprocation. The suggestion that solidarity be recognized comes more gracefully from the elder than from the younger, from the richer than from the poorer, from the employer than from the employee, from the noble than from the commoner, from the female than from the male.

In support of our claim that solidarity has largely won out over power we can offer a few quotations from language scholars. Littré (1882), writing of French usage, says: 'Notre courtoisie est même si grande, que nous ne dédaignons pas de donner du vous et du monsieur à l'homme de la condition la plus vile.' Grand (1930) wrote of the Italian V: 'On commence aussi à le donner aux personnes de service, à qui on disait tu autrefois'. We have found no authority who describes the general character of these many specific changes of usage: a shift from power to solidarity as the governing semantic principle.

The best evidence that the change has occurred is in our interviews and notes on contemporary literature and films and, most importantly, the questionnaire results. The six social dyads of Figure 2 were all represented in the questionnaire. In the past these would have been answered in accordance with asymmetrical power. Across all six of these dyads the French results yield only 11 per cent non-reciprocal power answers, the German 12 per cent, the Italian 27 per cent. In all other cases the usage is reciprocal, as indicated in Figure 2b. In all three of the languages, address between master and servant retains the greatest power loading. Some of the changes toward solidarity are very recent. Only since the Second World War, for instance, has the French Army adopted a regulation requiring officers to say V to enlisted men.

Finally, it is our opinion that a still newer direction of semantic shift can be discerned in the whole collection of languages studied. Once solidarity has been established as the single dimension distinguishing T from V the province of T proceeds to expand. The direction of change is increase in the number of relations defined as solidary enough to merit a mutual T and, in particular, to regard any sort of camaraderie resulting from a common task or a common fate as ground for T. We have a favorite example of this new trend given us independently by several French informants. It seems that mountaineers above a certain critical altitude shift to the mutual T. We like to think that this is the point where their lives hang by a single thread. In general, the mutual T is advancing among fellow students, fellow workers, members of the same political group, persons who share a hobby or take a trip together. We believe this is the direction of current change because it summarizes what our informants tell us about the pronoun usage of the 'young people' as opposed to that of older people.

Contemporary differences among French, Italian and German

While T and V have passed through the same general semantic sequence in these three languages, there are today some differences of detailed usage which were revealed by the questionnaire data. Conversations with native speakers guided us in the writing of questionnaire items, but the conversations themselves did not teach us the characteristic semantic features of the three languages; these did not emerge until we made statistical comparison of answers to the standard items of the questionnaire.

The questionnaire is in English. It opens with a paragraph informing the subject that the items below all have reference to the use of the singular pronouns of address in his native language. There are twenty-eight items in the full questionnaire, and they all have the form of the following example from the questionnaire for French students:

1a Which pronoun would you use in speaking to your mother?
            T (definitely)
            T (probably)
      Possibly T, possibly V
            V (probably)
            V (definitely)
1b Which would she use in speaking to you?
            T (definitely)
            T (probably)
      Possibly T, possibly V
            V (probably)
            V (definitely)

The questionnaire asks about usage between the subject and his mother, his father, his grandfather, his wife, a younger brother who is a child, a married elder brother, that brother's wife, a remote male cousin and an elderly female servant whom he has known from childhood. It asks about usage between the subject and fellow students at the university at home, usage to a student from home visiting in America, and usage to someone with whom the subject had been at school some years previously. It asks about usage to a waiter in a restaurant, between clerks in an office, fellow soldiers in the army, between boss and employee, army private and general. In addition, there are some rather elaborate items which ask the subject to imagine himself in some carefully detailed social situation and then to say what pronoun he would use. A copy of the full questionnaire may be had on application to the authors.

The most accessible informants were students from abroad resident in Boston in the fall of 1957. Listings of such students were obtained from Harvard, Boston University, MIT, and the Office of the French Consul in New England. Although we have data from a small sample of female respondents, the present analysis is limited to the males. All the men in the sample have been in the United States for one year or less; they come from cities of over 300,000 inhabitants, and these cities are well scattered across the country in question. In addition, all members of the sample are from upper-middle-class, professional families. This homogeneity of class membership was enforced by the factors determining selection of students who go abroad. The occasional informant from a working-class family is deliberately excluded from these comparisons. The class from which we draw shows less regional variation in speech than does the working class and, especially, farmers. At the present time we have complete responses from fifty Frenchmen, twenty Germans and eleven Italians; many of these men also sent us letters describing their understanding of the pronouns and offering numerous valuable anecdotes of usage. The varying numbers of subjects belonging to the three nationalities result from the unequal representation of these nationalities among Boston students rather than from national characterological differences in willingness to answer a questionnaire. Almost every person on our lists agreed to serve as an informant.

In analysing the results we assigned the number 0–4 to the five response alternatives to each question, beginning with 'Definitely V' as 0. A rough test was made of the significance of the differences among the three languages on each question. We dichotomized the replies to each question into: (a) all replies of either 'Definitely T' or 'Probably T'; (b) all replies of 'Definitely V' or 'Probably V' or 'Possibly V, possibly T'. Using the chi-squared test with Yates's correction for small frequencies we determined, for each comparison, the probability of obtaining by chance a difference as large or larger than that actually obtained. Even with such small samples, there were quite a few differences significantly unlikely to occur by chance ($P = 0.05$ or less). Germans were more prone than the French to say T to their grandfathers, to an elder brother's wife and to an old family servant. The French were more prone than the Germans to say T to a male fellow student, to a student from home visiting in America, to a fellow clerk in an office and to someone known previously as a fellow student. Italians were more prone than the French to say T to a female fellow student and also to an attractive girl to whom they had recently been introduced. Italians were more prone than the Germans to say T to the persons just described and, in addition, to a male fellow student and to a student from home visiting in America. On no question did either the French or the Germans show a significantly greater tendency to say T than did the Italians.

The many particular differences among the three languages are susceptible of a general characterization. Let us first contrast German and French. The German T is more reliably applied within the family than is the French T; in addition to the significantly higher T scores for grandfather and elder brother's wife there are smaller differences showing a higher score for the German T on father, mother, wife, married elder brother and remote male cousin. The French T is not automatically applied to remote relatives, but it is more likely than the German pronoun to be used to express the camaraderie of fellow students, fellow clerks, fellow countrymen abroad and fellow soldiers. In general it may be said that the solidarity coded by the German T is an ascribed solidarity of family relationships. The French T, in greater degree, codes an acquired solidarity not founded on family relationship but developing out of some sort of shared fate. As for the Italian T, it very nearly equals the German in family solidarity and it surpasses the French in camaraderie. The camaraderie of the Italian male, incidentally, is extended to the Italian female; unlike the French or German student the Italian says T to the co-ed almost as readily as to the male fellow student.

There is a very abstract semantic rule governing T and V which is the same for French, German and Italian and for many other languages we have studied. The rule is that usage is reciprocal, T becoming increasingly probable and V less probable as the number of solidarity-producing attributes shared by two people increases. The respect in which French, German and Italian differ from one another is in the relative weight given to various attributes of persons which can serve to generate solidarity. For German, ascribed family membership is the important attribute; French and Italian give more weight to acquired characteristics.

Semantics, social structure and ideology

A historical study of the pronouns of address reveals a set of semantic and social psychological correspondences. The non-reciprocal power semantic is associated with a relatively static society in which power is distributed by birthright and is not subject to much redistribution. The power semantic was closely tied with the feudal and manorial systems. In Italy the reverential pronoun *Lei* which has largely displaced the older *voi* was originally an abbreviation for *la vostra Signoria* 'your lordship' and in Spanish *vuestra Merced* 'your grace' became the reverential *usted*. The static social structure was accompanied by the Church's teaching that each man had his properly appointed place and ought not to wish to rise above it. The reciprocal solidarity semantic has grown with social mobility and an equalitarian ideology. The towns and cities have led the way in the semantic change as they led the way in opening society to vertical movement. In addition to these rough historical correspondences we have made a collection of lesser items of evidence favoring the thesis.

In France the non-reciprocal power semantic was dominant until the Revolution when the Committee for the Public Safety condemned the use of V as a feudal remnant and ordered a universal reciprocal T. On 31 October 1793, Malbec made a Parliamentary speech against V:

Nous distinguons trois personnes pour le singulier et trois pour le pluriel, et, au mépris de cette règle, l'esprit de fanatisme, d'orgueil et de féodalité, nous a fait contracter l'habitude de nous servir de la seconde personne du pluriel lorsque nous parlons à un seul (quoted in Brunot, 1927).

For a time revolutionary 'fraternité' transformed all address into the mutual *Citoyen* and the mutual *tu*. Robespierre even addressed the president of the Assembly as *tu*. In later years solidarity declined and the differences of power which always exist everywhere were expressed once more.

It must be asked why the equalitarian ideal was expressed in a universal T rather than a universal V or, as a third alternative, why there was not a shift of semantic from power to solidarity with both pronouns being retained. The answer lies with the ancient upper-class preference for the use of V. There was animus against the pronoun itself. The pronoun of the 'sans-culottes' was T (Gedike, 1794), and so this had to be the pronoun of the Revolution.

Although the power semantic has largely gone out of pronoun use in France today native speakers are nevertheless aware of it. In part they are aware of it because it prevails in so much of the greatest French literature. Awareness of power as a potential factor in pronoun usage was revealed by our respondents' special attitude toward the saying of T to a waiter. Most of them felt that this would be shockingly bad taste in a way that other norm violations would not be, apparently because there is a kind of seignorial right to say T to a waiter, an actual power asymmetry, which the modern man's ideology required him to deny. In French Africa, on the other hand, it is considered proper to recognize a caste difference between the African and the European, and the non-reciprocal address is used to express it. The European says T and requires V from the African. This is a galling custom to the African, and in 1957 Robert Lacoste, the French Minister residing in Algeria, urged his countrymen to eschew the practice.

In England, before the Norman Conquest, *ye* was the second person plural and *thou* the singular. *You* was originally the accusative of *ye*, but in time it also became the nominative plural and ultimately ousted *thou* as the usual singular. The first uses of *ye* as a reverential singular occur in the thirteenth century (Kennedy, 1915), and seem to have been copied from the French nobility. The semantic progression corresponds roughly to the general stages described in the first section of this paper, except that the English seem always to have moved more freely from one form to another than did the continental Europeans (Jespersen, 1905).

In the seventeenth century *thou* and *you* became explicitly involved in social controversy. The Religious Society of Friends (or Quakers) was founded in the middle of this century by George Fox. One of the practices setting off this rebellious group from the larger society was the use of Plain Speech, and this entailed saying *thou* to everyone. George Fox explained the practice in these words:

Moreover, when the Lord sent me forth into the world, He forbade me to put off my hat to any, high or low; and I was required to Thee and Thou all men and women, without any respect to rich or poor, great or small (quoted in Estrich and Sperber, 1946).

Fox (1660) wrote a fascinating pamphlet, arguing that T to one and V to many is the natural and logical form of address in all languages. Among others he cites Latin, Hebrew, Greek, Arabick, Syriack, Aethiopic, Egyptian, French and Italian. Fox suggests that the Pope, in his vanity, introduced the corrupt and illogical practice of saying V to one person. Farnsworth, another early Friend, wrote a somewhat similar pamphlet (Farnsworth, 1655), in which he argued that the Scriptures show that God and Adam and God and Moses were not too proud to say and receive the singular T.

For the new convert to the Society of Friends the universal T was an especially difficult commandment. Thomas Ellwood has described the trouble that developed between himself and his father:

But whenever I had occasion to speak to my Father though I had no Hat now to offend him; yet my language did as much: for I durst not say YOU to him, but THOU or THEE, as the Occasion required, and then would he be sure to fall on me with his Fists (Ellwood, 1714).

The Friends' reasons for using the mutual T were much the same as those of the French revolutionaries, but the Friends were always a minority and the larger society was antagonized by their violations of decorum.

Some Friends use *thee* today; the nominative *thou* has been dropped and *thee* is used as both the nominative and (as formerly) the accusative. Interestingly many Friends also use *you*. *Thee* is likely to be reserved for Friends among themselves and *you* said to outsiders. This seems to be a survival of the solidarity semantic. In English at large, of course, *thou* is no longer used. The explanation of its disappearance is by no means certain; however, the forces at work seem to have included a popular reaction against the radicalism of Quakers and Levellers and also a general trend in English toward simplified verbal inflection.

In the world today there are numerous examples of the association proposed between ideology and pronoun semantics. In Yugoslavia, our informants tell us, there was, for a short time following the establishment of Communism, a universal mutual T of solidarity. Today revolutionary *esprit* has declined and V has returned for much the same set of circumstances as in Italy, France or Spain. There is also some power asymmetry in Yugoslavia's 'Socialist manners'. A soldier says V and *Comrade General*, but the general addresses the soldier with T and surname.

It is interesting in our materials to contrast usage in the Afrikaans language of South Africa and in the Gujerati and Hindi languages of India with the rest of the collection. On the questionnaire, Afrikaans speakers made eight non-reciprocal power distinctions; especially notable are distinctions within the family and the distinctions between customer and waiter and between boss and clerk, since these are almost never power-coded in French, Italian, German, etc., although they once were. The Afrikaans pattern generally preserves the asymmetry of the dyads described in Figure 2, and that suggests a more static society and a less developed equalitarian ethic. The forms of address used between Afrikaans-speaking whites and the groups of 'coloreds' and 'blacks' are especially interesting. The Afrikaaner uses T, but the two lower castes use neither T nor V. The intermediate caste of 'coloreds' says *Meneer* to the white and the 'blacks' say *Baas*. It is as if these social distances transcend anything that can be found within the white group and so require their peculiar linguistic expressions.

The Gujerati and Hindi languages of India have about the same pronoun semantic, and it is heavily loaded with power. These languages have all the asymmetrical usage of Afrikaans and, in addition, use the non-reciprocal T and V between elder brother and younger brother and between husband and wife. This truly feudal pronominal pattern is consistent with the static Indian society. However, that society is now changing rapidly and, consistent with that change, the norms of pronoun usage are also changing. The progressive young Indian exchanges the mutual T with his wife.

In our account of the general semantic evolution of the pronouns, we have identified a stage in which the solidarity rule was limited to address between persons of equal power. This seemed to yield a two-dimensional system in equilibrium (see Figure 1a), and we have wondered why address did not permanently stabilize there. It is possible, of course, that human cognition favors the binary choice without contingencies and so found its way to the suppression of one dimension. However, this theory does not account for the fact that it was the rule of solidarity that triumphed. We believe, therefore, that the development of open societies with an equalitarian ideology acted against the non-reciprocal power semantic and in favor of solidarity. It is our suggestion that the larger social changes created a distaste for the face-to-face expression of differential power.

What of the many actions other than non-reciprocal T and V which express power asymmetry? A vassal not only says V but also bows, lifts his cap, touches his forelock, keeps silent, leaps to obey. There are a large number of expressions of subordination which are patterned isomorphically with T and V. Nor are the pronouns the only forms of non-reciprocal address. There are, in addition, proper names and titles, and many of these operate today on a non-reciprocal power pattern in America and in Europe, in open and equalitarian societies.

In the American family there are no discriminating pronouns, but there are non-reciprocal norms of address. A father says *Jim* to his son but, unless he is extraordinarily 'advanced' he does not anticipate being called *Jack* in reply. In the American South there are no pronouns to mark the caste separation of Negro and white, but there are non-reciprocal norms of address. The white man is accustomed to call the Negro by his first name, but he expects to be called *Mr Legree*. In America and in Europe there are forms of non-reciprocal address for all the dyads of asymmetrical power; customer and waiter, teacher and student, father and son, employer and employee.

Differences of power exist in a democracy as in all societies. What is the difference between expressing power asymmetry in pronouns and expressing it by choice of title and proper name? It seems to be primarily a question of the degree of linguistic compulsion. In face-to-face address we can usually avoid the use of any name or title but not so easily the use of a pronoun. Even if the pronoun can be avoided, it will be implicit in the inflection of the verb. 'Dites quelque chose' clearly says *vous* to the Frenchman. A norm for the pronominal and verbal expression of power compels a continuing coding of power, whereas a norm for titles and names permits power to go uncoded in most discourse. Is there any reason why the pronominal coding should be more congenial to a static society than to an open society?

We have noticed that mode of address intrudes into consciousness as a problem at times of status change. Award of the doctoral degree, for instance, transforms a student into a colleague and, among American academics, the familiar first name is normal. The fledgling academic may find it difficult to call his former teachers by their first names. Although these teachers may be young and affable, they have had a very real power over him for several years and it will feel presumptuous to deny this all at once with a new mode of address. However, the 'tyranny of democratic manners' (Cronin, 1958) does not allow him to continue comfortable with the polite 'Professor X'. He would not like to be thought unduly conscious of status, unprepared for faculty rank, a born lickspittle. Happily, English allows him a respite. He can avoid any term of address, staying with the uncommitted *you*, until he and his addressees have got used to the new state of things. This linguistic *rite de passage* has, for English speakers, a waiting room in which to screw up courage.

In a fluid society crises of address will occur more frequently than in a static society, and so the pronominal coding of power differences is more likely to be felt as onerous. Coding by title and name would be more tolerable because less compulsory. Where status is fixed by birth and does not change each man has enduring rights and obligations of address.

A strong equalitarian ideology of the sort dominant in America works to suppress every conventional expression of power asymmetry. If the worker becomes conscious of his unreciprocated polite address to the boss, he may feel that his human dignity requires him to change. However, we do not feel the full power of the ideology until we are in a situation that gives us some claim to receive deferential address. The American professor often feels foolish being given his title, he almost certainly will not claim it as a prerogative; he may take pride in being on a first-name basis with his students. Very 'palsy' parents may invite their children to call them by first name. The very President of the Republic invites us all to call him *Ike*. Nevertheless, the differences of power are real and are experienced. Cronin (1958) has suggested in an amusing piece that subordination is expressed by Americans in a subtle, and generally unwitting, body language. 'The repertoire includes the boyish grin, the deprecatory cough, the unfinished sentence, the appreciative giggle, the drooping shoulders, the head-scratch and the bottom-waggle.'

Group style with the pronouns of address

The identification of style is relative to the identification of some constancy. When we have marked out the essentials of some action – it might be walking or speaking a language or driving a car – we can identify the residual variation as stylistic. Different styles are different ways of 'doing the same thing', and so their identification waits on some designation of the range of performances to be regarded as 'the same thing'.

Linguistic science finds enough that is constant in English and French and Latin to put all these and many more into one family – the Indo-European. It is possible with reference to this constancy to think of Italian and Spanish and English and the others as so many styles of Indo-European. They all have, for instance, two singular pronouns of address, but each language has an individual phonetic and semantic style in pronoun usage. We are ignoring phonetic style (through the use of the generic T and V, but in the second section of the paper we have described differences in the semantic styles of French, German and Italian.

Linguistic styles are potentially expressive when there is covariation between characteristics of language performance and characteristics of the performers. When styles are 'interpreted', language behavior is functionally expressive. On that abstract level where the constancy is Indo-European and the styles are French, German, English and Italian, interpretations of style must be statements about communities of speakers, statements of national character, social structure or group ideology. In the last section we have hazarded a few propositions on this level.

It is usual, in discussion of linguistic style, to set constancy at the level of a language like French or English rather than at the level of a language family. In the languages we have studied there are variations in pronoun style that are associated with the social status of the speaker. We have seen that the use of V because of its entry at the top of a society and its diffusion downward was always interpreted as a mark of good breeding. It is interesting to find an organization of French journeymen in the generation after the Revolution adopting a set of rules of propriety cautioning members against going without tie or shoes at home on Sunday and also against the use of the mutual T among themselves (Perdiguier, 1914). Our informants assure us that V and T still function as indications of class membership. The Yugoslavians have a saying that a peasant would say T to a king. By contrast, a French nobleman who turned up in our net told us that he had said T to no one in the world except the old woman who was his nurse in childhood. He is prevented by the dominant democratic ideology from saying T to subordinates and by his own royalist ideology from saying it to equals.

In literature, pronoun style has often been used to expose the pretensions of social climbers and the would-be elegant. Persons aping the manners of the class above them usually do not get the imitation exactly right. They are likely to notice some point of difference between their own class and the next higher and then extend the difference too widely, as in the use of the 'elegant' broad [a] in 'can' and 'bad'. Molière gives us his 'précieuses ridicules' saying V to servants whom a refined person would call T. In Ben Jonson's *Everyman in his Humour* and *Epicoene* such true gallants as Wellbred and Knowell usually say *you* to one another but they make frequent expressive shifts between this form and *thou*, whereas such fops as John Daw and Amorous-La-Foole make unvarying use of *you*.

Our sample of visiting French students was roughly homogeneous in social status as judged by the single criterion of paternal occupation. Therefore, we could not make any systematic study of differences in class style, but we thought it possible that, even within this select group, there might be interpretable differences of style. It was our guess that the tendency to make wide or narrow use of the solidary T would be related to general radicalism or conservatism of ideology. As a measure of this latter dimension we used Eysenck's Social Attitude Inventory (Eysenck, 1957). This is a collection of statements to be accepted or rejected concerning a variety of matters – religion, economics, racial relations, sexual behavior, etc. Eysenck has validated the scale in England and in France on members of Socialist, Communist, Fascist, Conservative and Liberal party members. In general, to be radical on this scale is to favor change and to be conservative is to wish to maintain the *status quo* or turn back to some earlier condition. We undertook to relate scores on this inventory to an index of pronoun style.

As yet we have reported no evidence demonstrating that there exists such a thing as a personal style in pronoun usage in the sense of a tendency to make wide or narrow use of T. It may be that each item in the questionnaire, each sort of person addressed, is an independent personal norm not predictable from any other. A child learns what to say to each kind of person. What he learns in each case depends on the groups in which he has membership. Perhaps his usage is a bundle of unrelated habits.

Guttman (Stouffer, Guttman and Schuman, 1950) has developed the technique of Scalogram Analysis for determining whether or not a collection of statements taps a common dimension. A perfect Guttman scale can be made of the statements: (a) I am at least 5' tall; (b) I am at least 5' 4" tall; (c) I am at least 5' 7" tall; (d) I am at least 6' 1" tall; (e) I am at least 6' 2" tall. Endorsement of a more extreme statement will always be associated with endorsement of all less extreme statements. A person can be assigned a single score – a,b,c,d, or e – which represents the most extreme statement he has endorsed and, from this single score all his individual answers can be reproduced. If he scores c he has also endorsed a and b but not d or e. The general criterion for scalability is the reproducibility of individual responses from a single score, and this depends on the items being interrelated so that endorsement of one is reliably associated with endorsement or rejection of the others.

The Guttman method was developed during the Second World War for the measurement of social attitudes, and it has been widely used. Perfect reproducibility is not likely to be found for all the statements which an investigator guesses to be concerned with some single attitude. The usual thing is to accept a set of statements as scalable when they are 90 per cent reproducible and also satisfy certain other requirements; for example, there must be some statements that are not given a very one-sided response but are accepted and rejected with nearly equal frequency.

The responses to the pronoun questionnaire are not varying degrees of agreement (as in an attitude questionnaire) but are rather varying probabilities of saying T or V. There seems to be no reason why these bipolar responses cannot be treated like yes or no responses on an attitude scale. The difference is that the scale, if there is one, will be the semantic dimension governing the pronouns, and the scale score of each respondent will represent his personal semantic style.

It is customary to have a hundred subjects for a Scalogram Analysis, but we could find only fifty French students. We tested all twenty-eight items for scalability and found that a subset of them made a fairly good scale. It was necessary to combine response categories so as to dichotomize them in order to obtain an average reproducibility of 85 per cent. This coefficient was computed for the five intermediate items having the more-balanced marginal frequences. A large number of items fell at or very near the two extremes. The solidarity or T-most end of the scale could be defined by father, mother, elder brother, young boys, wife or lover quite as well as by younger brother. The remote or V-most end could be defined by 'waiter' or 'top boss' as well as by 'army general'. The intervening positions, from the T-end to the V-end, are: the elderly female servant known since childhood, grandfather, a male fellow student, a female fellow student and an elder brother's wife.

For each item on the scale a T answer scores one point and a V answer no points. The individual total scores range from 1 to 7, which means the scale can differentiate only seven semantic styles. We divided the subjects into the resultant seven stylistically homogeneous groups and, for each group, determined the average scores on radicalism-conservatism. There was a set of almost perfectly consistent differences.

In Table 1 appear the mean radicalism scores for each pronoun style. The individual radicalism scores range between 2 and 13; the higher the score the more radical the person's ideology. The very striking result is that the group radicalism scores duplicate the order of the group pronoun scores with only a single reversal. The rank-difference correlation between the two sets of scores is 0·96, and even with only seven paired scores this is a very significant relationship.

There is enough consistency of address to justify speaking of a personal-pronoun style which involves a more or less wide use of the solidary T. Even among students of the same socioeconomic level there are differences of style, and these are potentially expressive of radicalism and conservatism in ideology. A Frenchman could, with some confidence, infer that a male university student who regularly said T to female fellow students would favor the nationalization of industry, free love, trial marriage, the abolition of capital punishment, and the weakening of nationalistic and religious loyalties.

What shall we make of the association between a wide use of T and a cluster of radical sentiments. There may be no 'sense' to it at all, that is, no logical connection between the linguistic practice and the attitudes, but simply a general tendency to go along with the newest thing. We know that left-wing attitudes are more likely to be found in the laboring class than in the professional classes. Perhaps those offspring of the professional class who sympathize with proletariat politics also, incidentally, pick up the working man's wide use of T without feeling that there is anything in the linguistic practice that is congruent with the ideology.

On the other hand perhaps there is something appropriate in the association. The ideology is consistent in its disapproval of barriers between people: race, religion, nationality, property, marriage, even criminality. All these barriers have the effect of separating the solidary, the 'in-group', from the non-solidary, the 'out-group'. The radical says the criminal is not far enough 'out' to be killed; he should be re-educated. He says that a nationality ought not to be so solidary that it prevents world organization from succeeding. Private property ought to be abolished, industry should be nationalized. There are to be no more out-groups and in-groups but rather one group, undifferentiated by nationality, religion or pronoun of address. The fact that the pronoun which is being extended to all men alike is T, the mark of solidarity, the pronoun of the nuclear family, expresses the radical's intention to extend his sense of brotherhood. But

Table 1 Scores on the pronoun scale in relation to scores on the radicalism scale

Group pronoun score	Group mean radicalism score
1	5·5
2	6·66
3	6·82
4	7·83
5	6·83
6	8·83
7	9·75

we notice that the universal application of the pronoun eliminates the discrimination that gave it a meaning and that gives particular point to an old problem. Can the solidarity of the family be extended so widely? Is there enough libido to stretch so far? Will there perhaps be a thin solidarity the same everywhere but nowhere so strong as in the past?

The pronouns of address as expressions of transient attitudes

Behavior norms are practices consistent within a group. So long as the choice of a pronoun is recognized as normal for a group, its interpretation is simply the membership of the speaker in that group. However, the implications of group membership are often very important; social class, for instance, suggests a kind of family life, a level of education, a set of political views, and much besides. These facts about a person belong to his character. They are enduring features which help to determine actions over many years. Consistent personal style in the use of the pronouns of address does not reveal enough to establish the speaker's unique character, but it can help to place him in one or another large category.

Sometimes the choice of a pronoun clearly violates a group norm and perhaps also the customary practice of the speaker. Then the meaning of

R. Brown and A. Gilman 123

the act will be sought in some attitude or emotion of the speaker. It is as if the interpreter reasoned that variations of address between the same two persons must be caused by variations in their attitudes toward one another. If two men of seventeenth-century France properly exchange the V of upper-class equals and one of them gives the other T, he suggests that the other is his inferior since it is to his inferiors that a man says T. The general meaning of an unexpected pronoun choice is simply that the speaker, for the moment, views his relationship as one that calls for the pronoun used. This kind of variation in language behavior expresses a contemporaneous feeling or attitude. These variations are not consistent personal styles but departures from one's own custom and the customs of a group in response to a mood.

As there have been two great semantic dimensions governing T and V, so there have also been two principal kinds of expressive meaning. Breaking the norms of power generally has the meaning that a speaker regards an addressee as his inferior, superior or equal, although by usual criteria, and according to the speaker's own customary usage, the addressee is not what the pronoun implies. Breaking the norms of solidarity generally means that the speaker temporarily thinks of the other as an outsider or as an intimate; it means that sympathy is extended or withdrawn.

The oldest uses of T and V to express attitudes seem everywhere to have been the T of contempt or anger and the V of admiration or respect. In his study of the French pronouns Schliebitz (1886) found the first examples of these expressive uses in literature of the twelfth and thirteenth centuries, which is about the time that the power semantic crystallized in France, and Grand (1930) has found the same thing for Italian. In saying T, where V is usual, the speaker treats the addressee like a servant or a child and assumes the right to berate him. The most common use of the expressive V, in the early materials, is that of the master who is exceptionally pleased with the work of a servant and elevates him pronominally to match this esteem.

Racine, in his dramas, used the pronouns with perfect semantic consistency. His major figures exchange the V of upper-class equals. Lovers, brother and sister, husband and wife – none of them says T if he is of high rank, but each person of high rank has a subordinate confidante to whom he says T and from whom he receives V. It is a perfect non-reciprocal power semantic. This courtly pattern is broken only for the greatest scenes in each play. Racine reserved the expressive pronoun as some composers save the cymbals. In both *Andromaque* and *Phèdre* there are only two expressive departures from the norm, and they mark climaxes of feeling.

Jespersen (1905) believed that English *thou* and *ye* (or *you*) were more often shifted to express mood and tone than were the pronouns of the continental languages, and our comparisons strongly support this opinion. The *thou* of contempt was so very familiar that a verbal form was created to name this expressive use. Shakespeare gives it to Sir Toby Belch (*Twelfth Night*) in the lines urging Andrew Aguecheek to send a challenge to the disguised Viola: 'Taunt him with the license of ink, if thou thou'st him some thrice, it shall not be amiss.' In life the verb turned up in Sir Edward Coke's attack on Raleigh at the latter's trial in 1603 (Jardine, 1832–5): 'All that he did, was at thy instigation, thou viper; for I thou thee, thou traitor.'

The T of contempt and anger is usually introduced between persons who normally exchange V but it can, of course, also be used by a subordinate to a superior. As the social distance is greater, the overthrow of the norm is more shocking and generally respresents a greater extremity of passion. Sejanus, in Ben Jonson's play of that name, feels extreme contempt for the emperor Tiberius but wisely gives him the reverential V to his face. However, soliloquizing after the emperor has exited, Sejanus begins: 'Dull, heavy Caesar! Wouldst thou tell me. . . .' In Jonson's *Volpone* Mosca invariably says *you* to his master until the final scene when, as the two villains are about to be carted away, Mosca turns on Volpone with 'Bane to thy wolfish nature'.

Expressive effects of much greater subtlety than those we have described are common in Elizabethan and Jacobean drama. The exact interpretation of the speaker's attitude depends not only on the pronoun norm he upsets but also on his attendant words and actions and the total setting. Still simple enough to be unequivocal is the ironic or mocking *you* said by Tamburlaine to the captive Turkish emperor Bajazeth. This exchange occurs in Act IV of Marlowe's play:

TAMBURLAINE Here, Turk, wilt thou have a clean trencher?
BAJAZETH Ay, tyrant, and more meat.
TAMBURLAINE Soft, sir, you must be dieted; too much eating will make you surfeit.

Thou is to be expected from captor to captive and the norm is upset when Tamburlaine says *you*. He cannot intend to express admiration or respect since he keeps the Turk captive and starves him. His intention is to mock the captive king with respectful address, implying a power that the king has lost.

The momentary shift of pronoun directly expresses a momentary shift of mood, but that interpretation does not exhaust its meaning. The fact that a man has a particular momentary attitude or emotion may imply a great deal about his characteristic disposition, his readiness for one kind of feeling rather than another. Not every attorney-general, for instance, would have used the abusive *thou* to Raleigh. The fact that Edward Coke did so suggests an arrogant and choleric temperament and, in fact, many made this assessment of him (Jardine, 1832–5). When Volpone spoke to Celia, a lady of Venice, he ought to have said *you* but he began at once with *thee*. This violation of decorum, together with the fact that he leaps from his sick bed to attempt rape of the lady, helps to establish Volpone's monstrous character. His abnormal form of address is consistent with the unnatural images in his speech. In any given situation we know the sort of people who would break the norms of address and the sort who would not. From the fact that a man does break the norms we infer his immediate feelings and, in addition, attribute to him the general character of people who would have such feelings and would give them that kind of expression.

With the establishment of the solidarity semantic a new set of expressive meanings became possible – feelings of sympathy and estrangement. In Shakespeare's plays there are expressive meanings that derive from the solidarity semantic as well as many dependent on power usage and many that rely on both connotations. The play *Two Gentlemen of Verona* is concerned with the Renaissance ideal of friendship and provides especially clear expressions of solidarity. Proteus and Valentine, the two Gentlemen, initially exchange *thou*, but when they touch on the subject of love, on which they disagree, their address changes to the *you* of estrangement. Molière (Fay, 1920) has shown us that a man may even put himself at a distance as does George Dandin in the soliloquy beginning: 'George Dandin! George Dandin! Vous avez fait une sottise . . .'

In both French and English drama of the past, T and V were marvelously sensitive to feelings of approach and withdrawal. In terms of Freud's striking amoeba metaphor the pronouns signal the extension or retraction of libidinal pseudopodia. However, in French, German and Italian today this use seems to be very uncommon. Our informants told us that the T, once extended, is almost never taken back for the reason that it would mean the complete withdrawal of esteem. The only modern expressive shift we have found is a rather chilling one. Silverberg (1940) reports that in Germany in 1940 a prostitute and her client said *du* when they met and while they were together but when the libidinal tie (in the narrow sense) had been dissolved they resumed the mutual distant *Sie*.

We have suggested that the modern direction of change in pronoun usage expresses a will to extend the solidary ethic to everyone. The apparent decline of expressive shifts between T and V is more difficult to interpret. Perhaps it is because Europeans have seen that excluded persons or races or groups can become the target of extreme aggression from groups that are benevolent within themselves. Perhaps Europeans would like to convince themselves that the solidary ethic once extended will not be withdrawn, that there is security in the mutual T.

References

BAUGH, A. C. (1935), *A History of the English Language*, New York.

BRUNOT F. (1927). *La Pensée et la Langue*, Paris.

BRUNOT. F. (1937), *Histoire de la Langue Française*, Librairie Armand Colin.

BYRNE, SISTER ST G. (1936), 'Shakespeare's use of the pronoun of address', unpublished doctoral dissertation, Catholic University of America, Washington.

CHÂTELAIN, É. (1880), 'Du pluriel de respect en Latin', *Revue de Philologie*, vol. 4, pp. 129–39.

CRONIN, M. (1958), 'The tyranny of democratic manners', *New Republic*, vol. 137, pp. 12–14.

DEVEREUX, W. B. (1853), *Lives and Letters of the Devereux, Earls of Essex, in the Reigns of Elizabeth, James I and Charles I, 1540–1646*, London.

DIEZ, F. (1876). *Grammaire des Langues Romanes*, Paris.

ELLWOOD, T. (1714), *The History of the Life of Thomas Ellwood*, J. Sowle.

ESTRICH, R. M., and SPERBER, H. (1946), *Three Keys to Language*, Holt, Rinehart & Winston.

EYSENCK, H. J. (1957), *Sense and Nonsense in Psychology*, Penguin.

FARNSWORTH, R. (1655), *The Pure Language of the Spirit of Truth . . . or 'thee' and 'thou' in its place . . .*, London.

FAY, P. B. (1920), 'The use of "tu" and "vous" in Moliére', *University of California Publications in Modern Philology*, vol. 8, pp. 227–86.

FOX, G. (1660), *A Battle-Doore for Teachers and Professors to Learn Plural and Singular*, London.

GEDIKE, F. (1794), *Über du und sie in der Deutschen Sprache*, Berlin.

GRAND, C. (1930), '*Tu, Voi, Lei;' Étude des Pronoms Allocutoires Italiens*, P. Theodose.

GRIMM, J. (1898), *Deutsche Grammatik*, Vol. 4, Gütersloh.

HARRISON, G. B. (ed.) (1935), *The Letters of Queen Elizabeth*, London.

JARDINE, D. (1832–1835), *Criminal Trials*, Vols. 1–2, London.

JESPERSEN, O. (1905), *Growth and Structure of the English Language*, Teubner.

JOHNSTON, O. M. (1904), 'The use of "ella", "lei" and "la" as polite forms of address in Italian', *MPh*, vol. 1, pp. 469–75.

KENNEDY, A. G. (1915), *The Pronoun of Address in English Literature of the Thirteenth Century*, Stanford.

LITTRÉ, É. (1882), *Dictionnaire de la Langue Française*, Vol. 4, Librairie Hachette.

MEYER-LÜBKE, W. (1900), *Grammaire des Langues Romanes*, Vol. 3, Paris.

MULLER, H. F. (1914), 'The use of the plural of reverence in the letters of Pope Gregory I', *Romanic Review*, vol. 5, pp. 68–89.

PERDIGUIER, A. (1914), *Mémoires d'un Compagnon*, Moulins.

SCHLIEBITZ, V. (1886), *Die Person der Anrede in der französischen Sprache*, Jungfer.

SILVERBERG, W. V. (1940), 'On the psychological significance of "du" and "sie"', *Psychoanal. Q.*, vol. 9, pp. 509–25.

STIDSTON, R. O. (1917), *The Use of Ye in the Function of Thou: A Study of Grammar and Social Intercourse in Fourteenth-Century England*, Stanford.

STOUFFER, S. A., GUTTMAN, L. and SCHUMAN, E. A. (1950), *Measurement and Prediction*, Studies in Social Psychology in World War II, Vol. 4, Princeton.

6 R. Brown and M. Ford

Address in American English

R. Brown and M. Ford, 'Address in American English', *Journal of Abnormal and Social Psychology*, vol. 62, 1961, pp. 375-85.

When one person speaks to another, the selection of certain linguistic forms is governed by the relation between the speaker and his addressee. The principal option of address in American English is the choice between use of the first name (hereafter abbreviated to FN) and the use of a title with the last name (TLN). These linguistic forms follow a rule that is truly relational. Their use is not predictable from properties of the addressee alone and not predictable from properties of the speaker alone but only from properties of the dyad. Kinship terms of address (e.g. *dad*, *mom*, *son*) are also relational language, but they constitute a restricted language of relationship since most dyads that might be created in America would not call for any sort of kinship term. Proper names, on the other hand, constitute a nearly universal language of relationship; the semantic dimensions involved serve to relate to one another all of the members of the society.

Much of our knowledge of the dimensions that structure interaction has been obtained from paper-and-pencil performances such as the status ranking of acquaintances or the sociometric choice from among acquaintances. There can be no doubt that the dimensions revealed by such data are genuinely functional in ordinary life. However, performances elicited by the social scientist are not the everyday performances that reveal dimensions of social structure and cause each new generation to internalize such dimensions. It is always possible that a paper-and-pencil task imposes a dimension or encourages an unrepresentative consistency and delicacy of differentiation. It is desirable to study social structure in everyday life, but much of the everyday behavior that is governed by social dimensions is difficult to record and involves an uncertain number of significant contrasts (e.g. influencing decisions, smiling at someone, warmth of manner). Forms of address are speech and so there is a recording technique called writing which preserves most of the significant detail. English forms of address are reasonably well described by a single binary contrast: FN or TLN. These forms are ubiquitous and for any set of interacting persons it is possible to obtain a collection of address dyads from which the latent structuring dimensions can be inferred. The paper provides an example of the application of semantic analysis to the study of social structure. We begin by describing the norms of American address, then point out a certain pattern in these norms which is to be found in the forms of address of all languages known to us. This abstract speech pattern suggests a feature of social structure that may possibly be universal.

Method
Materials

To discover the norms of address in American English we require a large sample of usage. The range of the subject population is vast but the uniformity must be great. Some sensible compromise is required between the stratified national sample dictated by the scope of the problem and the unsystematic observation of one's friends dictated by the probable simplicity of its solution. Four kinds of data have been used.

Usage in modern American plays. There are more instances of address in plays than in any other form of literature. Thirty-eight plays written by American authors, performed since 1939, and anthologized in three volumes of *Best American Plays* (Gassner, 1947, 1952, 1958) were used. Of the plays in these volumes we omitted only those set in some remote time or in a country other than the United States. Without listing all the titles it is possible to indicate the range of American usage that it represented. By geographic region we move from *The Philadelphia Story* to the Southland of *The Member of the Wedding* through the midwest of *Picnic* to the Far West of *The Time of Your Life*; by social class from *The Rose Tattoo* and *A View from the Bridge* through *Death of a Salesman* and *Tea and Sympathy* to *The Solid Gold Cadillac*. For military usage there are such plays as *Mister Roberts* and *No Time for Sergeants*. The speech of Jewish, Italian and Negro minorities is represented and also that of such groups as politicians, corporation executives, narcotics addicts, college professors and policemen.

Of course these materials are not a record of actual speech from the characters named but are the speech constructed for such characters by playwrights. Probably playwrights accurately reproduce the true norms of address, and it is possible to check one author against another. In addition, however, there are three other kinds of data to catch possible inaccuracies in this first set.

Actual usage in a Boston business firm. For two months a man employed in a drafting firm took advantage of leisure moments to jot down for us instances of linguistic address overheard from his fellow workers. He collected address terms for 214 different dyads in which 82 different people are involved either as speaker or addressee. Each person is identified by full name, sex, age and position in a twelve-level occupational hierarchy. In addition, we benefited from our informant's good knowledge of friendship patterns among the dramatis personae.

Reported usage of business executives. Each year there is at MIT at group of Alfred P. Sloan Fellows; these are business executives between thirty and thirty-eight years of age, who are nominated by their respective employers to study for one year at the institute. The thirty-four Sloan Fellows designated for 1958–9 served as informants for this study. They come from many different parts of the country, most of them from very large corporations but a few from small companies.

By the time the Sloan Fellows served as informants the general pattern of the norms had become sufficiently clear to make possible the writing of a questionnaire designed to elicit the most important information. Each man was asked to write down the full names and positions of four persons whom he was accustomed to see nearly every day at his place of business, and he was to distribute his selections so as to include: one person equal to himself in the organization hierarchy with whom he was on close or intimate terms, one person equal to himself with whom he was on distant or formal terms, one person superior to himself in the organization hierarchy, one person subordinate to himself in the hierarchy. After listing the names the informant was asked to write down for each person listed the exact words that he (the informant) would customarily speak in greeting that person for the first time each day. In addition, the Sloan Fellows were asked some other questions that will be described when they become relevant.

Recorded usage in Midwest. The Psychological Field Station of the University of Kansas directed by Barker and Wright (1954) kindly allowed us to make an extended study of ten 'specimen records', each of which record the events and conversation in a full day of the life of a child. The station has also allowed us to work with a set of brief 'behavior settings observations' made on fifty-six children in the town called Midwest and on fifty-six children in Yoredale, England, matched with those in Midwest by sex and age. In these materials we have been primarily concerned with a grammatical analysis of the kinds of 'mands' addressed to children (for another study of the language of social relationship) but have, in addition, taken the opportunity to check our conclusions about American address against the Midwest records.

Procedure

For each of the thirty-eight plays every instance of address was recorded, together with an identification of the speaker and addressee. The method of study is a sort of controlled induction.[1] Approximately one-third of the plays were first examined in an effort to discover rules that would summarize all of the instances of address they contained. The resulting provisional rules were then tested against a second set of plays and underwent some revision. The revised rules proved adequate to the description of all instances of address in a third and final set of plays. The supplementary data from a business firm, from the Sloan Fellows, and from the Midwest records were used as additional checks on the rules induced from the plays and also to test several particular hypotheses.

Major patterns of address

If we consider only the FN and TLN there are just three logically possible dyadic patterns: the reciprocal exchange of FN, the reciprocal exchange of TLN and the non-reciprocal pattern in which one person uses FN and the other TLN. All three patterns occur with high frequency and the problem is one of inducing the semantic factors invariably associated with a given pattern and serving to distinguish it from the others.

In classifying instances of address into the three classes, FN was taken to include full first names (e.g. *Robert*), familiar abbreviations (e.g. *Bob*), and diminutive forms (e.g. *Bobbie*). It may be said at once that male first names in American English very seldom occur in full form (*Robert*, *James* or *Gerald*) but are almost always either abbreviated (*Bob*, *Jim*) or diminutized (*Jerry*) or both (*Bobbie*, *Jimmy*). Female first names are more often left unaltered. Titles for the purpose of this classification include, in addition to *Mr*, *Mrs* and *Miss*, such occupational titles as *Dr*, *Senator*, *Major*, and the like.

Two reciprocal patterns

The vast majority of all dyads in the plays exchange FN (Mutual FN). Indeed, where the actual name is not known there occur sometimes what may be called generic first names; these include the *Mack*, *Jack* and *Buddy* of taxi drivers. Mutual TLN is most commonly found between newly introduced adults. The distinction between the two patterns is

1. Since address involves two persons and, very often, a choice between two linguistic forms, we believe it should be possible to treat the complete set of address dyads for any group of persons as a matrix of paired comparisons from which the dimensions structuring the group could be rigorously derived. We are at present trying to develop such a method.

primarily one of degree of acquaintance with the degree required for the Mutual FN being less for younger people than for older people and less where the members of the dyad are of the same sex than where they are of different sex.

It seems likely that the two reciprocal patterns are on a dimension that ranges from acquaintance to intimacy. However, in modern American English the distance between the two points is small with the Mutual FN usually representing only a very small increment of intimacy over the Mutual TLN; as small sometimes as five minutes of conversation. Because the segment of the line that lies between the two patterns is usually so very short, it is not easy to make out its exact character. However, in English of the past[2] and in cognate languages today the Mutual FN is farther displaced from the Mutual TLN, and from these cases and other materials later to be presented we can hazard a characterization of intimacy. Intimacy is the horizontal line between members of a dyad. The principal factors predisposing to intimacy seem to be shared values (which may derive from kinship, from identity of occupation, sex, nationality, etc., or from some common fate) and frequent contact. Among the behavioral manifestations of intimacy, a relatively complete and honest self-disclosure is important.

Non-reciprocal pattern

In this case one member of the dyad says FN and the other TLN. There are two kinds of relation that can generate this pattern. The first is a difference of age: children say TLN to adults and receive FN; among adults an elder by approximately fifteen-or-more years receives TLN and gives FN to his junior. The second is a difference of occupational status: this may be a relation of direct and enduring subordination (e.g. master–servant, employer–employee, officer–enlisted man); it may be a relation of direct but temporary subordination, involving someone in a service occupation (e.g. waiter, bootblack) and a customer; it may be an enduring difference of occupational status that does not involve direct subordination (e.g. United States senators have higher status than firemen). If the intimacy dimension that governs reciprocal address is the horizontal of social relationship, then the status dimension that underlies the non-reciprocal pattern may be called the vertical of social relationship.[3]

2. In six American plays (Quinn, 1917) written between 1830 and 1911 the reciprocal FN between adults clearly implies a much longer and closer acquaintance than it does in contemporary usage.

3. Kinship terms of address in American English (Schneider and Homans, 1955) also show a non-reciprocality of status. Members of ascending generations are commonly addressed with kinship titles (mother, father, grandmother, grandfather, uncle, aunt) but respond by calling their children, grandchildren, nephews and nieces by FN.

Age and occupational status are correlated and most instances of non-reciprocal address involve congruent differences on the two dimensions. There is, however, proof that a difference on either dimension alone is able to generate the non-reciprocal pattern. The proof is the existence of non-reciprocal dyads matched on one dimension but not on the other.

Because there are two criteria for the assignment of status and, in addition, the correlation between the two criteria is not perfect, we must ask what happens to address in dyads where the elder has the humbler occupation. There are in the plays numerous instances in which the criteria oppose one another: an adolescent girl and her family's middle-aged cook, a young navy ensign and a middle-aged enlisted man, a young executive and an elderly janitor. In all such cases address is in accordance with occupational status and so it would appear that there is a normative rule of priority for the two criteria. It is to be expected in a society whose values are more strongly linked to achieved personal attributes than to ascribed attributes (Parsons, 1951) that occupation would prevail over age in the determination of deference.

The three sets of data in addition to the plays confirm the generalizations made above. Sloan Fellows call almost all of their business acquaintances by FN and expect this address to be reciprocated. In the few cases where one of these men would say TLN and expect to receive FN the other member of the dyad was invariably an organizational superior and was also the elder. In the Boston drafting firm, also, most address is on the pattern of Mutual FN. The few cases of Mutual TLN involved persons who were scarcely acquainted and who were well matched by age and position. There were forty different instances of non-reciprocal address. In thirty-six of these the recipient of TLN was the organizational superior and elder; in twenty-eight cases he was a member of one of the four top executive ranks whereas the recipient of FN was a member of one of the eight unionized ranks. In three cases the organizational superior was younger than his subordinate and it was the superior, not the elder, who received TLN. The single remaining case involved a pair matched by rank but not by age and in this case the elder received TLN. Midwest children participate in non-reciprocal address dyads with parents and teachers and in Mutual FN dyads with other children.

Variant forms of address

In this section are offered tentative characterizations of the several common forms other than FN and TLN. At a later point in the paper we will return to these variants and suggest the nature of their relationship with the major patterns.

Title without name

Commonly used titles (T) include *sir*, *madam*, *ma'am* and *Miss*. In general these forms are used like TLN; either reciprocally between new acquaintances or non-reciprocally by a person of lower status to a person of higher status. The address form T is probably a degree less intimate and a degree more deferential than TLN. It may, for instance, be used reciprocally where acquaintance is so slight that the last name is not known. In non-reciprocal military usage between ranks the TLN may be used to immediate superiors but the T to remote colonels, generals, commanders and admirals even though the names of these superiors are well known.

Beyond this general characterization as a minimally intimate and maximally deferential form particular varieties of T have their specialized uses. The form ma'am is most commonly heard from young men to mature women. Schoolchildren in Yoredale, England, preface almost all address to a teacher by saying: '*Please, Miss . . .*' In parallel circumstances Midwest children use TLN.

Last name alone

An occasional person is regularly addressed by LN. This seems usually to occur where the FN is polysyllabic and has no familiar abbreviation whereas the LN is either a monosyllable or easily transformed into a monosyllable. In these circumstances LN is simply a substitute for FN and patterns in identical fashion.

Where the LN is not the usual form for an addressee it represents a degree of intimacy greater than TLN but less than FN. In military usage enlisted men receive the LN from officers when they are little acquainted; increased familiarity leads to the FN downward though not upward. Elderly and very distinguished professors sometimes begin letters to junior colleagues whom they know fairly well: '*Dear Jones . . .*' The form is not reciprocated in this case.

Reciprocal LN is common between enlisted men until they become acquainted. The enduring reciprocal LN seems always to go with a mutual antagonism that blocks progression to intimacy. In *The Caine Mutiny Court Martial*, for instance, Greenwald and Keefer exchange LN though the degree of acquaintance and their ages would normatively produce Mutual FN. In the climax of this play Greenwald dashes a drink in Keefer's face. In *The Philadelphia Story* Kittredge and Haven exchange LN; the former is the husband-to-be of Tracy Lord and the latter her former-but-still-interested husband.

Multiple names

A speaker may use more than one form of the proper name for the same addressee, sometimes saying TLN, sometimes FN or LN or a nickname, sometimes creating phonetic variants of either FN or the nickname. We are not here interested in the business of temporal progression through the possible forms where earlier terms are dropped as new terms are taken up. The case of multiple names (MN) is the case in which two or more versions of the proper name are used in free variation with one another.

The instances of MN in the plays suggested that this form represented a greater degree of intimacy than the FN, but degrees of intimacy are not easily judged and so we decided to put the hypothesis to a more direct test. The test involved individual interviews with thirty-two MIT male undergraduates. Each subject was asked to think of four men of about his own age all of whom he had met for the first time approximately one year ago. In addition, it was to be the case that the subject had had about equal opportunity to get to know all of these men and yet now was to find himself on close, friendly terms with some of them and on more distant terms with others. The subject was asked to write down the full names of the four men and then to record the name by which he usually addressed each one. When this had been done, the subject was asked, for each acquaintance, whether he ever addressed the man in any other way and all the names currently being used were noted down.

In an earlier paragraph it was suggested that one of the meanings of intimacy is a relatively complete and honest disclosure of the personality. Jourard and Lasakow (1958) have devised a self-disclosure questionnaire which requires the subject to indicate whether or not he has discussed with a designated other person each of sixty topics classifiable under the headings: attitudes and opinions, tastes and interests, work (or studies), money, personality and body. Our thirty-two subjects filled out this questionnaire for each acquaintance. For each subject, then, we ranked the four acquaintances in order of decreasing self-disclosure and we take this to be an order of decreasing intimacy. It generally corresponds with the subjects' ordering of the four into friends and acquaintances.

Across all subjects we combined the thirty-two closest friends, those eliciting highest self-disclosure scores (self-disclosure 1) and also the thirty-two acquaintances with self-disclosure rank orders 2, 3 and 4. For each rank group we determined the number of cases addressed by MN (two or more proper names) and the number addressed by FN alone. The results appear in Table 1. The cases of MN decline as intimacy declines. Using the sign test and a one-tailed hypothesis it was determined that the

Table 1 **Frequencies of two forms of address to acquaintances at different levels of self-disclosure**

	Self-disclosure 1	Self-disclosure 2	Self-disclosure 3	Self-disclosure 4
Multiple names	18	10	7	3
First name	14	22	25	29

Note. Self-disclosure 1 v. Self-disclosure 2 by sign test, $p = 0.020$; Self-disclosure 1 v. Self-disclosure 4 by sign test, $p < 0.004$.

self-disclosure 1 group contained more cases of MN than did the next most intimate group (self-disclosure 2) with $p = 0.020$. The difference between the most intimate and the least intimate (self-disclosure 4) group shows more cases of MN in the former group with $p < 0.004$.

One informant addressed his closest friend whose name is Robert Williams as *Williams* or *Robert* or *Bob* or *Willie* and his next closest friend whose name is James Scoggin as *Scoggin*, *James*, *Jim* or *Scoggs*. Many informants reported that they sometimes playfully addressed a good friend by TLN. Others used playful, and usually pejorative, phonetic variations: *Magoo* for *Magee*, *Katool* for *Katell*, *Lice* for *Leis*.

The tendency to proliferate proper names in intimacy is interesting because it accords with a familiar semantic–psychological principle. For language communities the degree of lexical differentiation of a referent field increases with the importance of that field to the community. To cite a fresh example of this kind of thing, Conklin (1957) reports that the Hanunóo of the Philippine Islands have names for ninety-two varieties of rice which is their principal food. In naming ferns and orchids, with which they are little concerned, the Hanunóo combine numerous botanical species under one term whereas the rice they differentiate so finely is for the botanist a single species. Within a language community Brown (1958) has pointed out that a speaker more concerned with a given referent field will make finer lexical distinctions than a speaker less concerned with that field (botanists have more names for plants than do psychologists). In the referent field composed of other persons we have seen that where contact and concern are minimal and distance greatest, titles alone are likely to be used in address. To call someone *miss* or *sir* is to address the person on a categorical level which does not establish the addressee's individual identity. The proper name constitutes the individual as a unique organism. Beyond the single proper name, however, where interest is still greater the individual is fragmented into a variety of names. Perhaps this differentiation beyond individuality expresses various manifestations or ways of regarding someone who is close (Brown, 1959).

A general system of address

How are these various forms of address related to one another? Consider first only the three major patterns. The Mutual TLN goes with distance or formality and the Mutual FN with a slightly greater degree of intimacy. In non-reciprocal address the TLN is used to the person of higher status and the FN to the person of lower status. One form expresses both distance and deference; the other form expresses both intimacy and condescension. Within the limits of two dyadic address forms there is a formally or logically possible alternative pattern. The form used mutually between intimates could be used upward to superiors and the form used between distant acquaintances could be directed downward to subordinates. Because there is an alternative the pattern actually found is not a formal necessity but rather an empirical fact; a fact, we shall see, of great generality.

Several years ago we began our general studies of the language of social relationship with a selection point that does not occur in modern English but which does occur in the other Indo-European languages. In French, for example, a speaker must choose between two second person singular pronouns; his addressee may be addressed as *tu* or as *vous*. In German the comparable forms are *du* and *Sie*; in Italian *tu* and *Lei*. In English of the past, from about the thirteenth century until the eighteenth, there was a cognate option of address; the choice between *thou* and *ye*. We have studied the semantic rules governing these pronouns in twenty languages of Europe and India, comparing one language with another and the usage of earlier centuries with later (Brown and Gilman, 1960). For our present purposes the important point is that these pronouns in all the languages studied follow the same abstract pattern as the FN and TLN.

In discussing the pronouns of address let us use T as a generic designator for pronouns of the type of *tu* and *du* and V as a designator for pronouns of the type *vous* and *Sie*. Mutual V is the form of address for adult new acquaintances; it begins where TLN begins – at the temporal point of origin of the dyad. Mutual T like Mutual FN is an expression of increased intimacy but it is, for most Europeans, much farther along the line than is the Mutual FN of Americans. From medieval times into the present century non-reciprocal T and V was the pattern for those unequal in status with the superior receiving the V and the subordinate the T. In recent times the non-reciprocal use of the pronouns has much declined because of a conscious egalitarianism. The important point is, however, that when the non-reciprocal pattern has been used anywhere from southern India to Scandinavia the downward directed form has been the intimate T and the upward directed the distant V.

It may be that the abstract linkage in personal address of intimacy and condescension, distance and deference is a linguistic universal, but we certainly do not know that as yet. We do know that the linkage occurs also in some non-Indo-European languages (e.g. Japanese second person pronouns). Indeed, in those few languages for which we have found adequate descriptions of the semantics of address, no violations of the abstract pattern have yet appeared.

Table 2 Two forms of greeting for four classes of associate

	Equal and intimate	
	Good morning	Hi
Equal and distant		
Hi	0	4
Good morning	4	10
	Subordinate	
	Good morning	Hi
Superior		
Hi	1	3
Good morning	13	8

Note. With McNemar test for the significance of changes in related samples (employing Yates correction) χ^2 for intimate $v.$ distant $= 8\cdot10$, $p < 0\cdot0025$ and χ^2 for subordinate $v.$ superior $= 4\cdot00$, $p < 0\cdot025$.

It seems also that the pattern applies to more than names, titles and pronouns. The Sloan Fellows' greetings to their business associates almost invariably used the FN. However, the greetings themselves were quite varied; including *hi, morning, good morning, hello, howdy*, etc. Only *hi* and *good morning* occurred with sufficient frequency to make possible the discovery of a pattern. The Sloans reported on greetings to four classes of associate: equal and intimate, equal and distant, superior, and subordinate. In Table 2 appear the frequencies of *hi* and *good morning* for these various categories. *Hi* is more common to intimates and to subordinates while *good morning* is for distant acquaintances and superiors. Using the McNemar test for the significance of changes in related samples with the Yates correction for continuity, the difference between intimates and acquaintances is significant with $p < 0\cdot0025$ and the difference for subordinates and superiors with $p < 0\cdot025$. In both cases a one-tailed test was used since the direction of the differences was predicted by the abstract pattern of address. The records of actual usage in a Boston firm accord with this finding. In one revealing instance a workman was greeted 'Hi' and promptly answered 'Hi', but as he turned and recognized the boss, he added 'Good morning'.

Why should the abstract pattern described govern address between two persons? A curious fact about contemporary use of T and V provides a clue. While the non-reciprocal pattern for pronouns has generally been abandoned in Europe, inequality of status continues to affect one aspect of usage. Dyads begin at the Mutual V and, with time, may advance to the intimacy of Mutual T. For many the shift from V to T is an important rite of passage. The Germans even have a little informal ceremony they call the *Bruderschaft*. One waits for a congenial mood, a mellow occasion, perhaps with a glass of wine, and says: 'Why don't we say *du* to one another?' The new usage is, of course, to be reciprocal. However, there is one necessarily non-reciprocal aspect of the occasion – someone must make the suggestion. When there is a clear difference of status between the two the right to initiate the change unequivocally belongs to the superior – to the elder, the richer, the more distinguished of the two. The gate to linguistic intimacy is kept by the person of higher status.

The norms of English address also make a pattern in time. A dyad must, with time, either increase its total amount of contact or else dissolve. Since the Mutual TLN represents less contact than the Mutual FN if Mutual TLN is to occur in a given dyad it must occur at an earlier time than the Mutual FN. The place of the non-reciprocal pattern in time is between the other two and it may be understood as a step from Mutual TLN in the direction of Mutual FN; a step which, like the suggestion of the *Bruderschaft* is taken first by the superior. Many dyads will linger for a very long time – possibly the life of the dyad – in the non-reciprocal pattern. In this circumstance the pattern gives enduring expression to an inequality of status.

Consider a familiar sort of example. A prospective graduate student arrives at a university to meet some of the faculty of the psychology department and is interviewed by the chairman. Probably the two will initially exchange TLN. In the course of the day or, if not, shortly after the student enrolls, the chairman will begin to call him by FN. He extends the hand of friendship, but the student knows that it behooves him not to grasp it too quickly. The student will continue with the TLN for several years (four is probably the mode) and in this period the non-reciprocality of speech will express the inequality of status. If the chairman is neither very elderly nor very august the student will eventually feel able to reciprocate the FN and the dyad will have advanced to Mutual FN. The three patterns may be described as a progression in time (see upper portion of Figure 1) if we add several important qualifications.

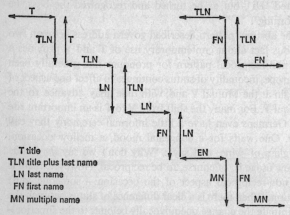

T title
TLN title plus last name
LN last name
FN first name
MN multiple name

Figure 1 Graphic models of the progression of address in time (from left to right). (The upper portion of the figure represents the major progression: the lower portion represents the full progression.)

Not every dyad passes through all three steps. There are some that begin at each of the three points: adults of equal status with Mutual TLN, master and servant with non-reciprocality, young people with Mutual FN. In addition, not every dyad that continues to exist will necessarily advance to Mutual FN. In North Carolina until 1860 the Negro slave said TLN to his master and was told FN (Eliason, 1956), and there was no change with time. There is a final qualification concerning the progression of address in time. Even when relationships do develop in intimacy they will not necessarily pass through the intermediate non-reciprocal stage. When the members of a dyad are not of clearly unequal status, they will advance at the same time to Mutual FN.

The general statement that can be made is: if an address pattern changes in time it will change in the direction of Mutual TLN → non-reciprocal TLN and FN → Mutual FN though a step may be skipped. Even this statement cannot stand without a little more explanation. There are special circumstances in which the direction of movement of address can be reversed. If a person of lower status seems to move too fast to the reciprocation of the FN a superior may step back from his use of FN to TLN. The day after a convivial office party a breezy young clerk calls out to the president: 'Morning, Jack!' and in icy tones the president replies: 'Good morning, *Mr* Jones.' The person of lower status must never use a more familiar form of address than the person of higher status and the backstep by the superior puts the subordinate in just that position from which he will usually withdraw to the propriety of TLN.

The variant forms of address discussed at an earlier point in this paper seem to function as additional optional steps in the progression of address.[4] Title alone (T) probably is the formal extreme since we find in our data that dyads which begin as Mutual T often change with time to non-reciprocal TLN downwards and T upwards. The last name alone (LN) must be intercalated between TLN and FN since LN downwards is found in combination with TLN upwards and LN upwards is found in combination with FN downwards. The use of multiple names (MN), we have seen, represents the intimate extreme. Making these additions to the major three-step progression we arrive at the full progression of Figure 1 (lower portion) in which each new step towards intimacy is initiated by the superior who is, therefore, not just the gatekeeper to Mutual FN but the pace-setter for all linguistic advances in intimacy.

The qualifications that apply to the major progression apply also to the full progression. Dyads may begin at any point, need not move at all, and if they move may skip steps. There is an additional qualification that results from the multiplication of forms. Any less formal term may be used downwards in a non-reciprocal pattern with any more formal term being used upwards. Thus we find not only the TLN with the LN but also the T with LN or even with FN as when a captain calls an enlisted man *Jones* or *John* but is called *captain*.

Is there any way to test the accuracy of the full progression pictured in Figure 1? We have found no dyads that pass through the entire progression but only dyads moving in one or another limited region. By the time the third and final set of plays was ready for analysis, the full progression had been constructed. If the progression, with all its qualifications, is accurately descriptive of American English practice, one should find certain kinds of address combinations and not others. Any address form can be used mutually (five possible combinations). When there is a clear difference of status we may have any non-reciprocal pattern that combines a less formal term downward with a more formal term upwards (ten possible combinations). With a clear status difference we may not have any non-reciprocal pattern that combines a more formal term downwards with a less formal term upwards (ten impossible combinations). In the last set of plays instances of all the possible combinations occur and no in-

4. This paper does not discuss all American English forms of address but only those that have clear positions in the intimacy and status pattern. There is, for instance, the use of the complete name (*John Jones* or even *John Montgomery Jones*) which is used as an intensifier and is particularly favored by mothers 'manding' disobedient children.

stances of the impossible combinations. The static predictions of the model are validated.

The construction also generates a set of dynamic predictions. When address changes (if there is not either a reproving or a jocular intent) movement must be in the direction from left to right in the drawing of Figure 1 though it need not be to the immediately adjacent position. Changes of address in the plays are surprisingly infrequent and seldom involve more than two steps. Only seven different kinds of change occurred but all of these are included among those defined as possible by the model. One 'impossible' change occurred in the play *Born Yesterday*. Billie Dawn, the junk dealer's mistress, in speaking with the wife of a United States Senator who is many years her senior initiates movement from Mutual TLN to a more intimate form. This violation of the norms is greeted with general shock and is a device that helps to establish Billie Dawn's ingenuous vulgarity. In so far as the limited occurrences of change in address permit, then, the model is confirmed in its dynamic aspect.

Status and intimacy in social relations

Two persons of unequal status may be conceived as two points on a generalized value scale of the sort used by Osgood and Tannenbaum (1955) for the congruity model which they have used to predict attitude change. The person of superior status has, of course, the greater value on such a scale. Movements towards intimacy of address in terms of the congruity model are acts of association. Such acts, the model predicts, will cause the objects of unequal value to move towards one another; in the case of address between persons this means that the value of the inferior is enhanced by intimate association with a superior while the value of the superior is diminished. The prediction is good intuitive sense. But now the interesting thing is that this model seems to call for the abstract pattern of address that does not occur. Since the person of lower status has a motive for initiating intimacy and the superior has none the intimate form ought, in non-reciprocal address, to be used upwards and the distant form to be used downwards. This is not the pattern which we have found in all of our materials but, is rather, the formal alternative to that pattern and we have nowhere found this alternative to be the operative norm.

The abstract design of address is not a direct expression of the realities of status and intimacy but is rather a denial of the realities. The pattern might have been designed to minimize the pain of invidious status distinctions. The person of lesser value may be presumed to be ever ready for association with a person of higher value but the person of higher value must be presumed to be less ready. If the person of lesser value were to initiate associative acts, he would run the risk of rebuff; if the person of higher value initiates such acts there is no such risk. The superior, then, must be the pacesetter in progression to intimacy. If there is to be no progression but rather an enduring non-reciprocal expression of inequality, this expression is not so disagreeable as it might be since the superior offers intimate address and it is the inferior who demurs. The abstract pattern minimizes the pain that could be involved when persons are to be related on two dimensions: the horizontal of intimacy and the vertical of status.

The person of higher status is, we believe, the pacesetter not in linguistic address alone but in all acts that increase intimacy. The Sloan Fellows who served as informants for us responded to two questions that concern non-linguistic moves towards intimacy. Each question was answered with reference to each of the four persons listed by the informant. One of these persons, you may remember, was a superior, one a subordinate, one equal and intimate, one equal and distant. The informant indicated on a scale from 1–5 how willing he would be to behave in the designated manner with reference to each person. The number 1 represents maximal willingness ('definitely would') and 5 minimal willingness ('definitely would not'). The questions are:

1. In ordinary circumstances would you be willing to ask 'X' for a loan of his comb?
2. Suppose 'X' were feeling very unhappy about something or other. Would you put your hand on his shoulder in a reassuring way?

The results appear in Table 3 and show a familiar pattern. Informants were more willing to borrow a comb from, and to put a hand on the shoulder of, an associate who was equal and intimate than one equal and distant and also more willing to initiate these acts of intimacy with subor-

Table 3 Comparative willingness to initiate acts of intimacy with four classes of associate

	More willing with equal and intimate than with distant associate	More willing with equal and distant than with intimate associate	More willing with subordinate than with superior	More willing with superior than with subordinate
Borrow comb	7	0	9	2
Hand on shoulder	11	3	24	1

Note. By sign test intimate v. distant on borrow comb, $p = 0.008$; on hand on shoulder, $p = 0.029$. Subordinate v. superior on borrow comb, $p = 0.033$; on hand on shoulder, $p < 0.002$.

dinates than with superiors. Using a sign test and a one-tailed hypothesis the comb question differentiates intimate from remote associates with a $p = 0.008$ and subordinates from superiors with a $p = 0.033$; the hand-on-shoulder question differentiates intimate from remote associates with a $p = 0.029$ and subordinates from superiors with a $p < 0.002$. These non-speech acts follow the pattern of TLN and FN; of T and V; and of *hi* and *good morning*. Perhaps all kinds of associative behavior can be placed on a rough scale of intimacy and in the progression over this scale of a dyad the superior may always be in advance.

With a good sized inequality of status the use of FN by the higher does not, of course, justify immediate reciprocation from the lower. The lower must wait for the initiation of additional acts of intimacy before taking a step on his own. It is very likely that the normative lag in intimacy increases with the degree of status inequality. However, the norms are not always perfectly clear; graduate students will sometimes be uncertain whether the time has come to say FN to a professor, employees will wonder whether they know their bosses well enough to use the familiar form. When someone is in this region of uncertainty, we find that he avoids the use of any sort of personal name and makes do with the uncommitted omnibus *you*.

Summary

The semantic rules governing address in American English are worked out, from a varied collection of data that includes usage in American plays, actual usage in a Boston business firm, reported usage of business executives from various cities in the United States and usage recorded in a midwestern American town. The most common address forms are the first name (FN) and the title plus last name (TLN). These function in three sorts of dyadic pattern: the Mutual TLN, the Mutual FN, and the non-reciprocal use of TLN and FN. The semantic distinction between the two mutual patterns is on the intimacy dimension with Mutual FN being the more intimate of the two patterns. In the non-reciprocal pattern a distinction is made in terms of status with the higher saying FN and the lower TLN. The practice of using the intimate form to a subordinate and the distant form to a superior also governs the use of pronouns of address in many languages as well as the use of certain conventional greetings. It is suggested that this very general pattern prevails because in the progression towards intimacy of unequals the superior is always the pacesetter initiating new moves in that direction. The superior is the pacesetter because the willingness of the person of lower status to enter into association can be taken for granted and there is little risk that a superior will be rebuffed whereas the risk would be great if the inferior were to initiate acts of association. Such variant forms of address as the title alone, the last name alone, and the use of multiple names are fitted into a model that purports to describe the temporal progression of address from acquaintance to friendship. Each new step towards friendship is, in this model, initiated by the person of higher status.

References

BARKER, R. G., and WRIGHT, H. F. (1954), *Midwest and Its Children*, Harper & Row.
BROWN, R. (1958), *Words and Things*, Free Press.
BROWN, R. (1959), 'Humbert's idiography', *Contemp. Psychol.*, vol. 4, pp. 172–4.
BROWN, R., and GILMAN, A. (1960), 'The pronouns of power and solidarity', in T. Sebeok (ed.), *Style in Language*, Wiley. [Reprinted in this book, pp. 103–27.]
CONKLIN, H. C. (1957), *Hanunóo Agriculture*, Food and Agriculture Organization of the United Nations.
ELIASON, N. E. (1956), *Tarheel Talk: An Historical Study of the English Language in North Carolina to 1860*, University of North Carolina Press.
GASSNER, J. (ed.) (1947), *Best Plays of the Modern American Theatre: Second Series*, Crown.
GASSNER, J. (ed.) (1952), *Best American Plays: Third Series*, Crown.
GASSNER, J. (ed.) (1958), *Best American Plays: Fourth Series*, Crown.
JOURARD, S. M., and LASAKOW, P. (1958), 'Some factors in self-disclosure', *J. abnorm. soc. Psychol.*, vol. 56, pp. 91–8.
OSGOOD, C. E., and TANNENBAUM, P. H. (1955), 'The principle of congruity in attitude change', *Psychol. Rev.*, vol. 62, pp. 42–55.
PARSONS, T. (1951), *The Social System*, Free Press.
QUINN, A. H. (ed.) (1917), *Representative American Plays*, Century.
SCHNEIDER, D. M., and HOMANS, G. C. (1955), 'Kinship terminology and the American kinship system', *Amer. Anthrop.*, vol. 57, pp. 1194–208.

7 B. Malinowski

Phatic Communion

Excerpt from B. Malinowski, 'The problem of meaning in primitive languages', supplement to C. K. Ogden and I. A. Richards, *The Meaning of Meaning*, Routledge & Kegan Paul, 1923.

So far, I have dealt mainly with the simplest problems of meaning, those associated with the definition of single words and with the lexicographical task of bringing home to a European reader the vocabulary of a strange tongue. And the main result of our analysis was that it is impossible to translate words of a primitive language or of one widely different from our own, without giving a detailed account of the culture of its users and thus providing the common measure necessary for a translation. But though an ethnographic background is indispensable for a scientific treatment of a language, it is by no means sufficient, and the problem of meaning needs a special theory of its own. I shall try to show that, looking at language from the ethnographic perspective and using our conception of *context of situation*, we shall be able to give an outline of a semantic theory, useful in the work on Primitive Linguistics, and throwing some light on human language in general.

First of all, let us try, from our standpoint, to form a view of the nature of language. The lack of a clear and precise view of linguistic function and of the nature of meaning, has been, I believe, the cause of the relative sterility of much otherwise excellent linguistic theorizing. The direct manner in which Ogden and Richards face this fundamental problem and the excellent argument by which they solve it, constitute the permanent value of their work.

The earlier study of a native text has demonstrated that an utterance becomes comprehensive only when we interpret it by its context of situation. The analysis of this context should give us a glimpse of a group of savages bound by reciprocal ties of interests and ambitions, of emotional appeal and response. There was boastful reference to competitive trading activities, to ceremonial overseas expeditions, to a complex of sentiments, ambitions and ideas known to the group of speakers and hearers through their being steeped in tribal tradition and having been themselves actors in such events as those described in the narrative. Instead of giving a narrative I could have adduced linguistic samples still more deeply and directly embedded in the context of situation.

Take for instance language spoken by a group of natives engaged in one of their fundamental pursuits in search of subsistence – hunting, fishing, tilling the soil; or else in one of those activities, in which a savage tribe express some essentially human forms of energy – war, play or sport, ceremonial performance or artistic display such as dancing or singing. The actors in any such scene are all following a purposeful activity, are all set on a definite aim; they all have to act in a concerted manner according to certain rules established by custom and tradition. In this, speech is the necessary means of communion; it is the one indispensable instrument for creating the ties of the moment without which unified social action is impossible.

Let us now consider what would be the type of talk passing between people thus acting, what would be the manner of its use. To make it quite concrete at first, let us follow up a party of fishermen on a coral lagoon, spying for a shoal of fish, trying to imprison them in an enclosure of large nets, and to drive them into small net-bags – an example which I am choosing also because of my personal familiarity with the procedure (Malinowski, 1918).

The canoes glide slowly and noiselessly, punted by men especially good at this task and always used for it. Other experts who know the bottom of the lagoon, with its plant and animal life, are on the lookout for fish. One of them sights the quarry. Customary signs, or sounds or words are uttered. Sometimes a sentence full of technical references to the channels or patches on the lagoon has to be spoken; sometimes when the shoal is near and the task of trapping is simple, a conventional cry is uttered not too loudly. Then, the whole fleet stops and ranges itself – every canoe and every man in it performing his appointed task – according to a customary routine. But, of course, the men, as they act, utter now and then a sound expressing keenness in the pursuit or impatience at some technical difficulty, joy of achievement or disappointment at failure. Again, a word of command is passed here and there, a technical expression or explanation which serves to harmonize their behaviour towards other men. The whole group act in a concerted manner, determined by old tribal tradition and perfectly familiar to the actors through life-long experience. Some men in the canoes cast the wide encircling nets into the water, other plunge, and wading through the shallow lagoon, drive the fish into the nets. Others again stand by with the small nets, ready to catch the fish. An animated scene, full of movement follows, and now that the fish are in their power the fishermen speak loudly, and give vent to their feelings. Short, telling exclamations fly about, which might be rendered by such words as: *Pull in*, *Let go*, *Shift further*, *Lift the net*; or again technical expressions completely untranslatable except by minute description of the instruments used, and of the mode of action.

All the language used during such a pursuit is full of technical terms, short references to surroundings, rapid indications of change – all based on customary types of behaviour, well-known to the participants from personal experience. Each utterance is essentially bound up with the context of situation and with the aim of the pursuit, whether it be the short indications about the movements of the quarry, or references to statements about the surroundings, or the expression of feeling and passion inexorably bound up with behaviour, or words of command, or correlation of action. The structure of all this linguistic material is inextricably mixed up with, and dependent upon, the course of the activity in which the utterances are embedded. The vocabulary, the meaning of the particular words used in their characteristic technicality is not less subordinate to action. For technical language, in matters of practical pursuit, acquires its meaning only through personal participation in this type of pursuit. It has to be learned, not through reflection but through action.

Had we taken any other example than fishing, we would have reached similar results. The study of any form of speech used in connection with vital work would reveal the same grammatical and lexical peculiarities: the dependence of the meaning of each word upon practical experience, and of the structure of each utterance upon the momentary situation in which it is spoken. Thus the consideration of linguistic uses associated with any practical pursuit, leads us to the conclusion that language in its primitive forms ought to be regarded and studied against the background of human activities and as a mode of human behaviour in practical matters. We have to realize that language originally, among primitive, non-civilized peoples was never used as a mere mirror of reflected thought. The manner in which I am using it now, in writing these words, the manner in which the author of a book, or a papyrus or a hewn inscription has to use it, is a very far-fetched and derivative function of language. In this, language becomes a condensed piece of reflection, a record of fact or thought. In its primitive uses, language functions as a link in concerted human activity, as a piece of human behaviour. It is a mode of action and not an instrument of reflection.

These conclusions have been reached on an example in which language is used by people engaged in practical work, in which utterances are embedded in action. This conclusion might be questioned by an objection that there are also other linguistic uses even among primitive peoples who are debarred from writing or any means of external fixation of linguistic texts. Yet even they, it might be urged, have fixed texts in their songs, sayings, myths and legends, and most important, in their ritual and magical formulae. Are our conclusions about the nature of language correct, when faced with this use of speech; can our views remain unaltered when, from speech in action, we turn our attention to free narrative or to the use of language in pure social intercourse; when the object of talk is not to achieve some aim but the exchange of words almost as an end in itself?

Anyone who has followed our analysis of speech in action and compares it with [. . .] narrative texts [. . .], will be convinced that the present conclusions apply to narrative speech as well. When incidents are told or discussed among a group of listeners, there is, first, the situation of that moment made up of the respective social, intellectual and emotional attitudes of those present. Within this situation, the narrative creates new bonds and sentiments by the emotional appeal of the words. In the narrative quoted, the boasting of a man to a mixed audience of several visitors and strangers produces feelings of pride or mortification, of triumph or envy. In every case, narrative speech as found in primitive communities is primarily a mode of social action rather than a mere reflection of thought.

A narrative is associated also indirectly with one situation to which it refers – in our text with a performance of competitive sailing. In this relation, the words of a tale are significant because of previous experiences of the listeners; and their meaning depends on the context of the situation referred to, not to the same degree but in the same manner as in the speech of action. The difference in degree is important; narrative speech is derived in its function, and it refers to action only indirectly, but the way in which it acquires its meaning can only be understood from the direct function of speech in action. To use the terminology of this work: the referential function of a narrative is subordinate to its social and emotive function, as classified by Ogden and Richards.

The case of language used in free, aimless, social intercourse requires special consideration. When a number of people sit together at a village fire, after all the daily tasks are over, or when they chat, resting from work, or when they accompany some mere manual work by gossip quite unconnected with what they are doing – it is clear that here we have to do with another mode of using language, with another type of speech function. Language here is not dependent upon what happens at that moment, it seems to be even deprived of any context of situation. The meaning of any utterance cannot be connected with the speaker's or hearer's behaviour, with the purpose of what they are doing.

A mere phrase of politeness, in use as much among savage tribes as in a European drawing room, fulfils a function to which the meaning of its words is almost completely irrelevant. Inquiries about health, comments on weather, affirmations of some supremely obvious state of things – all such are exchanged, not in order to inform, not in this case to connect people in action, certainly not in order to express any thought. It would be even incorrect, I think, to say that such words serve the purpose of establishing a common sentiment, for this is usually absent from such current phrases of intercourse; and where it purports to exist, as in expressions of sympathy, it is avowedly spurious on one side. What is the *raison d'être*, therefore, of such phrases as *How do you do? Ah, here you are. Where do you come from? Nice day today* – all of which serve in one society or another as formulae of greeting or approach?

I think that, in discussing the function of speech in mere sociabilities, we come to one of the bedrock aspects of man's nature in society. There is in all human beings the well-known tendency to congregate, to be together, to enjoy each other's company. Many instincts and innate trends, such as fear or pugnacity, all the types of social sentiments such as ambition, vanity, passion for power and wealth, are dependent upon and associated with the fundamental tendency which makes the mere presence of others a necessity for man.[1]

Now speech is the intimate correlate of this tendency, for, to a natural man, another man's silence is not a reassuring factor, but, on the contrary, something alarming and dangerous. The stranger who cannot speak the language is to all savage tribesmen a natural enemy. To the primitive mind, whether among savages or our own uneducated classes, taciturnity means not only unfriendliness but indirectly a bad character. This no doubt varies greatly with the national character but remains true as a general rule. The breaking of silence, the communion of words is the first act to establish links of fellowship, which is consummated only by the breaking of bread and the communion of food. The modern English expression, *Nice day today* or the Melanesian phrase, *Whence comest thou?* are needed to get over the strange and unpleasant tension which men feel when facing each other in silence.

After the first formula, there comes a flow of language, purposeless expressions of preference or aversion, accounts of irrelevant happenings, comments on what is perfectly obvious. Such gossip, as found in primitive societies, differs only a little from our own. Always the same emphasis of affirmation and consent, mixed perhaps with an incidental disagreement which creates the bonds of antipathy. Or personal accounts of the speaker's views and life history, to which the hearer listens under some restraint and with slightly veiled impatience, waiting till his own turn arrives to speak. For in this use of speech the bonds created between hearer and speaker are not quite symmetrical, the man linguistically active receiving the greater share of social pleasure and self-enhancement. But though the hearing

1. I avoid on purpose the use of the expression herd-instinct, for I believe that the tendency in question cannot strictly be called an instinct. Moreover the term herd-instinct has been misused in a recent sociological work which has, however, become sufficiently popular to establish its views on this subject with the general reader.

given to such utterances is as a rule not as intense as the speaker's own share, it is quite essential for his pleasure, and the reciprocity is established by the change of roles.

There can be no doubt that we have here a new type of linguistic use – *phatic communion* I am tempted to call it, actuated by the demon of terminological invention – a type of speech in which ties of union are created by a mere exchange of words. Let us look at it from the special point of view with which we are here concerned; let us ask what light it throws on the function or nature of language. Are words in phatic communion used primarily to convey meaning, the meaning which is symbolically theirs? Certainly not! They fulfil a social function and that is their principal aim, but they are neither the result of intellectual reflection, nor do they necessarily arouse reflection in the listener. Once again we may say that language does not function here as a means of transmission of thought.

But can we regard it as a mode of action? And in what relation does it stand to our crucial conception of context of situation? It is obvious that the outer situation does not enter directly into the technique of speaking. But what can be considered as *situation* when a number of people aimlessly gossip together? It consists in just this atmosphere of sociability and in the fact of the personal communion of these people. But this is in fact achieved by speech, and the situation in all such cases is created by the exchange of words, by the specific feelings which form convivial gregariousness, by the give and take of utterances which make up ordinary gossip. The whole situation consists in what happens linguistically. Each utterance is an act serving the direct aim of binding hearer to speaker by a tie of some social sentiment or other. Once more language appears to us in this function not as an instrument of reflection but as a mode of action.

I should like to add at once that though the examples discussed were taken from savage life, we could find among ourselves exact parallels to every type of linguistic use so far discussed. The binding tissue of words which unites the crew of a ship in bad weather, the verbal concomitants of a company of soldiers in action, the technical language running parallel to some practical work or sporting pursuit – all these resemble essentially the primitive uses of speech by man in action and our discussion could have been equally well conducted on a modern example. I have chosen the above from a savage community, because I wanted to emphasize that such and no other is the nature of *primitive* speech.

Again in pure sociabilities and gossip we use language exactly as savages do and our talk becomes the 'phatic communion' analysed above, which serves to establish bonds of personal union between people brought together by the mere need of companionship and does not serve any purpose of communicating ideas. 'Throughout the Western world it is agreed that people must meet frequently, and that it is not only agreeable to talk, but that it is a matter of common courtesy to say something even when there is hardly anything to say' (Ogden and Richards, 1923, p. 11). Indeed there need not or perhaps even there must not be anything to communicate. As long as there are words to exchange, phatic communion brings savage and civilized alike into the pleasant atmosphere of polite, social intercourse.

It is only in certain very special uses among a civilized community and only in its highest uses that language is employed to frame and express thoughts. In poetic and literary production, language is made to embody human feelings and passions, to render in a subtle and convincing manner certain inner states and processes of mind. In works of science and philosophy, highly developed types of speech are used to control ideas and to make them common property of civilized mankind.

Even in this function, however, it is not correct to regard language as a mere residuum of reflective thought. And the conception of speech as serving to translate the inner processes of the speaker to the hearer is one-sided and gives us, even with regard to the most highly developed and specialized uses of speech, only a partial and certainly not the most relevant view.

To restate the main position arrived at in this section we can say that language in its primitive function and original form has an essentially pragmatic character; that it is a mode of behaviour, an indispensable element of concerted human action. And negatively: that to regard it as a means for the embodiment or expression of thought is to take a one-sided view of one of its most derivative and specialized functions.

References

MALINOWSKI, B. (1918), 'Fishing and fishing magic in the Trobriand Islands', *Man*, vol. 18, pp. 87–92.
OGDEN, C. K., and RICHARDS, I. A. (1923), *The Meaning of Meaning*, Kegan Paul, Trench, Trubner & Co.

Part Three
Speech and Personal Characteristics

Non-verbal features in speech are a rich source of indexical information. Allport and Cantril (8), Kramer (9) and Laver (10) all discuss how listeners draw conclusions from various non-verbal aspects of speech about a speaker's physical, psychological and social characteristics.

Allport and Cantril give an account of their experiments on broadcast voices, where the listeners based indexical conclusions primarily on the voice quality of speakers reading standardized material. Kramer reviews an extensive body of literature in experimental psychology, and evaluates the validity of the experimental approaches and of the correlations claimed to exist between certain non-verbal factors in speech and particular speaker-characteristics. Laver offers a descriptive phonetic model of voice quality, and looks specifically at the capacity of voice quality as an extralinguistic feature to carry indexical information.

One important conclusion all three Readings agree upon is the stereotyped nature of the judgements reached by listeners about the characteristics of a speaker. Our judgements in this area seem to be cruder than the actual interpersonal differences between speakers would justify.

8 G. W. Allport and H. Cantril

Judging Personality from Voice

G. W. Allport and H. Cantril, 'Judging personality from voice', *Journal of Social Psychology*, vol. 5, 1934, pp. 37–55.

Each member of an ordinary congregate audience receives a clear impression of the personality of the speaker. Complex visual perceptions of his physical build, posture, clothes and movements, in addition to auditory perceptions derived from his speech and voice, make this impression seem accurate and complete. Over the radio the rich and informative visual pattern is absent; only the voice and speech remain. The resulting judgement is somewhat fragmentary and uncertain. This situation has already received popular recognition in jokes concerning the disillusionment of those who learn to their sorrow that the radio voice with which they fell in love does not reveal accurately either the appearance or the nature of its possessor.

In spite of such hazards, however, probably most people who listen to radio speakers feel assured that some of their judgements are dependable. Often the impression is nothing more than a feeling of favor or aversion, but sometimes it represents a surprisingly definite judgement concerning the speaker's physical, intellectual and moral qualities. One broadcasting official asserts:

The human voice, when the man is not making conscious use of it by way of impersonation, does in spite of himself reflect his mood, temper and personality. It expresses the character of the man. President Roosevelt's voice reveals sincerity, good-will and kindliness, determination, conviction, strength, courage and abounding happiness (*New York Times Magazine*, 18 June 1933).

Such statements, even when made with authority, require proof. It is plainly a problem for the psychologist to determine how accurate, on the average, such judgements are.

In spite of its obviousness and accessibility, the problem of judging personality by the radio voice has as yet received very little attention. Pear (1931) has made an auspicious beginning with the assistance of the British Broadcasting Company. Using nine speakers of different ages, sex and interests, he secured over 4000 listeners' judgements concerning the vocation, place of residence, age and birthplace of these speakers. Although

G. W. Allport and H. Cantril 155

Pear's chief interest was in such phonetic problems as accent and dialect, the free descriptions submitted by the auditors enabled him to make some tentative statements concerning the accuracy of judgements of other personal characteristics. Sex was stated correctly (except in the case of an eleven-year-old child); age, in spite of a strong central tendency in the judgements, was on the whole estimated with fair success. Physical descriptions seemed frequently to be apt and vocation was sometimes stated with surprising exactness. Since Pear did not prescribe the manner in which the judgements should be made or instruct the listeners concerning all of the features of personality which they might judge, his results are difficult to express quantitatively or to compare with chance.

The distinction drawn by Sapir (1927) between *voice* and *speech* is important in research of this type. Voice is expressive movement, an individual pattern composed of such inextricable factors as pitch, rhythm, intensity, inflection, volume and vocal mannerisms. Voice is, in brief, the external *form* of vocal expression. Speech, on the other hand, is its *content*. The subject matter of the discourse, the vocabulary employed, the language or dialect spoken, the grammatical structure of the sentences and the style of composition, are all peculiarities of *speech*. They are determined in large part by the cultural background of the speaker, and furnish considerable information useful in classifying him as a member of certain racial, regional or educational groups. It is true that in everyday life we judge a man by what he says and by his cultural affiliations quite as much as by his own individual vocal characteristics, but in research concerned with voice alone it is essential that all other cues be excluded or held constant. The same requirement confronts the psychologist working with handwriting. If individual differences in chirography alone are the object of the investigation, the context and subject matter, the quality of the stationery and mistakes in spelling must not be permitted to furnish an extra basis of judgement.

The ten experiments described below were all designed to determine to what extent the unanalysed natural *voice* is a valid indicator of various features of personality.[1] Certain precautions were taken to exclude the cues which might arise from individual differences in *speech*. In as much as uniform material was read from typewritten texts, differences in vocabulary, fluency of speech, grammatical accuracy and subject matter were virtually eliminated. Except in the case of one speaker (a native of South Africa) there were no appreciable differences in accent among our broadcasters.

1. A preliminary account of this research was reported at the Tenth International Congress of Psychology (Copenhagen) and has been published in *Education on the Air*, Columbus, Ohio State University, 1932, pp. 304–10.

No attempt was made to analyse voice into its various attributes, as Michael and Crawford (1927) and Sapir (1927) have suggested. To attempt to correlate pitch with one personal quality, speed with another, and intensity with a third, would be to make the whole problem absurdly atomistic, and, as is the case with all studies which seek correlations between mere meaningless fragments of well-structured personalities, the study would be foredoomed to failure (cf. Allport, 1933).

The method

In the main part of the investigation eight separate experiments were performed. Six of these took place in the Harvard Psychological Laboratory where a complete broadcasting and receiving unit had been installed. The other two experiments were conducted from the broadcasting studio of Station WEEI in Boston. In the six laboratory experiments students acted as judges, the number in the different experiments ranging from thirty-two to eighty-five. In the two WEEI experiments, the public was asked to send in judgements. From one of these appeals 190 replies were received; from the other, ninety-five. The total number of judges participating in these eight experiments was 587. The procedure employed in each of the laboratory experiments (I–VI) and in the two studio experiments (VII–VIII) was practically identical.

Certain features of personality which could be reliably measured or otherwise determined objectively were selected for study. The features chosen ranged from such definite physical attributes as age and height to certain complex traits and interests of the 'inner' personality. The meanings of two semi-technical expressions (extroversion–introversion and ascendance–submission) were carefully explained to the judges. In each of the eight experiments several of the following features of personality appeared.

Physical and expressive features ('outer' characteristics)

1. Age.
2. Height.
3. Complexion.
4. Appearance in photographs.
5. Appearance in person.
6. Handwriting.

Interests and traits ('inner' characteristics)

7. Vocation.
8. Political preference.
9. Extroversion–introversion.

10. Ascendance–submission.
11. Dominant values.
12. Summary sketch.

Three speakers were selected for each of these eight experiments. Eighteen different speakers took part; twelve participated only once, and six participated in two experiments. All of the speakers were male. In general, a diversity of voices and personalities was sought, although extreme eccentricities or abnormalities were avoided. Before each experiment, objective information for each speaker was obtained on all of the features included in that experiment. The objective criteria for the first eight features are obviously gathered from direct measurement, observation or questioning. The criterion for extroversion–introversion was the Heidbreder scale; for ascendance–submission, the Allport *A–S Reaction Study*; for dominant values, the Allport and Vernon *Study of Values*.

For experiments involving the matching of voice with handwriting or with appearance in photographs, slides were made of uniform samples and projected upon the screen for the duration of the experiment. Three photographs or three samples of handwriting would remain upon the screen while the three voices read their passages. For the experiments involving a matching of voice with appearance in person, simultaneous matching was impossible. After each reading all three of the speakers walked into the room where the audience was seated. An interval of perhaps half a minute elapsed between the voice and the appearance of the three speakers. Each speaker wore a symbol pinned to his coat, which was employed by the judges in indicating their matching.

At the beginning of each of the eight experiments there was one practice reading of the same passage by each of the three speakers, to accustom the judges to the voices. The passages which were used in both the practice reading and in each portion of the experiment averaged approximately ten lines in length, and were selected from Dickens, Lewis Carroll or similar sources.

In Experiments I–VI small record booklets were prepared for the judges, on each page of which the necessary information concerning one feature of personality was given. One page of the booklet, for example, appeared as follows:

Rating on a test for ascendance–submission

Voice – very ascendant
Voice – slightly ascendant
Voice – very submissive

The subjects were instructed to match each of the three voices they would hear (designated as voice no. 1, voice no. 2 and voice no. 3) with the items of information given. The three speakers read the same passage in rotation and the judges entered beside each of the three items the number of the voice which the characterization seemed to fit best. The listeners were instructed to make independent judgements for each feature represented on the separate pages of the record booklet. In no case were they allowed to turn back or ahead.

The final part of each of these experiments consisted of matching the voices with three summary sketches based upon all the information previously given for each voice. The final page of the record booklet in Experiment V, for example, read as follows:

Voice. A teacher of physics who is very interested in acquiring knowledge and in business, but who has little religious interest. He is extremely submissive but neither extroverted nor introverted. He is forty-one years old and six feet tall.

Voice. A supervisor of community centers who has social interest and likes power. He has very little artistic interest; is somewhat extroverted and slightly submissive. He is fifty-one years old and five feet eight inches tall.

Voice. An electrical engineer who is interested in business and learning but is not religious. He is slightly introverted and slightly submissive. Thirty-one years old and five feet ten inches tall.

In Experiments VII and VIII (from Station WEEI) this procedure had to be modified somewhat. The announcer first instructed the auditors how to make out their own reply cards, and then before each portion of the experiment gave the necessary information concerning the three speakers. The procedure was not complicated, and the replies which were sent in showed virtually no confusion.

Results

Table 1 presents the results obtained in these eight experiments. All figures indicate the reliability of the percentage of the correct judgements. This reliability was determined by subtracting the theoretical percentage for chance matching (33 per cent) from the percentage of correct responses obtained from the judges. This difference was then divided by the probable error of the percentage

(determined by the Yule formula, $P.E. = 0.6745 \sqrt{\dfrac{pq}{n}}$) (Yule, 1927, p. 337).

All quotients (here represented by the symbol Q) which are four or over may be considered statistically 'significant'. All such quotients are bold faced, and are positive unless otherwise indicated.

It can be seen from this table that twenty-five (44 per cent) of the coefficients are significantly positive; four (7 per cent) are significantly negative. Before drawing any conclusions, however, the results of matching each feature with voice should be inspected separately.

Table 1 Results of matching voice with various features of personality

Feature judged	Experiment number							
	(Laboratory)						(WEEI)	
	I	II	III	IV	V	VI	VII	VIII
Physical and expressive features								
1. Age					9·9		+	
2. Height			−3·3		4·3	−0·6	1·7	
3. Complexion			3·6	8·8	6·9		4·6	
4. Appearance in photographs	2·8	1·2						
5. Appearance in person			−2·8	1·0	6·0	2·8		
6. Handwriting	1·9		0·9	2·1	0·7	−2·2		
Interests and traits								
7. Vocation	−2·8		−5·9	6·4	−1·3	0·4	24·5	8·2
8. Political preferences	7·4		1·2	3·3				4
9. Extroversion–introversion	14	15	−5·4	−3·1	−3·8	−0·8		19·2
10. Ascendance–submission	13·5	14·5	17	8·8	−4·8		−8·7	

Feature judged	Experiment number (Laboratory)						(WEEI)	
	I	II	III	IV	V	VI	VII	VIII
11. Dominant values	7·4	6	−3·3	0·2	8·0	0·3		95
12. Summary sketch	14·7	13·5	−2	5·7	8·8	0·9	190	
Number of judges	55	85	34	46	50	32		
Voice number 1	A	A	D	G	K	N	Q	J
Voice number 2	B	B	E	H	L	O	R	H
Voice number 3	C	C	F	J	M	P	S	M

Age. The two experiments in which age was judged yielded positive results. In V the voices were matched to the ages given, while in VII the ages of the three speakers were merely estimated by the judges. The averages of the estimates in VII for the speakers were twenty-five, thirty-seven and forty-one and the actual ages were twenty-seven, thirty-six and fifty-one, respectively. There was thus a tendency to center the ages around a median of thirty-five to forty, corroborating Pear's discovery of a central tendency in judgements of age from voice.

Height. Herzog (1933) reported positive results in a study of the determination of height from voice.[2] Only one of our four experiments on height seems to support her finding. The comparatively large percentage of correct answers (45 per cent) for this item in V was due primarily to the case of a short, fat man whose voice was thick, mellow, and 'chuckling'. By 60 per cent of the listeners (instead of the 33 per cent expected by chance) this voice was judged to belong to the shortest speaker.

Complexion. The only experiment which included this feature yielded somewhat significant results. Little confidence can be placed in this finding, however, until it is confirmed.

Appearance in photographs. In all cases the results here are positive, and in two cases they are significantly so. The significant results in IV and V seem to be due chiefly to the distinctive appearance of one or two of the speakers in each experiment. For example, in IV, the photograph of speaker H, whose voice was correctly taken to be that of a poet, showed him with side-burns and a drawn, pointed face.

Appearance in person. It seems illogical that the results here are not quite so positive as those obtained from the use of photographs. This deficiency may be due to the time which necessarily elapsed between hearing the voice and making the judgement, with the result that there was a fading-out or confusion in the image of the voice before the matching could be made.

Handwriting. This matching has special significance for the problem of the consistency or harmony of an individual's expressive movements (Allport and Vernon, 1933). If the voice and the handwriting are both expressions of personality, should they not be matched with each other? Wolff (1930) found that voices recorded by means of a gramophone were

2. Herzog's study also includes results in judgements of sex, age, vocation and weight of voice. In general, they show that all these characteristics are judged more accurately than one would expect by chance.

correctly matched with handwriting about one and a half times as frequently as would be expected by chance. Although this matching was tried in five laboratory experiments, none of the results is significant. Four of the quotients are positive, however, and only one negative. The failure to obtain higher results may be due chiefly to the fact that untrained judges were employed, skilled neither in the judgement of voices nor of handwriting.

Vocation. Three of the experiments yielded significantly positive quotients, while one was significantly negative. The largest coefficient of successful matching obtained in the entire series of experiments came from the judgements of vocation made by 190 listeners in Experiment VII. In this experiment one speaker was an artist, one a business man and one a professor. The coefficient of correct matching was + 24·5. The negative results in III are also significant. Here one speaker was a professor of English, one a psychologist and one a journalist. The psychologist, however, was a native of South Africa and had an apparently 'English accent', and was therefore consistently judged to be a professor of English! It is evident that the auditors have decided opinions concerning the kinds of voices which are typical of the various professions. Such preconceptions are frequently, though by no means invariably, correct.

Political preferences. Like the matching with photographs, the determination of political preference from voice seems to be rather surprisingly successful. In the cases where 'significant' results were obtained, however, there were present in each group of speakers at least one or two distinctive voices which made matching easy. The 'poetic' voice of H, for example, was usually taken as belonging to a *socialist*.

Extroversion–introversion. In three experiments this matching was accomplished with signal success. The strikingly significant results were clearly due to the loud, boisterous, care-free voices which in these three experiments happened to fit the extroverts, and the gentle, restrained voices which happened to fit the introverts. In the other experiments, where slightly negative results were obtained, these vocal characteristics were either absent or else were actually deceptive. This extremely irregular result, very unlike chance, is quite typical of all our findings, and will be interpreted later.

Ascendance–submission. Every result for these traits is significant, four markedly positive and two moderately negative. Here, as in extroversion–introversion, the distribution of results does not in the least resemble chance. The voice gives very decided indications of traits, often correctly, but sometimes incorrectly. The degrees of ascendance–submission of the speakers in the first four experiments correctly fit into the picture of the forceful, aggressive voice as opposed to the passive, meek voice; while in Experiment VII the great majority of the incorrect answers were due to the fact that the submissive professor had cultivated (for classroom purposes) a typically ascendant manner of speaking.

Dominant values. In half the experiments the results were clearly positive and significant. In Experiment I two of the speakers were high in both aesthetic and religious interests (as measured by the *Study of Values*), and were often confused with each other. The positive result of this experiment is due therefore to the fact that these two speakers were scarcely ever mistaken for the third, whose voice clearly betrayed his political and economic interests.

Summary sketches. The single features just enumerated were summarized for the judges into one final thumb-nail sketch of each speaker. The purpose of this final matching was to determine whether or not the voice reveals a *complex pattern* of personality better than a single feature. The results are positive. *A pattern of qualities seems, on the average, rather more correctly matched with voice than does any single quality.*

Matching free descriptions of personality with voice

In Experiments IV, V, VII and VIII, the judges submitted free descriptions of the speakers to supplement their matchings. Many of these descriptions seemed even more accurate than the controlled judgements. The descriptions of six of the speakers were collated and arranged in the form of six brief sketches and employed in Experiment IX. All uncomplimentary and ambiguous items were deleted. Although such editing was to a certain extent arbitrary, each sketch was made to conform as faithfully as possible to the descriptions submitted. Qualities often mentioned were emphasized, and conflicting characterizations were proportionately included. Following is one of the final sketches employed.

Mr A. is characterized by his ascendant, aggressive behavior. He has drive and initiative, knows what he wants and gets it. He has decided opinions and likes to express them. He is extroverted, easily resists salesmen, and cares little what others think about him. He is wealthy and aristocratic, and has an appreciation of good literature.

Experiment IX was divided into two parts. In Part I three of the speakers participated. The radio audience was instructed by the station announcer that three speakers (voice A, voice B and voice C) would read three descriptions (descriptions 1, 2 and 3) intended to describe the speakers and that the radio audience should decide which description best characterized each speaker. The three speakers then read description 1, each speaker ending the passage with the question, 'Does this describe me?' Then description 2 was read by each speaker, and, finally, description 3. Part II was identical with Part I except that three other speakers and their corresponding descriptions were employed.

The numbers of answers (twenty-five) returned by the listeners was unfortunately small (*Amos 'n Andy* proving to be too great a competitor for science). The results, however, so far as they go, are significantly above chance in both parts of the experiment.

	Q
Part I	4·4
Part II	9

This experiment provides a kind of check upon the reliability of the impressions created by the six voices. Unlike Experiments I–VIII the judgements are not validated against objective criteria, but are compared with the judgements of other listeners who knew the speakers only by their voices. Whether the impressions are correct or incorrect, it is clear that they are essentially the same for *different* groups of listeners.

In a minor experiment (X) the free descriptions of the speakers sent in by the judges in Experiment VII were listed. The three lists of brief characterizations ('moody', 'nervous', 'precise', 'dapper', etc.) were then mimeographed on separate sheets. Copies were distributed to friends and acquaintances and they were asked to decide which list best described the speaker or speakers whom they knew. Fifty-six judgements were received and 91 per cent of these were correct.

The radio voice versus the normal voice

In order to determine whether the mechanical transmission of voice reduces the ability of the judges to make correct matchings, several control presentations were introduced in some of the laboratory experiments. In these presentations, the speakers read behind a curtain in the same room where the subjects were seated. The same features which were matched with the radio voice were likewise judged in this situation.

The comparative analysis of the results in Table 2, based on data obtained in four experiments, shows that there is an average difference of about 7 per cent in favor of the normal voice. To control the effect of practice the normal voice in some experiments was introduced before, and in others after, the voice had been heard over the radio. The order of presentation makes no appreciable difference.

Table 2 Comparative results of matching radio voice and natural voice with various features of personality

Feature judged	Radio voice % correct	Q	Normal voice % correct	Q
Experiment 1*				
Photograph	41	2·8	59	9·1
Handwriting	38	1·9	44	3·6
Vocation	27	−2·8	44	3·6
Political preference	53	7·4	51	6
Extroversion–introversion	67	14	70	13·6
Ascendance–submission	62	13·5	63	10·6
Dominant values	53	7·4	76	17
Summary sketch	70	14·7	64	10·9
average	51		59	
Experiment II				
Extroversion–introversion	63	15	37	1·7
Ascendance–submission	62	14·5	75	23
Dominant values	46	6	64	15·5
average	57		50	
Experiment V				
Height	46	4·3	50	5·9
Appearance	50	5·9	78	16·5
Ascendance–submission†	42	−4·8	63	2·9
Experiment VI				
Appearance	48	2·7	27	−1·2
Average (Exps. V, VI)	46		55	
Average in all exps.	51		58	

*In Experiment I, fifty-four judges participated in the radio presentation and forty-five judged the normal voice.

†Since two of the speakers obtained the same rating, the chance percentage for this feature is 5/9 rather than 1/3.

This finding has considerable theoretical and practical interest. From the theoretical point of view, it may be said that the listeners are quite successful in 'hearing through' the inevitable burr which accompanies a mechanical transmission of the human voice. Adaptation to the change in the quality which a voice undergoes in such transmission seems to be remarkably rapid and thoroughgoing. Even the subtlest inflections may be successfully analysed out from all extraneous sounds. The voice, as it were, becomes a distinct and well-identified figure upon the ground of subdued mechanical noise. (A very few people, however, seem incapable of negative adaptation to the ground, and persistently complain of the distortion of the voices or musical instruments which they hear. Such people usually dislike the radio for aesthetic reasons.)

Even though the broadcaster can be assured that most people readily adapt to the figure-ground situation which the radio creates, our experiments do show a slight loss in the accuracy of matching. On the average, the natural voice is somewhat more revealing of personal qualities than is the radio voice. The loss represents perhaps only such imperfections in transmission which mechanical improvements in the radio may in time remove. It should be reported here that the apparatus employed in these experiments lacked the dynamic or condenser microphone found in the newest broadcasting equipment. Except for its two-button carbon microphone the equipment used was modern in every respect.

Conclusions and interpretations

This analysis of the results now enables us to answer the two fundamental questions with which the investigation is concerned.

1. *Does voice convey any correct information concerning outer and inner characteristics of personality?* The answer is *Yes*. Not only are the majority of our coefficients positive (74 per cent), but 47 per cent are 'significantly' so, often by very large margins. If the judgements of the various features of personality were due entirely to chance we would, of course, expect an approximately equal number of positive and negative Q's and a very much smaller percentage of 'significant' results.

2. *Is there uniformity in the expression of personality through voice*, so that it might be said that certain personality qualities are consistently revealed and others not at all; or that certain types of individuals are always revealed by their voices, and others never? The answer is *No*. Results which are exclusively positive and significant were obtained for no single feature excepting age and complexion (and repeated experiments would be necessary to establish their reliabilities). Nor were the results for all of the personal characteristics of any one of our eighteen speakers always posi-

tive and significant. Therefore, the only certain generalization that can be made is that by and large *many features of many personalities can be determined from voice.*

This general conclusion requires supplementation and interpretation through the following additional findings.

3. The fact that 53 per cent of our coefficients are 'significant' (either positive or negative) and the fact that only 14 per cent fall within the range of $\pm$ 1 P.E. indicate that the judgements, even when they are erroneous, do not represent mere guesses. A voice seems to arouse a more or less uniform impression on a group of listeners even when the impression is incorrect. *The uniformity of opinion regarding the personality of radio speakers is somewhat in excess of the accuracy of such opinion.*

4. This discovery is evidence that stereotypes play an important part in making the judgements. In everyday life we frequently hear people say, 'He talks like a poet', 'He sounds like a politician', 'You can tell from his voice that he is timid'. Likewise, in the laboratory situation it appears that *for the various features of personality there is associated in the minds of the judges some preconception of the type of voice to which these features correspond.*

5. These preconceptions regarding the type of voice which 'should' accompany various features of personality are not equally definite for each feature. The results show that *the more highly organized and deep-seated traits and dispositions are judged more* CONSISTENTLY *than the more specific features of physique and appearance.* In the group of characteristics which includes physical features and handwriting only 33 per cent of the matchings were 'significant' (either correct or incorrect), while among the features classified as 'interests and traits' almost twice as many (64 per cent) were 'significant'.

6. *Not only are the more highly organized traits and dispositions judged more consistently than such outer characteristics as physique and appearance, but they are also judged more* CORRECTLY. One-third of the judgements on 'physical and expressive' features were significantly positive, whereas one-half of the judgements on 'traits and interests' were positive and significant. This finding should be taken as supporting a dynamic and personalistic theory of expression (Allport and Vernon, 1933, ch.7). It is clear that vocal expression is not specific and independent; it is associated to some extent with other physical and expressive features, but especially with the highly organized qualities of the 'inner' personality.

7. *If a voice arouses a stereotype of the speaker, it is likely that several features of personality will be subsumed under that stereotype.* Thus in Experiment

VII, speaker Q was correctly judged to be the artist by 71 per cent of the listeners (only 3 per cent said he was the business man). But the stereotype of an artist's voice was not confined to vocation alone. Fifty-six per cent of the listeners said that he was markedly submissive, 73 per cent thought he had a light complexion, and 44 per cent said he was tall. All of these judgements were significantly above chance and all of them wrong. Likewise in the same experiment, speaker R was correctly judged by 72 per cent of the listeners to be the business man. And 65 per cent believed (correctly in this case) that the business man had a dark complexion.

There is therefore a kind of totalizing effect which is prejudicial to accurate and detailed judgement. It is an aspect of the common tendency toward undue economy and simplicity encountered in much recent work upon judgement and attitudes. In the field of personality especially it seems that impressions are often oversimplified almost to the point of caricature.

8. The matching of voice with *summary sketches* was rather more successful than the matching with any single feature. *The more information given concerning the speaker, the more accurately is his voice identified.* Whereas the totalized stereotype is often prejudicial to correct estimates, the totalized portrait is helpful. This finding constitutes an argument against 'segmental' and 'atomistic' research upon arbitrarily isolated variables in personality. Studies which deal with the interplay and patterning of qualities are closer to the realities of organized vital processes, and for that reason yield more postive results.

9. *The success of judgement is inevitably influenced by the heterogeneity of the voices and personalities of the speakers.* It is quite clear that if any of our groups of three speakers contained a captain of industry, a prima donna and the village idiot, there would be almost no errors in matching. Too great a homogeneity among voices or personalities is equally prejudicial to representative results. The inconclusive findings in Experiment VI are to be explained by the lack of distinctive quality in the three voices. The striking results of certain other experiments (e.g. VII and VIII) are due to the use of contrasting types. Our eighteen speakers were of the same sex, and differed less than a random sampling of population in respect to age, educational status and racial background. On the other hand, the use of the matching method required that the personalities be at least distinguishable by the objective tests and measurements which were employed as the criteria. All in all, it is probably true that our groups were neither unusually heterogeneous nor homogeneous, but represented reasonable variations in type.

10. It must be remembered that the criteria chosen for these experiments are all 'objective', and are perfect neither in their reliability nor in their

validity (excepting only records of physical characteristics). Those who are familiar with the complexities of the task of measuring personality will find it rather remarkable that the human voice can be so accurately matched with results obtained from the available tests for ascendance–submission, extroversion–introversion and personal values. Such a degree of success with these objective criteria constitutes a peculiar kind of validation for the tests themselves and an encouragement to their further development. At the same time, since the criteria are imperfect, it must be borne in mind that the human voice may reveal even more concerning personality than our results indicate. *In our desire to keep the investigation objective and quantitative, we may have minimized the degree to which the voice expresses personal qualities.*

11. When some of the experiments were repeated, using a curtain rather than the radio to conceal the speaker, the average results were approximately 7 per cent higher. This finding seems to indicate that *there is a slight distortion of the voice due to the background of mechanical noise.* Further improvements in broadcasting may reduce or eliminate this distortion.

12. Strong supporting evidence for certain of our conclusions was obtained in two minor experiments (IX and X) which demonstrated that *free descriptions of personality from voice were successfully recognized by other listeners and by acquaintances of the speakers.*

Summary

Ten experiments were conducted in the Harvard Psychological Laboratory, where a complete broadcasting and receiving equipment had been installed, and from the studio of Station WEEI in Boston. Eighteen male speakers and over six hundred judges took part. The method consisted chiefly in matching objective information obtained for twelve features of personality (e.g. age, photographs, handwriting, dominance, extroversion) with the corresponding voices. In comparing these matchings with chance it was found that the majority were successful, often by large margins, but that no single feature was always matched correctly, nor was any individual speaker correctly judged in every respect. It was also found that the uniformity of opinion regarding the personalities of the speakers was somewhat in excess of the accuracy of such opinion, showing the importance of stereotypes. In general, better results were obtained from the use of summary sketches than from single features, and judgements were more often correct for the organized traits and interests of personality than for mere physical features. There is a discussion of the relation of successful matching to the heterogeneity of the voices and personalities participating in the experiments; likewise of the use of strictly objective criteria. When the speakers read from behind a curtain instead of over the radio it was found that on the average approximately 7 per cent higher results were obtained. Additional experiments showed that free descriptions of personality sent in by judges were in general successfully recognized by other listeners and by acquaintances of the speakers.

References

ALLPORT, G. W. (1933), 'The study of personality by the experimental method' *Character Person.*, vol. 1, pp. 259–64.

ALLPORT, G. W., and VERNON, P. E. (1933), *Studies in Expressive Movement*, Macmillan.

HERZOG, H. (1933), 'Stimme und Persönlichkeit', *Z. Psychol.*, vol. 130, pp. 300–379.

MICHAEL, W., and CRAWFORD, C. C. (1927), 'An experiment in judging intelligence by the voice', *J. educ. Psychol.*, vol. 18, pp. 107–14.

PEAR, T. H. (1931), *Voice and Personality*, Chapman & Hall.

SAPIR, E. (1927), 'Speech as a personality trait', *Amer. J. Sociol.*, vol. 32, pp. 892–905. [Reprinted in this book, pp. 71–81.]

WOLFF, W. (1930), 'Ueber Faktoren charakterologischen Urteilsbildung', *Z. Psychol.*, vol. 35, pp. 385–446.

YULE, G. U. (1927), *An Introduction to the Theory of Statistics* (8th edn), Griffin.

9 E. Kramer

Judgement of Personal Characteristics and Emotions from
Non-Verbal Properties of Speech

E. Kramer, 'Judgement of personal characteristics and emotions from non-verbal properties of speech', *Psychological Bulletin*, vol. 60, 1963, pp. 408–20.

A person's changing emotional state and relatively stable personal characteristics may be judged from non-verbal properties of his voice. These properties include such elements as timbre, inflection and stress, which accompany the actual words spoken but are not a direct part of them. Many studies have used inadequate measures as the independent criterion for the traits being judged, and no method of eliminating the verbal content has been wholly successful. The evidence does show, however, that some validity of judgement is possible. Acoustic analysis has been little used; it could increase the objectivity of studies. Individual differences among listeners and the relationship of voice to psychopathology have been particularly neglected areas in research.

In a fantasy novel by the poet Robert Graves, a man of the distant future asks a twentieth-century Englishman, 'Do I speak with correctitude?' 'With great correctitude,' he is assured, 'but without the modulations of tone we English use to express, or disguise, our feelings' (Graves, 1949, p. 1). All of us not only use such modulations ourselves, but also make judgements about others' current feelings and attitudes, as well as about more stable personal characteristics, partly on the basis of how they 'sound' to us. Sullivan has stated (1954, p. 7) that these 'sound accompaniments suggest what is to be made of the verbal propositions stated'. Whether or not we can interpret them correctly, whether or not speaker and listener would agree to their significance, these 'non-verbal but nonetheless primarily vocal aspects of the exchange' (Sullivan, 1954, p. 5) play an important part in the perception of persons.

The first major experiment on impressions of persons based on voice alone (Pear, 1931) analysed over 4000 reports from British radio listeners who had responded to questions about nine different readers they had heard on the air. Age and sex proved easiest to estimate correctly. An actor and a clergyman were most consistently identified correctly from among the nine professsions represented. The highest leadership ratings were given to the speakers whose voices were professionally important to them:

an actor, a judge and a clergyman. Birthplace of the speakers was not guessed with significant accuracy. Certain errors in guessing a speaker's profession showed significant consistency, suggesting that some voices provide a stereotype of a certain occupation even though this is not the actual occupation of this speaker. Such 'vocal stereotypes' have remained the most frequent finding in all studies of the relationship between voice and personality (Kramer, 1963).

The studies which followed are divided here into two major categories: those which called for judgements from voice of relatively stable characteristics of an individual, and those which asked for judgements of emotional or affective variables which change over relatively short periods of time. Both kinds of judgements involve problems of separating nonverbal aspects of the voice from the actual words spoken, and problems of adequate independent criteria for the traits being judged. Physical characteristics of an individual may usually be easily measured; but aptitudes, interests and personality traits present special problems. Such pencil-and-paper inventories as those by Bernreuter (1931) and Bell (1934), frequently used in such studies, have many limitations of their own (McKelvey, 1953; Tyler, 1953). If valid judgements are made from voice, a low correlation between such judgements and inventory scores might still be a frequent finding (Kramer, 1963). The problem of separating verbal and non-verbal aspects of speech is dealt with in the section below on voice and changing emotional states.

Voice and stable characteristics of an individual
Physical characteristics

A speaker's age can apparently be judged with better than chance accuracy from his voice (Allport and Cantril, 1934; Herzog, 1933; Pear, 1931), but two of the studies (Allport and Cantril, 1934; Pear, 1931) found a tendency for estimates of age to center in the thirties. On judgements of height, both positive (Herzog, 1933) and negative results (Allport and Cantril, 1934; Cantril and Allport, 1935) have been reported. Voice and the overall appearance of a speaker, both in person and in photographs, have been matched with statistically significant accuracy (Allport and Cantril, 1934). An attempt to match voices with photographs of the Kretschmerian body types (Kretschmer, 1925) found the pyknic type matched most accurately, then leptosomatic, and finally athletic (Bonaventura, 1935). Another study (Fay and Middleton, 1940c) asked judges to match speakers' voices with paragraphs describing the three body types. The athletic type was matched no better than chance, while low positive correlations were found for the others. No actual morphological measurements of the speakers was made, but each was assigned a Kretschmerian type merely on the basis of superficial appearance. Since such measurements were considered a necessary step in classification by Kretschmer (1925), the speakers may not have represented good examples of the classification given them.

Certain types of brain damage alter aspects of an individual's intonation pattern, which Monrad-Krohn (1947, 1957) has referred to as 'prosody'. He reported that these intonation changes give the listener the impression of a person speaking with a foreign accent. The importance of the pitch contour of speech – changing patterns in the fundamental frequency – in conveying impressions of accent and language was demonstrated by Cohen and Starkweather (1961). They found that English speaking listeners could judge whether or not they were hearing a recording made from English speech, even after the recording had been passed through a low-pass filter which removed all those higher frequencies required for recognition of words (French and Steinberg, 1947).

Aptitudes and interests

The one reported study on voice and intelligence (Fay and Middleton, 1940b) found a correlation of 0·33 between estimates of intelligence from voice and speakers' IQs on the Terman Group Test of Mental Ability (Terman, 1920). A voice in the 'average intelligence' group which was consistently judged to be that of a person of very low intelligence led the authors to conclude, 'Possibly all the ratings indicate voice stereotypes. The fact that some of them agree with test results of intelligence may be purely coincidental' (p. 190). In another study, Fay and Middleton (1943) had fifteen freshman fraternity men rated for leadership by ten fraternity seniors who had known them for six weeks. These ratings showed no correlation with ratings of leadership based solely on the freshmen's voices, although the interjudge reliability of the voice judgements was 0·41. The authors feel that this degree of social agreement, in the face of no accuracy compared to the criterion, suggests the presence of vocal stereotypes of leadership. The presence of stereotyped voices is given by Allport and Cantril (1934) to explain the unexpected success their listeners had in judging speakers' political preferences.

Judgements of speakers' dominant values were compared with the speakers' scores on the Allport–Vernon Study of Values (Allport and Vernon, 1931) in two studies (Allport and Cantril, 1934; Fay and Middleton, 1939b). The earlier found mixed results, while Fay and Middleton found that the types 'judged most accurately in terms of mean percentage superior to chance are: political, 46 per cent; esthetic, 29 per cent; social, 23 per cent' (p. 154). In another of their series of studies, Fay and Middleton (1939b) asked listeners to identify the vocations of speakers representing several vocations. Only the voice of a preacher was correctly identified consistently better than chance, and it was frequently mistaken for that of a lawyer. Earlier studies on voice and vocation reported more positive results (Allport and Cantril, 1934; Pear, 1931).

Personality

This section is divided into judgements from voice of personality traits, of personality in more global terms, and of personality adjustment and psychopathology. All three areas have suffered from a lack of adequate independent criteria for the success of vocal judgements. Attempts to specify what elements of voice are responsible for the judgements have often only served to illustrate the lack, noted by Sapir (1927), of an adequate vocabulary for describing voice.

Personality traits. Judgements of dominance were found to be significantly correlated with scores on the Allport A–S Reaction Study (Allport and Allport, 1928) by Allport and Cantril (1934), while Eisenberg and Zalowitz (1938) found no significant correlation between such judgements and their criterion measure, the Maslow Social Personality Inventory (Maslow, 1937). Fay and Middleton found that listeners had no success in estimating either introversion–extraversion (Fay and Middleton, 1942) or sociability (Fay and Middleton, 1941) from speakers' voices, with the speakers' scores on the Bernreuter Inventory (Bernreuter, 1931) as the criteria. In both cases, however, they found significant interjudge agreement, which they interpret as providing evidence for the presence of vocal stereotypes. It should be remembered that more recent consideration of the Bernreuter test – which is among the better validated of the criteria used in voice judgement studies – has shown that artifactual correlations within it seem to permit clear measurement of considerably fewer factors than the number of labeled scales, and adjusted and maladjusted subjects show much overlap on their test scores (Tyler, 1953).

Attempts to match both test scores and judgements on certain traits with the particular voice qualities involved have been made by Moore (1939) and Mallory and Miller (1958). Moore (1939) found that subjects with a 'breathy' tone of voice tended to be lower in dominance and higher in introversion. Mallory and Miller (1958) report that Bernreuter scores on introversion were negatively related to loudness, low pitch, and resonance in the voice. A 'slight positive association' is reported between dominance scores and the voice qualities of loudness, resonance and lower pitch.

Neither study provides the exact acoustical data which would be required to objectify the voice quality terms (cf. Ostwald, 1960b) and permit cross-validation of the relationships. The same problem exists with Stagner's (1936) finding that flow, poise and clearness in speech correlate positively with aggression and negatively with nervousness. At least part of the correlations may be spurious due to the fact that the same group of listeners made the judgements on both voice quality and the speakers' personality characteristics.

Personality as a whole. One of the earliest studies on judgements from voice (Allport and Cantril, 1934) found that, on the average, summary personality sketches of the speakers could be more accurately matched with their voices than could any single quality or trait. Taylor (1934) reported in the same year, however, no relationship between the speakers' scores on a questionnaire based chiefly on items from Thurstone's Personality Schedule (Thurstone and Thurstone, 1929) and the scores predicted for them by listener-judges. He did find significant interjudge agreement. Wolff (1943) reported both high agreement among listeners on matching voices with summary descriptions of personality, and significant agreement between these matchings and ratings by the speakers' friends. In an interesting variation, Wolff included the raters' own voices among those to be judged. Only 10·5 per cent recognized their own voices. The 'unconscious self-judgements' of the others agreed in general with the ratings given by other listeners, but they tended to judge each characteristic as more extreme or more obviously present than did others' ratings.

An attempt to define one aspect of how voices differ was made by Starkweather (1955b, 1956b), who compared speakers with high and low scores on a personality test (Harris, 1953) which distinguishes hypertensives from normals. His prediction that the hypertensive syndrome group would show greater incongruence between the verbal and non-verbal (roughly equivalent to tone of voice) aspects of their speech was not confirmed. His technique of removing those frequencies of the speech spectrum upon which word recognition depends (Fletcher, 1953; French and Steinberg, 1947; Licklider and Miller, 1951) is discussed below in the section on voice and changing emotional states, under 'low-pass filtering'. The role of expert judgement on determining personality from voice was investigated by Jones (1942). He gave the Rorschach protocol from an adolescent boy to a well-known Rorschach analyst, Piotrowski, and gave a recording of the boy's voice to Moses, a laryngologist who has had a strong interest in the interrelationships of voice and personality (Moses, 1941, 1942, 1954). The two independent analyses were considered to match well with each other. Moses (1942) has described from a clinical point of view the twenty-one voice variables he considered in making his analysis.

Personality adjustment and psychopathology. Although practising clinicians have been well aware of the importance of the non-verbal aspects of voice for problems of diagnosis and therapy (Shakow, 1959; Soskin, 1953; Sullivan, 1954), few experimental studies have been done. In the milder range of adjustment problems, Duncan (1945) had speakers rated for voice quality by fellow speech students after three weeks in class. Of the thirty descriptive terms used in the ratings, eleven could be used to identify whether the speaker had been low or high in his social adjustment score on the Bell Inventory (Bell, 1934). No cross-validation of the discriminating terms was reported. Monotonism seems likely to affect speech patterns; Ramm (1946) found that twenty-five fifth graders with monotonism showed inadequate social and emotional adjustment on a number of personality tests, especially the Rorschach. The lack of a control group in her study makes the criterion value of the Rorschach scores particularly tentative, since there is no adequate normative data on children's Rorschach performances as an indicator of general personality adjustment.

A study on schizophrenic children (Goldfarb, Braunstein and Lorge, 1956) reported that these youngsters, compared with a normal group, were ineffective in conveying mood or emotion vocally, giving the effect of either no emotion at all or one which was inappropriate to the verbal content. Cohen (1961) found that naïve judges could not separate schizophrenics from normals on the basis of voice quality and speech pattern. Experienced judges were used by Moskowitz (1952), but her report on the diagnostic significance in schizophrenia of 'monotonous, weak, gloomy and unsustained' voices seems chiefly a reminder of the difficulty in finding an adequate language for describing voice. A possible way out of that difficulty is suggested in the work of Ostwald (1960a, 1960b). He has done speech spectrum analyses of the voices of many patients and compared these spectrogram records with common terms for describing voices. Such comparisons should clarify which terms have some reliable meaning. He has also made some tentative suggestions (Ostwald, 1960a) about the relationships between certain types of psychiatric disorders and the spectrum analyses of the patients' speech.

The role of the expert judge is best illustrated in the work of Moses (1941, 1942, 1954) and Jones (1942). His *Voice of Neurosis* (Moses, 1954) presents most fully the foundations and implications of his belief that 'voice is the primary expression of the individual, and even through voice alone the neurotic pattern may be discovered' (p. 1). He stresses the need for using different frames of reference in different social and linguistic groups. Although he has attempted to set down the relevant voice variables and his method of judging them in the most objective manner possible, a large part of his work remains exclusively the analysis of the single expert. Some of his voice variables do seem quantifiable in terms which could be investigated in the laboratory; for example, 'range' as the range of the fundamental frequencies used, and 'rhythm' as a stress pattern of the changes in amplitude over time. Other categories, however, would need much redefining before they could be submitted to close experimental, laboratory investigation. Despite this, Moses's clinical acumen and experience are important in an area marked by the inadequacy of experimental studies.

Voice and changing emotional states

Soskin (1953) has described vocal communication in terms of two channels, each specializing in a different type of information. 'Semantic information' is carried in the channel consisting of the articulated patterns of sounds which we recognize as words and sentences. 'Affective information' is carried in the channel bearing the changing, non-verbal features of the voice.

The studies presented here on how successfully and under what conditions emotion is conveyed by the non-verbal parts of the voice are grouped below according to the method used for removing the influence of the particular words spoken – the 'semantic' channel – on the judgements of emotion. A grouping analogous to the previous section, where studies would be classified according to the emotions investigated, would make the unwarranted assumption that a label such as 'grief' or 'joy' meant the same thing to all experimenters who used it. In fact, no test of the purity of the emotional categories seems to have been done by any experimenter. In the range of studies, each covering many and variously labeled emotions, one man's joy may come close to being another man's poison.

Meaningless content

The chief forms of 'meaningless content' have been numerals and letters of the alphabet; however, the earliest reported study of this type (Skinner, 1935) requested subjects to say merely *Ah*. They were requested first to read a passage of emotional literature and listen to selected music that was designed to put them into a sad or happy emotional state. They then spoke, and the *ah*'s of happiness showed higher pitch and greater force than those of sadness. Dusenbury and Knower (1939) asked a group of speech students and instructors to 'try to feel the designated emotional state and to use a tonal code that would indicate their feelings' (p. 67) while reciting the letters A through K. Eleven emotions were designated, and eight sets of recitations were selected out of an initial twenty-two on the basis of pretests. All of these eight sets were matched with the emotion which the speaker had tried to represent with significantly greater than chance accuracy. In a later study (Knower, 1941) the speakers whispered the letters in an attempt to eliminate the effects of 'tone', since the fundamental frequency of the voice is not present in a whisper. Recognition of the intended emotions was still better than chance. These studies unfortunately cannot confirm whether these speakers, or any others, would use these same 'tonal codes' when experiencing the emotions in real life situations.

Similar material has been used for teaching psychotherapy (Thompson and Bradway, 1950). Two psychologists acted out a 'therapeutic interview' in which they actually spoke only numbers, although with the inflections which a genuine exchange between patient and therapist might have. The two participants each listened separately to recordings of the interview and made statements about the 'affective interchange'. The two sets of statements were found to be significantly correlated with each other. Numerals also formed the only verbal content in a study by Pfaff (1954) in which an 'experienced speaker' used numbers to express a variety of emotions. Out of various groups of listeners, junior high school students of low socio-economic status did least well at identifying the emotions being portrayed, which college oral interpretation students did best. A partial explanation of the results may be that the 'experienced speaker' drew from the same stock of stereotypes and stage techniques with which the oral interpretation students were most familiar. The low ranking of the junior high school students of low socio-economic status suggests the hypothesis that the 'tonal affect language' may be different, at least to some extent, for different classes in a society. Inexperienced readers from a Navy ROTC group were used by Black and Dreher (1955). They read a list of five-syllable phrases in a manner aimed at simulating certainty or uncertainty. Listeners, presumably of the same background as the speakers, were able to distinguish between the two types of reading with high reliability.

Recitations of the alphabet with varying expressions were used by Davitz and Davitz (1959a, 1959b) in work which focused on errors and relative ease in guessing various emotions. In their first study (1959a) all feelings were identified more consistently than chance alone would predict, but certain errors in identification showed significant consistency. When fear was mistakenly identified, it was most commonly taken for nervousness; love was most commonly misidentified as sadness, and pride for satisfaction. In their second study (Davitz and Davitz, 1959b), they selected from pretests two speakers who were particularly successful at communicating feelings through reciting the alphabet. These speakers each used the alphabet to express fifty different feelings. Thirty judges tried to match each recitation with the correct feeling. Ten judges rated each feeling from the list of fifty, checking each feeling on the list which was similar to it. A similarity score was based on the number of times a feeling was noted as being similar to any other feeling. Separate groups of judges rated the feelings on the list in order to derive 'strength', 'activity' and 'valence' scores for them. Findings were: (a) accuracy of identification of feelings was correlated − 0·29 with similarity scores (significant at the 0·025 level); (b) the degree to which one feeling is mistaken for another is related to the subjective similarity of the two; (c) for pairs of similar feelings, the stronger tends to be communicated more accurately; and (d) no significant realationships appeared involving the activity or the valence scores. The authors note, however, that 'since the relationships found were not high, the greater part of the variance in accuracy of communication is unaccounted for' (p. 116).

The longest units of 'meaningless content' were the eight neutral sentences used by Pollack, Rubenstein and Horowitz (1960a, 1960b); e.g. *The lamp stood on the table*. The sentences were read in various modes under increasing signal–noise ratios. The authors found that recognition of the emotional modes intended held up better under noise than did recognition of the particular sentences. Mode recognition was also possible with significant accuracy even when the fundamental frequency was eliminated by having the sentences whispered. Effects of temporal sampling were also explored; some recognition of the modes was still possible with extremely short samples and with sections of the recorded samples removed at periodic intervals.

Constant content

Another technique for eliminating the effects of the words spoken has been to use the same set of words for all the emotions represented – words which are ambiguous as to emotional content, rather than meaningless in the sense that numerals or separate letters are. Like the use of meaningless content, this method required the use of actors – experienced or inexperienced – and thus may capitalize on the presence of stereotyped representations of emotions which might not occur naturally. Fairbanks (1940; Fairbanks and Hoaglin, 1941; Fairbanks and Pronovost, 1939) had experienced student actors read five passages, each marked by a different emotion. Listeners heard only a set of sentences that was common to all five passages; they were asked to identify the emotion being represented on the basis of these excerpts. Some of the actors seemed to provide much clearer vocal differentiation of emotion than did others. Measurable pitch differences (Fairbanks and Pronovost, 1939) and differences in duration of phrases (Fairbanks and Hoaglin, 1941) were found among the different emotions, using average measures from the various readings. Fairbanks appears to have assumed that his common passage was ambiguous or neutral for the five emotions he studied. The present writer, in an unpublished study, presented the passage in typescript to a group of raters and found it significantly most frequently identified as anger. Expressing such a passage in various emotional styles may have required an exaggeration of pitch and duration characteristics which would not be found in natural emotional speech.

A standard passage was ready by 'tired' and 'rested' speakers in an attempt to see if listeners could distinguish between the two groups (Fay and Middleton, 1940a). The rested speakers had their normal amounts of sleep, while the tired group had gone without sleep for thirty hours. They were all free from speech defects, 'nor, in the opinion of the writers, did any of the speakers possess voices noticeably lacking in vitality' (p. 646). This opinion seems not to have corresponded with the perceptions of the listeners, whose accuracy in deciding whether the speaker was tired or rested proved to be significantly worse than chance. The authors feel that 'the existence of stereotyped tired and rested voices' (p. 649) accounted for the results.

Ignoring content

Brody (1943), attempting to focus his attention away from the patients' words, has called attention to subtle variations in voice during the course of psychoanalysis. He presented several cases in which vocal changes seemed to mark transitions between major emotional stages in therapy. He regards vocal expression as a relatively safe way to act out hostile feelings during analysis. Verbal content may be 'ignored' by measuring specific non-verbal properties of speech. Different aspects of speech rate and breathing rate were measured in a series of studies on non-content aspects of speech during psychotherapy (Goldman-Eisler, 1955, 1956a, 1956b). Rate of respiration and expulsion rate of syllables were correlated with a single psychiatrist's judgement of the emotional content of the patients' communications.

Experimental attention has been given to the role of silences and disturbances in speech as indicators of changing emotional states in psychotherapy (Dibner, 1956; Mahl, 1956, 1959). Mahl (1959) has sometimes referred to these as 'expressive aspects of . . . speech', but they have chiefly been treated as disruptions in the speech process rather than as part of the simultaneous non-verbal accompaniment to spoken words which is the center of focus in the present review. Krause (1961) has shown that Mahl's measures are highly similar to those used by Dibner (1956) as indicators of anxiety. Krause and Pilisuk (1961), using measures from both Mahl and Dibner, found that 'intrusive non-verbal sounds, mainly laughs and sighs' were the best speech indicators of transitory anxiety.

Linguistics has offered some schemes of analysis which consider non-verbal, or non-lexical, aspects of speech (Pittenger and Smith, 1957; Trager, 1958). These aspects, 'vocalization and voice qualities together are being called paralanguage' (Trager, 1958, p. 4). McQuown (1957) used these recently described categories in a detailed analysis of a single interview, where he characterized the effect involved; no independent measure of the affective aspects of the interview is reported. A highly detailed booklength analysis in these terms has been made of the first five minutes of a psychiatric interview (Pittenger, Hockett and Danehy, 1960). In a study by Eldred and Price (1958) four judges listened to tape recordings from various parts of intensive psychotherapy with a single patient and noted which linguistic and which emotional categories seemed to vary together. No cross-validation of the suggested relationships was reported. Some doubt has been cast on the utility of such approaches by a study using a larger number of judges (Dittman and Wynne, 1961). It was found that more traditional linguistic categories, such as juncture, stress and pitch, could be reliably coded but bore no relationship to the emotional state of the speakers. Paralinguistic categories were expected to be more emotionally relevant, but they could not be reliably coded.

Acoustical methods

Filtered speech. The studies noted here have eliminated verbal content by passing recorded speech through a low-pass filter designed to hold back those higher frequencies of speech upon which word recognition depends. It is expected, in such studies, that many of the non-verbal aspects, such as stress patterns and intonation patterns based on fundamental frequency, still remain. Little notice has been taken of the non-verbal information which is lost together with the verbal, although an acoustical study (Ochai and Fukumura, 1957) has shown that the upper as well as the lower overtones of speech contribute to the personal tone or timbre of a person's voice. Controls have also been lacking on the effectiveness of the filtering in eliminating content; the available material on frequency and intelligibility (Fletcher, 1953; French and Steinberg, 1947; Licklider and Miller, 1951) does not deal with intelligibility in connected discourse.

Fifteen speech samples were rated for emotional content by a group which heard them on normal recording, and separately by a group which heard them on recordings from which frequencies above 450 Hertz had been removed (Soskin and Kauffman, 1961). The two sets of ratings showed significant agreement. Kauffman (1954) had a professional actor record two readings of a series of short speeches. In one reading the actor read with an emotional expression which was appropriate to the words of each speech, while in the other reading he used an expression which was highly incongruent with the verbal content. The recordings were passed through a low-pass filter to remove the semantic content. One group of listeners judged the second series of speeches for incongruity by comparing the filtered recordings with typescripts of the speeches. Separate groups rated the typescripts alone, and the full range and filtered recordings. Kauffman classified the 'meanings' of the rating categories into two main divisions: (a) expressive, 'affect meanings relevant to the psychological state of the speaker', and (b) 'manipulative . . . meanings relevant to the purposive behavior of the speaker'. He found that both the vocal and verbal channels, corresponding to the affective and semantic channels of Soskin (1953), carry information about both the expressive and manipulative meanings in speech. There is, however, a tendency for the expressive function to be performed by the vocal channel and the manipulative by the verbal. Incongruence between vocal and verbal channels was reflected in greater heterogeneity of judgements, particularly in the judging of expressive meanings by those who heard only the filtered recordings. Heterogeneity of judgements was assumed to be a measure of ambiguity. There was, then, a consistent negative correlation between the degree of congruence of the vocal and verbal channels and the amount of ambiguity.

Starkweather (1955a, 1956a) sampled recordings of the 1954 Army-McCarthy hearings for three excerpts each, of the voices of McCarthy and Welch, and filtered out content by attenuating higher frequencies. Twelve clinical psychologists showed high interjudge agreement on rating emotional content although they insisted that they had no confidence in their own ratings. The raters were then given a normal, unfiltered presentation of the excerpts and asked to rate them again. A comparison of the categories assigned to the filtered and unfiltered recordings indicates that Welch's voice was judged appropriate to the verbal content, while McCarthy's voice was judged to be without variation.

Other acoustic techniques. Some possible experimental approaches to duration and other physical aspects of the speech signals which have not yet been directly used in voice and emotion studies have been noted (Starkweather, 1961). These may offer better ways of quantifying some of the dimensions of speech which change with changing emotions. Hargreaves and Starkweather (1961) present a case study where judges were able to use certain aspects of speech spectrograph records to identify changes in a patients' vocal behavior which had been considered significant by her therapist. The validity of the 'machine method' of identifying emotionally significant vocal changes still rests on the validity of the skilled listener who sets the criterion dimensions for it, but the authors feel that the method offers a great saving in effort over having a skilled listener consider separately every section of vocal behavior in an interview. Using set aspects of the spectrogram also avoids the effects of fatigue and the learning of wrong cues which might mar the judgements of the skilled listener alone. The authors point out that much information is present in the spectrogram, and a different selection of dimensions might have served as well as theirs for finding correlates to emotional changes in the patient. It may be necessary to use different dimensions for different individuals, as Krause (1961) has found different behavioral measures of vocal behavior to be important for subjects in identifying anxiety.

Conclusion

The abstract at the head of this review has summarized the main trends in the experimental studies on judging personal characteristics from voice. Twenty years ago, Sanford (1942) noted that common experience seems to accept the existence of connections between voice and personality, and if 'the analytic-experimental approach ... reveals no relationship, we should be forced to conclude that it may be the fault of the approach' (p. 838). Many details still remain to be explored (Kramer, 1962), but the 'analytic-experimental approach' has, by now, verified that such relationships exist.

References

ALLPORT, G., and ALLPORT, F. (1928), *A-S Reaction Study*, Houghton Mifflin.

ALLPORT, G., and CANTRIL, H. (1934), 'Judging personality from the voice', *J. soc. Psychol.*, vol. 5, pp. 37–55. [Reprinted in this book, pp. 155–71.]

ALLPORT, G., and VERNON, P. (1931), *Study of Values: A Scale for Measuring the Dominant Interests in Personality*, Houghton Mifflin.

BELL, H. M. (1934), *Adjustment Inventory*, Stanford University Press.

BERNREUTER, R. (1931), *Personality Inventory*, Stanford University Press.

BLACK, J. W., and DREHER, J. J. (1955), 'Non-verbal messages in voice communication', *United States Navy School of Aviation Medicine Research Reports*, No. NM001 104 500.45.

BONAVENTURA, M. (1935), 'Ausdruck der Personlichkeit in der Sprechstimme und in Photogramm', *Arch. ges. Psychol.*, vol. 94, pp. 501–70.

BRODY, M. W. (1943), 'Neurotic manifestations of the voice', *Psychoanal. Q.*, vol. 12, pp. 371–80.

CANTRIL, H., and ALLPORT, G. (1935) *The Psychology of Radio*, Harper & Row.

COHEN, A. (1961), 'Estimating the degree of schizophrenic pathology from recorded interview samples', *J. clin. Psychol.*, vol. 17, pp. 403–6.

COHEN, A., and STARKWEATHER, J. (1961), 'Vocal cues to language identification', *Amer. J. Psychol.*, vol. 74, pp. 90–93.

DAVITZ, J. R., and DAVITZ, L. J. (1959a), 'The communication of feelings by content-free speech', *J. Communication*, vol. 9, pp. 6–13.

DAVITZ, J. R., and DAVITZ, L. J. (1959b), 'Correlates of accuracy in the communication of feelings', *J. Communication*, vol. 9, pp. 110–17.

DIBNER, A. S. (1956), 'Cue-counting: a measure of anxiety in interviews' *J. consult. Psychol.*, vol. 20, pp. 475–8.

DITTMAN, A. T., and WYNNE, L. C. (1961), 'Linguistic techniques and the analysis of emotionality in interviews', *J. abnorm. soc. Psychol.*, vol. 63, pp. 201–4.

DUNCAN, M. H. (1945), 'An experimental study of some of the relationships between voice and personality among students of speech', *SpMon*, vol. 12, pp. 47–61.

DUSENBURY, D., and KNOWER, F. H. (1939), 'Experimental studies of the symbolism of action and voice: II. A study of the specificity of meaning in abstract tonal symbols', *QJSp*, vol. 25, pp. 67–75.

EISENBERG, P., and ZALOWITZ, E. (1938), 'Judgements of dominance-feeling from phonograph records of voice', *J. appl. Psychol.*, vol. 22, pp. 620–31.

ELDRED, S. H., and PRICE, D. B. (1958), 'A linguistic evaluation of feeling states in psychotherapy', *Psychiatry*, vol. 21, pp. 115–21.

FAIRBANKS, G. (1940), 'Recent experimental investigations of vocal pitch in voice', *J. accoust. Soc. Amer.*, vol. 11, pp. 457–66.

FAIRBANKS, G., and HOAGLIN, L. W. (1941), 'An experimental study of the durational characteristics of the voice during the expression of emotion', *SpMon*, vol. 8, pp. 85–90.

FAIRBANKS, G., and PRONOVOST, W. (1939), 'An experimental study of the pitch characteristics of the voice during the expression of emotions', *SpMon*, vol. 6, pp. 87–104.

FAY, P J., and MIDDLETON, W. C. (1939a), 'Judgement of occupation from the voice as transmitted over a public address system and over a radio', *J. appl. Psychol.*, vol. 23, pp. 586–601.

FAY, P. J., and MIDDLETON, W. C. (1939b), 'Judgement of Spranger personality types from the voice as transmitted over a public address system', *Character Person.*, vol. 8, pp. 144–55.

FAY, P. J., and MIDDLETON, W. C. (1940a), 'The ability to judge the rested or tired condition of a speaker from his voice as transmitted over a public address system', *J. appl. Psychol.*, vol. 24, pp. 645–50.

FAY, P. J., and MIDDLETON, W. C. (1940b), 'Judgement of intelligence from the voice as transmitted over a public address system', *Sociometry*, vol. 3, pp. 186–91.

FAY, P. J., and MIDDLETON, W. C. (1940c), 'Judgement of Kretschmerian body types from the voice as transmitted over a public address system', *J. soc. Psychol.*, vol. 12, pp. 151–62.

FAY, P. J., and MIDDLETON, W. C. (1941), 'The ability to judge sociability from the voice as transmitted over a public address system', *J. soc. Psychol.*, vol. 13, pp. 303–09.

FAY, P. J., and MIDDLETON, W. C. (1942), 'Judgement of introversion from the transcribed voice', *QJSp*, vol. 28, pp. 226–8.

FAY, P. J., and MIDDLETON, W. C. (1943), 'Judgement of leadership from transmitted voice', *J. soc. Psychol.*, vol. 17, pp. 99–102.

FLETCHER, H. (1953), *Speech and Hearing in Communication*, Van Nostrand.

FRENCH, N. R., and STEINBERG, J. C. (1947), 'Factors governing the intelligibility of speech sounds', *J. acoust. Soc. Amer.*, vol. 19, pp. 90–119.

GOLDFARB, W., BRAUNSTEIN, P., and LORGE, I. (1956), 'A study of speech patterns in a group of schizophrenic children', *Amer. J. Orthopsychiat.*, vol. 26, pp. 544–55.

GOLDMAN-EISLER, F. (1955), 'Speech-breathing activity: a measure of tension and affect during interviews', *Brit. J. Psychol.*, vol. 46, pp. 53–63.

GOLDMAN-EISLER, F. (1956a), 'The determinants of the rate of speech output and their mutual relations', *J. psychosom. Res.*, vol. 1, pp. 137–43.

GOLDMAN-EISLER, F. (1956b), 'Speech-breathing activity and content in psychiatric interviews', *Brit. J. med. Psychol.*, vol, 29, pp. 35–48.

GRAVES, R. (1949), *Watch the North Wind Rise*, Creative Age Press.

HANAWALT, N. (1953), 'Test review no. 28', in O. Buros (ed.), *The Fourth Mental Measurements Yearbook*, Gryphon Press.

HARGREAVES, W. A., and STARKWEATHER, J. A. (1961), 'Vocal behavior: an illustrative case study', paper read at Western Psychological Association, Seattle.

HARRIS, R. E. (1953), 'Dominance, assertiveness, and hostility in persons with high and low blood pressures: some similarities and some differences', unpublished manuscript, Institute of Personality Assessment and Research, University of California, Berkeley.

HERZOG, H. (1933), 'Stimme und Personlichkeit', *Z. Psychol.*, vol. 130, pp. 300–79.

JONES, H. E. (1942), 'The adolescent growth study: VI. The analysis of voice records', *J. consult. Psychol.*, vol. 6, pp. 255–6.

KAUFFMAN, P. E. (1954), 'An investigation of some psychological stimulus properties of speech behavior', unpublished doctoral dissertation, University of Chicago.

KNOWER, F. H. (1941), 'Analysis of some experimental variations of simulated vocal expressions', *J. soc. Psychol.*, vol. 14, pp. 369–72.

KRAMER, E. (1962), 'The non-verbal aspects of voice: a review and a call for further research', paper read at Michigan Academy of Arts, Sciences, and Letters, Ann Arbor.

KRAMER, E. (1963), 'Personality stereotypes in voice: a reconsideration of the data', *J. soc. Psychol.*, vol. 62, pp. 247–51.

KRAUSE, M. S. (1961), 'Anxiety in verbal behavior: an intercorrelational study' *J. consult. Psychol.*, vol. 25, p. 272.

KRAUSE, M. S., and PILISUK, M. (1961), 'Anxiety in verbal behavior: a validation study', *J. consult. Psychol.*, vol. 25, pp. 414–19.

KRETSCHMER, E. (1925), *Korperbau und Charakter*, W. J. H. Spratt (tr.), Harcourt. Originally published at Springer, Berlin, Germany, 1921.

LICKLIDER, J. C. R., and MILLER, G. A. (1951), 'The perception of speech', in S. S. Stevens (ed.), *Handbook of Experimental Psychology*, Wiley.

MCKELVEY, D. P. (1953), 'Voice and personality', *Western Speech*, vol. 17, pp. 91–4.

MCPHERSON, M. W. (1956), 'Speech behavior and egocentricity', *J. clin. Psychol.*, vol. 12, pp. 229–35.

MCQUOWN, N. A. (1957), 'Linguistic transcription and specification of psychiatric interview materials', *Psychiatry*, vol. 20, pp. 79–86.

MAHL, G. F. (1956), 'Disturbances and silences in the patient's speech in psychotherapy', *J. abnorm. soc. Psychol.*, vol. 53, pp. 1–15.

MAHL, G. F. (1959), 'Measuring the patient's anxiety during interview from "expressive" aspects of his speech', *Trans. N. Y. Acad. Sci.*, vol. 21, pp. 249–57.

MALLORY, E., and MILLER, V. (1958), 'A possible basis for the association of voice characteristics and personality traits', *SpMon*, vol. 25, pp. 255–60.

MASLOW, A. H. (1937), 'Dominance-feeling, behavior, and status', *Psychol. Rev.*, vol. 44, pp. 404–29.

MONRAD-KROHN, G. H. (1947), 'Dysprosody or altered "melody of language"' *Brain*, vol. 70, pp. 405–15.

MONRAD-KROHN, G. H. (1957), 'The third element of speech: prosody in the neuropsychiatric clinic', *J. ment. Sci.*, vol. 103, pp. 326–31.

MOORE, W. E. (1939), 'Personality traits and voice quality deficiencies', *J. Speech Hear. Disorders*, vol. 4, pp. 33–6.

MOSES, P. (1941), 'Social adjustment and voice', *QJSp*, vol. 27, pp. 532–6.

MOSES, P. (1942), 'The study of personality from records of the voice', *J. consult. Psychol.*, vol. 6, pp. 257–61.

MOSES, P. (1954), *The Voice of Neurosis*, Grune & Stratton.

MOSKOWITZ, E. W. (1952), 'Voice quality in the schizophrenic reaction type', *SpMon*, vol. 19, pp. 118–19.

OCHAI, Y., and FUKUMURA, T. (1957), 'On the fundamental qualities of speech in communication', *J. acoust. Soc. Amer.*, vol. 29, pp. 392–3.

OSTWALD, P. F. (1960a), 'A method for the objective denotation of sound of the human voice', *J. psychosom. Res.*, vol. 4, pp. 301–5.

OSTWALD, P. F. (1960b), 'Visual denotation of human sounds', *Archs. gen. Psychiat.*, vol. 3, pp. 117–21.

PAUL, J. E. (1951), 'An investigation of parent–child relationships in speech: intensity and duration', unpublished doctoral dissertation, Purdue University.

PEAR, T. H. (1931), *Voice and Personality*, Chapman & Hall.

PFAFF, P. L. (1954), 'An experimental study of communication of feeling without contextual material', *SpMon*, vol. 21, pp. 155–6.

PITTENGER, R. E., and SMITH, H. L. (1957), 'A basis for some contributions of linguistics to psychiatry', *Psychiatry*, vol. 20, pp. 61–78.

PITTENGER, R. E., HOCKETT, C., and DANEHY, J. (1960), *The First Five Minutes*, Martineau.

POLLACK, I., RUBENSTEIN, H., and HOROWITZ, A. (1960a), 'Communication of verbal modes of expression', *L&S*, vol. 3, pp. 121–30.

POLLACK, I., RUBENSTEIN, H., and HOROWITZ, A. (1960b), 'Recognition of "verbal expression" over communications systems', paper read at the Fifty-ninth Meeting of the Acoustical Society of America.

POTTER, R. K., KOPP, G. A., and GREEN, H. C. (1947), *Visible Speech*, Van Nostrand.

RAMM, K. (1946), 'Is monotonism an indication of maladjustment?', *Smith College Studies in Social Work*, vol. 17, pp. 264–84.

SANFORD, F. H. (1942), 'Speech and personality', *Psychol. Bull.*, vol. 39, pp. 811–45.

SAPIR, E. (1927), 'Speech as a personality trait', *Amer. J. Sociol.* vol. 32, pp. 892–905. [Reprinted in this book, pp. 71–81.]

SHAKOW, D. (1959), 'Discussion of papers by Leary and Gill, and Rogers', in E. A. Rubinstein and M. B. Parloff (eds.), *Research in Psychotherapy*, American Psychological Association.

SKINNER, E. R. (1935), 'A calibrated recording and analysis of the pitch, force and quality of vocal tones expressing happiness and sadness', *SpMon*, vol. 2, pp. 81–137.

SOSKIN, W. F. (1953), 'Some aspects of communication and interpretation in psychotherapy', paper read at the American Psychological Association, Cleveland.

SOSKIN, W., and KAUFFMAN, P. (1961), 'Judgement of emotion in word-free voice samples', *Journal of Communication*, vol. 11, pp. 73–80.

STAGNER, R. (1936), 'Judgements of voice and personality', *J. educ. Psychol.*, vol. 27, pp. 272–7.

STARKWEATHER, J. A. (1955a), 'The communication value of content-free speech', paper read at the Midwestern Psychological Association, Chicago.

STARKWEATHER, J. A. (1955b), 'Judgements of content-free speech as related to some aspects of personality', unpublished doctoral dissertation, Northwestern University.

STARKWEATHER, J. A. (1956a), 'The communication-value of content-free speech', *Amer. J. Psychol.*, vol. 69, pp. 121-3.

STARKWEATHER, J. A. (1956b), 'Content-free speech as a source of information about the speaker', *J. abnorm. soc. Psychol.*, vol. 52, pp. 394-402.

STARKWEATHER, J. A. (1961), 'Vocal communication of personality and human feelings', *J. Communication*, vol. 11, pp. 63-72.

SULLIVAN, H. S. (1954), *The Psychiatric Interview*, Norton.

TAYLOR, H. C. (1934), 'Social agreements on personality traits as judged from speech', *J. Soc. Psychol.*, vol. 5, pp. 244-8.

TERMAN, L. M. (1920), *Terman Group Test of Mental Ability*, World Book.

THOMPSON, C. W., and BRADWAY, K. (1950), 'The teaching of psychotherapy through content-free interviews', *J. consult. Psychol.*, vol. 14, pp. 321-3.

THURSTONE, L. L., and THURSTONE, T. G. (1929), *Personality Schedule*, University of Chicago Press.

TRAGER, G. L. (1958), 'Paralanguage: a first approximation', *SIL*, vol. 13, pp 1-12.

TYLER, L. (1953), 'Test review No. 77', in O. Buros (ed.), *The Fourth Mental Measurements Yearbook*, Gryphon Press.

WOLFF, W. (1943), *The Expression of Personality*, Harper & Row.

10 J. Laver

Voice Quality and Indexical Information

J. Laver, 'Voice quality and indexical information', *British Journal of Disorders of Communication*, vol. 3, 1968, pp. 43–54.

Introduction

As actors in a social world, we interact with other people by virtue of a constant interchange of information on many different levels. Perhaps the most explicit sort of information exchanged in social intercourse is language, and modern linguistic and phonetic theory has developed some elegant and effective concepts for the description of speech, the spoken medium of language. The description of the more narrowly linguistic aspects of speech does not, however, exhaust the possibilities of information carried in utterances. Any given utterance contains not only linguistic information, but also a great deal of information for the listener about the characteristics of the speaker himself. Abercrombie (1967) refers to the features in speech which convey this information as 'indexical' features. It is the purpose of this article to explore one major vehicle of such indexical information in speech, that of voice quality.

While the concepts available for linguistic description are well developed, it is only comparatively recently that phoneticians have begun to show more than a cursory interest in a descriptive theory of voice quality. For a long time other disciplines such as speech pathology, psychology and psychiatry have been more ready to acknowledge the relevance of the study of this topic. With the current expansion of research in the area, this may be an appropriate time to try to suggest the broad outline of an overall descriptive model of voice quality. One motive for attempting to set up such a descriptive model is to facilitate interdisciplinary discussion of the indexical function of voice quality; another is to incorporate the descriptive model into the wider theory of general phonetics. I hope to be able to show that general phonetics constitutes a legitimate framework for the study of this area, in that it offers an appropriate philosophy of analysis, and can make available an established and meaningful body of relevant descriptive concepts.

There has been a variety of usages in labelling voice qualities in the past. With the exception of some phonetically sophisticated systems developed by speech pathology, the majority of previous systems have used single impressionistic labels for given voice qualities. Typical labels have been 'husky', 'plummy', 'thin', 'rich', 'velvety', 'reedy', etc. Such labels are often vague to the point of meaninglessness, except in a metaphorical sense, or as arbitrary imitation labels. The great advantage of a general phonetic approach to the labelling problem is that, in its systems for describing the physiology of articulation, overall labelling is not attempted. The basic philosophy of phonetic analysis is that composite articulatory events are broken down into their component parts, and each independent physiological component is separately labelled. Thus, for example, the sound at the beginning of the English word *fat* is described not as a 'sort of "f"-sound', but as a 'pulmonic, egressive, voiceless, labiodental fricative with velic closure', with each important physiological component analytically isolated.

It is the principal thesis of the descriptive model put forward here that voice quality is similarly susceptible of description in terms of components, and that general phonetic theory can supply the concepts necessary for a physiologically meaningful description of each of the components.[1]

Outline of a descriptive model of voice quality

Voice quality, the quasi-permanent quality of a speaker's voice (Abercrombie, 1967, p. 91), can be thought of as deriving from two main sources: firstly, the anatomical and physiological foundation of a speaker's vocal equipment; and secondly, the long-term muscular adjustments, or 'settings' (Honikman, 1964), once acquired idiosyncratically, or by social imitation, and now unconscious, of the speaker's larynx and supralaryngeal vocal tract.

The anatomy and physiology of a speaker determine the width of the potential range of operation for any voice quality feature, and the long-term habitual settings of the larynx and the vocal tract restrict this feature to a more limited range of operation. For example, a man's voice may be physically capable of spanning a wide pitch range; in normal speech, however, he habitually selects a more restricted range within the total possibilities. Basic anatomy and physiology thus determine the possible extremes, and voluntary muscular settings determine habitual ranges between those extremes.

While factors of basic anatomy and physiology are beyond the speaker's control, and the habitual settings are to a certain extent within his control,

---

1. Abercrombie (1967), Garvin and Ladefoged (1963) and Fairbanks (1960) are among previous writers who have suggested a phonetic approach to voice quality. This article owes much, in particular, to Abercrombie's suggestions.

both these sources of voice quality can transmit indexical information, although of different sorts, as we shall see in a later section.

The anatomy and physiology of the vocal organs, and their habitual muscular settings, are all of legitimate professional interest to the phonetician, but for the moment the habitual muscular settings will be taken as the more direct focus of attention.

It is useful to divide the setttings into two groups:

Settings of the larynx.
Settings of the supralaryngeal vocal tract.

Settings of the larynx
Laryngeal settings fall into three sub-categories:
Phonation types.
Pitch ranges.
Loudness ranges.

Phonation types. Phonation types constitute an area which is still largely open to exploration. Certainly, some labels exist, and are used more or less widely in phonetics, but much research needs to be done before confident statements about the detailed physiology of a wide range of phonation types can be made. The phonation types relevant to this article about whose physiology something is known, besides 'normal voice', include 'breathy voice', 'whispery voice', 'creaky voice', 'falsetto voice', 'ventricular voice' and 'harsh voice'. One of the most valuable contributions to current phonetic knowledge about phonation types has been that of Catford (1964), and he has done much to give both physiological and aerodynamic definitions to many of the above labels.

Some combinations of these phonation types are possible, as in 'harsh, whispery voice', 'whispery, ventricular voice', 'creaky, falsetto voice', 'harsh, falsetto voice', 'harsh, whispery, falsetto voice', 'whispery, creaky voice', 'breathy, falsetto voice' and so forth (see Catford, 1964).

Pitch ranges. Pitch ranges within the total possible range in any phonation type can usefully be described on a five-point scale: 'very deep', 'deep', 'medium', 'high' and 'very high'.

Although the total pitch-possibilities for each phonation type can be divided into the five suggested ranges, there seems to be a tendency for speakers using a given phonation type to favour a particular pitch range. This happens, for instance, in the case of falsetto voice, where speakers typically select a high pitch range within the possibilities for falsetto voice, or in creaky voice, where the deeper ranges for creaky voice are often used. In acoustic terms, the absolute frequencies involved in deep falsetto voice and high creaky voice (which show less usual choices of pitch range within the possibilities for the particular phonation types), may overlap considerably. The 'normal-voice' phonation type does not show this tendency quite as much as the other phonation types, and the pitch ranges used are much more varied.

Loudness ranges. Loudness ranges can also be described as selections from a five-point scale: 'very soft', 'soft', 'medium', 'loud' and 'very loud'.

The habitual settings of the laryngeal and associated musculature which result in characteristic pitch and loudness ranges are of a different order from the settings for characteristic phonation types, in that while a person might be recognized solely by his phonation type in the utterance of a single syllable, a much longer stretch of utterance would be necessary for a listener to be able to recognize the speaker by his characteristic pitch and loudness ranges. However, partly because impressionistic labels for voice quality nearly always seem to contain an implicit reference to these features, and partly because of the quasi-permanent role of such features in characterizing the speaker, pitch and loudness ranges are included in this outline model as features integrally associated with the overall quality of a speaker's voice. In a theoretically more rigorous analysis one would abstract such 'dynamic' features separately from features of 'quality' (Abercombie, 1967, ch. 6).

Settings of the supralaryngeal vocal tract

Supralaryngeal settings of the vocal tract can be divided into four groups, referring to different sorts of modification of the shape and acoustic characteristics of the tract:
Longitudinal modifications.
Latitudinal modifications.
Tension modifications.
Nasalization.

Longitudinal modifications. Longitudinal modifications of the vocal tract can result from vertical displacements of the larynx upwards or downwards, from a neutral position, to give 'raised larynx voice' or 'lowered larynx voice'. Pouting forwards of the lips also effects changes in the length of the longitudinal axis of the vocal tract, and has auditory and acoustic correlates in voice quality.

Latitudinal modifications. Latitudinal modifications of the vocal tract involve quasi-permanent changes in the cross-sectional area at a particular location of the tract, which result in local constrictive or expansive tendencies. These modifications include: different sorts of labialization, with the space between the lips being narrowed either vertically or horizontally, or both; two types of pharyngalization, involving muscular constrictions of the pharynx, or in narrowing of the pharynx by backward displacement of the tongue from its central position in the mouth; and thirdly, settings of the tongue that result in a constrictive or expansive tendency somewhere in the oral cavity.

The settings of the tongue in the oral and pharyngeal cavity are parallel to many of the 'secondary articulations' of traditional phonetic theory. One could speak of overall tendencies towards maintaining a particular 'secondary articulation', but of course such settings are in no sense 'secondary' as far as voice quality, as distinct from segmental features, is concerned (Abercrombie, 1967, p. 93). A less prejudicial conceptualization of the general principle underlying these settings of the tongue, whether in the mouth or in the pharynx, is achieved if any local constrictive or expansive tendency is thought of as resulting from a shift, along one or both of the horizontal and vertical axes of the mouth, of the centre of gravity of the tongue away from the neutral position in which it would lie in an unmodified vocal tract. In this way, pharyngalization can be said to result from backing in the mouth of the centre of gravity of the tongue; velarization from backing and raising; palatalization from raising; alveolarization from fronting; and a quality which currently lacks a conventional phonetic term, but which is sometimes impressionistically called 'hot-potato voice', as if the speaker literally had a hot object in his mouth, is the result of lowering, and perhaps backing, of the centre of gravity of the tongue.

For convenience in the labelling system, instead of the more cumbersome 'tonge-raised-and-backed voice', etc., the more usual phonetic labels such as 'velarized voice' can be retained, provided that it is remembered that no implications of secondary status enter their definition, which would be in terms of the relative position of the centre of gravity of the tongue.

It is probable, because the tongue is of a relatively fixed volume, that any constrictive tendency in the mouth has a corresponding compensatory expansive tendency in other parts of the mouth and pharynx. Similarly, some longitudinal modifications of the vocal tract probably involve a latitudinal component as well; raised larynx voice, for example, has a component of slight pharyngalization. It is also probable that longitudinal modifications involving vertical displacements of the larynx and oral and pharyngeal latitudinal modifications of the vocal tract can affect the fine detail of the mode of vibration of the vocal cords within any phonation type, because of the interactions of the different muscle systems involved.

Tension modifications. In a detailed model of voice quality, account would have to be taken of the effect of variations in the degree of overall muscular tension of the vocal organs on the acoustic damping characteristics of the vocal tract, through factors of radiation and absorption of sound energy in the tract walls. Different degrees of muscular tension may contribute importantly, for example, to the auditory differences between the qualities of the impressionistically-labelled 'metallic voice' and 'muffled voice'. More research is needed in this area, and factors of overall muscular tension will be omitted from further discussion in this article.

Nasalization. It is customary, in phonetic usage in this area, to distinguish only between 'nasalized voice' and 'denasalized voice'. In a more detailed model, it would perhaps be necessary to re-scrutinize these two categories, and set up some finer subdivisions. Speech pathology, for example, has shown that there are a number of auditorily distinguishable kinds of nasalization arising from a variety of organic causes (Luchsinger and Arnold, 1965). Similarly, the term 'denasalized voice' seems to cover at least two different phenomena: firstly, a quality resulting from habitual velic closure, or, more accurately, from a complete lack of nasal resonance; secondly, the quality which is produced by a speaker with a severe cold in the head and nasal catarrh. The first can legitimately be called 'denasalized voice'; the second, speculatively, might be better thought of as a special case of 'nasalized voice', resulting from a partial or complete blockage of catarrhal mucus somewhere in the nasal cavity or naso-pharyngeal sphincter, which would allow the cavity to resonate, but in a highly damped manner. An auditory quality rather like that of velarization seems also to be a component of such 'cold-in-the-head' voices, perhaps because of some feature of muscular adjustment in the vocal tract walls near the soft palate in this special condition.

In this exploratory article, such subdivisions will be ignored, and the terms 'nasalized voice' and 'denasalized voice' used in the customary phonetic sense mentioned above.

Features of habitual nasalization may conceivably affect the setting of the vocal tract as a whole, and thereby the laryngeal settings also; this is because some of the depressor-relaxer muscles of the velum, *glossopalatinus* and *pharyngopalatinus* (Kaplan, 1960, p. 188), which serve to open the velic valve, have their point of origin in the tongue and pharynx, and these muscles, to be effective, have to exert a pull, in contraction, against their points of origin.

The use of a quantitative scale is helpful when describing supralaryngeal modifications of the vocal tract. At least, three degrees of modification can usually be auditorily distinguished – 'slight', 'moderate' and 'severe'.

Thus one may choose to refer to 'slightly pharyngalized voice', 'severely nasalized voice', 'moderately raised larynx voice', and so on.

Labelling system for voice quality

We are now in a position to offer more specific comments on the suggested labelling system. Instead of single-term impressionistic labels such as 'beery', 'brassy', 'sepulchral', etc., we can use composite labels made up of a number of phonetic terms each specifying a physiologically meaningful component of the voice quality in question. The labelling stystem concentrates, as a beginning to the problem, on the voluntary muscular settings rather than on the limitations imposed by the basic anatomy and physiology which underlie the settings.

As a convention, features of pitch range and loudness range are described first, then features of supralaryngeal modification, and lastly features of phonation type. Typical labels might then be 'deep, loud, nasalized, harsh voice', 'high, soft, velarized, raised larynx, falsetto voice', 'very soft, nasalized, whispery, creaky voice', 'very high, pharyngalized, harsh, falsetto voice', 'deep, nasalized voice', and so forth.

Medium pitch, medium loudness, an unmodified vocal tract and the 'normal-voice' phonation type can be left to be assumed if no contrary specification is explicitly made. Scalar quantities of different degrees of vocal tract modification can be incorporated, as in 'high, loud, severely nasalized voice', or 'deep, soft, slightly velarized, whispery, creaky voice'. If the degree of vocal tract modification is left unspecified, it could be assumed that a moderate degree was applicable.

It becomes possible to communicate fairly reliably about voices, with a phonetically meaningful descriptive system of this sort. The translation of some impressionistic labels can be attempted, and some illustrative examples are suggested in the following list:

Equivalence of labelling systems

Impressionistic label	Phonetic label
Ginny voice	Deep, (harsh), whispery, creaky voice
Husky voice	Deep, soft, whispery voice
Golden voice	Deep, soft, slightly nasalized voice
Piping voice	High, falsetto voice
Bleating voice	High, loud, (severely) nasalized voice
Light-blue voice	High, soft, raised larynx voice
Hoarse voice	Deep, (loud), harsh/ventricular, whispery voice
Gruff voice	Deep, harsh, whispery, creaky voice
Sepulchral voice	Very deep, pharyngalized, tongue-lowered, lowered larynx, (whispery), (creaky) voice
Adenoidal voice	Soft, denasalized, velarized voice

Because of the unreliability of reference of the impressionistic labels, not everyone might agree with the suggested translations, but at least the phonetic system, while not yet offering a complete specification, does allow positive statements to be made about assumed components. Communication in writing about voice qualities becomes much more feasible, because the phonetic labels in effect convey instructions for attempts at imitation of the voluntarily controllable components referred to.

Indexical information in voice quality

The descriptive model of voice quality put forward here can now facilitate the discussion of the sources of indexical information in voice quality; the information falls broadly into three categories:
Biological information.
Psychological information.
Social information.

Biological information in voice quality

Biological information about the speaker, derived from the effects, outside his control, of his anatomy and physiology, itself falls into three subcategories:
Size and physique.
Sex and age.
Medical state.

Size and physique. There seems to be a general correlation between a person's size and physique and the size of his larynx and vocal tract. If we hear a very deep loud voice over the telephone, we confidently expect the speaker to turn out to be a large strong male; and in general our expectations are fulfilled, within fairly wide margins of error (Moses, 1941; Fay and Middleton, 1940a). Exceptions to this rule are not uncommon, but they take one aback when they occur.

Sex and age. One usually forms fairly accurate impressions, from voice quality alone, of a speaker's sex and age (Mysak, 1959; Tarneaud, 1941; Zerffi, 1957). Deviations from 'normal' expectations about the correlation between a speaker's voice and his sex and age seem to have a powerful effect on impressions of personality.

Medical state. Voice quality supplies a surprisingly varied amount of indexical information about the medical state of the speaker. It is useful to distinguish between permanent and slightly more ephemeral, although still relatively long-term, medical states. Information about permanent aspects can include details of general health, with crude correlations between, for instance, phonaesthenia, or soft, whispery/breathy voices, and poor health, and between so-called 'strong', 'resonant' or 'rich' voices, (deep, loud, (nasalized) voices), and good health. Permanent abnormalities of anatomy and physiology can be revealed by voice qualities associated with cleft palates, deafness, and even exceptional singing voices, which are sufficiently rare to be thought abnormal in this sense.

More ephemeral, but still quasi-permanent states of health can be signalled by voice quality when the speaker is suffering from conditions of local inflammation of his vocal organs, as in laryngitis, pharyngitis, and tonsillitis, and from nasal catarrh, adenoids or a cold.

Other ephemeral factors in voice quality derive from changes in the hormonal state of the speaker, where, for example, these result in changes in the copiousness and consistency of the supply of lubricating mucus to the larynx, and in the characteristics of the mucous membrane covering the actual vocal cords. Such changes occur in the pregnant and premenstrual states in women (Perelló, 1962), and in conditions of sexual arousal in both men and women. These changes often seem to cause slight harshness, and whispery or breathy voice.

Clues in voice quality to other more permanent, but occasionally reversible, hormonal states are sometimes found in the case of voice disorders resulting from diseases of the thyroid, adrenal and pituitary glands (Luchsinger and Arnold, 1965). Systematic research into the possible use of voice quality as a diagnostic index to these and other medical states would be extremely valuable; so far, the area has only sporadically attracted investigation (McCallum, 1954; Palmer, 1956; Punt, 1959; Sonninen, 1960; Canter, 1963).

Examples of temporary states which can become more permanent, and which can be detected in voice quality, are the effects of intoxicating agents like alcohol and tobacco smoke. In excess, these agents tend to damage the vocal cords. 'Whisky voice', 'ginny voice' and 'rummy voice' are popular labels for the deep, harsh, whispery voices that tend to signal one result of excessive habitual consumption of alcohol (Luchsinger and Arnold, 1965) and 'smoker's larynx' is a fairly frequently used medical label for the pathological effect of excessive tobacco smoke on the vocal cords (Myerson, 1950; Devine, 1960).

Lastly, information about temporary states such as fatigue can sometimes be found in voice quality.

Psychological information in voice quality

We seem to be prepared, as listeners, to draw quite far-reaching conclusions from voice quality about long-term psychological characteristics of a speaker, in assessments of personality. In Western culture, we are ready to believe, for example, that a harsh voice is correlated with more aggressive, dominant, authoritative characteristics, and a breathy voice with more self-effacing, submissive, meek personalities. The belief that personality characteristics, both normal and psychopathological, are correlated with voice quality, has been tested experimentally by many writers, mainly in the medical and psychological fields (Allport and Cantril, 1934; Cohen, 1961; Diehl, White and Burle, 1959; Eisenberg and Zalowitz, 1938; Fay and Middleton, 1939b, 1940b; Froeschels, 1960; Goldfarb, Braunstein and Lorge, 1956; Mallory and Miller, 1958; Moore, 1939; Moses, 1954; Pear, 1957; Sapir, 1926-7; Starkweather, 1964; Taylor, 1934). Some controversy remains, but in general writers seem to agree that some such broad correlations do exist. Intuitively, one would agree with them, but one major obstacle in the way of reliable scientific statements has been the lack of any standard system of labelling the voice qualities concerned, and a related inability to attain more than a fairly crude quantification of the voice quality variables which act as the experimental stimuli.

If it is true that information about personality is conveyed by voice quality, then the information must be chiefly carried by aspects of the habitual muscular settings, rather than by the basically invariant anatomy and physiology of the speaker.

Social information in voice quality

Social behaviour is largely learned behaviour. Because of this, clues in voice quality to social information must lie mainly in those features of voice quality which can be acquired by imitation. In this sense, a particular accent often has a special voice quality associated with it, and the voice quality can thereby act as a partial clue to any social characteristics that are typical of speakers of that accent. Thus voice quality may serve as an index to features of regional origin, social status, social values and attitudes, and profession or occupation, where these features characterize speakers of the particular accent in question. Nasalization is a voice quality component very commonly associated with particular accents. It characterizes most speakers of Received Pronunciation in England, and many accents of the United States and Australia. Velarization is a regional marker in the speech of speakers from Liverpool and Birmingham, England, and some parts of New York.

Voice quality can also act as an index to membership of a group which is not necessarily an accent group (Fay and Middleton, 1939a). For example, some British male stage actors used to seem consciously to strive to attain a voice quality like that of Sir Laurence Olivier; similarly, military drill sergeants typically have harsh voices, and these are not necessarily the result of habitual vocal abuse, but rather acquired by imitation, in the hope of projecting the characteristic persona of their profession.

Stereotyped judgements in voice quality

We all act, as listeners, as if we were experts in using information in voice quality to reach conclusions about biological, psychological and social characteristics of speakers. Long experience of inferring such characteristics from voice quality, presumably often successfully confirmed by information from other levels, invests our implicit ideas about the correlations between voice quality and indexical information with an imagined infallibility. It is worth questioning the validity of this judgement process. We make judgements, and we act on them, but is the information we infer accurate, or is there a possibility that it is quite false? Since the correlations must be statistical in nature, and not always of a very high degree of statistical confidence, obviously listeners will sometimes be wrong in the conclusions they draw from particular voice qualities. There is a good deal of evidence that in such subjective judgements we operate with stereotypes (Cantril and Allport, 1935; Eisenberg and Zalowitz, 1938; Fay and Middleton, 1939b, 1940a, 1940b; Starkweather, 1964). Listeners, if they are from the same culture, tend to reach the same indexical conclusions from the same evidence, but the conclusions themselves may, on occasion, bear no reliable relation to the real characteristics of the speaker.

Of the three types of indexical information in voice quality, biological, psychological and social, it is the biological information which probably tends to lead to the most accurate conclusions, especially as to sex and age. Biological conclusions are possibly more reliable because of the fact that they derive principally from the involuntary, largely invariant aspects of a speaker's anatomy and physiology. Psychological and social conclusions are much more likely to be erroneous, because of their culturally relative nature, and because they derive from a more variable strand of the speaker's voice quality, the habitual muscular settings of the larynx and vocal tract.

Experimental investigation of voice quality

The descriptive model suggested in this article represents no more than an initial structuring of the area, and a good deal of work, both experimental and theoretical, will be necessary before the phonetic description of voice quality can approach adequacy. Happily, experimental phonetics is not lacking in appropriate techniques of investigation. Experimental research can follow two complementary lines of approach, in speech analysis and speech synthesis.

In the speech analysis approach to voice quality, data are needed on a number of different aspects. It would be valuable, for instance, to have anthropometric measurements of typical variations in anatomical dimensions, as well as acoustic and physiological information about long-term articulatory activity. Acoustic techniques currently available include a wide range of analytic devices, from spectrography for discovering the distribution in time and frequency of acoustic energy, to inverse filtering of the speech signal for recovery of the characteristics of the glottal waveform. Physiological techniques which might be utilized include cine-radiography, stroboscopic cinelaminography (Hollien, 1964), electromanometry and electromyography (Cooper, 1965).

Speech synthesis is a useful avenue of research, in that hypotheses about physiological activities and their acoustic and auditory correlates can be easily tested. It is particularly valuable in that voice qualities of narrowly defined specifications can be fairly precisely simulated (Wendahl, 1963; Laver, 1967), and psychophonetic perceptual tests and the training of judges in the phonetic labelling system can be correspondingly facilitated.

The relevance of voice quality for the disciplines concerned with speech

I have maintained that while it is the business of general phonetics to suggest a descriptive model of voice quality, the study of this area has relevance for a number of disciplines.

Speech pathology has a direct interest in voice quality, and various systems of descriptive terminology are used by workers in this field. These systems, moreover, are not necessarily lacking in implications of phonetic specificity, as in the use of terms like 'hyperrhinolalia' and 'hyperrhinophonia' as labels for 'severely nasalized voice', and 'dysphonia plicae ventricularis', for 'ventricular voice'. The limitation of such systems is in their emphasis on deviations, for whatever etiological reasons, from socially acceptable norms of voice quality. This is not to disparage such systems; in many areas of speech pathology attention is necessarily focused on abnormality. However, such systems are inherently too partial for general applicability to voice qualities of all kinds. The advantage of the more general type of system outlined in this article is in its being able to function without prejudice as to culturally-assessed factors of 'normality' or 'abnormality'. Both sorts of systems share the characteristic of analysing voice quality on a physiological, componential basis. Either system would be valuable, for instance, in the research area commented on earlier, that of the use of the voice as an indexical diagnostic clue to various pathological states.

Psychology and psychiatry have shown a frequent interest in voice quality research, because of the importance of the voice as an index to affective conditions, and to personality. Psychological experimentation in this area might benefit considerably from the techniques of synthetic simulation of voice qualities mentioned earlier, in that the voice quality stimulus variable in experiments investigating the correlations between voice quality and personality, for example, might be brought under more delicate, reliable and quantified control in this way.

Finally, considerations of voice quality are crucial for some aspects of the specifically linguistic study of speech. The distinction between voice quality and 'phonetic quality' is one of the most fundamental distinctions in linguistic phonetics (Ladefoged, 1962), since phonetic quality is the basic datum of the subject, in its capacity as the vehicle for the meaningful distinctions of phonology. It is sometimes thought that phonetic quality and voice quality are independent aspects of the phonic continuum, and that therefore phonetic quality can be related directly, as a simple abstraction, to the 'real world' of 'phonic quality'. A case can nevertheless be made for considering that phonetic quality and voice quality are not completely independent, and that phonetic quality can in fact only be judged against the previously assessed background of the voice quality of the speaker producing the utterance. Phonetic quality in this view would thus be a more abstract concept than is perhaps often believed.

One of the difficulties facing phoneticians and linguists investigating the phonology of a particular language arises from the general fact that voice quality and phonetic quality can rely for their manifestation on many similar activities of the speech organs. Activities used on a quasi-permanent basis, in some of the habitual laryngeal and supralaryngeal settings, can potentially also be used on a much shorter-term basis, in the contrastive articulations representing phonological units.

Thus many of the features discussed in this article in their role as contributors to voice quality, such as labialization, palatalization, velarization, pharyngalization, nasalization, breathy voice and creaky voice, have also been found in various languages as signals used to differentiate the phonetic quality of the sounds representing phonological units in those languages.

It is because of the potential linguistic utilization of such features that the phonetician or linguist conducting phonological research must take an early decision about the status of these features, when they occur in the speech of his informant.

Conclusion

The study of speech attracts the research attention of a number of different disciplines, each with its own professional interests. For the majority of these disciplines speech is a partial interest, and the main focus of the discipline lies outside speech as such, as in the case of psychology and psychiatry. Speech therapy, on the other hand, takes speech as its principal data, but brings a specialized interest to bear on a restricted area within the wider field of speech as a whole. The one subject which takes as its professional domain the study of *all* aspects of speech is phonetics. As such, phonetics should be able to offer, to these other interested disciplines comprehensive theoretical structures for the description of all aspects of speech. This article has outlined a general phonetic approach to the description of voice quality, as one particular aspect of speech, in the hope of facilitating inter-disciplinary discussion about this aspect, and about the indexical information conveyed by its different factors.

References

ABERCROMBIE, D. (1967), *Elements of General Phonetics*, Edinburgh University Press.

ALLPORT, G. W., and CANTRIL, H. (1934), 'Judging personality from voice', *J. soc. Psychol.*, vol. 5, pp. 37–55. [Reprinted in this book, pp. 155–71.]

CANTER, G. J. (1963), 'Speech characteristics of patients with Parkinson's disease: I. Intensity, pitch and duration', *J. Speech Hear. Disorders*, vol. 28, pp. 221–9.

CANTER, G. J. (1965), 'Speech characteristics of patients with Parkinson's disease: II. Physiological support for speech', *J. Speech Hear. Disorders*, vol. 30, pp. 44–9.

CANTRIL, H., and ALLPORT, G. W. (1935), *The Psychology of Radio*, Harper & Row.

CATFORD, J. C. (1964), 'Phonation types: the classification of some laryngeal components of speech production', in D. Abercrombie, D. B. Fry, P. A. D. MacCarthy, N. C. Scott and J. L. M. Trim (eds.), *In Honour of Daniel Jones*, Longman.

COHEN, A. (1961), 'Estimating the degree of schizophrenic pathology from recorded interview samples', *J. clin. Psychol.*, vol. 4, pp. 403–6.

COOPER, F. S. (1965), 'Research techniques and instrumentation: EMG', *American Speech and Hearing Association Reports*, vol. 1, pp. 153–68.

DEVINE, K. D. (1960), 'Pathologic effects of smoking in the larynx and oral cavity', *Proc. Staff Meet. Mayo Clin.*, vol. 35, pp. 349–52.

DIEHL, D. F., WHITE, R., and BURLE, K. (1959), 'Voice quality and anxiety', *J. Speech Hear. Res.*, vol. 2, pp. 282–5.

EISENBERG, P., and ZALOWITZ, E. (1938), 'Judgements of dominance feelings from phonograph records of the voice', *J. appl. Psychol.*, vol. 22, pp. 620–31.

FAIRBANKS, G. (1960), *Voice and Articulation Drillbook* (2nd edn), Harper & Row.

FAY, P. J., and MIDDLETON, W. C. (1939a), 'Judgement of occupation from the voice as transmitted over a public address system and over a radio', *J. appl. Psychol.*, vol. 23, pp. 586–601.

FAY, P. J., and MIDDLETON, W. C. (1939b), 'Judgement of Spranger personality types from the voice as transmitted over a public address system', *Character Person.*, vol. 8, pp. 144–55.

FAY, P. J., and MIDDLETON, W. C. (1940a), 'Judgement of Kretschmerian body types from the voice as transmitted over a public address system', *J. soc. Psychol.*, vol. 12, pp. 151–62.

FAY, P. J., and MIDDLETON, W. C. (1940b), 'Judgement of intelligence from the voice as transmitted over a public address system', *Sociometry*, vol. 3, pp. 186–91.

FROESCHELS, E. (1960), 'Remarks on some pathologic and physiologic conditions of the human voice', *A.M.A. Archs. Otolar.*, vol. 71, pp. 787–8.

GARVIN, P., and LADEFOGED, P. (1963), 'Speaker identification and message identification in speech recognition', *Phonetica*, vol. 9, pp. 193–9.

GOLDFARB, W., BRAUNSTEIN, P., and LORGE, I. (1956), 'A study of speech patterns in a group of schizophrenic children', *Amer. J. Orthopsychiat.*, vol. 26, pp. 544–55.

HOLLIEN, H. (1964), 'Stroboscopic laminography of the vocal folds', *PICPS V*, Münster.

HONIKMAN, B. (1964), 'Articulatory settings', in D. Abercrombie, D. B. Fry, P. A. D. MacCarthy, N. C. Scott and J. L. M. Trim (eds.), *In Honour of Daniel Jones*, Longman.

KAPLAN, H. M. (1960), *Anatomy and Physiology of Speech*, McGraw-Hill.

LADEFOGED, P. (1962), *The Nature of Vowel Quality*, Laboratorio de Fonetica Experimental, Coimbra.

LAVER, J. (1967), 'The synthesis of components in voice quality', *PICPS VI*, Prague.

LUCHSINGER, R., and ARNOLD, G. E. (1965), *Voice–Speech–Language*, Constable.

McCALLUM, J. R. (1954), 'Chronic laryngitis', *Speech*, vol. 18, pp. 48–50.

MALLORY, E. B., and MILLER, V. B. (1958), 'A possible basis for the association of voice characteristics and personality traits', *SpMon*, vol. 25, pp. 255–60.

MOORE, W. E. (1939), 'Personality traits and voice quality deficiencies', *J. Speech Hear. Disorders*, vol. 4, pp. 33–6.

MOSES, P. J. (1941), 'Theories regarding the relation of constitution and character through the voice', *Psychol. Bull.*, vol. 38, p. 746 (A).

MOSES, P. J. (1954), *The Voice of Neurosis*, Grune & Stratton.

MYERSON, M. C. (1950), 'Smoker's larynx – a clinical pathological entity?', *Ann. Otol. Rhinol. Lar.*, vol. 59, pp. 541–6.

MYSAK, E. D. (1959), 'Pitch and duration characteristics of older males', *J. Speech Hear. Res.*, vol. 2, pp. 46–54.

PALMER, J. M. (1956), 'Hoarseness in laryngeal pathology: a review of the literature', *Laryngoscope*, vol. 66, pp. 500–16.

PEAR, T. H. (1957), *Personality Appearance and Speech*, Allen & Unwin.

PERELLÓ, J. (1962), 'La disfonia premenstrual', *Acta oto-rino-lar. ibéro-am.*, vol. 23, pp. 561–3.

PUNT, N. A. (1959), 'Alteration in the voice', *Med. Press*, pp. 235–8.

SAPIR, E. (1926–7), 'Speech as a personality trait', *Amer. J. Sociol.* vol. 32, pp. 892–905. [Reprinted in this book, pp. 71–81.]

SONNINEN, A. (1960), 'Laryngeal signs and symptoms of goitre', *FPhon*, vol. 12, pp. 41–7.

STARKWEATHER, J. A. (1964), 'Variations in vocal behavior', in *Disorders of Communication*, Res. Publs., Ass. Res. nerv. ment. Dis., vol. XLII.

TARNEAUD, J. (1941), *Traité Pratique de Phonologie et de Phoniatrie*, Librarie Maloine.

TAYLOR, H. C. (1934), 'Social agreements on personality traits as judged from speech', *J. soc. Psychol.*, vol. 5, pp. 244–8.

WENDAHL, R. W. (1963), 'Laryngeal analog synthesis of harsh voice quality', *FPhon*, vol. 15, pp. 241–50.

ZERFFI, W. (1957), 'Male and female voices', *A.M.A. Archs. Otolar.*, vol. 65, pp. 7–10.

Part Four
Non-Vocal Communication

A major theme in the Introduction was that conversation involves many more strands of communication than speech alone. This section contains six Readings which make detailed comment on gesture, posture, proximity, spatial orientation and eye-contact behaviour, as non-vocal paralinguistic features of conversation. The Readings focus on the way these features convey indexical information about relationships between the participants, and also interaction-management information for controlling the temporal progress of the conversation.

The indexical use of paralinguistic features to signal the nature of the social and psychological relationships between the participants is discussed by Scheflen (12) for posture, Hall (14) for proximity, Sommer (15) for spatial orientation, and Argyle and Dean (16), and Sommer, for eye-contact behaviour.

Interaction-management information can be conveyed by all the above features, and Scheflen (12) in particular discusses the use of posture as a system of signals for giving an interaction its temporal structure.

La Barre (11) gives a comprehensive survey of the use of gesture in many different cultures. Hall (13) examines the various factors involved in conducting a microscopic analysis of the proximity between participants in an interaction. An important point raised by La Barre, and by Hall in both his Readings, is that features such as gesture and proximity constitute communicative codes, and that, as such, they have to be learned, and are necessarily culturally-relative, not universal for all cultures.

11 W. La Barre

The Cultural Basis of Emotions and Gestures

W. La Barre, 'The cultural basis of emotions and gestures', *Journal of Personality*, vol. 16, 1947, pp. 49–68.

Psychologists have long concerned themselves with the physiological problems of emotion, as for example, whether the psychic state is prior to the physiological changes and causes them, or whether the conscious perception of the inner physiological changes in itself constitutes the 'emotion'. The physiologists also, notably Cannon, have described the various bodily concomitants of fear, pain, rage, and the like. Not much attention, however, has been directed toward another potential dimension of meaning in the field of emotions, that is to say the *cultural* dimension.

The anthropologist is wary of those who speak of an 'instinctive' gesture on the part of a human being. One important reason is that a sensitivity to meanings which are culturally different from his own stereotypes may on occasion be crucial for the anthropologist's own physical survival among at least some groups he studies, and he must at the very least be a student of this area of symbolism if he would avoid embarrassment.[1] He cannot safely rely upon his own culturally subjective understandings of emotional expression in his relations with persons of another tribe. The advisability and the value of a correct reading of any cultural symbolism whatsoever has alerted him to the possibility of culturally arbitrary, quasilinguistic (that is, non-instinctual but learned and purely agreed-upon) meanings in the behavior he observes.

A rocking of the skull forward and backward upon its condyles, which rest on the atlas vertebra, as an indication of affirmation and the rotation upon the axis vertebra for negation have so far been accepted as 'natural' and 'instinctive' gestures that one psychologist at least[2] has sought an

---

1. The notorious Massey murder in Hawaii arose from the fact that a native beach boy perhaps understandably mistook the Occidental 'flirting' of a white woman for a *bona fide* sexual invitation. On the other hand, there are known cases which have ended in the death of American ethnographers who misread the cultural signs while in the field.

2. Holt (1931, p. 111), and personal conversations. The idea is originally Darwin's, I believe (Darwin, 1872), but he himself pointed out that the lateral shake of the head is by no means universally the sign of negation. Holt has further noted the interesting point that in a surprising number of languages, quite unrelated to each other, the word

explanation of the supposedly universal phenomenon in ascribing the motions of 'yes' to the infant's seeking of the mother's breast, and 'no' to its avoidance and refusal of the breast. This is ingenious, but it is arguing without one's host, since the phenomenon to be explained is by no means as widespread ethnologically, even among humans, as is mammalian behavior biologically.

Indeed, the Orient alone is rich in alternatives. Among the Ainu of northern Japan, for example, our particular head noddings are unknown: 'the right hand is usually used in negation, passing from right to left and back in front of the chest; and both hands are gracefully brought up to the chest and gracefully waved downwards – palms upwards – in sign of affirmation' (Landor, 1893, pp. 6, 233–4).

The Semang, pygmy Negroes of interior Malaya, thrust the head sharply forward for 'yes' and cast the eyes down for 'no' (Skeat and Blagden, 1906).

The Abyssinians say 'no' by jerking the head to the right shoulder, and 'yes' by throwing the head back and raising the eyebrows. The Dyaks of Borneo raise their eyebrows to mean 'yes' and contract them slightly to mean 'no'. The Maori say 'yes' by raising the head and chin; the Sicilians say 'no' in exactly the same manner (Klineberg, 1935, p. 283).

A Bengali servant in Calcutta rocks his head rapidly in an arc from shoulder to shoulder, usually four times, in assent; in Delhi a Moslem boy throws his head diagonally backward with a slight turning of the neck for the same purpose; and the Kandyan Singhalese bends the head diagonally forward toward the right, with an indescribably graceful turning in of the chin, often accompanying this with a cross-legged curtsey, arms partly crossed, palms upward – the whole performance extraordinarily beautiful and ingratiating. Indeed, did my own cultural difference not tell me it already, I would know that the Singhalese manner of receiving an object (with the right hand, the left palm supporting the right elbow) is not instinctive, for I have seen a Singhalese mother *teaching* her little boy to do this when I gave him a chunk of palm-tree sugar. I only regretted, later, that my own manners must have seemed boorish or subhuman, since I

for *mother* is a variant of the sound 'ma'. One can collect dozens of such instances, representing all the continents, which would seem to confirm his conjecture: the genuinely universal 'sucking reflex' which brings the lips into approximation (m), plus the simplest of the simple open vowel sounds (a), are 'recognized' by the mother as referring to her when the baby first pronounces them; hence they become the lexical designation of the maternal parent. Although this phenomenon becomes a linguistic one, it is only on some such physiological basis that one can explain the recurrence of the identical sound combinations in wholly unrelated languages referring to the same person, the mother. But there is no absolute semantic association involved: one baby boy I have observed used 'mama' both to connote and to denote older persons of either sex.

handed it to him with my right hand, instead of with both, as would any courteous Singhalese. Alas, if I had handed it to a little Moslem beggar in Sind or the Punjab with my *left* hand, he would probably have dashed the gift to the ground, spat, and called me by the name of an animal whose flesh he had been taught to dislike, but which I have not – for such use of the left hand would be insulting, since it is supposed to be confined to attending to personal functions, while the right hand is the only proper one for food.

Those persons with a passion for easy dominance, the professional dog-lovers, must often be exasperated at the stupidity of a dog which does not respond to so obvious a command as the pointed forefinger. The defence of man's best friend might be that this 'instinctively' human gesture does not correspond to the kinaesthesias of a non-handed animal. Nevertheless, even for an intelligent human baby, at the exact period when he is busily using the forefinger in exploring the world, 'pointing' by an adult is an arbitrary, sublinguistic gesture which is not automatically understood and which must be *taught*. I am the less inclined to berate the obtuseness to the obvious of either dog or baby, because of an early field experience of my own. One day I asked a favorite informant of mine among the Kiowa, old Mary Buffalo, where something was in the *ramada* or willow-branch 'shade' where we were working. It was clear she had heard me, for her eighty-eight-year-old ears were by no means deaf; but she kept on busying both hands with her work. I wondered at her rudeness and repeated the request several times, until finally with a puzzled exasperation which matched my own, she dropped her work and fetched it for me from in plain sight: she had been repeatedly pointing with her lips in approved American Indian fashion, as any Caucasian numbskull should have been able to see.

Some time afterward I asked a somewhat naïve question of a very great anthropologist, the late Edward Sapir: 'Do other tribes cry and laugh as we do?' In appropriate response, Sapir himself laughed, but with an instant grasping of the point of the question: In which of these things are men alike everywhere, in which different? Where are the international boundaries between physiology and culture? What are the extremes of variability, and what are the scope and range of cultural differences in emotional and gestural expression? Probably one of the most learned linguists who have ever lived, Sapir was extremely sensitive to emotional and sublinguistic gesture – an area of deep illiteracy for most 'Anglo-Saxon' Americans – and my present interest was founded on our conversation at that time.

Smiling, indeed, I have found may almost be mapped after the fashion of any other culture trait; and laughter is in some senses a geographic variable. On a map of the Southwest Pacific one could perhaps even draw lines between areas of 'Papuan hilarity' and others where a Dobuan, Melanesian dourness reigned. In Africa, Gorer noted that

laughter is used by the Negro to express surprise, wonder, embarrassment and even discomfiture; it is not necessarily, or even often a sign of amusement; the significance given to 'black laughter' is due to a mistake of supposing that similar symbols have identical meanings (Gorer, 1935, p. 10)

Thus it is that even if the physiological behavior be present, its cultural and emotional functions may differ. Indeed, even within the same culture, the laughter of adolescent girls and the laughter of corporation presidents can be functionally different things; so too the laughter of an American Negro and that of the white he addresses.

The behaviorist Holt 'physiologized' the smile as being ontogenetically the relaxation of the muscles of the face in a baby replete from nursing. Explanations of this order may well be the case, if the phenomenon of the smile is truly a physiological expression of generalized pleasure, which is caught up later in ever more complex conditioned reflexes. And yet, even in its basis here, I am not sure that this is the whole story: for the 'smile' of a child in its sleep is certainly in at least some cases the grimace of *pain* from colic, rather than the relaxation of pleasure. Other explanations such as that the smile is *phylogenetically* a snarl suffer from much the same *ad hoc* quality.

Klineberg (1935) writes:

It is quite possible, however, that a smile or laugh may have a different meaning for groups other than our own. Lafcadio Hearn has remarked that the Japanese smile is not necessarily a spontaneous expression of amusement, but a law of etiquette, elaborated and cultivated from early times. It is a silent language, often seemingly inexplicable to Europeans, and it may arouse violent anger in them as a consequence. The Japanese child is taught to smile as a social duty, just as he is taught to bow or prostrate himself; he must always show an appearance of happiness to avoid inflicting his sorrow upon his friends. The story is told of a woman servant who smilingly asked her mistress if she might go to her husband's funeral. Later she returned with his ashes in a vase and said, actually laughing, 'Here is my husband.' Her white mistress regarded her as a cynical creature; Hearn suggests that this may have been pure heroism (Hearn, 1894).

Many in fact of these motor habits in one culture are open to grave misunderstanding in another. The Copper Eskimo welcome strangers with a buffet on the head or shoulders with the fist, while the northwest Amazonians slap one another on the back in greeting. Polynesian men greet each other by embracing and rubbing each other's back; Spanish-American males greet one another by a stereotyped embrace, head over right shoulder of the partner, three pats on the back, head over reciprocal left shoulder, three more pats. In the Torres Straits islands 'the old form of greeting was to bend slightly the fingers of the right hand, hook them with those of the person greeted, and then draw them away so as to scratch the palm of the hand; this is repeated several times' (Haddon, 1904, p. 306; Whiffen, 1905, p. 259). The Ainu of Yezo have a peculiar greeting; on the occasion of a man meeting his sister, 'The man held the woman's hands for a few seconds, then suddenly releasing his hold, grasped her by both ears and uttered the Aino cry. Then they stroked one another down the face and shoulders' (Hitchcock, n.d., pp. 464–5; Landor, 1893, pp. 6, 233–4). Kayan males in Borneo embrace or grasp each other by the forearm, while a host throws his arm over the shoulder of a guest and strokes him endearingly with the palm of his hand. When two Kurd males meet, 'they grasp each other's right hand, which they simultaneously raise, and each kisses the hand of the other' (Perkins, 1851, p. 101; Hose and MacDougall, 1912, pp. 124–5). Among the Andaman Islanders of the Gulf of Bengal:

When two friends or relatives meet who have been separated from each other for a few weeks or longer, they greet each other by sitting down, one on the lap of the other, with their arms around each other's necks, and weeping or wailing for two or three minutes till they are tired. Two brothers greet each other in this way, and so do father and son, mother and daughter, and husband and wife. When husband and wife meet, it is the man who sits in the lap of the woman. When two friends part from one another, one of them lifts up the hand of the other towards his mouth and gently blows on it (Radcliffe-Brown, 1922, pp. 117, 74n. 1).

Some of these expressions of 'joy' seem more lugubrious than otherwise. One old voyager, John Turnbull, writes as follows:

The arrival of a ship brings them to the scene of action from far and near. Many of them meet at Matavai who have not seen each other for some length of time. The ceremony of these meetings is not without singularity; taking a shark's tooth, they strike it into their head and temples with great violence, so as to produce a copious bleeding; and this they will repeat, till they become clotted with blood and gore.

The honest mariner confesses to be non-plussed at this behavior.

I cannot explain the origin of this custom, nor its analogy with what it is intended to express. It has no other meaning with them than to express the excess of their joy. By what construction it is considered symbolical of this emotion I do not understand (1813, pp. 301–2).

Quite possibly, then, the weeping of an American woman 'because she is so happy' may merely indicate that the poverty of our gamut of physiological responses is such as to require using the same response for opposite meanings. Certainly weeping does obey social stereotypes in other cultures. Consider old Mary Buffalo at her brother's funeral: she wept in a frenzy, tore her hair, scratched her cheeks, and even tried to jump into the grave (being conveniently restrained from this by remoter relatives). I happened to know that she had not seen her brother for some time, and there was no particular love lost between them: she was merely carrying on the way a decent woman should among the Kiowa. Away from the grave, she was immediately chatting vivaciously about some other topic. Weeping is *used* differently among the Kiowa. Any stereotypes I may have had about the strong and silent American Indian, whose speech is limited to an infrequent *ugh* and whose stoicism to pain is limitless, were once rudely shattered in a public religious meeting. A great burly Wichita Indian who had come with me to a peyote meeting, after a word with the leader which I did not understand (it was probably permission to take his turn in a prayer) suddenly burst out blubbering with an abandon which no Occidental male adult would permit himself in public. In time I learned that this was a stereotyped approach to the supernatural powers, enthusiastic weeping to indicate that he was as powerless as a child, to invoke their pity, and to beseech their gift of medicine power. Everyone in the tipi understood this except me.

So much for the expression of emotion in one culture, which is open to serious misinterpretation in another: there is no 'natural' language of emotional gesture. To return a moment to the earlier topic of emotional expression in greetings: West Africans in particular have developed highly the ritual gestures and language of greeting. What Gorer says of the Wolof would stand for many another tribe:

The gestures and language of polite intercourse are stylized and graceful; a greeting is a formal litany of question and answer embracing everyone and everything connected with the two people meeting (the questions are merely formal and a dying person is stated to be in good health so as not to break the rhythm of the responses) and continuing for several minutes; women accompany it with a swaying movement of the body; with people to whom a special deference is due the formula is resumed several times during the conversation; saying goodbye is equally elaborate (Gorer, 1935, p. 38).[3]

But here the sublinguistic gesture language has clearly emerged into pure formalisms of language which are quite plainly cultural.

The allegedly 'instinctive' nature of such motor habits in personal relationships is difficult to maintain in the face of the fact that in many cases the same gesture means exactly opposite, or incommensurable things,

3. Cf. Hollis (1905, pp. 284–7); Torday and Joyce (1910, pp. 233–4, 284, *et passim*). West Africans have developed the etiquette and protocol of greeting to a high degree, adjusting it to sex, age, relative rank, relationship degrees, and the like. Probably there is no more than a trace of this ceremoniousness surviving in American Negro greetings in the South.

in different cultures. Hissing in Japan is a polite deference to social superiors; the Basuto applaud by hissing, but in England hissing is rude and public disapprobation of an actor or a speaker. Spitting in very many parts of the world is a sign of utmost contempt; and yet among the Masai of Africa it is a sign of affection and benediction, while the spitting of an American Indian medicine man upon a patient is one of the kindly offices of the curer. Urination upon another (as in a famous case at the Sands Point, Long Island, country club, involving a congressman since assassinated) is a grave insult among Occidentals, but it is part of the transfer of power from an African medicine man in initiations and curing rituals. As for other opposite meanings, Western man stands up in the presence of a superior; the Fijians and the Tongans sit down. In some contexts we put on more clothes as a sign of respect; the Friendly Islanders take them off. The Toda of South India raise the open right hand to the face, with the thumb on the bridge of the nose, to express respect; a gesture almost identical among Europeans is an obscene expression of extreme disrespect. Placing to the tip of the nose the projecting knuckle of the right forefinger bent at the second joint was among the Maori of New Zealand a sign of friendship and often of protection;[4] but in eighteenth-century England the placing of the same forefinger to the right side of the nose expressed dubiousness about the intelligence and sanity of a speaker – much as does the twentieth-century clockwise motion of the forefinger above the right hemisphere of the head. The sticking out of the tongue among Europeans (often at the same time 'making a face') is an insulting, almost obscene act of provocative challenge and mocking contempt for the adversary, so undignified as to be used only by children; so long as Maya writing remains undeciphered we do not know the meaning of the exposure of the tongue in some religious sculptures of the gods, but we can be sure it scarcely has the same significance as with us. In Bengali statues of the dread black mother goddess Kali, the tongue is protruded to signify great raging anger and shock; but the Chinese of the Sung dynasty protruded the tongue playfully to pretend to mock terror, as if to 'make fun of' the ridiculous and unfeared anger of another person.[5] Modern Chinese, in South China at least, protrude the tongue for a moment and then retract it, to express embarrassment at a *faux pas*.

Kissing, as is well known, is in the Orient an act of private loveplay and arouses only disgust when indulged in publicly: in Japan it is necessary to

4. Klineberg (1935, pp. 286–7) citing Lubbock (1872); Best (1924); Lowie (1929); Hollis (1905, p. 315).
5. *Chin P'ing Mei* (Shanghai, n.d.), introduction by Arthur Waley. The sixteenth-century Chinese also had the expressions to act 'with seven hands and eight feet' for awkwardness, and 'to sweat two handfuls of anxiety'.

censor out the major portion of love scenes in American-made movies for this reason. Correspondingly, some of the old *kagura* dances of the Japanese strike Occidentals as revoltingly overt obscenities, yet it is doubtful if they arouse this response in Japanese onlookers. Manchu kissing is purely a private sexual act, and though husband and wife or lovers might kiss each other, they would do it stealthily since it is shameful to do in public; yet Manchu mothers have the pattern of putting the penis of the baby boy into their mouths, a practice which probably shocks Westerners even more than kissing in public shocks the Manchu (Shiro-kogoreff, 1924, pp. 122–3). Tapuya men in South America kiss as a sign of peace, but men do not kiss women because the latter wear labrets or lip plugs. Nose-rubbing is Eskimo and Polynesian; and the Djuka Negroes of Surinam (Kahn, 1929, p. 473) show pleasure at a particularly interesting or amusing dance step by embracing the dancer and touching cheek to cheek, now on one side, now on the other – which is the identical attenuation of the 'social kiss' between American women who do not wish to spoil each other's makeup.

In the language of gesture all over the world there are varying mixtures of the physiologically conditioned response and the purely cultural one, and it is frequently difficult to analyse out and segregate the two. The Chukchee of Siberia, for example, have a phenomenal quickness to anger, which they express by showing the teeth and growling like an animal – yet man's snout has long ceased being functionally useful in offensive or defensive biting as it has phylogenetically and continuously retreated from effective prognathism. But this behavior reappears again and again: the Malayan pagans, for example, raise the lip over the canine tooth when sneering and jeering. Is this instinctual reflex or mere motor habit? The Tasmanians stamped rapidly on the ground to express surprise or pleasure; Occidentals beat the palms of the hands together for the same purpose ordinarily, but in some rowdier contexts this is accompanied by whistling and a similar stamping of the feet. Europeans 'snort' with contempt; and the non-Mohammedan primitives of interior Malaya express disgust with a sudden expiration of the breath. In this particular instance, it is difficult to rid oneself of the notion that this is a consciously controlled act, to be sure, but nevertheless at least a 'symbolic sneeze' based upon a purely physiological reflex which does rid the nostrils of irritating matter. The favorite gesture of contempt of the Menomini Indians of Wisconsin – raising the clenched fist palm down up to the level of the mouth, then bringing it swiftly downwards, throwing forth the thumb and first two fingers – would seem to be based on the same 'instinctual' notion of rejection.

However, American Indian gestures soon pass over into the undisputedly linguistic area, as when two old men of different tribes who do not know a word of each other's spoken language, sit side by side and tell each other improper stories in the complex and highly articulate intertribal sign language of the Plains. These conventionalized gestures of the Plains sign language must of course be learned as a language is learned, for they are a kind of kinaesthetic ideograph, resembling written Chinese. The written Chinese may be 'read' in the Japanese and the Korean and any number of mutually unintelligible spoken Chinese dialects; similarly, the sign language may be 'read' in Comanche, in Cheyenne or in Pawnee, all of which belong to different language families. The primitive Australian sign language was evidently of the conventionalized Plains type also, for it reproduced words, not mere letters (since of course they had no written language), but unfortunately little is known in detail of its mechanisms.

Like the writing of the Chinese, Occidental man has a number of ideographs, but they are sublinguistic and primarily *signs to action* or *expressions of action*. Thus, in the standard symbolism of cartoons, a 'balloon' encircling print has signified *speaking* since at least the eighteenth century. Interestingly in a Maya painting on a vase from Guatemala of pre-Columbian times, we have the same speech 'balloons' enclosing ideographs representing what a chief and his vassal are saying, though what that is we do not know (Vaillant, 1941, plate 7, top). In Toltec frescoes speech is symbolized by foliated or noded crooks or scrolls, sometimes double, proceeding out of the mouths of human figures, although *what* is said is not indicated (Vaillant, 1941, plate 24). In the later Aztec codices written on wild fig-bark paper, speech is conventionalized by one or more little scrolls like miniature curled ostrich feathers coming out of the mouths of human beings, while motion or walking is indicated by footprints leading to where the person is now standing in the picture (Vaillant, 1941, plates 42, 57, 61). In American cartoons the same simple idea of footprints is also used. The ideograph of 'sawing wood' indicates the action of *snoring* or *sleeping*. A light bulb with radial lines means that a 'bright idea' has just occurred in the mind of the character above whose head it is written. While even children learn in time to understand these signs in context, no one would maintain that the electric-light 'sign' could naturally be understood by an individual from another tribe than our own. Birds singing, a spiral, or a five-pointed star means unconsciousness or semiconsciousness through concussion. A dotted line, if curved, indicates the past trajectory of a moving object; if straight and from eye to object, the action of seeing. None of these visual aids to understanding are part of objective nature. Sweat drops symbolize surprise or dumbfounding, although the physiology of this sign is thoroughly implausible. And

]%!*/=#?[/c& very often says the unspeakable, quite as? signifies query and ! surprise.

Many languages have *spoken* punctuation marks, which English grievously lacks. On the other hand, the speakers of English have a few *phonetic* 'ideographs', at least two of which invite to action. An imitation of a kiss, loudly performed, summons a dog, if that dog understands this much of English. A bilateral clucking of the tongue adjures a horse to 'giddyap', i.e. to commence moving or to move more smartly; and in some parts of the country at least, it has a secondary semantic employment in summoning barnyard fowl to their feeding. The dental-alveolar repeated clicking of the tongue, on the other hand, is not a symbolic ideophone to action, but a *moral comment* upon action, a strongly critical disapprobation largely confined in use to elderly females preoccupied with such moral commentary. These symbolic ideophones are used in no other way in our language; but in African Bushman and Hottentot languages, of course, these three sounds plus two others phonetically classified as 'clicks' (as opposed to sonants like b, d, g, z and surds like p, t, k, s, etc.) are regularly employed in words like any other consonants. It is nonsense to suppose that dogs, horses or chickens are equipped for 'instinctive' understanding or response to these human-made sounds, as much as that speakers of English have an instinctive understanding of Hottentot and Bushman. Certainly the sounds used in the Lake Titicaca plateau to handle llamas are entirely different.[6]

Sublinguistic 'language' can take a number of related forms. Among the Neolithic population of the Canary Islands there was a curious auxiliary 'language' of conventionalized whistles, signals which could be understood at greater distances than mere spoken speech. On four bugle tones, differently configurated, we can similarly order soldiers to such various actions as arising, assembling, eating, lowering a flag, and burying the dead. The drum language of West Africa, however, is more strictly linguistic than bugle calls. Many West African languages are tonemic, that is, they have pitch-accent somewhat like Chinese or Navaho. Drum language, therefore, by reproducing not only the rhythm but also the tonal configurations of familiar phrases and sentences, is able to send messages of high semantic sophistication and complexity, as easily recognizable as our 'Star-Spangled Banner' sung with rhythm and melody, but without words. The Kru send battle signals on multiple-pitched horns, but these are not conventional tunes like our bugle calls, but fully articulated sentences and phrases whose tonemic patterns they reproduce on an

6. La Barre (1947). All the tribes of the Provincia Oriental of Ecuador had the 'cluck of satisfaction' (Simpson, 1886, p. 94), which among the tribes of the Issa-Japura rivers is a 'sign of assent and pleasure' (Whiffen, 1905, p. 249).

instrument other than the human vocal cords. The Morse and International telegraph codes and Boy Scout and Navy flag communication (either with hand semaphores or with strings of variously shaped and colored flags) are of course mere auditory or visual alphabets, tied down except for very minor conventionalized abbreviations to the *spelling* of a given language. (The advantages of a phonetic script, however, are very evident when it comes to sending messages via a Morselike code for Chinese, which is written in ideographs which have different phonetic pronunciations in different dialects; Japanese has some advantage in this situation over Chinese in that its ideographs are already cumbrously paralleled in *katakana* and *hiragana* writing, which is quasi-phonetic.) Deaf-and-dumb language, if it is the mere spelling of words, is similarly bound to an alphabet; but as it becomes highly conventionalized it approaches the international supralinguistic nature of the Plains Indian sign language. Of this order are the symbols of mathematics, the conventionalizations on maps for topography, the symbol language for expressing meteorological happenings on weather maps, and international flag signals for weather. Modern musical notation is similarly international: a supralinguistic system which orders in great detail what to do, and with what intensity, rhythm, tempo, timbre and manner. Possibly the international nature of musical notation was influenced by the fact that medieval neume notation arose at a time when Latin was an international lingua franca, and also by the international nature of late feudal culture, rather than being an internationally-agreed-upon consensus of scientific symbolism. Based on the principles of musical notation, there have been several experimental attempts to construct an international system of dance notation, with signs to designate the position and motions of all parts of the body, with diacritical modifications to indicate tempo and the like. But while the motions of the classical ballet are highly stereotyped, they are semantically meaningless (unlike *natya* dancing in India and Ceylon, and Chinese and other Asiatic theatrics), so that this dance notation is mere *orders to action* like musical notation, with no other semantic content. Western dancing as an art form must appear insipid in its semantic emptiness to an Oriental who is used to articulate literary *meaning* in his dance forms. This is not to deny, however, that Occidental kinaesthetic language *may* be heavily imbued with great subtleties of meaning: the pantomime of the early Charlie Chaplin achieved at least a pan-European understanding and appreciation, while the implicit conventionalizations and stereotypes of Mickey Mouse (a psychiatrically most interesting figure!) are achieving currently an intercontinental recognition and enjoyment.

If all these various ways of *talking* be generously conceded to be purely cultural behavior, surely *walking* – although learned – is a purely physiological phenomenon since it is undeniably a panhuman trait which has brought about far-reaching functional and morphological changes in man as an animal. Perhaps it is, basically. And yet, there would seem to be clear evidence of cultural conditioning here. There is a distinct contrast in the gait of the Shans of Burma versus that of the hill people: the Kachins and the Palaungs keep time to each step by swinging the arms from side to side in front of the body in semicircular movements, but the Shans swing their arms in a straight line and do not bring the arms in front of the body. Experts among the American missionaries can detect the Shan from the Palaung and the Kachin, even though they are dressed in the same kinds of garment, purely from observing their respective gaits, and as surely as the character in a Mark Twain story detected a boy in girl's clothes by throwing a rat-chunker in his lap (the boy closed his legs, whereas a girl would spread her skirt). If an American Indian and an adult American male stride with discernible mechanical differences which may be imputed to the kinds of shoes worn and the varying hardness of the ground in woods or city, the argument will not convince those who know – but would find it hard to describe – that the Singhalese and the Chinese simply and unquestionably just do walk differently, even when both are barefooted. Amazonian tribes show marked sexual contrasts in their styles of walking: men place one foot directly in front of the other, toes straight forward, while women walk in a rather stilted, pigeon-toed fashion, the toes turned inward at an angle of some thirty degrees; it is regarded as a sign of power if the muscles of the thighs are made to come in contact with each other in walking. To pick a more familiar example, it is probable that a great many persons would agree with Sapir's contention that there does exist a peculiarly East European Jewish gait – a kind of kyphotic Ashkenazim shuffle or trudge – which is lost by the very first generation brought up in this country, and which, moreover, may not be observed in the Sephardic Jews of the Iberian Peninsula. Similar evidence comes from a recent news article: 'Vienna boasts that it has civilized the Russians ... has taught them how to walk like Europeans (some Russians from the steppes had a curious gait, left arm and left foot swinging forward at the same time).'[7] The last parenthesis plays havoc with behavioristic notions concerning allegedly quadrupedal engrams behind our 'normal' way of walking!

It is very clear that the would-be 'natural' and 'instinctive' gestures of actors change both culturally and historically. The back-of-the-hand-to-

7. Hoffman (1947, p. 31). A related kind of motor-habit – which is of course conscious – was that of the Plains Indian men who wore the buffalo robe 'gathered ... about the person in a way that emphasized their action or the expression of emotion' (*Handbook of American Indians North of Mexico*, 1907–1910). For the Amazonians, see Whiffen (1905, p. 271).

the-forehead and sideways-stagger of the early silent films to express intense emotion is expressed nowadays, for example, by making the already expressionless compulsive sullen mask of the actress one shade still more flat: the former technique of exaggerated pantomime is no doubt related to the limitations of the silent film, the latter to the fact that even a raised eyebrow may travel six feet in the modern close-up. The 'deathless acting' of the immortal Bernhardt, witnessed now in ancient movies, is scarcely more dated than the middle-Garbo style, and hardly more artificially stylized than Hepburn's or Crawford's. Indeed, for whatever reason, Bernhardt herself is reported to have fainted upon viewing her own acting in an early movie of *Camille* (Bardèche and Brasillach, 1938, p. 130). There are undoubtedly both fashions and individual styles in acting, just as there are in painting and in music composition and performance, and all are surely far removed from the instinctual gesture. The fact that each contemporary audience can receive the communication of the actor's gestures is a false argument concerning the 'naturalness' of that gesture: behavior of the order of the 'linguistic' (communication in terms of culturally agreed-upon arbitrary symbols) goes far beyond the purely verbal and the spoken.

That this is true can be decisively proved by a glance at Oriental theatrics. Chinese acting is full of stylized gestures which 'mean' to the audience that the actor is stepping over the threshold into a house, mounting a horse, or the like; and these conventionalizations are just as stereotyped as the colors of the acting masks which indicate the formalized personalities of the stock characters, villains or heroes or supernaturals. In Tamil movies made in South India, the audience is quickly informed as to who is the villain and who the hero by the fact that the former wears Europeanized clothing, whereas the latter wears the native *dhoti*. But this is elementary: for the intricate *natya* dancing of India, the postural dance dramas of Bali, and the sacred *hula* of Polynesia are all telling articulated stories in detailed gestural language. That one is himself illiterate in this language, while even the child or the ignorant countryman sitting beside one on the ground has an avid and understanding enjoyment of the tableau, leaves no doubt in the mind that this *is* a gestural language and that there *are* sublinguistic kinaesthetic symbolisms of an arbitrary but learnable kind.

Hindu movies are extraordinarily difficult for the Occidental man to follow and to comprehend, not only because he must be fortified with much reading and knowledge to recognize mythological themes and such stereotypes as the *deus-ex-machina* appearance of Hanuman the monkey-god, but also because Americans are characteristically illiterate in the area of gesture language. The kinaesthetic 'business' of even accomplished and imaginative stage actors like Sir Laurence Olivier and Ethel Barrymore is limited by the rudimentary comprehension of their audiences. Americans watch enthusiastically the muscular skills of an athlete in *doing* something, but they display a proud muckerism toward the dance as an art form which attempts to *mean* something. There are exceptions to this illiteracy, of course, notably among some psychiatrists and some ethnologists. H. S. Sullivan, for example, is known to many for his acute understanding of the postural tonuses of his patients. Another psychiatrist, E. J. Kempf, evidences in the copious illustrations of his 'Psychopathology' a highly cultivated sense of the kinaesthetic language of tonuses in painting and sculpture, and can undoubtedly discover a great deal about a patient merely by glancing at him. The linguist Stanley Newman, has a preternatural skill in recognizing psychiatric syndromes through the individual styles of tempo, stress and intonation.[8] The gifted cartoonist, William Steig, has produced, in *The Lonely Ones*, highly sophisticated and authentic drawings of the postures and tonuses of schizophrenia, depression, mania, paranoia, hysteria, and in fact the whole gamut of psychiatric syndromes. Among anthropologists, W. H. Sheldon is peculiarly sensitive and alert to the emotional and temperamental significance of constitutional tonuses.[9] I believe that it is by no means entirely an illusion that an experienced teacher can come into a classroom of new students and predict with some accuracy the probable quality of individual scholastic accomplishment – even as judged by other professors – by distinguishing the unreachable, unteachable *Apperceptions masse*-less sprawl of one student, from the edge-of-the-seat starved avidity and intentness of another. Likewise, an experienced lecturer can become acutely aware of the body language of his listeners and respond to it appropriately until the room fairly dances with communication and counter-communication, head-noddings, and the tenseness of listeners soon to be prodded into public speech.

8. Newman (1941; 1933; 1939; 1944); Newman and Mather (1938). The Witoto and Bororo have a curious motor habit: 'When an Indian talks he sits down – no conversation is ever carried on when the speakers are standing unless it is a serious difference of opinion under discussion; nor, when he speaks, does the Indian look at the person addressed, any more than the latter watches the speaker. Both look at some outside objects. This is the attitude also of the Indian when addressing more than one listener, so that he appears to be talking to someone not visibly present.' A story-teller turns his back on the listener and talks to the wall of the hut (Whiffen, 1905, p. 254).

9. Sheldon (1942). The argument of one variety of athletosome or somatotonic scientist that Sheldon is unable or unconcerned to muscle his findings into manageable, manipulable statistical forms wherewith to bludgeon and compel the belief of the unperceiving, is of course peculiarly irrelevant. The psychiatrist soaked in clinical experience is similarly helpless in his didactic relations with a public that either has not, or cannot, or will not see what he has repeatedly observed clinically.

The 'body language' of speakers in face-to-face conversation may often be seen to subserve the purposes of outright linguistic communication. The peoples of Mediterranean origin have developed this to a high degree. In Argentina, for example, the gesture language of the hands is called 'ademanes' or 'with the hands' (Daniels, 1941). Often the signs are in no need of language accompaniment: 'What a crowd!' is stated by forming the fingers into a tight cluster and shaking them before you at eye level; 'Do you take me for a sucker?' is asked by touching just beneath the eye with a finger, accompanying this with appropriate facial expressions of jeering or reproach as the case might be; and 'I haven't the faintest idea' is indicated by stroking beneath the chin with the back of the palm. One Argentine gentleman, reflecting the common notion that ademanes have the same vulgarity and undignified nature as slang – appropriate only for youngsters or lower-class folk – nevertheless, within five minutes of this statement, had himself twirled an imaginary moustache ('How swell!') and stroked one hand over the other, nodding his head wisely ('Ah ha! there's hanky-panky going on there somewhere!'). Argentine gesture-language is nearly as automatic and unconscious as spoken language itself, for when one attempts to collect a 'vocabulary' of ademanes, the Argentine has to stop and think of situations first which recall the ademanes that 'naturally' follow. The naturalness of at least one of these might be disputed by Americans, for the American hand-gesture meaning 'go away' (palm out and vertical, elbow somewhat bent, arm extended vigorously as the palm is bent to a face-downward horizontal position, somewhat as a baseball is thrown and in a manner which could be rationalized as a threatened or symbolic blow or projectile-hurling) is the same which in Buenos Aires would serve to summon half the waiters in a restaurant, since it means exactly the opposite, 'Come here!' When the Argentines use the word mañana in the familiar sense of the distant and improbable future, they accompany the word by moving the hand forward, palm down, and extending the fingers lackadaisically – a motion which is kinaesthetically and semantically related perhaps to the Argentine 'come here!' since this symbolically 'brings', while mañana 'pushes off'. Kissing the bunched fingertips, raising them from the mouth and turning the head with rolled or closed eyes, means 'Wonderful! Magnificent!', basically perhaps as a comment or allusion to a lady, but in many remotely derived senses as well. 'Wonderful!' may also be expressed by shaking one of the hands smartly so that the fingers make an audible clacking sound, similar to the snapping of the fingers, but much louder. But this gesture may signify pain as well as enjoyment, for if one steps on an Argentine's toes, he may shake his fingers as well as saying Ai yai for 'ouch!' The same gesture, furthermore, can be one of impatience, 'Get a move on!' Were one to define this gesture semantically, then, in a lexicon of *ademanes*, it would have to be classified as a nondescript intensificative adverb whose predication is indicated by the context. In fast repartee an Argentine, even though he may not be able to get a word in edgewise, can make caustic and devastating critiques of the speaker and his opinions, solely through the subtle, timed use of *ademanes*.

A study of conventional gesture languages (including even those obscene ones of the *mano cornuta*, the thumbed nose, the *mano fica*, the thumbnail snapped out from the point of the canine tooth, and so forth,[10] as well as those more articulated ones of the Oriental dance dramas), a study of the body language of constitutional types (the uncorticated, spinal-reflex spontaneity and *legato* feline quality of the musclebound athletosome, his body knit into rubbery bouncing tonuses even in repose; the collapsed colloid quality of the epicurean viscerotonic whose tensest tonus is at best no more than that of the chorion holding the yolk advantageously centered in the albumen of an egg, or the muscle habituated into a tendon supporting a flitch of bacon; and the multiple-vectored, tangled-stringiness of the complex 'high-strung' cerebrotonic, whose conceptual alternatives and nuances of control are so intricately involved in his cortex as to inhibit action), and the study of psychiatric types (the Egyptian-statue grandeur and hauteur of the paranoiac's pose; the catatonic who offers his motor control to the outsider because he has withdrawn his own executive ego into an inner, autistic cerebral world and has left no one at the switchboard; the impermanent, varying, puppet-on-a-string, spastic tonuses of the compulsive neurotic which picture myotonically his ambivalence, his rigidities and his perfectionism; the broken-lute despair of the depressive; and the distractable, *staccato*, canine, benzedrine-muscledness of the manic) – all might offer us new insights into psychology, psychiatry, ethnology and linguistics alike.

10. The only place I have seen this discussed recently is in an article by Feldman (1941). In the same periodical is an exquisitely sensitive interpretation of one person's interpretation of the signs of the zodiac in terms of positions and tonuses of the human body (Webster, 1940). Other papers of the few that could be cited with relevance to the present problem, would include: Critchley (1939); Allport and Vernon (1933); Hayes (1940); Deutsch (1947); Schilder (1935); Pear (1935); Flugel (1929); La Meri (c. 1940); von Laban (c. 1928).

References

ALLPORT, G. W., and VERNON, P. E. (1933), *Studies in Expressive Movement*, Macmillan.

BARDÈCHE, M., and BRASILLACH, R. (1938), *The History of Motion Pictures*, New York.

BEST, E. (1924), *The Maori*, Wellington, N.Z.

BUREAU OF AMERICAN ETHNOLOGY (1907–1910), *Handbook of American Indians North of Mexico*, Bulletin 30, Washington, D.C.

CRITCHLEY, M. (1939), *The Language of Gesture*, Edward Arnold.

DANIELS, A. (1941), 'Hand-made repartee', *New York Times*, 5 October.

DARWIN, C. (1872), *The Expression of the Emotions in Man and Animals*, Murray.

DEUTSCH, F. (1947), 'Analysis of postural behavior', *Psychoanal. Q.*, vol. 16, pp. 195–213.

FELDMAN, S. (1941), 'The blessing of the Kohenites', *American Imago*, vol. 2, pp. 315–18.

FLUGEL, J. C. (1929), 'On the mental attitude to present-day clothing', *Brit. J. med. Psychol.*, vol. 9, p. 97.

GORER, G. (1935), *African Dances*, New York.

HADDON, A. C. (ed.) (1904), *Report on the Cambridge Expedition to the Torres Straits*, IV, Cambridge.

HAYES, F. C. (1940), 'Should we have a dictionary of gestures?', *Southern Folklore Quarterly*, vol. 4, pp. 239–45.

HEARN, L. (1894), 'The Japanese smile', in *Glimpses of Unfamiliar Japan*, New York.

HITCHCOCK, R., 'The Ainos of Yezo', in *Papers on Japan*.

HOFFMAN, P. (1947), 'Twilight in the Heldenplatz', *Time*, 9 June.

HOLLIS, A. C. (1905), *The Masai, Their Language and Folklore*, Oxford.

HOLT, E. B. (1931), *Animal Drive and the Learning Process*, New York.

HOSE, C., and MACDOUGALL, W. (1912), *The Pagan Tribes of Borneo*, I, London.

KAHN, M. C. (1929), 'Notes on the Saramaccaner Bush Negroes of Dutch Guiana', *Amer. Anthrop.*, vol. 31, p. 473.

KLINEBERG, O. (1935), *Race Differences*, New York.

LA BARRE, W. (1947), *The Aymara Indians of the Lake Titicaca Plateau*, Memoir 68, American Anthropological Association.

LA MERI, (c. 1940), *Gesture Language of the Hindu Dance*, New York.

LANDOR, A. H. S. (1893), *Alone with the Hairy Ainu*, London.

LOWIE, R. H. (1929), *Are We Civilized?*, New York.

LUBBOCK, J. (1872), *Prehistoric Times*, New York.

NEWMAN, S. S. (1933), 'Further experiments in phonetic symbolism', *Am. J. Psychol.*, vol. 45, pp. 53–7.

NEWMAN, S. S. (1939), 'Personal symbolism in language patterns', *Psychiatry*, vol. 2, pp. 177–84.

NEWMAN, S. S. (1941), 'Behavior patterns in linguistic structure, a case study', in L. Spier, A. T. Hallowell and S. S. Newman (eds.), *Language, Culture and Personality, Essays in Memory of Edward Sapir*, Banta.

NEWMAN, S. S. (1944), 'Cultural and psychological features in English intonation', *Trans. N. Y. Acad. Sci.*, ser. II, vol. 7, pp. 45–54.

NEWMAN, S. S., and MATHER, V. G. (1938), 'Analysis of spoken language of patients with affective disorders', *Amer. J. Psychiat.*, vol. 94, pp. 913–42.

PEAR, T. (1935), 'Suggested parallels between speaking and clothing', *Acta psychol.*, vol. 1, pp. 191–201.

PERKINS, J. (1851), 'Journal of a tour from Oroomish to Mosul, through the Koordish Mountains, and a visit to the ruins of Nineveh', *J. Amer. orient. Soc.*, vol. 2.

RADCLIFFE-BROWN, A. R. (1922), *The Andaman Islanders*, Cambridge.

SCHILDER, P. (1935), *The Image and Appearance of the Human Body*, Psyche Monographs.

SHELDON, W. H. (1942), *The Varieties of Temperament*, New York & London.

SHIROKOGOREFF, S. M. (1924), *Social Organization of the Manchus*, Extra Vol. III, North China Branch, Royal Asiatic Society, Shanghai.

SIMPSON, A. (1886). *Travels in the Wilds of Ecuador and Exploration of the Putumayo River*.

SKEAT, W. W., and BLAGDEN, C. O. (1906), *Pagan races of the Malay Peninsula*, London.

TORDAY, E., and JOYCE, T. A. (1910), *Notes Ethnographiques sur les Peuples Communément Appelés Bakuba, ainsi que sur les Peuplades Apparentées, les Bushonga*, Brussels.

TURNBULL, J. (1813), *A Voyage Round the World*, London.

VAILLANT, G. C. (1941), *The Aztecs of Mexico*, New York.

VON LABAN, R. (c. 1928), *Laban's Dance Notations*, New York.

WEBSTER, D. (1940), 'The origin of the signs of the zodiac', *American Imago* vol. 1, pp. 31–47.

WHIFFEN, T. (1905), *The North West Amazons*, London.

12 A. E. Scheflen

The Significance of Posture in Communication Systems

A. E. Scheflen, 'The significance of posture in communication systems'
Psychiatry, vol. 27, 1964, 316–31.

In the course of research in psychotherapy, my colleagues and I have turned up an unexpected finding: configurations of posture or body positioning indicate at a glance a great deal about what is going on in an interaction. This paper will discuss these postural configurations, which are reliable indicators of the following aspects of communication:

1. They demarcate the components of individual behavior that each person contributes to the group activities.
2. They indicate how the individual contributions are related to each other.
3. They define the steps and order in the interaction – that is, the 'program'.

All English-speaking people (who also move 'in English') seem to utilize this postural information *unconsciously* for orienting themselves in a group. A *conscious* knowledge of these postural functions is of great value in research in human behavior and in studying or conducting a psychotherapy session informedly.

Cultural determination of behavior

In recent years social scientists have belatedly come to realize the importance of non-lexical behaviors in human communication. Although there are many who still believe that non-lexical communicative behaviors – such as postures – are individual, unique expressions which occur in an infinite variety of forms, our research leads us to quite another view: such behaviors occur in characteristic, standard configurations, whose common recognizability is the basis of their value in communication. That these behaviors are regular, uniform entities within a culture tremendously simplifies both research into human interaction and practical understanding of it. These forms are so familiar that a description of them leads to immediate recognition by most people, without elaborate details or measurements.

There are only twenty-six letters in the English alphabet, with no normally-occurring intermediate forms. Similarly, we estimate that there are no more than about thirty traditional American gestures. There is an even smaller number of culturally-standard postural configurations which are of shared communicative significance for Americans. The regularity of the communicative system extends not only to the form of the configurations, but to the contexts in which they appear. Each of these units occurs – and, for non-deviant, acculturated Americans, occurs *only* – in a limited and standard number of situations. Just as in English the letter 'p' does not occur in sequences like 'spn' or 'tpz', so a posture such as sitting back in a chair rarely occurs in subordinate males who are engaged in selling an idea to a male of higher status.

These generalizations obviously do not mean that all Americans behave exactly alike in manifesting a particular communicative pattern. A unit identified as standard includes a *range* of behaviors which are recognizable as the expected configuration. Variations occur within subgroupings in a culture – for example, within institutions such as medicine or religion, within geographic regions, within social classes, and so forth. Variations in style also occur, related to differences in personality. Finally, there is specialization according to gender, age, status, position, health, and so on. The units that are performed must be familiar to all members of the group, but all members of the group do not necessarily *use* all of the units. A male of thirty from New England who is a graduate in engineering will have a repertoire appropriate to his background. His repertoire will be similar to that performed by others of the same social niche, but different from that of a Midwestern housewife. It is quite possible for a specialist in communication to determine precisely what part of Pennsylvania a speaker comes from by his dialect, and he can also detect a native of Wisconsin by the manner in which he moves his brow in conversation. But even a lay observer is aware of gross cultural differences. The pantomimist knows instinctively that English and American males cross their legs differently (though he may not know that he knows), and the audience knows immediately whether he is portraying an Englishman or an American.

Now, the theoretical point is this: human social behavior is neither universal for all members of Homo sapiens nor individual and unique for each person. The musculoskeletal underpinnings of human behavior are determined by biological form and transmitted by genetic mechanisms, but every culture molds the raw actions according to its own traditions. Intromission and ejaculation are universal human behaviors, but *none* of the other activities involved in mating is universal. The forms of how coitus is performed differ from culture to culture. The ability to speak is universal, but language is culturally determined. Thus, to understand the meaning of gestures, postures, inflections and even affective expressions, it is necessary to look critically across cultures, across classes, across institutions.

To examine human behavior in this way – that is, to examine its common range within a traditional group – is to take a cultural view. This approach has been less common in behavioral science than looking at unique personality factors, but it has been used in research such as Pike's (1954), and very recently has been used to study the mental hospital (Goffman, 1957, 1961). This cultural approach underlies the research that my coworkers and I have been doing in psychotherapy and communication, and it will be from this viewpoint that the findings about posture will be reported here.

Intention and function in communication

In psychiatry, human group behavior has traditionally been examined in terms of the personal, unique life experiences and behavioral expressions of each subject. This is a psychological view. More recently, the interaction *between* individuals has become of interest to psychiatrists. The social psychological approach to such interaction examines how one person's behavior affects another. The sociological viewpoint considers the organization of individuals as a group. All of these approaches focus upon the individual or group, in contrast with the cultural approach, which emphasizes the discovery of the traditional formats or templates, learned and used by each member of a culture, that determine behavior. These varying views in no way represent in themselves competitive or alternative truths; but whichever one is used determines how researchers approach the quest for the function or meaning of an element of human behavior.

The psychological approach traditionally answers any question about meaning with a statement about the motivations or intention of the individual who performs the actions. But this type of explanation is too narrow in itself to account for the meaning or *function* of behavior in a group. In the first place, human behavior can be communicative whether or not it is *intended* to communicate. To one who recognizes it, the rash of measles is informative, but does not, of necessity, signify that the patient means to convey that he is ill. If a psychotherapist traditionally makes a summarizing interpretation at the end of each session, the patient soon learns that the onset of the interpretation period indicates the imminent termination of the session. But the intent of the interpretation was not necessarily to end the session. *The intent of an interactant and the function that a behavior actually has in a group process must be conceptually distinguished.*

The behaviors in a group combine to serve social purposes beyond the instinctual aims of any member. The fact that the activities of a group ultimately satisfy the needs of an individual member is not construed to mean that this is the purpose of the group. Group activity is concerned primarily with minute-by-minute control, negotiation of aims and relationships, adherence to form, and so on – the equilibrium of the group itself.

As specific groups have evolved, each has developed traditional forms of interaction which the individual must learn to use and recognize if he is to meet his personal needs. He must negotiate his position within the given forms of a given society.

Thus, every American speaker generally raises his head slightly at the end of statements to which he expects an answer. He does so because all other Americans recognize this postural form for eliciting an answer. It may be that raising the head has other, strictly personal or fanciful meanings for a particular person; but this is beside the point in terms of what is commonly understood by the communicative signal of head-raising. To elicit an answer to his question, the speaker must perform the head movement in the customary and recognized manner. If he wishes the personal meaning of the movement to be understood, he will have to learn another way of communicating it.

Communication, then, includes *all behaviors by which a group forms, sustains, mediates, corrects and integrates its relationships*. In the flow of an interaction, communicative behaviors serve to give continuous notification of the states of each participant and of the relationships that obtain between them. Individuals growing up in a culture must learn these communicative behaviors and perform them correctly if they are to be comfortable, perhaps even if they are to survive, in their world.

The method of research

The research that my colleagues and I have been doing has involved a comparative study of therapists conducting sessions. We have examined about eighteen therapists, representing a wide range of theoretical and doctrinal viewpoints, from orthodox psychoanalysis to very active and manipulative schools. We make sound motion picture recordings of selected sessions and analyse these films according to a method known as Context Analysis in order to determine the common denominators of communicative behavior in psychotherapy. In this way, we hope to determine what the currently prevailing psychotherapy practices are. We have found so far that all psychotherapy is strikingly similar in basic configurations, regardless of the identity of the therapist or the school of psychotherapy that he espouses.[1]

Context analysis – which has evolved out of traditional natural history

1. In our view, the major differences in psychotherapy systems are not to be found in what happens, but in the conceptions or theories about what happens. What a psychotherapist or a group says about the activities of a session may differ enormously from what others believe is occurring. This seems to be the case in all human activities. Einstein once pointed out that to learn what physicists do, one must observe them at work rather than ask them what they do (1933, pp. 34–40).

methods – has provided systematic ways of testing how elements of behavior are organized in the natural structure of a communicational system.[2]
The function of a behavior is determined by comparing what happens in
a situation when it is present, with what happens in the same situation
when it is absent. To determine the function of thyroxin, a physiologist
might excise the thyroid from living dogs and examine the physiological
changes that invariably occur. To be more certain of his data, he could
then inject dogs with thyroxin and cross-compare the resultant third
physiological state with that of the intact and that of the thyrodectomized
animals. Similarly, to determine the meaning of a type of behavior such as
interpretation in psychotherapy, one can examine the systems of individual
behavior and relationships that inhere at times when interpretations
occur, and compare them with those that inhere at times when the interpretations do not occur. This is the way I have derived the meaning of
the postural activities to be described.

All too often, research into the meaning of 'non-verbal' elements of
communication has consisted merely of isolating a fragment, counting its
frequency, and then free-associating or asking subjects to free-associate
about its meaning, as if elements of behavior carried meaning in and of
themselves. Consequently, the literature is filled with untested speculations
that such and such a gesture or postural shift reveals this or that instinctual
motivation. My coworkers and I believe that the essential discipline for
determining meaning is *to examine the relations of an element to its context*.
The physiologist could not determine the function of the thyroid if he
threw away the dog and examined only the isolated thyroid. Behavioral
scientists could go through endless rituals of counting and measuring and
speculating about the meaning of an event and having judges vote on the
most popular speculation. But the chance to determine experimentally
the function of an element is lost if the system in which it functions is
scrapped.

This paper will present the findings about the significance and function of
posture in American interactions in general, and in psychotherapy in
particular, from three points of view, all within the cultural frame of
reference:

1. A focus upon the behaviors of one participant and an indication of the
   units or parts he contributes.
2. A structural view of the interaction as a whole, and the relationship of
   each of the parts to the others.

2. Birdwhistell and I have described these methods in detail in the following publications: Birdwhistell (1952; 1963; forthcoming); Scheflen (1963; 1965); Scheflen *et al.*
(forthcoming).

3. An analysis of the steps or order of progression of the format for a group through time.

Postural indicators of units

Observed through time, the behaviors that make up communicative programs appear to be a continuous stream of events, but actually they are grouped into standard units of structure. These units are not arbitrary divisions made up spontaneously by an interactant or imposed presumptively by an investigator; *they are specific constellations of behavior built into a culture, learned and perceived in communication as Gestalten.*

The structure of language provides a familiar example of this kind of arrangement. Every school child learns about units of language.[3] Syllables are formed into words, and the words are arranged in a given order (identifying them as parts of speech) that occurs in a given context from which meaning can be derived. These characteristics – components, organization and context – allow identification of the structural units of language, and their hierarchical arrangement.

This type of hierarchical arrangement is characteristic for any phenomenon of nature. Planets are part of solar systems, which, in turn, are parts of galaxies. Organizations of molecules make up cells, which, in turn, are parts of larger structural units called organs, which make up organisms and so on (Bertalanffy, 1950, 1960). In music, certain combinations of rests and notes constitute a measure, so many measures a passage, so many passages a movement, and so on.

Just as language consists of a hierarchy of increasingly more inclusive units, so a communications system as a whole is an integrated arrangement of structural units deriving from kinesic, tactile, lexical and other elements. This extended view of communication beyond language is new and only slightly bolstered by research, but investigators already note that the system is organized hierarchically into larger and larger structural units. I have designated the units that we have identified beyond the syntactic sentence as the point, the position[4] and the presentation.[5]

These complex units seem to occur generally in American communication. I am going to describe each of them briefly here, and show how posture and postural shifts mark their duration and termination. Even a sketchy knowledge of them enables one to make practical use of postural observa-

3. In linguistics, the hierarchical order is as follows: phone, phoneme, morpheme, syntactic sentence.
4. My use of the term 'position' is not to be confused with the term 'posture'. I use position to designate one type of structural unit; posture, as one modality of communication.
5. In another publication I have described these structural units of communication as they occurred, in a psychotherapy session (Scheflen *et al.*, forthcoming).

tions in understanding interactions such as psychotherapy. Such knowledge brings into awareness what American interactants know unconsciously – when the steps of a communicative stream begin and end and how long each unit is in effect.

It is well known in structural linguistics that the unit known as the syntactic sentence is marked by a terminal change in pitch (Hockett, 1958; Gleason, 1955). These 'markers' are called junctures. There are three types in English: a rise in pitch, indicating a question; a fall in pitch, indicating completion; and a holding of pitch, indicating that the speaker will continue.

In 1962 Birdwhistell demonstrated that these junctures were also accompanied by a movement of the head, eyes or hands (Birdwhistell, research seminars, 1962–3). While the attitudes of head, eyes and hands are not in traditional usage considered 'posture', such actions are analogous to the use of posture in the larger units to be described. The occurrence of this pitch and kinesic activity at the termination of each syntactic sentence is illustrated in Figure 1.

The point

When an American speaker uses a series of syntactic sentences in a conversation, he changes the position of his head and eyes every few sentences. He may turn his head right or left, tilt it, cock it to one side or the other, or flex or extend his neck so as to look toward the floor or ceiling. Regardless of the kind of shift in head posture, the attitude is held for a few sentences, then shifted to another position. Each of these shifts I believe marks the end of a structural unit at the next level higher than the syntactic sentence. This unit I have tentatively named a 'point' because it corresponds crudely to making a point in a discussion. The maintenance of head position indicates the duration of the point. The use of head-eye postural markers in points is illustrated in Figure 2.

Most interactants in a given psychotherapy session show a repertoire of three to five points, which they use over and over. For example, the therapist in Figure 2 used two points repeatedly.

While there may be great variety in the manifest content of the speech accompanying each type of point, it is usually possible to abstract some theme that belongs with each category. For instance, explanations may occur with one type of head position, interruption with another, interpretations with yet another, and listening with a fourth. Or there may be different modes of relating corresponding to each type of point. The patient in Figure 2 accompanied head cocking to the right with baby talk and other regressive behavior, while in head-erect postures he spoke aggressively and in stilted formal language.

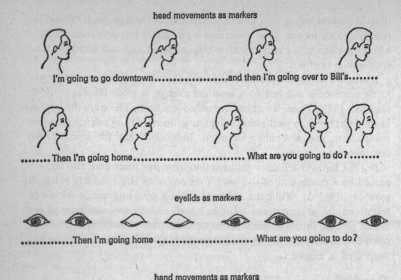

head movements as markers

I'm going to go downtown......................and then I'm going over to Bill's........

.... Then I'm going home................................. What are you going to do? ....

eyelids as markers

...............Then I'm going home .... What are you going to do?

hand movements as markers

.... Then I'm going home.................... What are you going to do?

Figure 1 Postural-kinesic markers of American syntactic sentences

It is difficult to believe that the head-eye points for a person during a thirty-minute interview are this stereotyped and repetitive. Yet, the participants in this and other interactions that I have studied rarely show greater range or variability. They use the same cluster of postures again and again.

The position

A sequence of several points constitutes a larger unit of communication that I call the 'position'. This unit corresponds roughly to a point of view that an interactant may take in an interaction. The position is marked by a gross postural shift involving at least half the body. Positions generally last from about half a minute to five or six minutes, although psychoanalytic therapists may hold the position in which they listen without speaking or moving grossly twenty minutes or more. Most interactants in the social situations that we have observed show about two to four positions.

The psychotherapist

Point 1: Head slightly downward, cocked to the right, averting eyes from patient. Used while listening to patient.

Marker: Head tilted up. Marks termination of Point 1 and transition to Point 2. Signals preparation to interpret.

Point 2: Head erect, looking directly at patient. Used while making an interpretation.

Marker: Head turned far to the right, away from patient. Marks termination of Point 2.

The patient

Point 1: Head erect, turned to his right. Used while therapist is interpreting and avoids her gaze.

Point 2: Head facing directly toward therapist. Used during response to interpretation. Stares at therapist as he minimizes interpetation's importance.

Point 3: Head cocked, gaze to therapist's left. Patient takes up narrative of another incident not manifestly related to therapist's interpretation, accompanied by childlike manner of speech.

Figure 2 Head placements and markers of points in a psychotherapist and patient

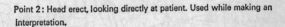
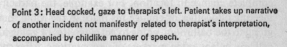

Everyone is familiar in a general way with the markers of positions. Imagine a participant in a conference, leaning back in his chair, smoking, remaining silent as another person expresses a point of view. The listener experiences growing disagreement and decides finally that he must state his viewpoint. His shift begins. He stamps out his cigarette, uncrosses his legs, leans forward, and, perhaps with some gesture, begins his exposition. Two markers of positions for a psychotherapy session are illustrated in Figure 3.

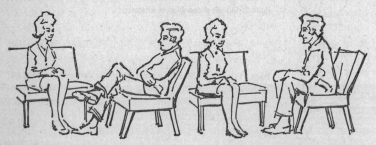

The therapist begins the session seated, with legs and arms crossed, and leaning backward, away from the patient. In this posture, he uses the clinical tactic of not answering and 'eliciting free associations'.

After about five minutes, he leans toward the patient, uncrossing his legs. After this postural shift, he is more active-reassuring, interpreting, conversing. He is likely to think of his tactic as 'establishing rapport'.

Figure 3 Body postures of a psychotherapist indicating positions

In Figure 3 the therapist shifted from an initial position in which he listened to free associations, to a position in which he interpreted and reassured the patient actively. Later he shifted back to his original position and resumed clinical 'inactivity'. This is a characteristic sequence in psychotherapy.

The presentation

The largest unit we have studied, the presentation, consists of the totality of one person's positions in a given interaction. Presentations have a duration of from several minutes to several hours, and the terminals are a complete change in location. For example, the participant may leave the meeting altogether or change his place in the room. Such familiar acts as going to the bathroom, going to get cigarettes or going to make a telephone call are, in fact, often markers of presentations. After such an interruption, the re-entrant usually assumes a different role or engages in a new type of interaction.

There appear, then, to be at least three levels of structural units above the syntactic sentence that are marked by postural activities. Whether or not there are other actions that can substitute for postural markers we do not yet know, nor do we know for certain whether or not there are other levels or larger units that have not yet been visualized. And we do not yet have clear-cut knowledge about differences incident to ethnic backgrounds or class.

Our research shows that the function of an individual's posture in communication is to mark or punctuate the units at multiple levels.[6] The unconscious observation of postures and shifts seems to help American communicants orient themselves in interaction. An explicit knowledge of the markers can increase the psychotherapist's awareness of what is happening and of what kind of unconscious boundaries both he and the patient are observing.

The clinical significance of postural markers

The occurrence of markers allows identification of the boundaries of different states of an individual in social relations. For instance, Peter Knapp (personal communication, 1964) told me of a patient who shifted his posture on the couch at the middle of every session, thus having two basic postural orientations per session. Knapp noted that the patient had very different affects, memories and attitudes in one than in the other. I have often noted similar behavior in my own practice. Each state represents a structural unit, probably at the level of the position.

One can quickly observe the association of characteristic positions and presentations with such clinical states as autism, depression, hysteria or hypomania. I also believe that different presentations are accompanied by different orders of consciousness. Often, for instance, the memory of what was said or done in certain positions or presentations becomes limited when a speaker moves into a second position or presentation. Certain positions are associated with what is clinically regarded as regressive behavior. Each of the multiple identifications of a person may be accompanied by some particular position and its postural markers. The clinician, once alerted to the function of posture, will quickly collect his own observations as to *what* postures are used in various clinical states.

6. Studies of posture have previously been done from two quite different viewpoints: (1) speculations about the psychological or psychodynamic implications of posture, and (2) comparisons of postures in different cultures. Deutsch (1951) studied the psychodynamics of posture in psychotherapy. Berger (1958) reviewed aspects of positioning in group psychotherapy. Hewes (1957) has made the most exhaustive cross-cultural studies. La Barre (1947) has discussed the role of movement and posture in cultural anthropology. Charney (forthcoming) has taken up the investigation of posture in communication.

Just as the markers of the syntactic sentences indicate that a speaker expects a response or has not completed his thought, so the markers of larger units also seem to indicate the type of response expected. For example, postural shifts involving movement away from others often seem to indicate completion and temporary disengagement.

But the markers must not be overloaded with significances they do not have. They mark the natural divisions in a behavioral stream. They advise the observer to search the stream for the divisions of some interval, for some shift in activity. They do not as yet, however, indicate what the behavior or shift is. The postural shift is like the referee's whistle at the end of a play in football. It means that some unit is ended, but does not identify the unit. Or it can be likened to the ringing of the church bell in a small Italian town. The townsmen are told that something is happening. Unless they have additional information they do not know *what* is happening.

The meaning or function of an event is not contained in itself but in its relation to its context (Bateson, forthcoming). A letter of the alphabet does not carry meaning until it is part of a word, which is part of a sentence, which is part of a discourse and a situation. Just as psychoanalysts now avoid listing dream symbols and their meanings without regard to the life situations, transference and past experiences, so social investigators must avoid a glossary in which one kind of postural shift 'means' this and another kind means that.

Researchers must also avoid assigning special psychological or psycho-pathological significance to the markers. To be sure, individuals add their own styles to the performance of markers. Psychotics may perform them ever so slowly or in exaggerated excursion or rapidity, but so far no pathognomonic markers have been identified. The markers used correspond to cultural divisions. They are rarely, if ever, idiosyncratic. Like other kinesic activities, they appear to be primarily ethnic, but they may also – though less clearly – be related to age, class, gender, status and occupation. Dampening the excursion of postural shifts, for example, can be Irish, Southeastern European Jewish and psychoanalytic. There is every evidence that markers and other kinesics vary from culture to culture. The limitations of generalization legislate against assigning purely individual significance on the one hand and universal meaning on the other. When a therapist has identified the postural markers for his ten o'clock patient, he cannot extrapolate them willy-nilly to his eleven o'clock patient. One patient might be a Midwestern German and the other a Southern Protestant Anglo-Saxon, and there might be differences on other grounds, too. The markers must always be seen in the context of the individual's background and the situation.

However, one vital aspect of the applicable generalizations is worth repeating: a sociocultural point must not be confused with a personality point. Unless there is individual deviation these markers are not personality matters at all, but points of cultural structure. I do not need to explain postural shifting psycho-dynamically any more than I need to explain wearing clothes or speaking English from the psychological point of view. Each of us has internalized these aspects of culture and our use of them involves psychological processes, but the fact that one performs postural markers is of cultural derivation – they are part of being American or being a psychotherapist. Any intuitive speculation about unique motivation or psychopathology in performing them may be correct, but misses the point. What a postural shift signifies is *not a personality quality but a communicative structural event.*

Postural indicators of relationships

If one directs attention away from individuals in a group and toward the relations between and among members, one finds that posture has another order of communicative significance. At this level, the research question is not how the posture of Mr X relates to his other activities, but how the posture of Mr X relates to that of Mr Y. At this level of relationship one again finds that postural configurations are orderly and standard for a culture.

Although at first glance there seems to be an infinite variety of postural relationships, these can be abstracted to a few basic types, which are regularly associated with given social activities. In fact, even when no words are being spoken (or the sound track of a movie is turned off) it is possible to identify the kinds of human relationship that are in progress by means of the postural configurations and other kinesic movements.

The markers of re chanically the same postures and shifts that are used b nark units. But here postural shifts mark the beginning an ts and some aspects of the relationship as well. It is not unusuai for multiple units or activities to be continuous, so that one and the same marker signals the completion of one or more structural divisions and a change in the relationship. For instance, the gun at the end of a football game may mark the end of a play, a quarter, a game and a season, and at the same time mark the end of a particular relationship between two quarterbacks and another between two teams.

There are three basic dimensions of postural relations in interaction, ly observable, that grossly indicate aspects of the relationships. The dimensions, which occur simultaneously, are not different types of ral relation but are abstractable from any configuration of posture. re:

1. Inclusiveness or non-inclusiveness of posture – defines the space for the activities and delimits access to and within the group.
2. *Vis-à-vis* or parallel body orientation – gives evidence about the types of social activities.
3. Congruence or non-congruence of stance and positioning of extremities – indicates association, non-association or dissociation of group members.

Inclusiveness–non-inclusiveness

Whenever a group is meeting, especially if others are present who are not at that moment engaged in the group activity, the group members tend to define or delimit their immediate group by the placement of their bodies or extremities. When they are standing or have freedom to move furniture, they tend to form a circle. If they are located in a line, the members at each end turn inward and extend an arm or a leg across the open space as if to limit access in or out of the group. This effect we call 'bookending'. In American groups, it is not unusual for males to sit or stand on the flanks of a seated group; if a number of men are present, those of the highest status usually assume the end positions.

Very often the members of a group act as though there were reason to prevent or discourage certain subgroups from forming or to keep certain participants apart. This is seen in situations in which particular dyads – for example, pairs that might engage in courtship or flirtation, taboo relationships, or arguments – might interfere with other purposes of the group. The access of such members to each other is limited by the body placement and posture of a third participant, who may stand with a part of his body placed between the two who are to be kept separated. In a seated posture, someone may extend a leg or prop it up on a piece of furniture in order to form a barrier. Blocking of this type is also carried out in the following manner: The person on each side of the member to be controlled crosses his legs in such a way as to box in the center person.

It is often noted in established groups that the participants will place their chairs or bodies in such a way as to limit access of a newcomer to those members of the group who are of the opposite sex. For example, in a seminar room, several rows of male staff members are likely to be found between a male visitor and the women members of the group.

In family therapy, it seems to be an unwritten rule that the manifest or designated patient in the family will sit next to the therapist. In all cases that we have observed, any exception to this rule was preceded by some explicit rearrangement.

A final instance of barrier behavior is seen whenever people are placed more closely together than is customary in the reciprocals of their culture.

Figure 4 Basic body orientations in a psychotherapy group, with splitting

will hold their extremities and heads in homologous rather than identical positions, so that they sit or stand in mirror-imaged postural relationship. Both the direct and mirror-imaged postures which are shown in Figure 5 are subtypes of what I have called congruent postures.

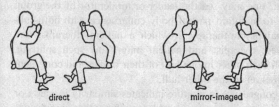

direct   mirror-imaged

Figure 5 Congruent postural relations

Congruent body postures may occur in either a *vis-à-vis* or a parallel postural orientation.[7]

Since an individual in a given culture can sit in only a limited number of postures, one immediately wonders whether postural congruence is purely coincidental. But even a very few continued observations of a group quickly end any theory of coincidence. Two, four, even six people often sit in postural congruence. When one member of a congruent set shifts posture the others often quickly follow suit, so that the congruence is maintained through repeated changes of body positioning. In a group of three or more, it is common for two basic configurations of position to be used, with one subgroup maintaining congruence in one kind of positioning and another subgroup maintaining congruence in another. If one *listens* to such a group

7. Many activities involve transient movements that may break the postural configuration temporarily. But unless there is a shift into another basic configuration, such transient movements are not to be regarded as breaking configural continuity. So long as the configuration returns to the basic postures, a continuity in attitudes of the persons involved is assumed.

and examines what it is doing, one often finds that two points of view or approaches to an issue are being debated or advocated. Even in cases where opposing or alternate issues have not yet been formulated, one can notice that often one postural set is maintained by those on one side of the table, another by those on the opposite side of the table.

Old friends or colleagues who have long-term ties sometimes shift into postural congruence at times when they are temporarily arguing or taking opposing sides, as if to indicate the ultimate continuity of their relationship. In family psychotherapy one child often maintains postural congruence with one parent, while the other children do so with the other parent. In such cases one finds that the clinical material indicates sharp ideational or affective divisions of the family into these two subgroups.

Just as there is a tendency to split postural orientation, so there is a tendency to split postural congruence. A person may maintain postural congruence with one person in his upper body, and with another in his lower body. In a large group, where two quite different sets of postural positioning are used, one may see the leader or moderator of the group using such splitting to maintain partial body congruence with both subgroups. In individual psychotherapy in which a patient, therapist and observer are involved, therapist and patient may show such splitting, being congruent with each other in one half of their bodies and congruent with the research observer in the other half.

In a general way congruence in posture indicates similarity in views or roles in the group. There is, however, evidence of another significance of congruence or non-congruence – indication of status. When some member of an alliance differs markedly in social status from the others, he may maintain a posture quite unlike that of the others. When the basic activities of a *vis-à-vis* orientation involve relations of equality or peer relations, the postures are often congruent. In doctor–patient, parent–child or teacher–student reciprocals, where it is important to indicate different status, congruence is less likely to occur. In situations where congruence is absent, there are often other evidences of non-association. The posturally non-congruent member might look out of the window, fail to look at the others, refrain from conversation, or simply give indications of being lost in his own thoughts.

Non-association must be distinguished from dissociation. In dissociation there is marked postural congruence at the same time that there are signals of alienation. Unlike the case in non-association, the dissociated member signals that he is to be *considered* unassociated. For example, dissociated members fail to move out of congruence even when they turn their backs to each other or turn their heads away from each other. They often do not talk, or they state their unwillingness to have anything to do with each other, yet their association is quite clearly signaled by their postural congruence. This relationship is often seen in a parent and child who, from a clinical standpoint, are regarded as showing inhibition or denial of a considerable unconscious incestuous fixation. It is also seen in quarreling lovers, in a patient who is strongly resisting the development of transference, and in schizophrenic patients who are mistakenly regarded as autistic or withdrawn.

The psychoanalytic reader will immmediately think of identification as he reads this description of postural congruence. It seems to me that postural congruence is indeed a manifestation of mutual identification and is possibly one of the cues upon which the interpretation of identification is based. But caution is necessary in using this concept. That two people engage in the same behavior does not necessarily mean that one has copied or identified with the other. It may be that both are, in common, following an internalized unconscious program of behavior which at that moment calls for identical behavior. In such a case, the cause of one's behaving like the other is to be found in the preceding and succeeding steps in the program or form – not in what the other partner has just done.

For example, in some groups there is an oscillating rhythm in the alignments and realignments of the participants, which appears to prevent a breakdown of the total group into persisting splinter subgroups. In unconscious compliance with such a rhythm, the participant may find himself falling into congruence, the act being dictated by the format of the interaction rather than by any motivation to identify or copy.

Postural indicators of the steps in a program

The units of communication are also organized through time as a series of steps. Since each interactant has internalized these steps, the interaction has an orderly, prescribed sequence. The culturally abstracted formats or templates for this order or sequence, Birdwhistell and I have called a 'cultural program'. In any culture there are programs, explicit or unconscious, for holding a meeting, greeting a friend, serving dinner, courting or bathing a baby. Both a psychotherapy session and a course of psychotherapy have a program.

If one looks at communicative events as a series of units through time, one sees that the postural markers that note the end of units also mark the stages in a program. The types of postures also indicate given stages. For example, in a church service, some stages are marked by kneeling, some by standing, some by sitting, some by the congregation's sitting while the minister is standing, and so on. In courtship, stages are indicated by physical proximity, closed relations of posture, placement of arms, and so on.

Individual psychotherapy has a program of tactics which is associated with a series of postures, at least on the part of the therapist. Most obvious of these relations between tactics and posture is the shift by the therapist from leaning backward with arms or legs crossed to leaning forward with arms and legs uncrossed when he stops listening and takes up interrupting, confronting or reassuring. The subjective experience of rapport also occurs in connection with the assumption of a characteristic pattern of postures. The shifts of the program of a psychotherapy hour move toward the rapport constellation, which in a sense is a 'climax'. In sessions of about forty minutes' duration, this usually develops at about the twentieth to the twenty-fifth minute. Then, in most of the sessions we have studied, the entire series is repeated.

Progressions typical of psychoanalytically oriented psychotherapists

(1) Progressive uncrossing of extremities

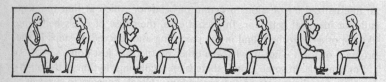

(2) Progressive movement toward the patient

Less conventional progression, leading to physical contact

Figure 6 Types of progressions of therapists' positions

In a program there may be a progression of units at various levels. For example, there may be an orderly sequence of maneuvers which make up a larger tactic. These tactics, in turn, have an order. The postures of the therapist indicate or mark these progressions of maneuvers and tactics. For example, maneuvers can be equated with points, which are indicated by head-eye postures. Tactics can be equated with positions, which are marked by total body posture. A progression of tactics (positions) characteristically seen in psychotherapy sessions of any type is illustrated in Figure 6. The progressive uncrossing of extremities and movement toward the patient – with or without physical contact – are combined, and each shift is followed by increased clinical activity and lexical engagement, such as interpretation, reassurance or instruction.

This progressional posture does *not* occur when the interaction with a patient is not a therapeutic session – for example, a demonstration interview for students, or a consultation in which the therapist is examining another psychiatrist's patient. In psychoanalytic language, the therapist in these situations does not encourage transference.

According to the level of behavior, postures indicate the beginnings and endings of units of communicative behavior, the ways in which participants are related to each other, and the steps in a program. Although research has so far only sketched broad outlines of communicative behavior, it is already possible to use this information in clinical practice and everyday life. The briefest glance at postural configurations has great value in identifying the participants' location in a flow of social events and the nature of their relationships.

References

BATESON, G. (1958), *Naven* (2nd edn), Stanford University Press.
BATESON, G. (forthcoming), chapter 1, in N. McQuown (ed.), *The Natural History of an Interview*, Grune & Stratton.
BERGER, M. M. (1958), 'Nonverbal communication in group psychotherapy', *Int. J. Grp. Psychother.*, vol. 8, pp. 161–78.
BERTALANFFY, L. W. (1950), 'An outline of general systems theory', *Brit. J. Philos. Sci.*, vol. 1, pp. 134–65.
BERTALANFFY, L. W. (1960), *Problems of Life*, Harper & Row.
BIRDWHISTELL, R. L. (1952), *Introduction to Kinesics*, University of Louisville Press.
BIRDWHISTELL, R. L. (1963), 'Body signal: normal and pathological', address to American Psychological Association.
BIRDWHISTELL, R. L. (forthcoming), chapter 3, in N. McQuown (ed.), *The Natural History of an Interview*, Grune & Stratton.
CHARNEY, E. J. (forthcoming), 'Postural configurations in psychotherapy'.
DEUTSCH, F. (1951), 'Thus speaks the body: III. Analytic posturology', *Psychoanal. Q.*, vol. 20, pp. 338–9.
EINSTEIN, A. (1933), 'On the methods of theoretical physics', in A. Einstein (ed.), *The World As I See It*, Covici & Friede.
GLEASON, H. A. (1955), *An Introduction to Descriptive Linguistics*, Holt, Rinehart & Winston.
GOFFMAN, E. (1957), 'Interpersonal persuasion', in B. Schaffner (ed.), *Group Processes*, Vol. III, Josiah Macy Jr Foundation.

GOFFMAN, E. (1961), *Asylums*, Doubleday.

HEWES, G. (1957), 'The anthropology of posture', *Scient. Amer.*, vol. 196, pp. 123–32.

HOCKETT, C. F. (1958), *A Course in Modern Linguistics*, Macmillan.

LA BARRE W. (1947), 'The cultural basis of emotions and gestures', *J. Personality*, vol. 16, pp. 49–68. [Reprinted in this book, pp. 207–24.]

PIKE, K. L. (1954), *Language*, Summer Institute of Linguistics, Glendale, California.

SCHEFLEN, A. E. (1963), 'Communication and regulation in psycho-therapy', *Psychiatry*, vol. 26, pp. 126–36.

SCHEFLEN, A. E., 'Natural history method in psychotherapy: communicational research', in L. A. Gottschalk and A. Auerbach (eds.), *Methods of Research in Psychotherapy*

SCHEFLEN, A. E., ENGLISH, O. S., HAMPE, W. W., and AUERBACH, A. (forthcoming), *Strategy and Structure: Three Research Approaches to Whitaker and Malone's Multiple Therapy*, Commonwealth of Pennsylvania Monograph Press.

13 E. T. Hall

A System for the Notation of Proxemic Behavior

E. T. Hall, 'A system for the notation of proxemic behavior', *American Anthropologist*, vol. 65, 1963, pp. 1003–26.

Introduction

This is one of a series of papers of Proxemics,[1] the study of how man unconsciously structures microspace – the distance between men in the conduct of daily transactions, the organization of space in his houses and buildings, and ultimately the layout of his towns.

The aim of this paper is to present a simple system of observation and notation with a view to standardizing the reporting of a narrow range of microcultural events. The system is far from perfect; but if it directs attention to certain behavior, it will have achieved its purpose. However, before proceeding to the descriptive portion of this paper, certain theoretical matters have to be dealt with.

The writer began systematic observations in a proxemic frame of reference when it became apparent that people from different cultures interacting with each other could not be counted on to attach identical meanings to the same or similar measured distances between them (Hall, 1955, 1959, 1963, 1964). What was close to an American might be distant to an Arab.

Without a systematic observational and recording technique for such encounters, pinpointing interferences[2] is a slow, somewhat uncertain procedure requiring highly developed observational skills. Not all observers are equally skilled.

1. When this research was conceived, no suitable designation had been found for the study of microspace as a system of bio-communication. *Human topology*, *chaology* (the study of boundaries), *choriology* (the study of organized space), and others were considered. *Proxemics* was chosen because it suggests the subject to the reader.

2. In an inter-cultural encounter the structural details of the two culture systems combine in one of three ways: They can mesh or complement, so that the transaction (Kilpatrick, 1961) continues or is reinforced. They can clash or interfere which has an inhibiting effect on the transaction. They can be unrelated so they neither reinforce nor inhibit the transaction.

Even within the broader context of American culture, it is possible to observe these three types of interaction; for example, the Utah Mormon's version of time – in which there is virtually no leeway for being late – meshes nicely with the US military system. *Interference* can be observed whenever there is an attempt to integrate two groups of

Levels of awareness

Any culture characteristically produces a simultaneous array of patterned behavior on several different levels of awareness. It is therefore important to specify which levels of awareness one is describing.

Unlike much of the traditional subject matter of anthropological observation, proxemic patterns, once learned, are maintained largely out of conscious awareness and thus have to be investigated without resort to probing the conscious minds of one's subjects. Direct questioning will yield few if any of the significant variables, as it will with kinship and house type, for example. In proxemics one is dealing with phenomena akin to tone of voice, or even stress and pitch in the English language. Being built into the language, these are hard for the speaker to consciously manipulate.

Values of proxemic study

Indeed, the very absence of conscious distortion is one of the principal reasons for investigating behavior on this level[3] for any step taken to

individuals, one having internalized the diffuse point pattern while the other uses the displaced point pattern (Hall, 1959).

As a general rule, the time systems of middle-class men and women from the same subculture tend to operate in such a way that there is a minimum of interference, even though the two systems differ. During the day, and for business, male time takes precedence. In the late afternoon and evening – particularly for meals and social occasions – women's time is the dominant pattern. Cultural interference is analogous to linguistic interference as described by Weinreich (1953).

3. Reducing distortion and minimizing contamination of data has long been considered a basic feature of the methodology of the physical sciences. Possibly because of the great complexity of our data, most anthropologists until recently have avoided the issue of distortion. Distortion, incidentally, should not be confused with accuracy of reporting, or lack of accuracy. Reporting is something the anthropologist does. Distortions are in the hands of the informant.

One might argue that the distortions on the overt level are distortions of content only and do not hide the patterns, that anything an informant tells the anthropologist is grist for the anthropologist's mill, or that the distortions themselves provide insights into the culture – all of which is often true.

Nevertheless, if one is seeking to construct a theory of the culture one is studying (Goodenough, 1956), this process proceeds more rapidly if the building blocks used to construct that theory are reasonably stable. It should be noted that the stories made up by an informant are of necessity rooted in his experience and as such are representations of his culture. However, the *design* he creates is of short duration, i.e. tomorrow he will tell a slightly different story. The basic distinction between out-of-awareness patterns that cannot be cut to conform to situational demands and the conscious screening of the truth from an outsider is in the time that two types of events remain stable. In addition to the desirability of increasing stability of the components that go to make up one's theory of a given culture, there is the practical matter of building confidence in one's subjects. In most instances ability to control the communications systems marks one as an insider; absence of this control marks one as an outsider. Any field anthropologist who has experienced the pride his subjects show in his own increased know-

eliminate a subject's conscious manipulation of the facade[4] presented to the world is desirable.[5] Boas (1911) stressed this same point as the principal reason for integrating linguistics and ethnological research. There are, however, other reasons for studying proxemic behavior. Why is it, for example, that an American[6] who is approached too closely by a foreigner will feel annoyed? Why is it that the discomfiture often fails to pass when he gets to know the culture better, in spite of conscious striving to suppress these feelings? Why do these interferences commonly last a lifetime, and why do people take this sort of interference so personally? Why is there so little they apparently can do to relieve their feelings? One subject (an anthropological colleague), after twelve years of working with the French, still couldn't stand being approached as closely as Frenchmen normally do in conversation and used to barricade himself behind his desk, because he felt the French were still getting too familiar.

Considering the architect's persisting preoccupation with space, why is it that 2400 years since the building of the Parthenon Western man still lacks a method for noting and describing the experience of space?[7] Some of the answers to these paradoxes can be derived from the art and literature of our own culture.[8]

---

ledge of, and skill in, controlling their culture, knows the importance of being able to use a given system correctly. Reduction of distortions and levels of awareness constitute the topic of another publication. The subject is mentioned here only to indicate that the writer is not unaware of the complexities and as a reminder that the most mundane and taken-for-granted assumptions often turn out to be most difficult to come to grips with.

4. Goffman (1959) describes still another level of awareness that deals with the mask one wears in order to play the proper parts in daily transactions.

5. Hymes, in commenting on this paper (also see Hymes, 1962), suggests how some 'functionally relevant dimensions' can be identified from the discomfiture of the subject when patterns have been broken.

6. Individual and regional diversity in proxemic patterns is comparable to that encountered in the use of time, materials and language. Distinctions on these levels are not relevant to this presentation. Instead, a more basic pattern should be mentioned: Americans of European ancestry fall generally into two groups – contact and non-contact. Non-contact Americans minimize physical contact – touch or holding during encounters when the transaction is social or consultative in nature. Contact Americans, on the other hand, employ touching and holding which is sufficiently different from the former pattern as to cause comments. Hereafter, whenever the term 'American' is used, it refers only to the dominant non-contact group.

7. Thiel (1961) has recently developed and published a system for describing the kind of space architects and landscape architects deal with (see also Goldfinger, 1941; 1942).

8. Benedict (1946) describes how the anthropologist not only uses informants but draws upon every other available expression of the culture, including art forms, movies and literature. It is in the tradition of anthropology, therefore, that the anthropologists look to other fields, particularly art and literature, as a means of checking their own observations.

Acute observers from other fields – often neglected or ignored – also provide the anthropologist with helpful cues.

Significant work in related fields

Hediger (1955), the Swiss ethologist, pioneered in the systematic observation of distance in vertebrates. He distinguishes between contact and non-contact species and was the first to describe personal and social distance in animals. His work continues to be of interest to anthropologists (Hediger, 1961).

Dorner (1958) gives structure to the artist's continuous quest – from the neolithic to the present – to discover new and more satisfying means for portraying spatial relationships. From him we get a new slant on how man has organized and re-organized his actual perceptions.

Lynch (1960), after interviewing inhabitants of three major US cities (Boston, Jersey City and Los Angeles), identified five elements intrinsic to the image of the city: paths, districts, edges, landmarks and nodes. These represented the subjects' own categories.

Grosser (1951), addressing himself solely to intimate, personal and social distance, describes how and why portraits in the Western world are painted at certain specific distances. The distance employed by an artist when he paints a human subject is designed to communicate specific features of the personality and at the same time screen out all other features. Grosser pins his observations down to feet and inches.

Among the psychologists, the transactional group (Kilpatrick, 1961) has made particular progress in isolating the principal means by which people judge the relationship and distances of objects, and in so doing has provided insight into how man unconsciously participates in the molding of his own perceptions. Gibson (1950) goes a long way in explaining how the total visual process stabilizes and synthesizes the ever-changing mosaic of images cast on the retina, converting them into a solid visual world.[9]

Barker and Wright (1954) have contributed significantly to the study of human ecology through their identifications of what they term standing behavior settings and objects (frames) for analysing and describing the behavior of a community. These frames can be further analysed in terms of constituent parts and categories that are subsumed under each heading. Barker and Barker (1961) discovered that attempts to impose categories of 'behavior settings' on their English subjects were much less productive than deriving the categories from the subject's own preferences, and also

9. See Gibson (1950). This process, however, seems to be different from the constant process of adjustment to another person who does not stand still but moves. Little is known about the former, even less of the latter.

that once established, these behavior setting categories tended to be self-perpetuating.

The combined insights of these writers – plus many more who could be cited – still leave several questions unanswered. By what means other than visual do people make spatial distinctions? How do they maintain such uniform distances from each other? And how do they teach these distances to the young?

Methodological considerations

Foreign students studying in the United States comprised one group of our proxemic research subjects.

An unanticipated consequence of these interviews was added insight into what Goffman (1957) terms 'the stuff of encounters' which was highlighted whenever there was interference between two patterns, or a perceived absence of patterning, during an encounter. These subjects reported suffering repeated alienations in encounters with Americans. There are many forms of alienation, but a frequent variety found was that which has been termed *lack of involvement*. Misinterpretation of American responses was traced to differences in the definition of what constituted proper listening behavior, some of which centered on use of the eyes. Further investigation revealed that there was also a virtual absence of skill in reading the minor cues as to what was going on behind the American facade (Goffman, 1957).

In a broader context involving older subjects, Arabs complained of experiencing alienation particularly when interacting with that segment of the US population which can be classed as non-contact (predominantly of North European origin, where touching strangers and casual acquaintances is circumscribed with numerous proscriptions). When approached too closely, Americans removed themselves to a position which turned out to be outside the olfactory zone (to be inside was much too intimate for the Americans). Arabs also experienced alienation traceable to a 'suspiciously' low level of the voice, the directing of the breath away from the face, and a much reduced visual contact. Two common forms of alienation reported by American subjects were *self-consciousness at the cost of involvement* and *other-consciousness*. Americans were not only aware of uncomfortable feelings, but the intensity and the intimacy of the encounter with Arabs was likely to be anxiety provoking. The Arab look, touch, voice level, the warm moisture of his breath, the penetrating stare of his eyes, all proved to be disturbing. The reason for these feelings lay in part in the fact that the relationship *was not defined as intimate*, and the behavior was such that in the American culture is only permissible on a non-public basis with a person of the opposite sex.

In a different cultural setting, a Chinese experienced alienation during an interview when he was faced directly and seated on the opposite side of a desk, for this was defined as *being on trial.*

Research in proxemics has been restricted to culturally-specific behavior and it does not encompass other environmental or personality variables, such as noise level, temperature and personality variables, all of which are important.[10] There are, nevertheless, a number of conceptual tools the anthropologist has at his disposal.

For example, the anthropologist knows that in spite of their *apparent* complexity, cultural systems are so organized that their content can be learned and controlled by all *normal* members of the group. Anything that can be learned has structure and can ultimately be analysed and described. The anthropologist also knows that what he is looking for are patterned distinctions that transcend individual differences and are closely integrated into the social matrix in which they occur.

Proper observation can tease from the data the patterning that man gives to a behavioral system in order that he may use it and transmit it to others. The notation system which is given in this paper will help the field worker to focus his observations in such a way as to clarify the various structure points of a given proxemic system.

Only the notation system itself is given here. The history of how it was developed will be treated at length in later publications, along with the rather complex matter of arriving at definitions of such systems. The process of making explicit the rules that combine isolates into sets and patterns (Hall, 1959) will be treated elsewhere.

In making observations of the sort required, and devising the notation system described below, this investigator owes a debt to several disciplines. Included in these are descriptive linguistics[11] and kinesics (Birdwhistell, 1952), ethology, and the various psychoanalytic schools starting with Freud and ending with Fromm and Harry Stack Sullivan.[12] Even the writer's experience as a weather observer in the Second World War

10. Concerning the relationship between the encounter and the setting, or between fixed feature space and dynamic space (Hall, 1963), there seems little doubt that such a relationship exists. The evidence of the animal psychologist and the ethologist is firmer than for man. However, on the human level, data from widely scattered sources points in the same direction (Hall, mss.). Until now, man's behavior in space has been treated from a strictly physical-anatomical point of view, and with the implicit assumption that cultural differences did not exist, and that if they did they were unimportant.

11. Specifically, the work of linguists in the tradition of Edward Sapir, Leonard Bloomfield and Benjamin Lee Whorf.

12. My contact with the various psychoanalytic movements has been eclectic. The out-of-awareness features of communications and the use of one's self as a control are so important that it is difficult to credit them sufficiently. Both are pivotal in any research this investigator undertakes (see Fromm, 1941 and Sullivan, 1940).

taught him the extremely useful nature of numerical codes in which information is associated not only with a numerical value but also with a position in the code. Weather codes were learned by thousands of men in a matter of weeks.

Proxemic notation system

Proxemic behavior can be seen as a function of eight different 'dimensions' with their appropriate scales. Complex as proxemic behavior is in the aggregate, by proceeding one at a time, these dimensions can be recorded quickly and simply in the following order:

1. Postural – sex identifiers.
2. Sociofugal – sociopetal orientation (SFP axis).
3. Kinesthetic factors.
4. Touch code.
5. Retinal combinations.
6. Thermal code.
7. Olfaction code.
8. Voice loudness scale.

Given the present meager state of our knowledge, a total of eight classes of events is sufficient to describe the distances (and the means of determining distances) employed by man. The systems are bio-basic, rooted in the physiology of the organism (Hall, 1959; Hall and Trager 1953). With slight modifications, this system could also be used to describe distance behavior of other mammals. It conforms to Wallace's number eight given for basic building blocks of cultural systems (Wallace, 1961). It is consistent with the criteria set by Goodenough in which observed units are ordered and interrelated according to contrasts inherent in the data (Goodenough, 1956, 1957; Frake, 1962).[13]

Each factor complex comprises a closed behavioural system which can be observed, recorded and analysed in its own right. On the proxemic level, however, each system is treated as a complex of isolates that will result in proxemes which combine into sets and patterns in larger systems.[14] For example, there are almost endless variations on posture. One observer (Hewes, 1955) records empirically some ninety positions. However, it is not necessary to note all variations. For example, in proxemic notation it

13. Frake, reviewing Goodenough's thesis (1962), sets forth many of the conditions which must be met in the writing of 'productive ethnographies' and the absolute necessity of tapping the *cognitive world of one's informants*, and avoidance of 'a priori notions of pertinent descriptive categories' (italics mine).

14. The proxeme equates with the phoneme of language, but on a much lower and simpler organizational level (cf. Hall, 1959, chs. 6–8).

is important to record only the sex of the subjects and whether they are standing, sitting or squatting, or lying down (prone).

Not all of the eight factors are of equal complexity, nor do all of them function at all times. The thermal and olfaction inputs are present only at close distances. Vision is more complex than either of these, and it is normally screened out only at very close distances.[15]

In the interest of speeding recording and with a view to future application of factorial analysis and computers to field records, every attempt has been made to be parsimonious. At each of the eight steps it is necessary for the observer to make only a few discriminations, in no case more than seven at one time. The present version of the system enables recording in thirty to sixty seconds; with practice, familiarity and improvements, it should be possible to reduce the recording time to as little as ten to fifteen seconds.[16]

The notation system which follows is designed to systematize observation in the simplest possible way and at the same time to provide a record so that similar events can be compared across time and space.

Postural-sex identifiers

One of the most essential operations in proxemic notation is to determine the sex and basic posture of the two individuals (whether they are standing, sitting or squatting, or prone). These distinctions are kept to a minimum in order to maintain congruity throughout the proxemic analytic level. On other analytic levels much greater detail has been observed and noted. For example, Birdwhistell, who named and developed the field of kinesics and worked in close cooperation with descriptive linguists, including McQuown and Hockett, notes an extraordinary number of events (Birdwhistell, 1952; McQuown, 1957; Hockett, 1958). The most recent number given[17] was over thirty different lines of recordings, each representing a possible analytic level.

Sex and basic posture can be noted by any one of three systems depending on the needs of the investigator: a pictographic mnemonic (iconic) symbol, a syllabic mnemonic, or simple number code. These are:

15. Linguistic style (Joos, 1962) associated with each distance represents the most recent and least known and also apparently the most complex of the subsystems linked to proxemic patterns. At present, Joos's type of analysis is only available for English. It is mentioned here as a reminder to the field worker, since other languages may have been subjected to similar analysis.

16. The information is considerably less than that transmitted for one weather station code used to plot the basic data for weather maps. These codes can be transcribed on a weather map as fast as a man can enscribe the simple weather symbols.

17. Figure given in response to question at Interdisciplinary Work Conference on Paralanguage and Kinesics, University of Indiana, 1962.

man prone	m/pr	1
man sitting or squatting	m/si	3
man standing	m/stg	5
female prone	f/pr	2
female sitting or squatting	f/si	4
female standing	f/stg	6

Once memorized, the number code is the easiest and quickest to use. Throughout the system, the active subject is indicated first. A man talking to a woman while both are standing is recorded as 56, while 65 means the woman is talking to the man. When it is not possible to tell which subject is more active, parentheses are used. Whenever there are extremes in age, size or status, these should be noted.

The sociofugal-sociopetal axis (SFP axis)

Osmond (1957) used the terms *sociofugal* and *sociopetal* to describe spatial arrangements or orientations that push people apart and pull them in – orientations that separate and combine people, that increase interaction or decrease it.

As can be seen, the SFP axis is a function of the relations of the bodies to each other. In theory, there are endless variations in the orientation of two bodies in relation to each other. However, in proxemic transcription the observer is interested in recording only those distinctions which are operationally relevant to the participant. After experimenting unsuccessfully with a number of overly sensitive systems, an eight-point compass face was finally selected as the most appropriate model (see Figure 1).

Zero and 8 are placed at North, 2 at East, 4 at South, 6 at West. Zero represents two subjects face to face (maximum sociopetality), 8 two subjects back to back (sociofugal), 2 two subjects slightly facing but at right angles so they can either see each other peripherally if they look straight ahead or look in each others' eyes. Position 4, in which the subjects stand side by side with the north–south axis running through a parallel to their shoulders, is also very common in the United States. Orientation six is definitely sociofugal because the subjects' shoulders are at right angles but with the faces pointing out and away; in order to see each other, they must crane their necks.

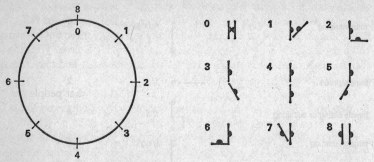

Figure 1 SFP axis notation code

Which components of the SFP axis are favored and for what transactions, is largely culturally determined. These components are also linked with the social setting and the age, status and sex of the two parties. On the basis of continuous observation over the past three years, it is possible to offer some generalizations concerning the principal structure points of the American system. In interpreting these generalizations the reader should keep in mind that, like other communications, proxemic communications are always read in context and have no meaning independent of context.

Zero, 1, 2, 4 and 8 are most frequently observed. Zero is for direct communications where the intent of one or both of the participants is to reach the other with maximum intensity.

Two is more casual and less involved. A subject of common interest is often discussed using this axis. The subjects may shift to 0 or 4, depending on how involved or uninvolved they become.

Four – the shoulder-to-shoulder axis – is one in which two people are normally watching and/or discussing something outside themselves, such as an athletic event or the girls going by on a Saturday afternoon, without necessarily being involved with each other. This is the axis for very informal, transitory communications.

Position 6 is used as a means of disengaging oneself. It is not quite, but almost as, sociofugal as 8.

The kinesthetic factors

One of the most basic forms of relating in space, one which is deeply imbedded in man's philogenetic past, is the potential to strike, hold, caress or groom. In threatening situations among animals, enemies and potential enemies are not permitted within striking distance (Hediger, 1955).

This applies in intra-species as well as interpersonal relations. A cowboy walking around a horse illustrates this principle; he uses three different distances. With a strange horse he follows an arc just outside the radius of the horse's hoofs when kicking. With familiar horses – those not known to be dangerous – he walks inside this circle but not too close. With his own horse he uses a much closer (more intimate) distance and may even brush the horse's tail as he passes.

The kinesthetic code and notation system is based on what people can do with their arms, legs and bodies, and the memory of past experiences with one's own as well as other bodies. Another person is perceived as close (as we shall see later) not only because one may be able in some instances to even feel the heat radiating from him, but also because there is the potential for holding, caressing, or of being struck.

Basically there are four ways of relating with the body.[18] These are a function of four basic inventories of potential actions:

1. Touching with the head or trunk.
2. Touching with forearms, elbows, or knees.
3. Touching with arm fully extended.
4. With the arm and the leg extended and body leaning, i.e. stretching (far apart but still able to touch). These are noted and/or symbolized as follows:

Each increment symbolizes a progressively greater distance. The *measured* distance depends largely on the size and shape of the individuals involved and the SFP axis, so that the figures given below are approximations, empirically derived from a small sample of medium-sized persons. The important feature is that, to the persons involved, the distance is perceived in terms of the capabilities of the two bodies. The observer therefore will have to revise the figures upward or downward depending on his own body build, particularly in relation to the larger distances.

18. Given the great flexibility of the body it may seem strange that the number of relational possibilities is so small. The situation is comparable to that noted earlier under sex and posture. Four is sufficient to record all distinctive features in the kinesthetic inventory. Any more would be too complex, as each of the four is coded digitally (touching or not touching) which yields sixty-four possible combinations, only eleven of which are really essential.

#1 0″−3″   #2 15″±2″   #3 22″±3″   #4 40″±4″

It is possible to code kinesthetic relationships in two ways: (a) As one of the four distances, or (b) as one of the four distances plus some space. This provides an inventory of eight distances which can be recorded in the following manner using a number code:

1 Within body contact distance.
#10 Just outside body contact distance.
2 Within easy touching distance with only forearm extended.
#20 Just outside forearm distance ('elbow room').
3 Within touching or grasping distance with the arms fully extended.
#30 Just outside this distance.
4 Within reaching distance.
#40 Just outside reaching distance.

Symbols	code
	11
	101
	12
	102
	22
	13
	103
	33
	303
	44
	404

••• outside the system when extensions are introduced,   55
such as swords, bolos, blow guns and modern arms.

Figure 2 Kinesthetic code and notation system

Since two parties are involved and each has his own repertoire of the eight kinesthetic distances listed, it is possible to construct a matrix with eight dimensions on a side (one for each kinesthetic distance) which contains sixty-four different slots (8 × 8). Because such a matrix is nothing more than a mechanical way of insuring that all possible combinations have been accounted for, there is considerable duplication (thirteen and thirty-one for example). From these sixty-four combinations eleven basic distinctions have proved sufficient to account for all the space transactions observed to date. These are given in Figure 2 (p. 258).

Touching

Cultures vary greatly in the amount of touching which occurs between people. Even in the United States, there are groups which participate in considerable touching and others whose members assiduously avoid touching anyone but those with whom they are intimate.

A seven-point scale seems sufficient for the moment to code the majority of contact-non-contact situations. Since it is possible for each person to touch the other, all combinations can be recorded on a 7 × 7 grid.

This proceeds from 00 mutual caressing to 66 in which there is no contact by either party (see Figure 3).

	0	1	2	3	4	5	6
0	00	01	02	03	04	05	06
1	10	11	12	13	14	15	16
2	20	21	22	23	24	25	26
3	30	31	32	33	34	35	36
4	40	41	42	43	44	45	46
5	50	51	52	53	54	55	56
6	60	61	62	63	64	65	66

0 = caressing and holding
1 = feeling or caressing
2 = extended or prolonged holding
3 = holding
4 = spot touching (hand peck)
5 = accidental touching (brushing)
6 = no contact whatever

Figure 3 Touch code

Vision

The role of vision in judging distance and in communication is incredibly complex. The non-specialist looking at the field as an outsider finds conflicting statements concerning not only the eye itself but the entire process of vision. There is agreement, however, that the visual sense is the most complex and highly evolved of the senses. Depending on the source one chooses, and using the size of the channel of the brain as a rough index of capacity, the eye feeds from six to twenty times as much information to the brain as the ear (Gibson, 1950; Le Grand, 1957). How the eye is used as a function of one's culture is regulated formally, informally, and technically (Hall, 1959). That is, the culture specifies at what, at whom, and how one looks, as well as the amount of communication that takes place via the eye.

For example, a Navaho is taught to avoid gazing directly at others during conversations. He also avoids looking at his mother-in-law, but distinguishes between these two events. The Greeks, on the other hand, emphasize the use of the eyes and look for answers in each other's eyes (their intent gaze can be disturbing to the American). Americans often convey the impression to the Arabs that they are ashamed. The way Americans look at the other person during conversations is the principal reason given by Arabs for this impression.

Given the above distinctions and the fact that culture is learned, the anthropologist must pose the following question: Is it possible, by some simple means, to distinguish operationally between these different events? Part of the answer lies in the structure of the retina. The fact that the retina provides for three distinct and easily identifiable types of vision makes it possible to make distinctions of the type indicated, and at the same time provides us with the basis for a notation system.

The three areas of the retina. In the middle of the visual field there is a small pit in the retina called the fovea. It subtends a visual angle of only one degree. Some idea of the fineness of visual detail made possible by this structure can be gained by considering the fact that there are 25,000 closely packed cones, each of which is connected to a single bipolar nerve cell. (There are no rods in the fovea.)

Surrounding the fovea is an oval area called the macula, with a vertical visual angle of approximately 3° and a horizontal visual angle of approximately 12°. This is the area of clear vision. From the macula on out, vision becomes less and less distinct. According to Dr Milton Whitcomb, secretary to the National Research Council's Committee on Vision, approximately half of 130,000,000 rods and all the 7,000,000 cones are concentrated in a central portion of the retina covering a visual angle of 20°. Peripherally it is possible for most people to perceive motion laterally on the temporal side of each eye at 180° or better.

The eye therefore provides three different ways of viewing, depending on where the image falls on the retina: the fovea, the macula or the periphery. A fourth alternative is to screen out vision.

Therefore it is possible to code these as:

f   foveal (sharp)   1
m   macular (clear)   2
p   peripheral   3
0   no visual contact   8

	f	m	p	o
f	ff	fm	fp	fO
m	ms	mm	mp	mO
p	pf	pm	pp	pO
o	Of	Om	Op	OO

	1	2	3	8
1	11	12	13	18
2	21	22	23	28
3	31	32	33	38
8	81	82	83	88

Figure 4 Visual code

A 4 × 4 grid illustrates the sixteen combinations of the ways that people look at each other (see Figure 4).

In constructing the visual scale and notation system it was deemed advisable to depart from previous practice and allow space for later additional notations. Therefore the numbers 0, 4, 5, 6 and 7 were reserved for this purpose.

To return to our earlier examples, two Navahos talking would be recorded as 33 (pp). A Navaho and his mother-in-law as 88 or 38 (38 because, while neither is supposed to look at the other, the mother-in-law is apparently dominant, since others will tell the son-in-law when she is around so he can leave or turn his back).[19]

Both Arabs and Greeks tend to read the other person's eye (11) much more than Americans.

In making a record of the way that people look at each other, it will be necessary for the field worker to develop recording techniques consistent with visual interaction patterns of the culture under observation. The capacity of virtually any subject to determine where another person is looking is extraordinarily well developed. According to Gibson the 'gaze line' can be calculated with accuracy approaching sensory acuity.[20]

The field worker can therefore rely on his own ability to determine where subjects are looking. The point is, however, that the topic of looks and of looking must be completely explored with one's subjects and backed up by observations. Practice will improve one's capacity to record visual interactions. The technique used by this field worker is to try to catch the most characteristic sequence of looks for a given type of transaction recording three or four, one above the other pp

19. The ethnographic data was obtained during field work with the Navaho some thirty years ago in the Pinyon Black Mesa region of the reservation. It is possible that the details of the mother-in-law taboo have changed since that time.

20. Gibson, J. J., letter to the investigator dated 5 September 1962.

mm 22
pp 33
mm 22

Virtually nothing is known of vision as a factor in human transactions. The most critical need is for data.

The thermal factors

Although not much is known about the thermal zone or zones, heat gain and loss apparently influence the structuring of close distances.[21] As indicated elsewhere, responses to heat flow in the subtle sense are not usually considered in a distance-regulating context. Operating as it does, almost totally out-of-awareness, heat flow is traditionally thought of as strictly a matter of comfort. Nevertheless it has been observed and commented on by some subjects that the sensing of heat from another body can result in a movement either towards or away from the source.

The degree to which this type of response occurs out-of-awareness is illustrated in the recording of a trivial event that might well have otherwise gone unnoticed. The ambient situation was a dinner party. There was the usual semi-crowding with the attention on conversation. This observer, hand resting on table, was suddenly aware of a rapid reflex-withdrawal of his hand. There was no immediate sensation such as pain or touch. Visual examination and quick review of the preceding few seconds revealed two things:

1. The hand of another guest approximately 2½ inches (6·5 cm) from where his own hand had been a moment before.
2. A memory trace of having detected heat in the hand. A replacing of the observer's hand in the same area revealed that heat flowing from the other person's still stationary hand was definitely detectable.

It is possible to code heat flow (digitally) as either being detected or not, depending on whether the two parties are within each other's thermal sphere or not. Heat flow is detected in two ways, by radiation and by conduction.

21. Recent studies in thermography (the study of infra-red radiation) demonstrate that human skin is an ideal emitter and receiver of infra-red energy (Barnes, 1963). How effective it is can be seen by looking at a scale of emissivities of various substance in which emissivity values have been given:

Mirrors and polished metals	0·02–0·03
Polished lead and cast iron	0·21–0·28
Black loam and fire brick	0·66–0·69
Wool and lumber	0·78
Lamp black and soot	0·95
Human skin	0·99

The thermal code and notation system is as follows:

Conducted heat detected	thc	1
Radiant heat detected	thr	2
Heat probably detected	th	3
Heat not detected	th	8

Because so little is known about thermal responsiveness to others, numbers 0, 4, 5, 6 and 7 are reserved for future use. The field worker will have to experiment until he has subjects who can tell him when they have detected heat. As with the level of loudness of the voice, there is considerable range in heat output. Clothing of course reduces sensitivity somewhat. One is dealing, however, with a primitive communication system that has been overlooked by social scientists but may have common currency. A limited number of subjects, for example, stated they were fully aware of the significance of changes in body temperature in others which could be interpreted as readily as though words had been used. One example will illustrate this point. The subject, a rather voluptuous young female, noted that when she danced with certain young males she could detect a rise in temperature in the abdominal region which foreshadowed genital tumescence and which could be differentiated from a temperature rise due to exertion. What is more, this rise in temperature could be detected several inches from the dance partner.

It should be noted that the body does not heat uniformly, but in specific areas depending on the situation. The whole subject of mapping the geography of heat output of the body under different emotional states remains to be explored.

Olfaction

In the United States advertisements extolling the virtues of not offending by the odor of one's body or breath are a prominent feature of American mass media. That is, the olfactory sense is culturally suppressed to a greater degree than any of the other senses.

Pleasant odors, such as perfume on women or bay rum on men, are desirable but should not be detectable at more than intimate distance for the middle class. In fact, when olfaction is present it usually signals intimacy.

Sexual odors, bad-smelling feet and flatus are definitely taboo in all but a very limited number of situations and relationships. The degree to which American culture has dulled, repressed, or dissociated the olfactory capacities is not known; much more comparative data is needed.

Also, as with vision and hearing, there is a great range of olfactory acuity. It is highly probable that sensitivity to different odors may be selective in a culturally patterned way, so that what is quite obvious or even overwhelming to a foreigner may not be *significant* to a local subject. Because of our own taboos, American research workers will have to be particularly careful to check their own observations with local colleagues.

In light of all this, and given the meager state of our present knowledge of olfaction as a proxemic indicator, it was decided to simplify the recording procedure as much as possible.

At any given distance, only four observations and accompanying notations are made:

Olfactory code

Differentiated body odor detectable	dbo or 1
Undifferentiated body odor detectable	ubo or 2
Breath detectable	br or 3
Olfaction probably present	oo or 4
Olfaction not present	Ø or 8

In essence, the investigator looks for boundaries and whether they have been crossed or not. Everyone is surrounded by a small cloud or haze of smell, varying in size according to physical setting, emotional state, and culturally prescribed norms. The investigator must determine at what point the smell is unmistakable and where this fits into the total proxemic picture. Usually there is little ambiguity. Most transactions occur either inside or outside these boundaries.

In recording breath, it must be determined at what point people feel free about directing their breath and whether the warmth and moisture of the breath is sought after or not.

Use code designation 4 (oo) when it is pretty certain that olfaction is present but otherwise unspecified. The numbers 0, 5, 6 and 7 are reserved for future refinements.

Questioning subjects on olfaction has not proved a problem to date. All Arabs interviewed spoke freely about bad breath and feet odors and how these must be avoided. Friends and relatives tell them when they should not stand too close to people. Normally they do not feel close to people until they can detect the heat, moisture and smell of breath. There seems to be little doubt that the Arab employs olfactory cues to set distance. The principal difference between the Arab and the American patterns is that for Americans to be within smelling distance is to introduce intimacy, whereas with the Arab it apparently only makes them feel 'at home'. Without smell, Arabs apparently feel somewhat 'left out'. It should be noted, however, that the Arab data is based on such a small segment of the overall culture that any interpretations made at this point must be tentative.

Voice loudness

The loudness of the voice is modified to conform to culturally prescribed norms for (a) distance, (b) relationship between the parties involved, and

(c) the situation or subject being discussed. Cultural norms can vary for any one of the three as well as for all three. The same applies to subcultures within a larger cultural frame. Voice level, therefore, is relevant as a significant variable in judging distance.

Holding the other two dependent variables – relationship and situation – neutral and constant, an American will normally code a whisper as close and a shout as distant. Similarly, Brodey's blind subjects judge the distance of a speaker by the loudness of his voice.[22] This is, of course, not the only means by which the blind judge distance; it is, however, an important one.

The culture of one's upbringing has a good deal to do with how loudness is perceived. For example, as a general rule Arabs sound loud to Americans. Arabs, on the other hand, will comment among themselves that the American's voice is too low and sounds insincere. Subjects' unguarded comments on ethnically associated loudness of voice are not the only source of data on this subject. Children have to be systematically taught not only what is correct and incorrect usage but how to modulate properly the loudness of the voice.

The investigator can provide a good deal of clinical data from his own past. No standards have been established for judging voice loudness *except* those people learn and against which they judge the behavior of others. There is no alternative except to code the loudness of voice employing the investigator's own culturally calibrated measuring device.

Using the investigator as a measuring device may not satisfy the rigid requirements of all scientists. It should be kept in mind, however, that this is what all people do whenever they respond to loudness or softness of the voice. The principle of measurement is the same as two people standing back to back to see who is the taller. The field investigator should test his own evaluations against those of others. This can be accomplished easily

Voice loudness scale

Descriptive level	Mnemonic code	Number code
silent	0	0
very soft	vs	1
soft	s	2
normal	n	3
normal+	n+	4
loud	l	5
very loud	vl	6

22. The perceptual world of five blind subjects has been investigated systematically for the past two and a half years by Dr Warren Brodey of the Washington School of Psychiatry. This investigator has participated in the research.

by having two or more observers record the same transaction separately and comparing notes.

Seven degrees of loudness have proved sufficient to code all vocal transactions to date. (A zero for silence increases the number from six to seven.)

Cautions and reminders

It is important not to overcomplicate the recording of voice loudness. As with other features of vocalization, overall loudness varies with the individual.

Most people are aware, however, when the speakers of another language in any given setting sound louder or softer than the speech they are used to hearing at home or when a person of their own culture speaks overly slowly or softly, as this may signify anger. One of the best ways of bringing home the point that voice level conforms to cultural norms is to be around small boys at the dinner table before they have learned to modulate their voices. While this task seems endless to parents, the seal of culture is well impressed by age eleven to fourteen for most normal situations.

In the field one should ask one's subjects for an appraisal of voice loudness. 'Are those people – or is he – or she talking in a normal tone of voice?' This will usually elicit a comment if there is anything unusual about the level of voice and provides added information. It is possible, for example, that variations of voice loudness is not as important as it is in the United States, or is, perhaps, more important. One English subject interviewed over a long period of time turned out to have a remarkable capacity to modulate and direct his voice in such a way that it was difficult to tell how far away he was.

Language style

Traditionally any layman will affirm that what one talks about and the manner of talking are linked with distance and situation, but he will be unable to describe what the differences are.

The linguist Joos (1962) has provided Americans with an analysis of their own linguistic behavior as viewed through a situational screen. The degree to which other cultures recognize and talk about situational styles or dialects is not known.

Joos lists five styles, each used for a different situation. They are: intimate, casual, consultative, formal and frozen, and while the matching with distance zones seems close but not perfect, more needs to be known about the proxemic aspects of style.

If different styles of speech are recognized and used in specific situations (classical and colloquial Arabic, for example), these should be noted also by the observer of proxemic behavior.

Proxemic systems as communication

Hockett (1958) defines communication as any event that triggers another organism. While many other life forms communicate (as for example when a bee informs another where honey is, by means of an orientating series of dance steps), language is characteristically human. Hockett lists seven principal features of language: duality, productivity, arbitrariness, interchangeability, specialization and displacement, and cultural (not genetic) transmission.

Proxemic behavior is obviously *not* language and will not do what language will do. Nevertheless a careful analysis demonstrates that proxemic communication as a culturally elaborated system incorporates more features named by Hockett than one might suppose. For example, language is both 'plerematic' and 'cenematic' – i.e. has both sets and isolates (Hall, 1959) or units that build up, or combine, to form a different kind of unit.

Proxemics lacks none of the seven features of language listed by Hockett. Its arbitrariness is not obvious at first, because proxemic behavior tends to be experienced as iconic – e.g. a feeling of 'closeness' is often accompanied by physical closeness – yet it is the very arbitrariness of man's behavior in space that throws him off when he tries to interpret the behavior of others across cultural lines. For example, the fact that Europeans name streets (the lines that connect points) and the Japanese name the points and ignore the lines, is arbitrary. The fact that in the European cultures people arrange objects whereas in Japan they arrange spaces, is arbitrary. American supression and repression of olfaction in proxemic behavior is also arbitrary. The arbitrariness operates on a Whorfian level rather than a more conscious level. Hence it is even more difficult to come to grips with than lexical items.

Proxemics demonstrates duality of a primitive but nevertheless readily identifiable sort. The units (cenemes) build up. For example, the elimination or introduction of visual contact can completely redefine physical closeness. The operating principle behind the confessional booth is that it makes it possible to bring a man and woman together in an intimate setting but without the ability to touch or see each other. Removing the partitions in the confessional would completely redefine the situation, particularly if it were an enclosed confessional.

Interchangeability means that subject 'A' can play 'B's' part and vice versa. In other words, the subject and the communication are not irrevocably tied together, as is the case with the male peacock and his display. A feature of proxemic communication is its interchangeability.

Displacement refers to the capacity of language to deal with displacements in time or space. In the animal world territorial markers (particularly the olfactory ones) characteristically feature displacement. In man fixed and semi-fixed features also feature displacement (see Hall, 1963). Boundary markers, fences, closed doors, chairs placed in a conversational group, the arrangement of furniture in an auditorium, the psychiatrist's couch, and the layout of offices all enable someone *who knows the system* to interpret what has taken place or the message that is intended. As Hazard notes: 'Walk into an empty courtroom and look around. The furniture arrangement will tell you at a glance who has what authority' (Hazard, 1962). Only dynamic space (the actual distances between people when they are interacting such as *tone of voice*) lacks the displacement features.

Specialization refers to the fact that language tends to refer to specific items or events, i.e., to become 'specialized'. Proxemic behavior is *not* as highly specialized as language. Nevertheless it contains great capacities for specialization. The American pattern for comforting and lovemaking are seldom confused, even though both involve great closeness. The fact that 'duality' is present, that there are differences in the interplay of receptors in these two instances (avoidance of olfaction in comforting for one thing) makes incipient specialization possible. Nothing could be more specialized than the sacredness or taboos associated by all people with certain specified places like Mecca, the Navaho mountain, or the Chindi hogan. What is more specialized than a boundary, or father's chair, the 'head' of the table, the tokonoma in the Japanese house, the proper distance to be maintained when attracting attention of someone without intruding, or the distinction between the relative and non-relative side of the office in the Middle-East (Hall, 1959, ch. 10)?

In other words, proxemic behavior parallels language, feature for feature. It is, however, much *less* specialized and more iconic. It tends to be treated as though certain features associated with language were lacking. The iconic features of proxemics are exaggerated in the minds of those who have not had extensive and deep cross-cultural experience. In fact, when a subject stops treating proxemic behaviour as iconic and sees its arbitrariness, he is beginning to experience the overall arbitrariness of culture.

Sebeok (1962) presents the hypothesis that animal communication is most often 'coded analogly', whereas speech is coded both digitally and analogly. Proxemic behavior is also coded both digitally and analogly.

The knowledge of the relationship of language to other cultural systems – not to mention the communications systems of lower life forms – is in a state of flux. Better understanding of how these other systems function and how best to study and describe them, in part awaits the development of improved procedures for discourse analysis.

Language is most commonly treated as an instrument for communicating *from* one person *to* another, rather than as a transaction; Hockett (1958), Hymes (1962) and Sebeok (1962) are exceptions though for different reasons. Joos (1962) comes closest to a transactional view with his five linguistic styles of English. Proxemic behavior, on the other hand, by its very nature inevitably is reduced to a transaction – a transaction between two or more parties, or one or more parties, and the environment. It is this very feature that makes it difficult to relate proxemics at all significant levels to current linguistic models.

Concerning the relationship of the *etic* level of analysis to the *emic* level and how one proceeds from the former to the latter (Hymes, 1962), it will be apparent to the reader that this presentation is concerned more with the proxetics than proxemics, and is therefore only the first of a series of steps in a long complex process.

In the course of this investigation attempts to classify behavior on the emic level were not successful until a system of observations and notations had been developed that enabled the observer to account for two types of differences: (a) between events in contrasting systems, and (b) between one proxeme and another within a given system. Thus one of the points of contrast observed by Americans overseas when interacting with a variety of peoples in the Mediterranean culture areas, is in the direction of the breath during personal (but not intimate) conversations. Americans are taught not to breathe on people, particularly strangers or people of higher status, and are made aware of this when others breathe on them. (Attention to the structure points of the system is also drawn during acculturation of the young, so that the anthropologist can learn a good deal about the American system while correcting his children.)

Within the bounds of the American system there is considerable variation in the use of the eyes and the degree of touching that is permissible by strangers. Touching or looking of a type that falls outside one's familiar pattern may be coded as unusual in the same manner that we treat unfamiliar allophones of a given phoneme and still recognize as a permissible variant of a familiar form. In one encounter, for example, items 5 (accidental brushing) and 6 (no contact) of the touch code (scale #4), were alloproxes of the same proxeme for the writer, but were coded as different proxemes by an upper-middle-class Dutch subject.

Summary

The notation system presented here is designed to provide a way of being rather specific when talking about observations of a very limited nature. No claim is made for the superiority of this stytem. It has proved to be reasonably workable and simple. If it persists at all as a tool in the hands

1. postural – sex identifier

male
1
3
5
2

female
4
6

2. orientation of bodies (SFP axis)

0
1 5
2 6
3 7
4 8

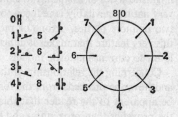

3. kinesthetic factors

11	33
101	14
12	303
102	34
22	44
13	404
103	

4. touch code

caressing and holding	0
feeling or caressing	1
prolonged holding	2
holding or pressing against	3
spot touching	4
accidental brushing	5
no contact	6

5. retinal combinations (visual code)

foveal	f	1
macular (clear)	m	2
peripheral	p	3
no contact	nc	8

6. thermal code

contact heat	thc	1
radiant heat	thr	2
probable heat	th	3
no heat	th	8

7. olfaction code

differentiated body odors detectable	do	1
undifferentiated body odors detectable	udo	2
breath detectable	br	3
olfaction probably present	oo	4
olfaction not present	o	8

8. voice loudness scale

silence	si	0
very soft	vs	1
soft	s	2
normal	n	3
normal+	n+	4
loud	l	5
very loud	vl	6

Figure 5 Key to combined proxemic notation system

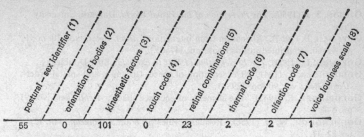

1. Two men standing.
2. Facing each other directly.
3. Close enough so that hands can reach almost any part of the trunk.
4. Touch does not play any part.
5. Man speaking looking at, but not in the eye, partner only viewing speaker peripherally.
6. Close enough so that radiant heat would have deen detected.
7. Body odour but not breath detectable.
8. Voice very soft.

Figure 6 Recorded transaction and key

of the ethnographer, it will undoubtedly go through transformations as use reveals its defects. Currently the visual dimension stands out, out of all those described, as the one most requiring additional treatment.

The following visual aids have been prepared to summarize the data of this article:

Figure 5 shows the entire code with all its component parts in the order in which they should be recorded.

Figure 6 shows a sample of a record of a transaction.

References

BARKER, R. G., and BARKER, L. S. (1961), 'Behavior units for the comparative study of cultures', in B. Kaplan (ed.), *Studying Personality Cross-culturally*, Harper & Row.

BARKER, R. G., and WRIGHT, H. F. (1954), *Midwest and Its Children; the Psychological Ecology of an American Town*, Harper & Row.

BARNES, R. B. (1963), 'Thermography of the human body', *Science*, vol. 140, no. 3569, pp. 870–77, 24 May.

BENEDICT, R. (1946), *The Chrysanthemum and the Sword*, Houghton Mifflin.

BIRDWHISTELL, R. (1952), *Introduction to Kinesics*, University of Louisville Press.

BOAS, F. (1911), *Introduction, Handbook of American Indian Languages, Bulletin of of the Bureau of American Ethnology*, Smithsonian Institution.

DORNER, A. (1958), *The Way Beyond Art*, New York University Press.

FRAKE, C. (1960), 'Family and kinship among the eastern Subanun', in G. P. Murdock (ed.), *Social Structure in Southeast Asia*, Viking Fund Publications in Anthropology no. 29.

FRAKE, C. (1962), 'Cultural ecology and ethnography', *Amer. Anthrop.*, vol. 64, pp. 53–9.

FROMM, E. (1941), *Escape from Freedom*, Holt, Rinehart & Winston.

GIBSON, J. J. (1950), *The Perception of the Visual World*, Harvard University Press.

GOFFMAN, E. (1957), 'Alienation from interaction', *Hum. Relat.*, vol. 10, no. 1, pp. 47–60. [Reprinted in this book, pp. 347–63.]

GOFFMAN, E. (1959), *The Presentation of Self in Everyday Life*, Doubleday.

GOLDFINGER, E. (1941), 'The sensation of space. Urbanism and spatial order', *Archit. Rev.*, vol. 90, pp. 129–31.

GOLDFINGER, E. (1942), 'The elements of enclosed space', *Archit. Rev.*, vol. 91, pp. 5–8.

GOODENOUGH, W. H. (1956), 'Residence rules', *S West. J. Anthrop.*, vol. 12, pp. 22–37.

GOODENOUGH, W. H. (1957), in *Seventh Annual Round Table Meeting on Linguistics and Language Study*, P. Garvin (ed.), Institute of Languages and Linguistics, Georgetown University, Washington, Monograph Series on Languages and Linguistics no. 9.

GROSSER, M. (1951), *The Painter's Eye*, Holt, Rinehart & Winston.

HALL, E. T. (1955), 'The anthropology of manners', *Scient. Amer.*, vol. 192, pp. 85–9.

HALL, E. T. (1959), *The Silent Language*, Doubleday.

HALL, E. T. (1963), 'Proxemics: the study of man's spatial relations', in I. Galdston (ed.), *Man's Image in Medicine and Anthropology*, International Universities Press.

HALL, E. T. (1964), 'Spatial features of man's biotope', *Proceedings of the Association for Research in Nervous and Mental Diseases*.

HALL, E. T., and TRAGER, G. (1953), *The Analysis of Culture*, American Council of Learned Societies.

HAZARD, J. (1962), 'Furniture arrangement and judicial roles', *ETC.*, vol. 19, pp. 181–8.

HEDIGER, H. (1955), *Studies of the Psychology and Behaviour of Captive Animals in Zoos and Circuses*, Butterworths Scientific Publications.

HEDIGER, H. (1961), 'The evolution of territorial behavior', in S. L. Washburn (ed.), *Social Life of Early Man*, Viking Fund Publications in Anthropology no. 31.

HEWES, G. (1955), 'World distribution of certain postural habits', *Amer. Anthrop.*, vol. 57, pp. 231–4.

HOCKETT, C. (1958), *A Course in Modern Linguistics*, Macmillan.

HYMES, D. (1962), 'The ethnography of speaking', in T. Gladwin and W. C. Sturtevant (eds.), *Anthropology and Human Behavior*, The Anthropological Society of Washington.

JOOS, M. (1962), 'The five clocks', *IJAL*, vol. 28, part 5.

KILPATRICK, F. (ed.) (1961), *Explorations in Transactional Psychology*, New York University Press.

LE GRAND, Y. (1957), *Light, Color and Vision*, Chapman & Hall.

LYNCH, K. (1960), *The Image of the City*, Technology Press; Harvard University Press.

MCQUOWN, N. (1957), 'Linguistic transcription and specification of psychiatric interview materials', *Psychiatry*, vol. 20, pp. 79–86.

OSMOND, H. (1957), 'Function as the basis of psychiatric ward design', *Mental Hospitals*, pp. 23–9.

SEBEOK, T. (1962), 'Evolution of signalling behavior', *Behavioral Science*, vol. 7, pp. 430–42.

SULLIVAN, H. S. (1940 and 1945). *Conceptions of Modern Psychiatry*, William Alanson White Foundation.

THIEL, P. (1961), 'A sequence-experience notation for architectural and urban space', *Town Plann. Rev.*, pp. 33–52.

WALLACE, A. (1961), 'On being just complicated enough', *Proc. natn. Acad. Sci.*, vol. 47, pp. 458–64.

WEINREICH, U. (1953), *Languages in Contact*, The Linguistic Circle of New York, Publication no. 1.

14 E. T. Hall

Silent Assumptions in Social Communication

E. T. Hall, 'Silent assumptions in social communication', in D. McK. Rioch and E. A. Weinstein (eds.), *Disorders of Communication*, Research Publications, Association for Research in Nervous and Mental Diseases, vol. 42, 1964, pp. 41–55.

The investigations reported briefly in this paper deal with *proxemics*, the study of ways in which man gains knowledge of the content of other men's minds through judgements of behavior patterns associated with varying degrees of proximity to them. These behavior patterns are learned, and thus they are not genetically determined. But because they are learned (and taught) largely outside awareness, they are often treated as though they were innate. I have found this type of behavior to be highly stereotyped, less subject to distortion than consciously controlled behavior and important to individuals in the judgements they form as to what is taking place around them at any given moment in time.

Thoreau (1929) wrote *Walden* over one hundred years ago. Yet in a section entitled 'Visitors' he describes how conversational distance and subject matter are functions of each other and, what is even more remarkable, he names some of the variables by means of which people unconsciously set distances.

One inconvenience I sometimes experienced in so small a house, is the difficulty of getting to a sufficient distance from my guest when we began to utter the big thoughts in big words. You want room for your thoughts to get into sailing trim and run a course or two before they make their port. The bullet of your thought must have overcome its lateral and ricochet motion and fallen into its last and steady course before it reaches the ear of the hearer, else it may plough out again through the side of his head. Also our sentences wanted room to unfold and form their columns in the interval. Individuals, like nations, must have suitable broad and natural boundaries, even a considerable neutral ground, between them. I have found it a singular luxury to talk across the pond to a companion on the opposite side. In my house we were so near that we could not begin to hear – we could not speak low enough to be heard; as when you throw two stones into calm water so near that they break each other's undulations. If we are merely loquacious and loud talkers, then we can afford to stand very near together, cheek by jowl, and feel each other's breath; but if we speak reservedly and thoughtfully we want to be farther apart, that all animal heat and moisture may have a chance to evaporate. If we could enjoy the most intimate society with that in each of us which is without, or above being spoken to, we must not only be silent, but commonly so far apart bodily that we cannot possibly hear each other's voice in any case. Referred to this standard, speech is for the convenience of those who are hard of hearing; but there are many fine things which we cannot say if we have to shout. As the conversation began to assume a loftier and grander tone, we gradually shoved our chairs farther apart till they touched the wall in opposite corners, and then commonly there was not room enough.

The insights and sensitive observations of Thoreau are helpful in pointing up certain consistencies in behavior in heretofore unsuspected areas, such as perceptions of body heat. They strengthened my original premise that man's behavior in space is neither meaningless nor haphazard. Yet there are paradoxes associated with proxemic behavior that need explaining.

Some paradoxes

A casual observer confronted with American reactions to being touched or approached too closely by foreigners is likely to dismiss such reactions as minor annoyances that will disappear as people get to know each other better. More careful investigation reveals, however, several puzzling questions, or anomalies, which suggest that there is more to behavior patterns based on interpersonal distance than meets the eye.

An anthropologist becomes accustomed to resistance to and denial of the idea that there are regularities in human behavior over which the individual has little or no control. But why do so many people, when faced with other people's behavior, take 'interference' with space patterns so personally? And why is there apparently so little that they can do to relieve their feelings?

One of my interview subjects, a colleague, quite typically explained that, after twelve years of working with French culture, he still could not accustom himself to the French conversational distance. He found it 'uncomfortably' close, and he found himself annoyed with Frenchmen, possibly because he felt they were getting too familiar. Like other Americans who have been brought up to resent being crowded, he used the device of barricading himself behind his desk.

Another anomaly is associated with architecture. Why is it that, even with a history of building dating back to predynastic Egypt, with surveying developed somewhere around 2500 BC and with the magnificence of the Parthenon achieved by the fifth century before Christ, architects have failed to develop a way of describing the experience of space? Recently Thiel (1961) published a notation system for describing open spaces.

By what means do people make spatial distinctions? How do people judge distance from each other and teach it to their young with such uniformity and still apparently not know that they are teaching it at all?

Technically the work of transactional psychologists answered some questions and raised others (Kilpatrick, 1961), while Gibson's (1950) approach is the most comprehensive treatment of how man perceives space visually. Asking subjects how they differentiate between distances or why they feel so strongly about matters of space, doesn't help – even the most cooperative subjects can give you only bits of information. Most people have only the vaguest notion of the rules governing the use of their immediate and distant receptors.

In approaching any new problem, the anthropologist must constantly remind himself that, even though he is faced with complexity on all sides, the components that go to make up the complexity must of necessity not be overly complex. Cultural systems are organized in such a way that the basic components (structure points) can be controlled by all *normal* members of the group. For example, varied and rich as languages are, all normal members of a group learn to speak and understand them.

In essence, one looks for simple distinctions that can be made by any normal person and go beyond individual differences.

This is a report of a study in progress. Additional data will undoubtedly result in revisions. If the data seem obvious, I can only say that to me they seemed obvious *after* I had identified the principal structure points of the system. Then I wondered why it had taken so long to reach this particular point. Recently Bruner (1959) stressed something the linguistic scientist has known for a long time: that people do not necessarily have to know the structure of a system of behavior in order to control it.

Research strategy

A combination of research strategies was employed during this study. Techniques included observation, participant's observations, interviews – structured and unstructured – and biweekly sessions with four blind subjects.[1] Normal subjects were drawn predominantly from the Washington area from the educated-professional group. Fifteen Americans and eighteen foreign subjects were interviewed in depth. Interviews lasted from three to fifteen hours in increments of two to three hours. Data were gathered from one hundred additional subjects in unstructured, natural situations. Foreign subjects included English, French, German, Swiss, Dutch, Spanish, Arab, Armenian, Greek and West Africans studying in the United States. These subjects were used in much the same way as subjects are used by the linguist, i.e. as examples of their own particular systems. A few hours with one subject does little more than provide some of the basic and

1. These sessions were conducted in cooperation with Dr Warren Brodey of the Washington School of Psychiatry in the winter of 1961 to 1962.

most obvious structure points as well as contrasting examples of proxemic behavior.

Since people apparently cannot describe the patterns that enable them to discriminate between one distance and another, it is next to useless to question them directly about how they go about perceiving spatial relations. It has been necessary to resort to various projective-type devices as a means of getting subjects started thinking about their own spatial experiences. Some of the most valuable leads were gathered as a result of casual conversations when a subject would 'warm up' and begin talking about an experience he had had with a particular person.

'Boy, you ought to see a guy we have in our office; everybody talks about it. They even kid him a lot. He comes right up to you, breathes in your face. I sure don't like seeing his face so close, with pop eyes and nose distorted all over the place. He feels you a lot, too. Sometimes we wonder if there isn't something wrong with him.'

'He breathes down my neck; why can't he keep his hands off you?'

'Did you ever notice how close he stands to you – it gives me the willies.'

'She's one of those who's always pawing you; did you ever notice how some people stand much too close?'

Many of these utterances are virtually stream-of-consciousness. They are valuable because they provide clues to what specific events in other people's behavior stand out as significant.

The Arabs and the English complain (for different reasons) because Americans do not listen. Greeks experience a great flatness in our interaction with them – like eating unsalted rice, they say. In each complaint there lie valuable data concerning the nature of the feedback mechanisms used by *both* parties.

In research of this sort one is faced with a paradox, namely, it is the commonplace that makes the difference when confronted with someone else's 'commonplace'. Another paradox is that, in writing and talking about one's reactions to being touched and breathed upon by a stranger, the description loses much of the immediate effect. The reactions are so obscure, so small and so seemingly inconsequential that at times it is difficult to realize they may add up to something.

The distinction that Hediger (1955) makes between 'contact' and 'non-contact' species can also be made for man or groups of men. Indeed, it seems to be the first and possibly the most basic distinction between groups.

As the term implies, the 'contact' group is characterized by considerable touching, both in private and public. The 'non-contact' group perceives the contact group as overly familiar and sometimes 'pushy', while the contact group refers to the non-contact as 'standoffish', 'high-hat', 'cold' or 'aloof'.

In addition to the contact, non-contact category, man seems to share a number of features of the generalized mammalian pattern described by Hediger (1955). Personal distance and social distance are certainly present though – inasmuch as a certain amount of confusion exists because of misunderstanding of Hediger's terminology – it may eventually become necessary to define operationally what is meant by these terms. The observations which follow refer to the non-contact group.

Distance sets

For the American non-contact group, and possibly for others as well, four distance sets seem to encompass most, if not all, behavior in which more than one person is involved. These are referred to as intimate, casual-personal, social-consultative and public. Each distance set is characterized by a close and a far phase.

The perception of distance and closeness apparently is the result of an interplay of the distant and immediate receptor systems (visual, auditory, olfactory), the systems in the skin that record touch and heat flow and those in the muscles that feed back information concerning where a part of the body is at any given moment in time. *The transition from one group of receptors to another is the boundary point between distance sets*, as will be shown subsequently.

For Americans, space judgements seem to depend principally on the tactile-kinesthetic and visual senses, although the olfactory, heat-radiation and oral-aural systems are also involved.

The two most commonly observed sets are *casual-personal distance* and *social-consultative distance*.[2] The descriptions which follow are idealized stereotypes for subjects in non-excited or non-depressed states with 20–20 vision, without excessive background noise and at average comfortable temperature (55° to 85° F).

Social-consultative distance

The distinguishing features of this distance (close phase: four to seven feet plus or minus six inches at each end; far phase: seven to twelve feet plus or minus six inches at each end) are that intimate visual detail in the face is not perceived and that nobody touches or expects to touch unless there is some special effort. Voice level is normal for Americans. There is little

2. Not to be confused with 'social distance', a term used by both Hediger (1955) and Bogardus (1959). 'Social-consultative distance' as used here is not at all like Bogardus's 'social distance', which is the distance separating two members of a group in a social hierarchy. It is much closer in meaning to Hediger's term 'social distance'.

change between the far and the close phases, and conversations can be overheard at a distance of up to twenty feet. (There is no loudness scale for the voice that is adaptable to descriptions such as these.)

I have observed that in overall loudness, the American voice at these distances is under that of the Arab, the Spaniard, the South Asian Indian and the Russian; and it is somewhat above that of the English upper class, the South-East Asian and the Japanese.

Close phase; social-consultative distance. The boundary between social-consultative and casual-personal distance lies at a point just beyond where the extended arms can no longer touch (four to seven feet).

Foveal vision (area of sharpest focus of the eye) at four feet covers an area of just a little larger than one eye (Table 1); at seven feet the area of sharp focus extends to nose and parts of eyes, or mouth, eye and nose are sharply seen. In many Americans, this sharp vision shifts back and forth, or around the face. Details of skin texture and hair are clearly perceived. At 60° visual angle, head, shoulders and upper trunk are seen at four feet distance; the same sweep includes the whole figure at seven feet. Feet are seen peripherally, even if standing. Head size is perceived as normal. As one moves away from the subject, the foveal area can take in an ever-increasing amount.

A good deal of impersonal business takes place at this distance. In the close phase there is much greater implication of involvement than in the distant phase. People who work together a good deal tend to use close social-consultative distance. It is also a very common distance for people who are attending a casual social gathering.

Looking down at a person at this distance is to dominate him almost completely, as when a man talks to his secretary or receptionist on leaving or entering the office.

Distant phase: social-consultative distance. Business and social discourse conducted at this distance (seven to twelve feet) has a more formal character than in the close phase. Desks in offices of 'important' people are large enough to hold anyone at this distance. In most instances, even with more or less standard desks, the chair opposite the desk is at about eight or nine feet from the man behind the desk.

At social-consultative distance, the finest details of the face, such as the capillaries in the eyes, are lost. Otherwise skin texture, hair, condition of teeth and condition of clothes are all readily visible. Neither heat nor odor from another person's body is apparently detectable at this distance. At least, none of my subjects mentioned either factor.

Table 1 Areas covered at eight distances by four visual angles

Distances		Visual angles			
		1°*	15° × 3°†	60° sweep‡	180°
Intimate					
	6″	0·1″	2·5″ × 0·3″ eye, mouth	6″ the face	Head and shoulders
	18″	0·3″ central iris	3·75 × 1″ upper or lower face	18″ head	Upper body and arms
Casual-personal					
close	30″	0·5″ tip of nose	6·25″ × 1·5″ upper or lower face	30″ head, shoulders	Whole figure
far	48″	0·8″ one eye	10″ × 2·5″ upper or lower face	48″ waist up	
Social consultative					
close	7′	1·7″ mouth, eye plus nose; nose plus parts of eye	20″ × 5″ the face	7′ whole figure	
far	12′	2·5″ two eyes	31″ × 7·5″ faces of two people	12′ figure w/ space around it	
Public					
	30′	6·3″ the face	6′ 3″ torso of 4 or 5 people	30′	
	340′	6′			
	500′	9′			
	1500′	26′			

* Computed to nearest 0·1 inch.   † Computed to nearest 0·25 inch.
‡ Varies with culture.

The full figure – with a good deal of space around it – is encompassed in a 60° angle. This is the distance which people move to when someone says 'Stand away so I can look at you.' Also, at around twelve feet, accommodation convergence ceases[3]; the eyes and the mouth are contained in the area

3. Gibson (1950), and M. Whitcomb, Vision Committee, National Academy of Sciences, personal communication.

of sharp vision so that it is not necessary to shift the eyes to take in the face. During conversations of any significant length, visual contact has to be maintained and subjects will peer around intervening objects.

If one person is standing and another seated, the seated person may push his or her chair back to about twelve feet in order to reduce the tilt of the head. Several subjects mentioned that 'looking up' accentuated the higher status of the other person. In the days of servants it was taken for granted that none would approach a seated employer so close as to make him look up. Today it may be that motorcycle policemen use the device of resting one foot on a running board and looking down on an offender as a way of increasing their psychological leverage. Judges' benches often accentuate differences in elevation.

The voice level is noticeably louder than for the close phase and can usually be heard easily in an adjoining room if the door is open. As the term implies, social-consultative distance is employed for professional and social transactions as long as there is an emotionally neutral effect. Raising the voice or shouting can have the effect of reducing social-consultative distance to personal distance.

I have observed some interviews start at the far end of this scale and move in; in others this process is reversed.

One of the functions of this distance is to provide for flexibility of involvement so that people can come and go without having to talk.[4] A receptionist in an office can usually work quite comfortably if she is ten or more feet from people waiting to see her boss; if she is any closer, she will feel she should talk to those waiting.

A husband coming back from work often finds himself sitting and relaxing reading the paper at ten or more feet from his wife. He may also discover that his wife has arranged the furniture back-to-back (a favorite device of the cartoonist, Chick Young, creator of *Blondie*). The back-to-back arrangement is an appropriate solution to minimum space, or a shortage of reading lights.

The social-consultative distance has the advantage of permitting an easy shifting back and forth between one's activity and whoever else is in the room. Participation with others at this distance is spotty and brief. Questions and answers and introductory or opening remarks are what one hears most often. Likewise, it is easy for one of several participants to disengage himself without offending.

Casual-personal distance

'Personal distance' (close phase: eighteen to thirty inches; far phase: thirty to forty-eight inches) is the term originally used by Hediger to

4. In other countries the circle of involvement cannot be counted on to be the same as in the United States.

designate the distance consistently separating the members of non-contact species. It might be thought of as a small protective sphere that an organism maintains between itself and others (Hediger, 1955).

Far phase: casual-personal distance. Keeping someone 'at arm's length' is one way of expressing this distance (two and a half to four feet). It begins at a point that is just outside easy touching distance on the part of one person to a point where two can touch easily if they extend both arms.

Details of subject's features are clearly visible. Fine detail of skin, gray hair, 'sleep' in eye and cleanliness of teeth are easily seen. Head size is perceived as normal.

Foveal vision covers only an area the size of the tip of the nose or one eye, so that the gaze must wander around the face; 15° clear vision covers the upper *or* lower face. Details of clothing – frayed spots, small wrinkles or dirt on cuffs – can be seen easily; 180° peripheral vision takes in the hands and the whole body of a seated person. Movement of the hands is detected, but fingers cannot be counted.

The voice is moderately low to soft.

No body heat is perceptible. The olfactory factor is not normally present for Americans. Breath odor can sometimes be detected at this distance, but Americans are trained to direct it away from others.

The boundary line between the far phase of the casual-personal distance and the close phase of social-consultative distance marks, in the words of one subject, 'the limit of domination'.

This is the limit of physical domination in the very real sense, for beyond it, a person cannot easily get his hands on someone else. Subjects of personal interest and involvement are talked about at this distance.

For a woman to permit a man inside the close personal zone when they are by themselves makes her body available to touch. Failure to withdraw signifies willingness to submit to touching.[5]

Close phase: casual-personal distance. There appears to be a distinct shift from the far phase to the close phase of casual-personal distance (one and a half to two and a half feet). The distance roughly is only half that of the former. Olfaction begins to enter in, as well as heat gain and loss from the other person. The kinesthetic sense of closeness derives from the possibilities that are opening up in regard to what each participant can do to or with the other's body. At this distance one can hold or grasp the extremities.

5. One female subject from a Mediterranean country repeatedly miscued American men who misinterpreted her failure to respond quickly (virtually with reflex speed) to a reduction in distance from *personal* to *close-personal*.

A visual angle of 15° (clear vision) takes in the upper or lower face which is seen with exceptional clarity. The planes of the face and its roundness are accentuated; the nose projects and the ears recede; fine hair of the face and back of neck, eyelashes and hair in nose, ears and pores are clearly visible.

This is as close as one can get without real distortions of the features. In fact, it is the distortion and the enlargement of the features that one encounters in the next closer zone – the intimate – that make it intimate.

Intimate distance

At intimate distance (full contact to eighteen inches), two subjects are deeply involved with each other. The presence of the other person is unmistakable and may at times be overwhelming because of the greatly stepped-up sensory inputs. Olfaction, heat from the other person's body, touch or the possibility of touch, not only by the hands but also by the lips and the breath, all combine to signal in unmistakable ways the close presence of another body.

Far phase: intimate distance. Hands can reach and grasp extremities but, because of the space between the bodies (six to eighteen inches), there is some awkwardness in caressing. The head is seen as enlarged in size and its features are distorted.

Ability to focus the eye easily is an important feature of this distance for Americans.[6]

In foveal vision the iris of the eye is enlarged over life size. Small blood vessels in the sclera are seen. Pores are enlarged. This is the distance at which personal services, such as removal of splinters, are provided. In apes it is the 'grooming distance'.

Fifteen degree clear vision includes the upper or lower portion of the face which is perceived as enlarged. When looking at the eye, the nose is overlarge, distorted and exaggerated. So are other features, such as lips, teeth and tongue. During conversations, the hands tend to come in and move up toward the face so they will be included in the peripheral field.

Peripheral vision, 180°, includes the outline of head and shoulders and very often, hands.

6. American Optical Company Phoroptor Test Card no. 1985-1A (20–20 vision at 0·37 m) was used to test subjects in a variety of situations including subjects chosen from audiences during lectures. The distance at which the smallest type (0·37 m) could be read was in all cases the same distance at which the investigator was told that he was now 'too close'. Twenty diopter lenses fitted to the eye reduced this distance from fifteen inches to nineteen inches to as little as seven inches. Subjects were chosen in the thirty-five to forty-five-year age bracket. Two subjects with presbyopia failed to respond in this way. With them sharp vision ceased to be featured in the intimate zone.

The voice is normally held at a low level, and Joos's (1962) 'intimate style'[7] prevails.

Heat as well as odor of breath may be detected, even though it is directed away from subject's face. Heat loss or gain from the other person's body begins to be noticed by some subjects if their attention is directed to heat.

Sensory input from all previously used sources has been stepped up considerably. New channels (such as the olfactory) are just beginning to come into play.

Close phase: intimate distance. This is the distance (full contact to six plus or minus two inches) of lovemaking and wrestling, comforting and protecting. Physical contact is featured. Use of the distance receptors is greatly reduced except for olfaction and sensitivity to radiant heat, both of which are stepped up.

Vocalization at intimate distances plays a very minor part in the communications process, which is carried mainly by other channels. A whisper has the effect of expanding the distance. The moans, groans and grunts that escape involuntarily during fighting or sex are produced by the action. The two parties act as one as it were.

In the most close (maximum contact) phase, the muscles communicate. Pelvis, thighs and head can be brought into play, arms can encircle. Except at the outer limits, sharp vision is blurred at this distance, although this is not true of the highly plastic eye of the very young or of the extraordinarily nearsighted.

Much of the physical discomfort that Americans experience when others are inappropriately inside the intimate sphere is expressed as distortions of the visual system. One subject said in regard to people that got 'too close' – 'these people get so close, you're crosseyed! It really makes me nervous they put their face so close it feels like they're *inside you*.'

The expressions, *'get your face out of mine'*, and *'he shook his fist in my face'* apparently express how many Americans perceive their body boundaries. That is, there is a transition between inside and the outside. At that point where sharp focus is lost, one feels the uncomfortable muscular sensation of being crosseyed from looking at something too close.

When close vision is possible within the intimate range – as with the young – the image is greatly enlarged and stimulates a significant portion (if not the total) of the retina. The detail that one sees at this distance is extraordinary. This, plus the felt pull of the eye muscles, structures the

7. '. . . an intimate utterance pointedly avoids giving the addressee information from outside of the speaker's skin. The point . . . is simply to remind (hardly 'inform') the addressee of some feeling . . . inside the speaker's skin.'

visual experience in a way that it cannot be confused with the less intense personal, social-consultative and public distances.

Intimate distance is not favored in public among the American middle class. However, it is possible to observe the young in automobiles and on beaches using intimate distances. Crowded subways and buses may bring strangers into what would ordinarily be coded as intimate spatial relations, if it were not for several characteristically isolating compensatory devices. The correct behavior is to be as immobile as possible and, when part of the trunk or extremities contact another, to withdraw if possible. If this is not possible, the muscles in the affected area are kept tense. For members of the non-contact group it is taboo to relax and enjoy the contact. In crowded elevators the hands are kept at the side or used to steady the body by grasping railings and overhead straps. The eyes are fixed at infinity and should not be brought to bear on anyone for more than a passing glance. Men who take advantage of the crowded situation in order to feel or pinch women violate an important cultural norm dealing with the privacy of the body and the right of a person to grant or withhold from others access to it. Middle-Eastern subjects do not express the outraged reactions to palpation in public places that one encounters among the non-contact American group.

Public distance: outside the circle of involvement

Several important shifts occur in the transition from the personal, consultative and social distances to public distances (close phase: twelve feet to twenty-five feet plus or minus five feet; far phase: thirty feet to maximum carrying distance of voice).

Close phase: public distance. In this phase of public distance (twelve to twenty-five feet) participants cannot touch or pass objects to each other. Possibly some form of flight reaction may be present subliminally. At twelve feet an alert subject can take evasive or defensive action if a threatening move is made.

The voice is loud but not full volume. Rice[8] suggests that choice of words and phrasing of sentences is much more careful and there may be grammatical (or syntactic) shifts that differentiate speech at this distance from the closer, less formal distances. Joos's (1962) choice of the term 'formal style' is appropriately descriptive: 'formal texts ... demand advance planning ... the speaker is correctly said to think on his feet'.

Because angular accommodation of the eyes is no longer necessary, there is an absence of feedback from the ocular muscles. The angle of sharpest vision (1°) covers the whole face. Fine details of the skin and eyes

8. F. Rice, Institute for Applied Linguistic Research, personal communication.

are no longer visible. The color of the eyes begins to be imperceivable (at sixteen feet only the whites of the eyes are visible). Also at sixteen feet the body begins to lose its roundness and to look flat.

Head size is perceived as considerably under life size. The 15° cone of clear vision includes the faces of two people (at twelve feet), 60° the whole body with a little space around it. Peripheral vision includes other persons if they are present.

Far phase: public distance. The far phase of public distance begins somewhere around thirty feet. It is the distance that is automatically set around important public figures. White's description of the spatial treatment accorded John F. Kennedy when his nomination became certain is an excellent example:

Kennedy loped into the cottage with his light, dancing step, as young and lithe as springtime, and called a greeting to those who stood in his way. Then he seemed to slip from them as he descended the steps of the split-level cottage to a corner where his brother Bobby and brother-in-law Sargent Shriver were chatting, waiting for him. The others in the room surged forward on impulse to join him. Then they halted. A distance of perhaps thirty feet separated them from him, but it was impassable. They stood apart, these older men of long-established power, and watched him. He turned after a few minutes, saw them watching him, and whispered to his brother-in-law. Shriver now crossed the separating space to invite them over. First Averell Harriman; then Dick Daley; then Mike DiSalle; then, one by one, let them all congratulate him. Yet no one could pass the little open distance between him and them uninvited, because there was this thin separation about him, and the knowledge they were there not as his patrons but as his clients. They could come by invitation only, for this might be a President of the United States (White, 1961).

At this distance body stance and gestures are featured; facial expression becomes exaggerated as does the loudness of the voice. The tempo of the voice drops; words are enunciated more clearly. Joos's (1962) *frozen style* is characteristic: 'Frozen style is for people who are to remain strangers.' The whole man may be perceived as *quite small* and he is *in a setting.* Foveal vision takes in more and more of the man until he is entirely within the small cone of sharpest vision. At this point, contact with him as a human being begins to diminish.

The 60° cone of vision takes in the setting. Peripheral vision seems to have as its principal function the alerting of the individual to movement at the side, which may represent danger.

Meaning and distance

What significance do people attach to different distances? The very term 'closeness' conjures up different images than 'distance'. 'Getting *next to*' someone implies a number of things about your relationship. The expression, '*I can't get together with him on that*', has a literal, in addition to a figurative, meaning. In the world of actions from which words take their meaning, a wife who sees another woman standing too close to her husband gets the message loud and clear.

For that matter, anyone confronted with a person whose space pattern varies from his own, finds himself asking the following questions: Who does this man think he is? What is he trying to say? Is he trying to push me around, or why does he have to be so familiar?

Yet one of the first things one discovers in this research is that very similar spatial relationships can have entirely different meanings. What one makes of how others treat him in space is determined by one's ethnic past. This is *not* a matter, however, of generalizing about Latinos standing closer than North Americans, of moving each space zone up a notch as it were. Rather it is a matter of entirely different systems, in which some items are shared but many others are not, including the order and selection of transactions that occur in the different distance sets (Hall, 1962). Thus, it does not necessarily imply any existing or intended relationship if an Arab walks up and places himself inside one's personal sphere in a public place. It may only mean that he wants the spot you are standing on for himself. Since there is no relationship or chance of one, he does not care what you think. The point, however, is so basic and so subtle that it is apt to be lost.

Summary

This paper has dealt with some rather specific aspects of how we gain knowledge as to the content of the minds of other men by means which function almost totally outside awareness. Proxemics represents one of several such out-of-awareness systems which fall within the general rubric of paracommunication.[9]

Communication of this sort, operating outside awareness as it does, appears to be an extraordinarily persistent form of culturally specific behavior which is responded to with considerable effect whenever people encounter patterns which are at variance with their own. It is also apparently a rather basic form of communication, many features of which are shared with other vertebrates.

How man codes distance is a function of which combinations of receptors he uses. These do not always seem to be the same from culture to culture and vary even within subcultures. Visual and kinesthetic cues are

9. Paracommunication is the term suggested as an appropriate designation by Joos (1962) and Trager (1958) to refer to communicative behavior which does not have its base in language but is often synchronized with linguistic and paralinguistic phenomena.

prominent in non-contact Americans. Olfactory and tactile cues are emphasized in Eastern Mediterranean urban Arab culture.

Recording of cues used to distinguish one distance from another is possible. It should be noted, however, that proxemic research is in its infancy and suffers from many obvious flaws. This report represents a summary of some of what has been accomplished to date rather than a definitive statement of the field.

References

BOGARDUS, E. S. (1959), *Social Distance*, Antioch Press.

BRUNER, J. (1959), *The Process of Education*, Harvard University Press.

GIBSON, J. J. (1950), *The Perception of the Visual World*, Riverside Press.

HALL, E. T. (1962), 'Sensitivity and empathy at home and abroad', Three Leatherbee Lectures, given at Harvard University Graduate School of Business Administration, Boston.

HEDIGER, H. (1955), *Studies of the Psychology and Behavior of Captive Animals in Zoos and Circuses*, Butterworth Scientific Series.

JOOS, M. (1962), 'The five clocks', *IJAL*, vol. 28, part 5.

KILPATRICK, F. P. (ed.) (1961), *Explorations in Transactional Psychology*, New York University Press.

THIEL, P. (1961), 'A sequence-experience notation for architectural and urban space', *Town Plann. Rev.*, pp. 33–52.

THOREAU, H. D. (1929), *Walden*, Macmillan Co.

TRAGER, G. L. (1958), 'Paralanguage: a first approximation', *SIL*, vol. 13, pp. 1–12.

WHITE, T. H. (1961), *The Making of the President 1960*, Atheneum.

15 R. Sommer

Further Studies of Small-Group Ecology

R. Sommer, 'Further studies of small-group ecology', *Sociometry*, vol. 28, 1965,
pp. 337–48.

To learn how groups arrange themselves, pairs of students were observed
in a cafeteria where interaction was encouraged and in a library where
interaction was discouraged. In the former situation, people chose to sit
across from one another while in the library people chose a distant seating
pattern. Several paper-and-pencil instruments were used to gauge seating
preference in casual, cooperating, competing and co-acting groups. In
general, casual groups prefer corner seating, cooperating groups to sit
side-by-side, co-acting in a distant arrangement, and competing groups
opposite one another. The role of eye contact in regulating spatial arrangements of small groups is discussed.

The study of ecology covers both the distribution and the density of organisms. Within the social sciences the major ecological studies have taken
place at the societal rather than at the small-group level (e.g. demography)
although it has been known for a long time that the arrangement of individuals in face-to-face groups is not accidental. In American society,
leaders tend to occupy the head positions at a table with their lieutenants
at their sides, while opposition factions frequently are found at the other
end of the table (Hall, 1959; Sommer, 1961; Strodtbeck and Hook, 1961).
Numerous accounts of these phenomena are found in observational studies
such as those by Whyte (1956) and Wilmer (1957). Considering the number of studies concerned with small discussion groups, relatively few have
made the arrangement of people a variable. The early studies by Steinzor
(1950) and Bass and Klubeck (1952) were primarily concerned with other
factors (e.g. leadership) and only afterwards was the physical arrangement
of individuals examined for its effects upon interaction. This is also the
procedure followed by Strodtbeck and Hook (1961) who reanalysed their
jury trial data to learn the effects of table position on contribution to the
discussion, and more recently Hare and Bales (1963) who reexamined
group discussion data for positional effects.

One of the oldest problems in social psychology concerns the classification of face-to-face groups (Allport, 1920). A heuristic taxonomy of

groups resolved some of the contradictory findings of experiments concerned with 'social facilitation', some of whose results indicated a social increment while others showed a social decrement. It was Allport (1920) who made the distinction between cooperating, competing and co-acting groups. Since most of the small group research of the last decades has concerned itself with discusssion groups, this distinction has been largely neglected. The goal of the present study is to learn how people in different types of face-to-face groups arrange themselves. Observational methods are used in seeking out groups whose members have a strong desire to interact and, in another condition, whose members want to remain apart. In a later phase these conditions were simulated through the use of paper and pencil tests.

Observational studies
The situation where people desire to interact

Over a fourteen-months period, observations were made during non-eating hours in the student-union cafeteria at a California university. During these hours the cafeteria is used by students for casual conversation and studying (and to a lesser extent by faculty and non-teaching staff for coffee breaks). The observations were made irregularly and there was some bias in these times in that the writer's schedule led him to pass this way at certain times rather than others but most of the daylight non-eating hours were covered. Records were kept of the seating of pairs of people. In the first series of observations, no distinction was made whether the people were conversing, studying together, or studying separately. The only category specifically excluded from the study was a pair where one or both people were eating. This cafeteria contained two different table sizes: single pedestal square tables (36 inches per side) each surrounded by four chairs, one to a side; double pedestal rectangular tables (36 × 54 inches) each surrounded by six chairs, two on the long sides and one at each end.

The fifty pairs seated at the small square tables showed a preference for corner rather than opposite seating (thirty-five pairs sat corner to corner while fifteen sat across from one another).[1] The double pedestal tables permit side-by-side and distant seating as well as corner and opposite seating. During the course of the observations, sixty pairs were observed at double tables. Table 1 shows clearly that side-by-side and distant seating were infrequent. The vast majority of pairs chose to occupy the corners or sit across from one another.

1. A similar preference for corner seating was found in a subsequent study of eating pairs in a hospital cafeteria. Of the forty-one pairs, twenty-nine sat corner-to-corner while twelve pairs sat across from one another.

Table 1 **Arrangement of pairs at rectangular tables (as percentage)**

Seating arrangement	Series 1 (N = 50)	Series 2 Conversing (N = 74)	Co-acting (N = 18)
Corner	40	54	0
Across	43	36	32
Side	8	6	0
Distant	10	4	68
Total	100	100	100

It was planned to continue these observations for another six months, but in February 1965 the furniture of the cafeteria was changed. In order to accommodate more people the management moved in new tables and rearranged others. Rather than combine these new observations with the previous ones, it seemed preferable to look upon them as a new series in which additional information could be gained. In the next four months fifty-two additional observations were made in which the *major activity* of the people as well as their seating arrangement was recorded. A distinction was made between those pairs who were interacting (conversing, studying together) and those who were co-acting (occupying the same table but studying separately). In order to keep the data comparable to the previous observations, the present analysis focused upon the square tables (36 × 36 inches) observed previously, as well as rectangular tables (36 × 72 inches) which were made by pushing two of the small square tables together. The situation at the other rectangular tables (36 × 54 inches) was confused since these tables now accommodated anywhere from four to eight people, sometimes with end chairs and sometimes without, so these are excluded from the analysis.

Of the 124 pairs seated at the small square tables, 106 were conversing or otherwise interacting while eighteen were co-acting. The interacting pairs showed a definite preference for corner seating, with seventy seated corner-to-corner compared to thirty-six seated across from one another. However, co-acting pairs chose a very different arrangement, with only two pairs sitting corner-to-corner and eighteen sitting opposite one another. These results support the previous studies in which corner seating was preferred over opposite and side-by-side seating in a variety of conditions where individuals interact. It suggests that corner seating preserves the closeness between individuals and also enables people to avoid eye contact since they do not sit face to face. The co-acting pairs use the distance across the table for books, handbags and other belongings, and can avoid visual contact by looking down rather than across the table.

Seating at the rectangular tables is shown in the second and third columns of Table 1. The interacting groups prefer corner-to-corner seating, and to a lesser extent opposite seating, with little use made of side-by-side or distant seating. On the other hand, more than two-thirds of the co-acting groups chose a distant seating arrangement which separated the people geographically and visually.

The situation where interaction is discouraged

One set of observations took place in the reading area adjacent to the reserve room of a university library. This is a large room (29 × 83 feet) containing thirty-three rectangular tables (48 × 64 inches) in the main area. Each table has a capacity of four persons, two sitting on opposite sides with the ends free. The room was generally quiet even when filled to capacity. This made it a good place to study how people arranged themselves when they did *not* want to interact. All observations took place when the room was relatively uncrowded since this provided some choice as to seating. Due to the size of the room, it was not possible to record the arrangements at all the tables in the room without appearing conspicuous. Thus the observer randomly selected some location in the room and diagrammed the seating arrangements within the visible portion of the room on a prepared chart.

A pilot study[2] had shown that the majority of people who came alone sat alone if there were an empty table. This trend was more marked for the males (70 per cent) than for the females (55 per cent). The next largest group arranged themselves diagonally across from whoever already occupied the table. Only 10 per cent of the students sat opposite or beside another student (i.e. in either of the two near positions) when there were empty seats available elsewhere.

Following this, there were nineteen occasions when the seating patterns of those individuals presently in the reserve room were recorded, including people who came alone as well as those who came with friends. The sample consisted of 193 males and 304 women. Again it was found that a higher percentage of males (34 per cent) than females (25 per cent) sat alone. However, the major focus of the study was on those students who sat two at a table (since there is only one possible way that people can arrange themselves three or four to a table). The results showed that 30 per cent of the pairs sat across from one another, 15 per cent sat side-by-side, while 56 per cent used the diagonal or distant arrangement. Although the observations were cross-sectional and spanned only several minutes each, a record was made of any conversations at the table. Conversations were observed among 8 per cent of the pairs sitting across from one another,

2. This study was carried out by David Addicott.

3 per cent of those pairs sitting in a diagonal or distant arrangement, and 37 per cent of those sitting side-by-side.

A second set of observations was made independently in the Periodical Room of the same library. The same general technique was followed in that the arrangement of all pairs was diagrammed on fourteen occasions over a two-month period. This room, excluding the magazine and transit areas, was 36 × 74 feet and contained two types of rectangular tables, one (48 × 64 inches) with two chairs on each side and the ends free, and the other (48 × 90 inches) with three chairs on each side and the ends free. The arrangements of pairs at the two types of tables were similar; and the pooled data show that of the seventy-four pairs, 19 per cent sat across from one another, 13 per cent sat side-by-side and 68 per cent sat in a distant arrangement. Conversations were noted between 14 per cent of the people sitting opposite one another, 6 per cent of those people sitting in a distant relationship and 60 per cent of those pairs sitting side-by-side.

Questionnaire studies
Rectangular-table ecology

To learn something of the way that a group task influences the way people arrange themselves, a paper-and-pencil test was administered to 151 students in an introductory psychology class. Each student was asked to imagine how he and a friend of the same sex would seat themselves under four different conditions: (a) to chat for a few minutes before class; (b) to study together for the same exam; (c) to study for different exams; and (d) to compete in order to see which would be the first to solve a series of puzzles. Each time the student was asked to indicate his own seating and that of his friend on a diagram showing a table and six chairs (see Figure 1). There was one chair at the head and one at the foot and two chairs on each of the sides. In order to maximize the realism of the test, the hypothetical activity was located in the student-union cafeteria during *non*-eating hours (which is, as has been noted, actively used for casual conversation, studying, etc., and has similar rectangular tables). The tasks set for the students included cooperating, co-acting and competing activity. In addition, a distinction was made between casual interaction such as conversation and structured cooperative activity (joint studying for an exam). The different tasks were presented in random order in the test booklet.

There were no significant differences between the sexes in seating arrangements under any of the conditions. This was unexpected since previous studies have shown that females make greater use of side-by-side seating while males prefer to sit across from other people.

seating arrangement	condition 1 (conversion)	condition 2 (cooperating)	condition 3 (co-acting)	condition 4 (competing)
X◻X (side-by-side top)	42	19	3	7
X◻X (side opposite)	46	25	3	41
X◻X (corner)	1	5	43	20
X◻X (opposite corners)	0	0	3	5
XX◻ (both left)	11	51	7	8
X◻X (head-foot)	0	0	13	18
total	100	100	100	99

Figure 1 Seating preferences at rectangular tables

Figure 1 shows the seating preferences for the total group of 151 students. If we take 'near seating' to include side-by-side, corner and opposite arrangements, and let 'distant seating' refer to all other patterns, Figure 1 shows that distant seating was rarely used by casual or cooperating goups. People who want to converse or work together use the near arrangements. On the other hand distant seating is the dominant pattern in co-acting groups. The most common distant pattern shows people sitting on opposite sides of the table but not directly facing one another rather than the more physically distant head–foot arrangement. This suggests that it is the visual contact between people rather than bodily presence that is the major source of distraction in co-acting groups. Distant seating is important in competing groups although the dominant arrangement here is opposite seating.

People conversing overwhelmingly chose a corner-to-corner or opposite arrangement. On the other hand, those studying together strongly prefer to sit side-by-side. In no other condition is side seating used anywhere near this frequency. There is a metaphorical quality to these arrangements with people competing sitting 'in opposition', people cooperating sitting 'on the same side', people conversing sitting 'in a corner' and people co-acting choosing a 'distant' arrangement.

The identical questionnaire was given to twenty-six students in a social psychology class. After the students completed the questionnaire in the usual way, each was asked to go through his responses and explain why he chose this particular arrangement.

For the *casual group*, the dominant preference was for corner seating, and the students' explanations were: 'We would be sitting close to each other and yet be able to see each person.' 'It's nice to be close when chatting but you should face each other instead of side-by-side.' 'You would be closer with only a corner than across the table, you'd have to turn less than side-by-side.' 'The corner arrangement is the most intimate. You wouldn't have to shout *across* the table, but, sitting adjacent you could still face the person. Sitting beside the person it is hard to look at them when you're talking.' Those people who chose to sit across from one another emphasized the desirability of a direct face-to-face arrangement.

In the *cooperating group*, those people who liked the corner arrangement mentioned the ease of conversing in corner chairs ('Because we could look at each other's notes with the least change of place and effort.') while those people who chose the side arrangement emphasized the ease of sharing things in this position.

For the *co-acting group*, the dominant arrangement was a distant one and these students emphasized the need to be apart yet feel together ('This would allow for sitting far enough apart so we wouldn't interfere with each other, but if we wanted to pass comments we are close enough.' 'Effectively divides table into two halves yet allows brief remarks without having to raise voice. Also allows staring into space and not at neighbor's face.').

As in the previous study, opposite, distant-opposite and distant seating were preferred by *competing groups*. The way that a face-to-face arrangement stimulates competition was frequently mentioned: e.g. 'Able to see how friend is doing but there's enough room'; or, 'In this situation the friend can be watched to determine his progress.' The reason given most frequently by people preferring the distant-opposite arrangement was that it reduced the temptation to look at the other person's answers while the long distance aided concentration. Those people electing a distant arrangement explained that this would minimize distraction. Two of the three people preferring a side arrangement mentioned that it was easier to concentrate when not looking directly at the other person.

Round-table ecology

In order to learn how the group task would affect the arrangement of people at a round table, 116 students in another introductory psychology class were asked to fill out a questionnaire similar to that of the preceding study except that the diagram showed a *round* table surrounded by six chairs. The same four situations were described (i.e. conversing with a friend, studying for the same exam, for different exams or competing). Since the results showed no significant difference between the sixty-five females and fifty-one males, the composite totals are presented in Figure 2. People can sit in only three possible arrangements under these conditions (see Figure 2), these three arrangements comprising a rank order of physical distance.

percentage of Ss choosing this arrangement

seating arrangement	condition 1 (conversion)	condition 2 (cooperating)	condition 3 (co-acting)	condition 4 (competing)
	63	83	13	12
	17	7	36	25
	20	10	52	63
total	100	100	100	100

Figure 2 Seating preferences at round tables

Figure 2 shows that casual and cooperating groups made greatest use of adjacent chairs. This trend was most marked among the cooperating groups where 83 per cent chose adjacent chairs. Although the co-acting group makes heavy use of an arrangement where one empty chair is left between the people, the majority of co-acting groups places a gap of two seats between them (i.e. sit directly opposite one another). The trend for opposite seating is most pronounced in the competing group.

If we make certain assumptions on the basis of our previous study with rectangular tables, it is possible to formulate hypotheses as to how positions at a round table compare with those at a rectangular table. Adjacent seating at a round table seems somewhere between side and corner seating. Physically, it places people side-by-side at a lesser angle than in a corner arrangement. Sitting one seat away from another person at a round table does not seem to be as 'distant' an arrangement as leaving the same gap at a rectangular table. This suggests that people at a round table are psychologically closer than at a corresponding position at a rectangular table. Opposite seating in the round table arrangement used here seems to serve some of the functions of both distant and opposite seating at a rectangular table.

The same questionnaire was given to eighteen students who, after filling out the questionnaire in the usual way, explained why they arranged themselves as they did. Most of the students in the *conversing condition* selected adjacent seats: 'I want to chat with my friend, not the whole cafeteria, so I sit next to her'; 'More intimate, no physical barriers between each other.' In the *cooperating group*, the vast majority chose to sit in adjacent chairs. Their explanations stressed the advantages of this arrangement for comparing notes and sharing materials. Most students in the *co-acting condition* chose to sit two seats away from one another, the greatest physical distance permitted in this diagram. Of those who chose to sit one seat away, several mentioned that this 'Doesn't put us directly opposite each other . . . keep looking at each other if we look up from studying', and 'Not directly across from each other because we'd have more of a tendency to talk then.' In the *competing condition*, most students chose to leave two seats between them which placed them directly opposite one another. The explanations emphasized the need to keep separate in order to avoid seeing each other's material. Several mentioned that opposite seating permitted them to see how the other person was doing and enhanced feelings of competition.

Discussion

These results indicate that different tasks are associated with different spatial arrangements; the ecology of interaction differs from the ecology of co-action and competition. Exactly why these particular arrangements are chosen we do not know for certain. On the basis of what our subjects report, eye contact seems an important factor in spatial arrangements. Under certain conditions direct visual contact represents a challenge to the other, a play at dominance. Among chickens and turkeys in confinement, McBride (1964) has shown that the dominant bird in the flock has the most eye space. When he looks at a submissive bird, the latter looks away. When birds are crowded together, they stand at the wire of the coop facing outward to avoid the stress that would be generated by extended visual contact. We may only speculate as to the extent to which eye contact regulates spatial arrangements, though it is interesting to note that the only questionnaire condition in which opposite seating was chosen over other distant alternatives was in the competitive task where the subject indicated a desire to 'keep an eye on what the other person was doing'. It is hypothesized that gestures of threat (agonistic displays) are more appropriate in competitive conditions than cooperative or strictly social tasks. On the other hand, agonistic displays are stressful to both parties, and in the animal kingdom are generally terminated by ritualized submissive behavior rather than actual combat. In a previous pilot study,[3] people were asked how they would seat themselves at a table already occupied by someone they disliked. It was found that people chose to sit at some distance from the disliked person, but *not* directly opposite him, i.e. in a distant-side position. In this way they were removed visually as well as geographically from the source of stress. The relationship between distance and aggressive behavior among chaffinches has been studied nicely by Marler (1956). Placing the cages of chaffinches various distances apart, he found the point at which aggressive displays began. Female chaffinches tolerated closer presence than males, while females whose breasts were dyed to resemble males were kept at the typical male distance by other birds.

Most stressful encounters are avoided through spatial segregation. The orbits in which people travel tend to remove them from contact with those with whom they disagree or dislike. Avoidance is the first line of defence against interpersonal stress but when this is not possible or effective, an individual develops alternate methods. Limiting the range of visual contact through social conventions or actual physical barriers are other possibilities. The present studies all took place in settings whose furnishings consisted solely of tables and chairs. No attempt was made to explore the role of physical barriers such as posts, partitions, tables, etc. in regulating interaction. The ways in which people gain privacy in public areas warrants further exploration in a society in which more and more

3. This study was conducted by Vera Stevens and Corinne Sundberg.

people share a finite amount of space. In settings such as libraries, study rooms and large open offices, it is exceedingly important to develop methods whereby unwanted or stressful interpersonal contact is avoided.

Chapin (1951), in his discussion of housing factors related to mental hygiene, indicated the importance of ease of circulation as well as areas that can be closed off from the main traffic flow. Just as people moving about a house require resting places for solitude or individual concentration, people rooted to a given spot in a public area require places where their eyes can rest without stress. There is the apocryphal story of the stress produced by the newspaper strike in New York City where the seated men were unable to 'retreat into' newspapers and had to look at the other occupants, particularly women standing above them. Subway officials believe that the advertisements on the wall provide safe resting places for the patrons' eyes.

Since the topological similarities between different arrangements of people make it unnecessary to experiment with every conceivable physical arrangement, it seems most fruitful to isolate the socially and psychologically genotypic arrangements. The two most obvious ones are near and distant seating. In ordinary social intercourse, near seating is the rule. In American society it is only among strangers, co-acting individuals or schizophrenic mental patients that one finds distant seating patterns in any frequency.

One can divide seating patterns into several important subclasses. One possible category involves arrangements which maximize direct visual contact between individuals. According to Goffman (1963), Hall (1964) and Birdwhistell (1952), direct visual contact can be exceedingly uncomfortable and disconcerting under ordinary conditions, producing feelings of anxiety in the person upon whom the eyes are directly centered. There are cultural differences in the use of visual contact such as the middle-class Southern girl described by Birdwhistell who 'uses her eyes more' than does the Northern or Western girl. One can also disinguish between near arrangements according to the extent to which they facilitate tactile or olfactory contact. The number of possible arrangements is still small enough to permit clear categorization and conceptualization.

References

ALLPORT, F. H. (1920), *Social Psychology*, Houghton-Mifflin.
BASS, B. M., and KLUBECK, S. (1952), 'Effects of seating arrangements in leaderless group discussions', *J. abnorm. soc. Psychol.*, vol. 47, pp. 724–7.
BIRDWHISTELL, R. (1952), 'Field methods and techniques', *Hum. Org.*, vol. 11, pp. 37–8.
CHAPIN, F. S. (1951), 'Some housing factors related to mental hygiene', *J. Social Issues*, vol. 7, pp. 164–71.
GOFFMAN, E. (1963), *Behavior in Public Places*, Free Press.

HALL, E. T. (1959), *The Silent Language*, Doubleday.

HALL, E. T. (1964), 'Silent assumptions in social communication', *Disorders of Communication*, vol. 42, pp. 41–55. [Reprinted in this book, pp. 274–88.]

HARE, A. P., and BALES, R. F. (1963), 'Seating position and small-group interaction', *Sociometry*, vol. 26, pp. 480–86.

MCBRIDE, G. (1964), *A General Theory of Social Organization and Behavior*, University of Queensland Press.

MARLER, P. (1956), 'Studies of fighting in chaffinches: proximity as a cause of aggression', *Brit. J. Animal Behav.*, vol. 4, pp. 23–30.

SOMMER, R. (1961), 'Leadership and group geography', *Sociometry*, vol. 24, pp. 99–110.

STEINZOR, B. (1950), 'The spatial factor in face-to-face discussion groups', *J. aborm. soc. Psychol.*, vol. 45, pp. 552–5.

STRODTBECK, F. L., and HOOK, L. H. (1961), 'The social dimensions of a twelve-man jury table', *Sociometry*, vol. 24, pp. 397–415.

WHYTE, W. H. (1956), *The Organization Man*, Simon & Schuster.

WILMER, H. A. (1957), 'Graphic ways of representing some aspects of a therapeutic community', *Symposium on Preventive and Social Psychiatry*, Government Printing Office, Washington.

16 M. Argyle and J. Dean

Eye Contact, Distance and Affiliation

M. Argyle and J. Dean, 'Eye contact, distance and affiliation', *Sociometry*, vol. 28, 1965, pp. 289–304.

Previous evidence suggests that eye contact serves a number of different functions in two-person encounters, of which one of the most important is gathering feedback on the other person's reactions. It is further postulated that eye contact is linked to affiliative motivation, and that approach and avoidance forces produce an equilibrium level of physical proximity, eye-contact and other aspects of intimacy. If one of these is disturbed, compensatory changes may occur along the other dimensions. Experiments are reported which suggest that people move towards an equilibrium distance, and adopt a particular level of eye contact. As predicted, there was less eye contact and glances were shorter, the closer two subjects were placed together (where one member of each pair was a confederate who gazed continuously at the other). The effect was greatest for opposite-sex pairs. In another experiment it was found that subjects would stand closer to a second person when his eyes were shut, as predicted by the theory.

During social interaction, people look each other in the eye, repeatedly but for short periods. If we may anticipate, people look most while they are listening, and use glances of about three to ten seconds in length. When glances are longer than this, anxiety is aroused. Without eye contact (EC), people do not feel that they are fully in communication. Simmel (1921) has described it as 'a wholly new and unique union between two people', and remarked that it 'represents the most perfect reciprocity in the entire field of human relationship'. A certain amount is already known about the empirical determinants of EC, and this will be reviewed below. Rather less is known about the psychological processes which produce EC, or the functions which it serves; the most important alternatives are discussed in the third section. We shall develop a set of hypotheses relating EC to the need for affiliation, and then report some experiments which test these hypotheses.

The determinants of EC

The amount of EC which takes place in an encounter varies from zero to 100 per cent of the time available, and some of the sources of variation are known. In some of the experiments cited it is more appropriate to speak of 'gaze-direction', since what was measured was whether the subject looked up, regardless of whether the other person was looking back. In other experiments, a confederate was used who gazed all the time at the subject, so that gaze-direction is the same as eye contact.

1. *Point in the conversation.* In all investigations where this has been studied it is found that there is more EC when the subject is listening than when he is speaking, typically with a ratio of $2\frac{1}{2}$ or $3:1$. Furthermore people look up, at the end of their speeches and of phrases within them, and look away at the start of long utterances (Kendon, 1964; Exline, Gray and Schuette, 1965; Nielsen, 1962).

2. *Nature of topic.* There is more EC when less personal topics are discussed (Exline, Gray and Schuette, 1965), and when the material is cognitively straightforward. There is less during unfluent and hesitating passages (Exline, 1963).

3. *Individual differences* in EC are very great. Women are found to engage in more EC, in a variety of situations (Exline, 1963). Some patients suffer from 'aversion of gaze' (Riemer, 1955), and it has been found that autistic children avoid masks of human faces too (Hutt and Ounstead, 1964). There are cross-cultural differences, varying from taboos on EC, to much greater amounts of intimacy than are common in Western countries.

4. *Relations between a pair of people.* There is more gaze direction if A likes B (Exline and Winters, 1965), and if they are cooperating rather than competing (Exline, 1963). There is less EC if there is tension in the relationship, as when a soldier is being disciplined by an officer (Goffman, 1963, p. 96), or if A has recently deceived B (Exline *et al.*, 1961).

5. *The developmental history of EC.* Observations of infants show that the smiling response to certain aspects of the human face develops in the first weeks of life. Spitz (1946) carried out experiments with masks, and found that in the second month a representation of the top of the head, including the eyes, would produce smiling. Wolff (1963, pp. 122–3) observed that EC first appeared between the twenty-fifth and twenty-eighth day; when this occurred it stopped the baby's random activity, and was found rewarding by the mothers, who now regarded the baby as 'fun to play with'. Just as the young of other species imprint the mother and follow her around, it has been suggested that the immobile human infant follows the mother's face with its eyes (Gray, 1958).

Functions of EC

There is no one theory that can explain all of the above findings. It has been pointed out that EC can have a variety of subjective meanings – such as friendship, sexual attraction, hate and a struggle for dominance (Feld-man, 1959, p. 233). We shall consider here the main functions which EC may serve.

Information-seeking. If social behavior is looked at as a kind of motor skill, we must inquire how the performer obtains the necessary feedback on the reactions of the other. Speech and paralinguistic material convey a great deal, but it is possible to get a lot more by careful inspection of the other's face, especially in the region of the eyes. Such feedback is needed most at the end of speeches, to see how these have been received. The speaker looks away at the beginning of his speeches and when he has to think about what he is saying, because the extra input from EC is distracting.

Signalling that the channel is open. During EC each person knows that the other is attending primarily to him, and that further interaction can proceed. A flicker of the eye towards a third party may indicate that the channel is closed. This can be regarded as a rather special case of the first process, in that information is obtained about the other's direction of attention. EC also places a person under some obligation to interact; thus, when a chairman or waiter allows his eye to be caught he places himself under the power of the eye-catcher (Goffman, 1963, p. 94).

Concealment and exhibitionism. Some patients, according to Laing, lack adequate feelings of self-regard and ego-identity, and have a great desire to be seen, in order to be 'loved and confirmed as a person' (Laing, 1960a, chapter 8). Some people want to be seen, and EC is the proof that they are being seen. Others do not want to be seen, and feel 'impaled before the glance of another' (Scheutz, 1948), feel they are depersonalized or turned to stone by becoming an object for another's perception (Laing, 1960b, pp. 48f., 78f.). This fear of being seen may be due to a fear of being rejected, based on past experience, or a desire to conceal inner states – which in turn would lead to rejection. The latter is supported by the finding that subjects who had been induced to cheat gazed less (Exline *et al.*, 1961, p. 396).

Establishment and recognition of social relationship. If A gazes at B, this will have a different impact, depending on his facial expression. If there is EC, both may know that A's attitude to B is one of sexual attraction, friendship, hate, dominance or submission. There may be a rapid sequence of communications, in which EC plays a central part, and which serves to establish the relationship between A and B. For example, suppose A wants to dominate B: A stares at B with the appropriate expression; B may accept A's dominance by a submissive expression and looking away; or B may outstare A, or simply withdraw by looking coldly away. Hess (1965) has found that emotional arousal leads to enlargement of the pupils, and that men are more attracted by girls with enlarged pupils (hence the use of belladonna), though they are quite unaware that this is the cue to which they are responding.

The affiliative-conflict theory. In this section we shall introduce some ideas which will explain some of the EC phenomena which are so far unexplained.

1. There are both approach and avoidance forces behind EC. The approach forces include the need for feedback, discussed above, and sheer affiliative needs: for example, EC can be used as a reinforcer in the operative conditioning of verbal behavior (Krasner, 1958). It may be innately satisfying as suggested above. The avoidance components include the fear of being seen, the fear of revealing inner states, and the fear of seeing the rejecting responses of others, which were discussed above.

2. If there are both approach and avoidance drives behind EC, Miller's conflict analysis is applicable (Miller, 1944), and it would be expected that there should be an equilibrium level of EC for a person coming into social contact with some second person, and that if EC rises above that amount it will be anxiety-arousing. (Of course the equilibrium amount of EC, and the equilibrium distance may not be the same for the two people; they will then work out some compromise solution, more or less satisfactory to both. In the experiments to be reported here, however, we shall hold the behavior of one person constant.)

3. It is supposed that similar considerations apply to other types of behavior which are linked with affiliative motivation. Thus there will be an equilibrium point of physical closeness, of intimacy of conversation, and of amount of smiling. The more these behaviors occur, the more affiliative motivation is satisfied, but if they go too far, anxiety is created.

4. It is suggested that an equilibrium develops for 'intimacy', where this is a joint function of eye contact, physical proximity, intimacy of topic, smiling, etc. This equilibrium would be at a certain degree of intimacy for any pair of people. We deduce that if one of the components of intimacy is changed, one or more of the others will shift in the reverse direction in order to maintain the equilibrium. Thus,

$$\text{Intimacy} = f \begin{cases} \text{eye contact} \\ \text{physical proximity} \\ \text{intimacy of topic} \\ \text{amount of smiling} \\ \text{etc.} \end{cases}$$

5. Twelve empirical deductions follow from this formulation. For example if amount of smiling is reduced, and intimacy of topic and physical proximity are held constant, EC should be increased to restore the equilibrium level of intimacy.

6. If equilibrium for intimacy is disturbed along one of its dimensions, attempts will first be made to restore it by adjusting the others. If this is not possible because all are held constant, or because the deviation is too extreme, the subject will feel uncomfortable in one of two ways. If the disturbance is in the direction of too much intimacy, the avoidance forces will predominate, and the subject will feel anxiety about rejection or revealing inner states; if in the direction of less intimacy, he will simply feel deprived of affiliative satisfactions.

An experiment has already been reported that confirms one of these twelve deductions. Exline, Gray and Schuette (1965) found that there was more EC when the topic of conversation was less intimate. We shall report two experiments testing two more of these deductions. Another experiment by Exline confirms the postulated connection between EC and 'intimacy': those who were caused to like a confederate engaged in more EC with him (Exline and Winters, 1965).

An experiment on EC and equilibrium for distance

There is some evidence for an equilibrium level of physical proximity. For the purposes of any particular form of interaction, people take up a position a certain distance from one another. Hall (1955) reports that Americans will not stand nearer than eighteen to twenty inches when talking to a stranger of the same sex. If they have to stand closer than this preferred distance, they will turn and face each other at right angles, or stand side-to-side. Steinzor (1950) found that subjects in groups of ten were least likely to speak to those nearest to them, and most likely to address those two or three places away. As well as minimum distances for EC and social interaction, there are also maximum ones. Sommer (1962) found that people did not like sitting more than five and a half feet apart when conversing in a rather large hall, and would move to another position if further apart. The preferred position for conversation at a table was at two corner seats, so that the participants were physically close, but not directly facing one another.

Americans may stand at eighteen to twenty inches, but people from Latin America and the Middle East will stand much closer. Hall (1955) reports how conversations at international gatherings result in Americans retreating backwards or gyrating round in circles. Members of some primitive societies in Africa and Indonesia come closer still and maintain bodily contact during conversation (E. Ardener, personal communication). Every animal species has its characteristic individual distance, closer than which they will not go, as well as a maximum social distance between members of the group. For some the minimum distance is zero, as for some kinds of monkeys; for the flamingo it is two feet, and so on (Hediger, 1955, pp. 66, 83).

In order to carry out the later experiment it was necessary to know where the equilibrium point was for local subjects and conditions. And it was predicted from the affiliative conflict theory that the equilibrium point for approach would be closer if the other person's eyes were shut.

Method

Subjects were invited to take part in a perceptual experiment, and asked to stand 'as close as is comfortable to see well' to two physical objects, both the same size as a human head (a book, and a plaster head of William McDougall). Then followed three other displays in different orders for different subjects: (1) a cut-out life-sized photograph of the face of the first author, (2) the first author with eyes shut and (3) with eyes open. In (1) and (3) the object was looking straight at the subject with a pleasant-to-neutral expression; in (2) and (3) the object was seated in a chair. Displays 1–3 were given in all six orders. The subjects were six adult acquaintances (three male, three female), and six child acquaintances (three male, three female, aged five to twelve). Distances eye-to-eye were measured by a long ruler. It was hoped that the disguise of the experiment as a study of vision would prevent such measurements being disturbing.

Results and discussion

As is shown in Table 1, subjects stand eleven inches closer to the photograph than to the person, and six inches closer to a person whose eyes are shut than to a person whose eyes are open. The second effect is more marked for adults than for children, and children stand closer in all three conditions.

Table 1 **Position in inches of nearest approach under different conditions**

Subjects	n	Photo	Eyes shut	Eyes open
Adults	6	35·7	34·0	42·7
Children	6	16·9	27·6	31·4
Total	12	26·3	30·8	37·1

There were no reversals for the six adults, and only one for the six children. Applying a binomial test, both the photo/eyes-open differences and the eyes-open/eyes-shut differences are significant at $p < 0.003$. Other tests of significance give a rather lower value in view of the large individual differences, but for adults only on a Mann-Whitney test the eyes-open/eyes-shut difference is significant at $p < 0.05$.

The main effect of order is that it makes a difference whether the 'eyes-shut' condition follows or precedes the 'eyes-open' condition. The finding is that when 'eyes-shut' comes first, both distances are less ($p < 0.05$). This suggests a persistence of the social system which is first established.

An experiment to determine the effects of distance on eye contact

There is some evidence that EC is reduced when proximity is greater. When proximity is very great, as in lifts and buses, interaction and EC often cease entirely. Goffman reports that EC is common when approaching a stranger on a pavement, while it is decided on which side to pass, but that 'civil inattention' is given when the stranger gets to a distance of eight feet (Goffman, 1963, p. 95).

The present experiment was designed to test one of the twelve deductions from our affiliative theory of EC, viz. that if spatial proximity is increased, EC will be reduced. If it is assumed that intimacy is a function of length of glance as well as of total EC, it follows that with greater proximity glances will become shorter.

Method

The method first employed by Exline was used, in which two people take part in a conversation, one of whom is a confederate who gazes continually at the other, a genuine subject.

Subjects were asked to come and take part in an 'experiment on conversations'. They were introduced to a person who appeared to be another subject but who was actually a confederate of the experimenter. The two were asked to discuss a TAT card and make up a story about it in three minutes. Three conversations were held, and the chairs were placed so that the distance between them was two, six and ten feet, eye-to-eye, in different orders for different pairs. In two preliminary experiments, the pairs were placed facing one another. In the final version of the experiment to be reported here, they were placed at 90°, behind tables; this has the advantage that EC is more 'voluntary', and the gazing of the confederate is less apparent.

The independent variable was the distance between subjects. Each pair held three conversations, at distances of two, six and ten feet. The chairs and tables were placed so that subjects could not deviate very far from these distances by leaning backwards or forwards. Subject and confederate were asked to move their chairs between conditions to positions marked by chalk. The experimenter said 'And for the next conversation I'd like you to move your chairs and sit . . . here . . . and . . . here.'

The dependent variables were the amount of EC in three minutes, and the average length of glances. Since the confederate gazed continuously, the amount of EC engaged in by the subject depended entirely on him, and it was only necessary to record the duration of his looking at the confederate. The observers were placed behind a one-way screen as shown in Figure 1.

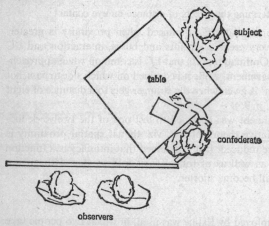

subject

table

confederate

observers

Figure 1 Arrangement of subjects and observers

The observers were looking directly into the eyes of the subject, and could tell with some accuracy when he looked at the confederate. The amount of EC in the three-minute conversations was recorded on cumulative stop watches. During the early trials two observers were used, but the agreement was so close that later we relied on one. A second observer counted the number of glances made by the subject during the three minutes. It has been suggested that at greater distance it is less clear whether the subject is really looking at the eyes of the confederate, or at other parts of his head, so that the amount of EC at greater distances may be over-estimated. However Gibson and Pick (1963) have found that subjects can tell with considerable accuracy whether a second person is looking them in the eye: when the other was two metres distance, shifts of fixation of ten cm were clearly discriminable. Exline found that an observer agreed highly with a confederate as to whether EC was taking place (Exline, Gray and Schuette, 1965), and that there was very high agreement between observers, (r = 0·98). It was our experience that for the majority of subjects there was no difficulty in telling whether EC was occurring or not; they did not spend much time fixating other parts of the head. In later studies with schizophrenics we have had greater difficulty. We also found that a subject's eyes were very stable when he was engaging in EC, rather than scanning the rest of the confederate's face. During EC there is a steady fixation, and this can generally be identified.

Instructions given to each pair were as follows: 'This is an experiment to find out how two people come to an agreement during a conversation. We would like you both to look at this picture, and then you will have three minutes to make up a joint story about what you think is happening. We shall be listening to your discussion from the next room.'

Eighty subjects were used, twenty-four of them in the main experiment, half of each sex. The subjects in the main experiment were all graduate students in subjects other than psychology. There were four confederates, two of each sex, and these were young people of similar age and background to the subjects. Some deception was used to make it appear that they were genuine subjects: they were instructed to talk about half the time and to adopt a pleasant-to-neutral expression.

At the end of the experiment, subjects were interviewed, mainly to discover if they had noticed that the confederate was gazing all the time, or whether they had guessed the point of the experiment, and to explain the experiment to them.

Results

The experimental procedure was thought to be satisfactory, in that perfectly normal conversations took place, and only one or two persons realized that they were being gazed at, or that they were talking to a confederate; and their results were no different from those of other subjects. The main findings on total EC and length of glance are given in the analyses of variance shown in Table 2 and Figure 2.

The experiment has been replicated four times, with variations in task and conditions, and using different subjects, confederates, observers and experimenters. The first two experiments used a head-on position of the subjects: the effects of this are discussed later. The third experiment is the one reported here, and incorporated a number of improvements in technique, such as using tables and chairs that prevented the subjects from changing the distance between them. The fourth is an experiment by E. R. Porter using pairs of males throughout, and varying certain other conditions. The effect of distance was similar in all these rather different versions of the experiment.

Distance and total EC. The prediction that EC will decrease with spatial proximity is confirmed for all four combinations of sexes ($p < 0.001$). It is

Table 2 Analysis of variance for main experiment on total EC and length of glance

Source	Total eye contact					Average length of glances				
	s.s.	df	m.s.	F	p	s.s.	df	m.s.	F	p
Distance	20,824	2	10,412	16·12	0·001	211·4	2	105·7	8·13	0·01
Sex of Subject (SS)	1271	1	1271	1·97	n.s.	10·0	1	10·0	0·77	n.s.
Sex of Confed. (SC)	263	1	263	0·41	n.s.	13·1	1	13·1	1·01	n.s.
Sequence (Seq.)	16,230	5	3246	5·03	0·025	145·3	5	29·1	2·24	0·06
Distance × SS	64	2	32	0·05	n.s.	8·3	2	4·2	0·32	n.s.
Distance × SC	40	2	20	0·03	n.s.	6·1	2	3·0	0·23	n.s.
Distance × Seq.	905	10	91	0·14	n.s.	40·5	10	4·1	0·31	n.s.
SS × SC	22,349	1	22,349	34·59	0·001	219·6	1	219·6	16·90	0·01
SS × Seq.	14,758	5	2952	4·57	0·025	479·4	5	95·9	7·38	0·01
SC × Seq.	22,779	5	4556	7·05	0·01	676·6	5	135·3	10·41	0·01
Dist. × SS × SC	1423	2	711	1·10	n.s.	16·7	2	8·4	0·64	n.s.
Dist. × SS × Seq.	2795	10	280	0·43	n.s.	85·8	10	8·6	0·66	n.s.
Dist. × SC × Seq.	3673	10	367	0·57	n.s.	64·5	10	6·5	0·50	n.s.
SS × SC × Seq.	19,450	5	3890	6·02	0·01	316·7	5	63·3	4·87	0·025
Residual	6460	10	646			130·0	10	13·0		
Total	133,284	71				2424·1	71			

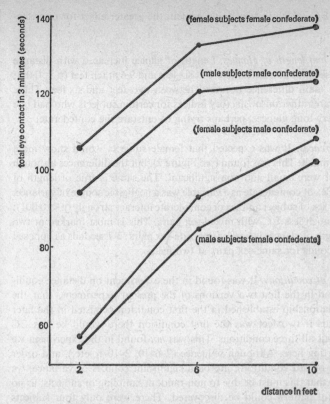

Figure 2 Relation between EC and distances for different combinations of confederates and subjects

somewhat more marked for opposite-sex pairs. These results are shown in Figure 2. It can be seen that EC varies from about 30 per cent to 75 per cent of the time in the different conditions, i.e. we are dealing with major sources of variance. These results were replicated in the preliminary experiments, using a different angle between subjects. The effects of distance were more marked at 90° than 180° between the subjects (p < 0·05, females only).

It was found that the effect of distance is greatest for subjects with short EC (averaged for all three distances): $\rho = -0.38$ (p < 0·05). Is this due to the greater shift and lower EC for opposite-sex pairs? If separate correlations are calculated, it is found that the shift/EC correlation is −0·30 (n.s.) for opposite-sex pairs, and 0·00 for same-sex pairs. It appears that the more fundamental relation is between sensitivity to distance

M. Argyle and J. Dean 311

and low EC, which in turn could explain the greater effect for opposite-sex pairs.

Distance and length of glances. Length of glance increased with distance from 5·5 seconds at two feet to 8·8 at six feet and 9·6 at ten feet (p < 0·01); Thus the main difference occurred between two feet and six feet. These averages are rather unsatisfactory indices for certain subjects who had one or two very long glances, perhaps trying to outstare the confederate.

Sex differences. It was expected that female subjects would show more EC than males. This was found (see Figure 2), but the differences although consistent were small and non-significant. The same is true of length of glances. Sex of confederate as a variable was a negligible source of variance. However sex of subject and sex of confederate interact strongly (p < 0·001): there is much less EC with mixed-sex pairs. This is most marked at two feet. Length of glances is less for opposite-sex pairs: 3·7 seconds as opposed to 7·2 seconds for same-sex pairs at two feet.

Sequence of conditions. It was found in the experiment on distance equilibrium, and in the first two versions of the present experiment, that the social relationship established in the first condition persisted in the later ones. Thus if two feet was the first condition there would be less EC throughout all three conditions. This was *not* found in the experiment we are reporting here. Although sequence (2–6–10, 2–10–6, etc.), and order (1st, 2nd or 3rd condition), are both significant sources of variance, we conclude that this must be due to non-random sampling of subjects, as no meaningful pattern could be discovered. There were only four subjects for each of the six sequences compared.

Observational results concerning equilibrium tendencies. It was expected that at very close distances efforts would first be made to reduce intimacy by reducing EC etc., but that anxiety would be shown if such steps were not enough. In the two feet condition, EC never quite fell to zero, but signs of tension were observed in all subjects, especially when facing each other directly. They tried to increase the distance – by leaning backwards – which was prevented by chairs in the main experiment. They engaged in various gestures apparently to reduce EC or to distract attention: looking down, shading the eyes with the hand, narrowing the eyes, scratching the head, smoking (prevented in final version), blowing the nose, etc. At the ten feet position, on the other hand, subjects were inclined to lean forwards as would be expected from the equilibrium theory. This was prevented by tables in the main experiment.

We should consider how far the conditions of the experiment may have distorted the results. The situation was odd in at least one respect; namely the confederate stared continuously. This would probably be interpreted by the subject as seeking greater intimacy; had the confederate adopted a more hostile expression, it might have been seen as an attempt to dominate. Thus the amount of intimacy in the situation was entirely under the control of the subject. However, many subjects were not aware that the confederate *was* gazing continuously; and this was particularly true of subjects with short EC, for whom the effect of distance was most marked.

Discussion

How far do our results support the existence of equilibrium positions for distance or EC? The first experiment found that subjects would only approach to a certain degree of physical proximity; the second experiment found that those at two feet tried to increase the distance, and those at ten feet to reduce it, by leaning backwards and forwards respectively. Subjects at two feet were in a state of discomfort and tension. There are no comparable data to demonstrate an equilibrium for EC, but in our second experiment, where EC was entirely under the subject's control, we found a consistent level of EC for each subject, and that this was a function of our experimental conditions, varying from 30–75 per cent of the time. There were very great individual differences, from 0 to 100 per cent of the time.

How far have our tests of hypotheses, derived from the theory, confirmed that theory? In the first experiment it was found (for adults) that A would stand 8·7 inches nearer B when B's eyes were shut – a difference of about 23 per cent of the mean distance. In the second experiment, it was found that EC was reduced at closer distances. The effect was greatest between two and six feet, for subjects who were low in EC, and for opposite-sex pairs, this being possibly a special case of the former. EC changed from 30 per cent to 58 per cent of the time for opposite-sex pairs, from 55 per cent to 72 per cent for same-sex pairs. Clearly this hypothesis is also confirmed, though there are further complications not envisaged by the theory.

There is an apparent difficulty over the finding that EC did not fall to zero in the two feet condition. Placing two people two feet apart is a major disturbance of equilibrium, and considerable reduction of EC, smiling, etc., would be needed in compensation. The fact that subjects were very uncomfortable at two feet shows that equilibrium was not satisfactorily restored. There seem to be two possibilities:

1. There is a separate equilibrium for EC, distance etc., and they cannot *fully* compensate for one another, as our theory supposed.

2. There are such strong positive forces behind EC that it is difficult to reduce it to zero.

These forces are the need for *some* feedback, to ensure that the channel is still open, and to avoid sheer rudeness in view of the conventional social pressures to engage in some EC. In the preliminary experiments, in which subjects sat directly facing each other, there was nearly as much EC at two feet as at six feet. We thought that this might be due to the difficulty of avoiding EC without rudeness at two feet, and we used a 90° position in the main experiment to make EC more voluntary. In fact there was a much greater drop in EC between six feet and two feet with this arrangement, which supports the interpretation above. In subsequent studies with schizophrenics, to be reported elsewhere, some subjects *did* reduce their EC to zero at two feet.

The finding that opposite-sex pairs show *less* EC and use shorter glances is contradictory to the general expectations of the theory, since it may be presumed that the approach drives are stronger with opposite-sex pairs. In fact, there was rather more arousal in the opposite-sex pairs, and conversation was more lively. Of course, opposite-sex pairs in other contexts *do* engage in a lot of EC, but this may be only when intimacy really has developed. In our situation the subjects were initially strangers. Another aspect of EC may need to be postulated to account for our result. EC between opposite-sex pairs of this age, in this culture, probably carries the additional implication of sexual attraction, and this may be especially true of long glances. In order to keep this attraction within bounds in the laboratory setting, EC may have been reduced.

Since the information and feedback-seeking aspects of EC are reasonably well established, it is worth inquiring whether our results could be explained in these terms. The greater EC at greater distances could perhaps be due to the increased difficulty of perception. It may also be more necessary to keep signalling to the other that one is still attending, i.e. that the channel is still open. We found that EC invariably fell off in the second half of each three-minute conversation. This could be because the necessary feedback had by then been obtained; in addition, subjects were at this stage thinking hard for more ideas, and EC would have constituted a distraction. On the other hand, this theory offers no explanation for the existence of an equilibrium position, or for the emotional aspects of EC, and it is believed that the affiliative-conflict theory is required in addition to the information-seeking analysis.

Summary

Previous evidence on the determinants of eye contact was reviewed, and it was concluded that EC serves a number of functions. One of the most important of these is the quest for feedback during social interaction, together with that of signalling that the channel is open.

A second theory was proposed, that EC is a component of intimacy and is equivalent to physical proximity. These, and other aspects of intimacy are governed by both approach and avoidance forces, and are kept in a condition of equilibrium for any two people. Experiments were reported which provide evidence of such an equilibrium for physical proximity and for eye contact.

It is postulated that if this equilibrium is disturbed along one of its constituent dimensions, e.g. by increasing physical proximity, there will be compensatory changes along the other dimensions. It has already been shown that greater intimacy of topic leads to less eye contact. We have now shown that reducing eye contact makes greater proximity possible, and that greater proximity reduces eye contact.

References

EXLINE, R. V. (1963), 'Explorations in the process of person perception: visual interaction in relation to competition, sex and the need for affiliation', *J. Personality*, vol. 31, pp. 1–20.

EXLINE, R. V., and WINTERS, L. C. (1965), 'Affective relations and mutual glances in dyads', in S. Tomkins and C. Izzard (eds.), *Affect, Cognition and Personality*, Springer.

EXLINE, R. V., GRAY, D., and SCHUETTE, D. (1965), 'Visual behavior in a dyad as affected by interview content and sex of respondent', *Journal of Personality and Social Psychology*, vol. 1, pp. 201–9.

EXLINE, R. V., THIBAUT, J., BRANNON, C., and GUMPERT, P. (1961), 'Visual interaction in relation to Machiavellianism and an unethical act', *Amer. Psychol.*, vol. 16, p. 396.

FELDMAN, S. S. (1959), *Mannerisms of Speech and Gesture in Everyday Life*, International University Press.

GIBSON, J. J., and PICK, A. D. (1963), 'Perception of another person's looking behavior', *Amer. J. Psychol.*, vol. 76, pp. 386–94.

GOFFMAN, E. (1963), *Behavior in Public Places*, Free Press.

GRAY, P. H. (1958), 'Theory and evidence of imprinting in human infants', *J. Psychol.*, vol. 46, pp. 155–66.

HALL, E. T. (1955), 'The anthropology of manners', *Scient. Amer.*, vol. 192, pp. 84–90.

HEDIGER, H. (1955), *Studies of the Psychology and Behaviour of Captive Animals in Zoos and Circuses*, Butterworth.

HESS, E. H. (1965), 'Attitude and pupil size', *Scient. Amer.*, vol. 212, pp. 46–54.

HUTT, C., and OUNSTED, C. (1964), 'The significance of gaze-aversion in children', unpublished manuscript.

KENDON, A. (1964), 'The distribution of visual attention in two-person encounters', Report to Department of Scientific and Industrial Research, London.

KRASNER, L. (1958), 'Studies on the conditioning of verbal behavior', *Psychol. Bull.*, vol. 55, pp. 148–70.

LAING, R. D. (1960a), *The Self and Others*, Tavistock.

LAING, R. D. (1960b), *The Divided Self*, Tavistock.

MILLER, N. E. (1944), 'Experimental studies in conflict', in J. McV. Hunt (ed.), *Personality and the Behavior Disorders*, vol. 1, Ronald.

NIELSEN, G. (1962), *Studies in Self Confrontation*, Monksgaard.

RIEMER, M. D. (1955), 'Abnormalities of the gaze: a classification', *Psychiat. Q.*, vol. 29, pp. 659–72.

SCHEUTZ, A. (1948), 'Sartre's theory of the alter ego', *Philosophy phenom. Res.*, vo.. 9, pp. 181–99.

SIMMEL, G. (1921), 'Sociology of the senses: visual interaction', in R. E. Park and E. W. Burgess (eds.), *Introduction to the Science of Sociology*, University of Chicago Press.

SOMMER, R. (1962), 'The distance for comfortable conversations: a further study', *Sociometry*, vol. 25, pp. 111–16.

SPITZ, R. A. (1946), 'The smiling response: a contribution to the ontogenesis of social relations', *Genet. Psychol. Monogr.*, vol. 34, pp. 57–125.

STEINZOR, B. (1950), 'The spatial factor in face to face discussion groups', *J. abnorm. soc. Psychol.*, vol. 45, pp. 552–5.

WOLFF, P. H. (1963), 'Observations on the early development of smiling', in B. M. Foss (ed.), *De erminants of Infant Behavior*, vol. 2, Methuen.

Part Five
Strategies of Interaction

When people participate in conversational interaction, at least three objectives are usually being served. Firstly, to involve oneself in conversation is an act of social integration with other human beings of basic psychological importance. Secondly, individuals use conversation to stake indexical claims to particular social identities and attitudes. And thirdly, the speakers involved are often trying to achieve some specific goal requiring concerted group activity. The four Readings in this section explore some of the different interactional strategies by which these objectives can be reached.

Goffman, in Reading 18, shows how group interactions are subject to strong conventions about each participant's obligation to demonstrate involvement in the interaction. In Reading 17, he discusses how participants exploit various strategies in announcing their social identities, in terms of establishing a particular *face*. In both cases, the individual's actions have to be consistent with the expectations of the rest of the group. When his degree of involvement is seen to be inadequate, the individual becomes *alienated* from the interaction; and when the group remains unconvinced by the image he projects, he *loses face*. In such cases, alienation and loss of face can be minimized by the use of certain strategies available to the individual and the other members of the group.

Schegloff (20) discusses a special form of two-person interaction, telephone conversation. In the absence of non-vocal cues such as gesture, posture and eye contact behaviour, participants in a telephone conversation must rely on vocal cues alone to manage the progress of the interaction. Taking telephone conversation as a paradigm of 'natural' face-to-face conversation, Schegloff looks specifically at the strategies employed by participants to organize the sequencing of their contributions in opening a conversation. Thus he shows that the strategies the participants use to control who speaks first follow strict conventional rules.

Bales (19) examines the behaviour of members of small groups who are trying to reach a consensus decision. He identifies the different strategic acts which typically take place, and shows how the members of the group each come to play a different contributory role in the group's progress towards a decision.

17 E. Goffman

On Face-Work: an Analysis of Ritual Elements in Social Interaction

E. Goffman, 'On face-work: an analysis of ritual elements in social interaction', *Psychiatry*, vol. 18, 1955, pp. 213–31.

Every person lives in a world of social encounters, involving him either in face-to-face or mediated contact with other participants. In each of these contacts, he tends to act out what is sometimes called a *line* – that is, a pattern of verbal and non-verbal acts by which he expresses his view of the situation and through this his evaluation of the participants, especially himself. Regardless of whether a person intends to take a line, he will find that he has done so in effect. The other participants will assume that he has more or less willfully taken a stand, so that if he is to deal with their response to him he must take into consideration the impression they have possibly formed of him.

The term *face* may be defined as the positive social value a person effectively claims for himself by the line others assume he has taken during a particular contact.[1] Face is an image of self delineated in terms of approved social attributes – albeit an image that others may share, as when a person makes a good showing for his profession or religion by making a good showing for himself.

A person tends to experience an immediate emotional response to the face which a contact with others allows him; he cathects his face; his 'feelings' become attached to it. If the encounter sustains an image of him that he has long taken for granted, he probably will have a few feelings about the matter. If events establish a face for him that is better than he might have expected, he is likely to 'feel good'; if his ordinary expectations are not fulfilled, one expects that he will 'feel bad' or 'feel hurt'. In general, a person's attachment to a particular face, coupled with the ease with which disconfirming information can be conveyed by himself and others, provides one reason why he finds that participation in any contact with others is a commitment. A person will also have feelings about the face sustained for the other participants, and while these feelings

1. For discussions of the Chinese conception of face see the following: Hsien Chin Hu (1944); Yang (1945, pp. 167–172); Macgowan (1912, pp. 301–12); Smith (1894, pp. 16–18). For a comment on the American Indian conception of face, see Mauss (1954, p. 38).

may differ in quantity and direction from those he has for his own face, they constitute an involvement in the face of others that is as immediate and spontaneous as the involvement he has in his own face. One's own face and the face of others are constructs of the same order; it is the rules of the group and the definition of the situation which determine how much feeling one is to have for face and how this feeling is to be distributed among the faces involved.

A person may be said to *have*, or *be in*, or *maintain* face when the line he effectively takes presents an image of him that is internally consistent, that is supported by judgements and evidence conveyed by other participants, and that is confirmed by evidence conveyed through impersonal agencies in the situation. At such times the person's face clearly is something that is not lodged in or on his body, but rather something that is diffusely located in the flow of events in the encounter and becomes manifest only when these events are read and interpreted for the appraisals expressed in them.

The line maintained by and for a person during contact with others tends to be of a legitimate institutionalized kind. During a contact of a particular type, an interactant of known or visible attributes can expect to be sustained in a particular face and can feel that it is morally proper that this should be so. Given his attributes and the conventionalized nature of the encounter, he will find a small choice of lines will be open to him and a small choice of faces will be waiting for him. Further, on the basis of a few known attributes, he is given the responsibility of possessing a vast number of others. His coparticipants are not likely to be conscious of the character of many of these attributes until he acts perceptibly in such a way as to discredit his possession of them; then everyone becomes conscious of these attributes and assumes that he willfully gave a false impression of possessing them.

Thus while concern for face focuses the attention of the person on the current activity, he must, to maintain face in this activity, take into consideration his place in the social world beyond it. A person who can maintain face in the current situation is someone who abstained from certain actions in the past that would have been difficult to face up to later. In addition, he fears loss of face now partly because the others may take this as a sign that consideration for his feelings need not be shown in the future. There is nevertheless a limitation to this interdependence between the current situation and the wider social world: an encounter with people whom he will not have dealings with again leaves him free to take a high line that the future will discredit, or free to suffer humiliations that would make future dealings with them an embarrassing thing to have to face.

A person may be said to *be in wrong face* when information is brought forth in some way about his social worth which cannot be integrated, even with effort, into the line that is being sustained for him. A person may be said to *be out of face* when he participates in a contact with others without having ready a line of the kind participants in such situations are expected to take. The intent of many pranks is to lead a person into showing a wrong face or no face, but there will also be serious occasions, of course, when he will find himself expressively out of touch with the situation.

When a person senses that he is in face, he typically responds with feelings of confidence and assurance. Firm in the line he is taking, he feels that he can hold his head up and openly present himself to others. He feels some security and some relief – as he also can when the others feel he is in wrong face but successfully hide these feelings from him.

When a person is in wrong face or out of face, expressive events are being contributed to the encounter which cannot be readily woven into the expressive fabric of the occasion. Should he sense that he is in wrong face or out of face, he is likely to feel ashamed and inferior because of what has happened to the activity on his account and because of what may happen to his reputation as a participant. Further, he may feel bad because he had relied upon the encounter to support an image of self to which he has become emotionally attached and which he now finds threatened. Felt lack of judgemental support from the encounter may take him aback, confuse him, and momentarily incapacitate him as an inter-actant. His manner and bearing may falter, collapse and crumble. He may become embarrassed and chagrined; he may become shamefaced. The feeling, whether warranted or not, that he is perceived in a flustered state by others, and that he is presenting no usable line, may add further injuries to his feelings, just as his change from being in wrong face or out of face to being shamefaced can add further disorder to the expressive organization of the situation. Following common usage, I shall employ the term *poise* to refer to the capacity to suppress and conceal any tendency to become shamefaced during encounters with others.

In our Anglo-American society, as in some others, the phrase *to lose face* seems to mean to be in wrong face, to be out of face, or to be shame-faced. The phrase *to save one's face* appears to refer to the process by which the person sustains an impression for others that he has not lost face. Following Chinese usage, one can say that *to give face* is to arrange for another to take a better line than he might otherwise have been able to take,[2] the other thereby gets face given him, this being one way in which he can gain face.

2. See for example, Smith (1894, p. 17).

As an aspect of the social code of any social circle, one may expect to find an understanding as to how far a person should go to save his face. Once he takes on a self-image expressed through face he will be expected to live up to it. In different ways in different societies he will be required to show self-respect, abjuring certain actions because they are above or beneath him, while forcing himself to perform others even though they cost him dearly. By entering a situation in which he is given a face to maintain, a person takes on the responsibility of standing guard over the flow of events as they pass before him. He must ensure that a particular *expressive order* is sustained – an order which regulates the flow of events, large or small, so that anything that appears to be expressed by them will be consistent with his face. When a person manifests these compunctions primarily from duty to himself, one speaks in our society of pride; when he does so because of duty to wider social units, and receives support from these units in doing so, one speaks of honor. When these compunctions have to do with postural things, with expressive events derived from the way in which the person handles his body, his emotions, and the things with which he has physical contact, one speaks of dignity, this being an aspect of expressive control that is always praised and never studied. In any case, while his social face can be his most personal possession and the center of his security and pleasure, it is only on loan to him from society; it will be withdrawn unless he conducts himself in a way that is worthy of it. Approved attributes and their relation to face make of every man his own jailer; this is a fundamental social constraint even though each man may like his cell.

Just as the member of any group is expected to have self-respect, so also he is expected to sustain a standard of considerateness; he is expected to go to certain lengths to save the feelings and the face of others present, and he is expected to do this willingly and spontaneously because of emotional identification with the others and with their feelings.[3] In consequence, he is disinclined to witness the defacement of others.[4] The person

3. Of course, the more power and prestige the others have, the more a person is likely to show consideration for their feelings, as Dale suggests. 'The doctrine of "feelings" was expounded to me many years ago by a very eminent civil servant with a pretty taste in cynicism. He explained that the importance of feelings varies in close correspondence with the importance of the person who feels. If the public interest requires that a junior clerk should be removed from his post, no regard need be paid to his feelings; if it is a case of an Assistant Secretary, they must be carefully considered, within reason; if it is a Permanent Secretary, his feelings are a principal element in the situation, and only imperative public interest can override their requirements' (1941, p. 126n.).

4. Salesmen, especially street 'stemmers', know that if they take a line that will be discredited unless the reluctant customer buys, the customer may be trapped by considerateness and buy in order to save the face of the salesman and prevent what would ordinarily result in a scene.

who can witness another's humiliation and unfeelingly retain a cool countenance himself is said in our society to be 'heartless', just as he who can unfeelingly participate in his own defacement is thought to be 'shameless'.

The combined effect of the rule of self-respect and the rule of considerateness is that the person tends to conduct himself during an encounter so as to maintain both his own face and the face of the other participants. This means that the line taken by each participant is usually allowed to prevail, and each participant is allowed to carry off the role he appears to have chosen for himself. A state where everyone temporarily accepts everyone else's line is established.[5] This kind of mutual acceptance seems to be a basic structural feature of interaction, especially the interaction of face-to-face talk. It is typically a 'working' acceptance, not a 'real' one, since it tends to be based not on agreement of candidly expressed heartfelt evaluations, but upon a willingness to give temporary lip service to judgements with which the participants do not really agree.

The mutual acceptance of lines has an important conservative effect upon encounters. Once the person initially presents a line, he and the others tend to build their later responses upon it, and in a sense become stuck with it. Should the person radically alter his line, or should it become discredited, then confusion results, for the participants will have prepared and committed themselves for actions that are now unsuitable.

Ordinarily, maintenance of face is a condition of interaction, not its objective. Usual objectives, such as gaining face for oneself, giving free expression to one's true beliefs, introducing deprecating information about the others, or solving problems and performing tasks, are typically pursued in such a way as to be consistent with the maintenance of face. To study face-saving is to study the traffic rules of social interaction; one learns about the code the person adheres to in his movement across the paths and designs of others, but not where he is going, or why he wants

5. Surface agreement in the assessment of social worth does not, of course, imply equality; the evaluation consensually sustained of one participant may be quite different from the one consensually sustained of another. Such agreement is also compatible with expression of differences of opinion between two participants, provided each of the disputants shows 'respect' for the other, guiding the expression of disagreement so that it will convey an evaluation of the other that the other will be willing to convey about himself. Extreme cases are provided by wars, duels and bar-room fights, when these are of a gentlemanly kind, for they can be conducted under consensual auspices, with each protagonist guiding his action according to the rules of the game, thereby making it possible for his action to be interpreted as an expression of a fair player openly in combat with a fair opponent. In fact, the rules and etiquette of any game can be analysed as a means by which the image of a fair player can be expressed, just as the image of a fair player can be analysed as a means by which the rules and etiquette of a game are sustained.

to get there. One does not even learn why he is ready to follow the code, for a large number of different motives can equally lead him to do so. He may want to save his own face because of his emotional attachment to the image of self, which it expresses, because of his pride or honor, because of the power his presumed status allows him to exert over the other participants, and so on. He may want to save the others' face because of his emotional attachment to an image of them, or because he feels that his coparticipants have a moral right to this protection, or because he wants to avoid the hostility that may be directed toward him if they lose their face. He may feel that an assumption has been made that he is the sort of person who shows compassion and sympathy toward others, so that to retain his own face, he may feel obliged to be considerate of the line taken by the other participants.

By *face-work* I mean to designate the actions taken by a person to make whatever he is doing consistent with face. Face-work serves to counteract 'incidents' – that is, events whose effective symbolic implications threaten face. Thus poise is one important type of face-work, for through poise the person controls his embarrassment and hence the embarrassment that he and others might have over his embarassment. Whether or not the full consequences of face-saving actions are known to the person who employs them, they often become habitual and standardized practices; they are like traditional plays in a game or traditional steps in a dance. Each person, subculture and society seems to have its own characteristic repertoire of face-saving practices. It is to this repertoire that people partly refer when they ask what a person or culture is 'really' like. And yet the particular set of practices stressed by particular persons or groups seems to be drawn from a single logically coherent framework of possible practices. It is as if face, by its very nature, can be saved only in a certain number of ways, and as if each social grouping must make its selections from this single matrix of possibilities.

The members of every social circle may be expected to have some knowledge of face-work and some experience in its use. In our society, this kind of capacity is sometimes called tact, *savoir-faire*, diplomacy or social skill. Variation in social skill pertains more to the efficacy of face-work than to the frequency of its application, for almost all acts involving others are modified, prescriptively or proscriptively, by considerations of face.

If a person is to employ his repertoire of face-saving practices, obviously he must first become aware of the interpretations that others may have placed upon his acts and the interpretations that he ought perhaps to place upon theirs. In other words, he must exercise perceptiveness.[6] But even if he is properly alive to symbolically conveyed judgements and is socially skilled, he must yet be willing to exercise his perceptiveness and his skill; he must, in short, be prideful and considerate. Admittedly, of course, the possession of perceptiveness and social skill so often leads to their application that in our society terms such as politeness or tact fail to distinguish between the inclination to exercise such capacities and the capacities themselves.

I have already said that the person will have two points of view – a defensive orientation toward saving his own face and a protective orientation toward saving the other's face. Some practices will be primarily defensive and others primarily protective, although in general one may expect these two perspectives to be taken at the same time. In trying to save the face of others, the person must choose a tack that will not lead to loss of his own; in trying to save his own face, he must consider the loss of face that his action may entail for others.

In many societies there is a tendency to distinguish three levels of responsibility which a person may have for a threat to face that his actions have created. First, he may appear to have acted innocently; his offence seems to be unintended and unwitting, and those who perceive his act can feel that he would have attempted to avoid it had he foreseen its offensive consequences. In our society one calls such threats to face *faux pas*, *gaffes*, boners or bricks. Secondly, the offending person may appear to have acted maliciously and spitefully, with the intention of causing open insult. Thirdly, there are incidental offences; these arise as an unplanned but sometimes anticipated by-product of action – action which the offender performs in spite of its offensive consequences, although not out of spite. From the point of view of a particular participant, these three types of threat can be introduced by the participant himself against his own face, by himself against the face of the others, by the others against their own face, or by the others against himself. Thus the person may find himself in many different relations to a threat to face. If he is to handle himself and others well in all contingencies, he will have to have a repertoire of face-saving practices for each of these possible relations to threat.

The basic kinds of face-work
The avoidance process

The surest way for a person to prevent threats to his face is to avoid contacts in which these threats are likely to occur. In all societies one can

6. Presumably social skill and perceptiveness will be high in groups whose members frequently act as representatives of wider social units such as lineages or nations, for the player here is gambling with a face to which the feelings of many persons are

observe this in the avoidance relationship[7] and in the tendency for certain delicate transactions to be conducted by go-betweens.[8] Similarly, in many societies, members know the value of voluntarily making a gracious withdrawal before an anticipated threat to face has had a chance to occur.[9]

Once the person does chance an encounter, other kinds of avoidance practices come into play. As defensive measures, he keeps off topics and away from activities which would lead to the expression of information that is inconsistent with the line he is maintaining. At opportune moments he will change the topic of conversation or the direction of activity. He will often present initially a front of diffidence and composure, suppressing any show of feeling until he has found out what kind of line the others will be ready to support for him. Any claims regarding self may be made with belittling modesty, with strong qualifications, or with a note of unseriousness; by hedging in these ways he will have prepared a self for himself that will not be discredited by exposure, personal failure, or the unanticipated acts of others. And if he does not hedge his claims about self, he will at least attempt to be realistic about them, knowing that otherwise events may discredit him and make him lose face.

Certain protective maneuvers are as common as these defensive ones. The person shows respect and politeness, making sure to extend to others any ceremonial treatment which might be their due. He employs discretion; he leaves unstated facts which might implicitly or explicitly contradict and embarrass the positive claims made by others.[10] He employs

---

attached. Similarly, one might expect social skill to be well developed among those of high station and those with whom they have dealings, for the more face an interactant has, the greater the number of events that may be inconsistent with it, and hence the greater the need for social skill to forestall or counteract these inconsistencies.

7. In our own society an illustration of avoidance is found in the middle- and upper-class Negro who avoids certain face-to-face contacts with whites in order to protect the self-evaluation projected by his clothes and manner. See for example Johnson (1943, ch. 13). The function of avoidance in maintaining the kinship system in small preliterate societies might be taken as a particular illustration of the same general theme.

8. An illustration is given by Latourette (1942) vol. 2, p. 211: 'A neighbor or a group of neighbors may tender their good offices in adjusting a quarrel in which each antagonist would be sacrificing his face by taking the first step in approaching the other. The wise intermediary can effect the reconciliation while preserving the dignity of both.'

9. In an unpublished paper Harold Garfinkel has suggested that when the person finds that he has lost face in a conversational encounter, he may feel a desire to disappear or 'drop through the floor', and that this may involve a wish not only to conceal loss of face but also to return magically to a point in time when it would have been possible to save face by avoiding the encounter.

10. When the person knows the others well, he will know what issues ought not to be raised and what situations the others ought not to be placed in, and he will be free to introduce matters at will in all other areas. When the others are strangers to him, he will often reverse the formula, restricting himself to specific areas he knows are safe.

circumlocutions and deceptions, phrasing his replies with careful ambiguity so that the others' face is preserved even if their welfare is not.[11] He employs courtesies, making slight modifications of his demands on or appraisals of the others so that they will be able to define the situation as one in which their self-respect is not threatened. In making a belittling demand upon the others, or in imputing uncomplimentary attributes to them, he may employ a joking manner, allowing them to take the line that they are good sports, able to relax from their ordinary standards of pride and honor. And before engaging in a potentially offensive act, he may provide explanations as to why the others ought not to be affronted by it. For example if he knows that it will be necessary to withdraw from the encounter before it has terminated, he may tell the others in advance that it is necessary for him to leave, so that they will have faces that are prepared for it. But neutralizing the potentially offensive act need not be done verbally; he may wait for a propitious moment or natural break – for example, in conversation, a momentary lull when no one speaker can be affronted – and then leave, in this way using the context instead of his words as a guarantee of inoffensiveness.

When a person fails to prevent an incident, he can still attempt to maintain the fiction that no threat to face has occurred. The most blatant example of this is found where the person acts as if an event which contains a threatening expression has not occurred at all. He may apply this studied non-observance to his own acts – as when he does not by any outward sign admit that his stomach is rumbling – or to the acts of others, as when he does not 'see' that another has stumbled.[12] Social life in mental hospitals owes much to this process; patients employ it in regard to their own peculiarities, and vistors employ it, often with tenuous desperation, in regard to patients. In general, tactful blindness of this kind is applied

---

On these occasions, as Simmel suggests, '. . . discretion consists by no means only in the respect for the secret of the other, for his specific will to conceal this or that from us, but in staying away from the knowledge of all that the other does not expressly reveal to us' (see Wolff, 1950, pp. 320–21).

11. The Western traveller used to complain that the Chinese could never be trusted to say what they meant but always said what they felt their Western listener wanted to hear. The Chinese used to complain that the Westerner was brusque, boorish, and un-mannered. In terms of Chinese standards, presumably, the conduct of a Westerner is so gauche that he creates an emergency, forcing the Asian to forgo any kind of direct reply in order to rush in with a remark that might rescue the Westerner from the compromising position in which he had placed himself (see Smith, 1894, ch. 8, 'The Talent for Indirection'). This is an instance of the important group of misunderstandings which arise during interaction between persons who come from groups with different ritual standards.

12. A pretty example of this is found in parade-ground etiquette which may oblige those in a parade to treat anyone who faints as if he were not present at all.

only to events which, if perceived at all, could be perceived and interpreted only as threats to face.

A more important, less spectacular kind of tactful overlooking is practised when a person openly acknowledges an incident as an event that has occurred, but not as an event that contains a threatening expression. If he is not the one who is responsible for the incident, then his blindness will have to be supported by his forbearance; if he is the doer of the threatening deed, then his blindness will have to be supported by his willingness to seek a way of dealing with the matter which leaves him dangerously dependent upon the cooperative forbearance of the others.

Another kind of avoidance occurs when a person loses control of his expressions during an encounter. At such times he may try not so much to overlook the incident as to hide or conceal his activity in some way, thus making it possible for the others to avoid some of the difficulties created by a participant who has not maintained face. Correspondingly, when a person is caught out of face because he had not expected to be thrust into interaction, or because strong feelings have disrupted his expressive mask, the others may protectively turn away from him or his activity for a moment, to give him time to assemble himself.

The corrective process

When the participants in an undertaking or encounter fail to prevent the occurrence of an event that is expressively incompatible with the judgements of social worth that are being maintained, and when the event is of the kind that is difficult to overlook, then the participants are likely to give it accredited status as an incident – to ratify it as a threat that deserves direct official attention – and to proceed to try to correct for its effects. At this point one or more participants find themselves in an established state of ritual disequilibrium or disgrace, and an attempt must be made to re-establish a satisfactory ritual state for them. I use the term *ritual* because I am dealing with acts through whose symbolic component the actor shows how worthy he is of respect or how worthy he feels others are of it. The imagery of equilibrium is apt here because the length and intensity of the corrective effort is nicely adapted to the persistence and intensity of the threat.[13] One's face, then, is a sacred thing, and the expressive order required to sustain it is therefore a ritual one.

The sequence of acts set in motion by an acknowledged threat to face and terminating in the re-establishment of ritual equilibrium, I shall call

13. This kind of imagery is one that social anthropologists seem to find naturally fitting. Note, for example, the implications of the following statement by Mead (1934, p. 274): 'If a husband beats his wife, custom demands that she leave him and go to her brother, real or officiating, and remain a length of time commensurate with the degree of her offended dignity.'

an *interchange*.[14] Defining a message or move as everything conveyed by an actor during a turn at taking action, one can say that an interchange will involve two or more moves and two or more participants. Obvious examples in our society may be found in the sequence of *Excuse me* and *Certainly*, and in the exchange of presents or visits. The interchange seems to be a basic concrete unit of social activity and provides one natural empirical way to study interaction of all kinds. Face-saving practices can be usefully classified according to their position in the natural sequence of moves which comprise this unit. Aside from the event which introduces the need for a corrective interchange, four classic moves seem to be involved.

There is, first, the challenge, by which participants take on the responsibility of calling attention to the misconduct; by implication they suggest that the threatened claims are to stand firm and that the threatening event itself will have to be brought back into line.

The second move consists of the offering, whereby a participant, typically the offender, is given a chance to correct for the offence and re-establish the expressive order. Some classic ways of making this move are available. On the one hand, an attempt can be made to show that what admittedly appeared to be a threatening expression is really a meaningless event, or an unintentional act, or a joke not meant to be taken seriously, or an unavoidable 'understandable' product of extenuating circumstances. On the other hand, the meaning of the event may be granted and effort concentrated on the creator of it. Information may be provided to show that the creator was under the influence of something and not himself, or that he was under the command of somebody else and not acting for himself. When a person claims that an act was meant in jest, he may go on and claim that the self that seemed to lie behind the act was also projected as a joke. When a person suddenly finds that he has demonstrably failed in capacities that the others assumed him to have and to claim for himself – such as the capacity to spell, to perform minor tasks, to talk without malapropisms, and so on – he may quickly add, in a serious or unserious way, that he claims these incapacities as part of his self. The meaning of the threatening incident thus stands, but it can now be incorporated smoothly into the flow of expressive events.

As a supplement to or substitute for the strategy of redefining the offensive act or himself, the offender can follow two other procedures: he can provide compensations to the injured – when it is not his own face that he has threatened; or he can provide punishment, penance and expiation for himself. These are important moves or phases in the ritual interchange.

14. The notion of interchange is drawn in part from Chapple (1940, especially pp. 26–30), and from Horsfall and Arensberg (1949, especially p. 19). For further material on the interchange as a unit see Goffman (1953, especially chs. 12 and 13, pp. 165–95).

Even though the offender may fail to prove his innocence, he can suggest through these means that he is now a renewed person, a person who has paid for his sin against the expressive order and is once more to be trusted in the judgemental scene. Further, he can show that he does not treat the feelings of the others lightly, and that if their feelings have been injured by him, however innocently, he is prepared to pay a price for his action. Thus he assures the others that they can accept his explanations without this acceptance constituting a sign of weakness and a lack of pride on their part. Also, by his treatment of himself, by his self-castigation, he shows that he is clearly aware of the kind of crime he would have committed had the incident been what it first appeared to be, and that he knows the kind of punishment that ought to be accorded to one who would commit such a crime. The suspected person thus shows that he is thoroughly capable of taking the role of the others toward his own activity, that he can still be used as a responsible participant in the ritual process, and that the rules of conduct which he appears to have broken are still sacred, real and unweakened. An offensive act may arouse anxiety about the ritual code; the offender allays this anxiety by showing that both the code and he as an upholder of it are still in working order.

After the challenge and the offering have been made, the third move can occur: the persons to whom the offering is made can accept it as a satisfactory means of re-establishing the expressive order and the faces supported by this order. Only then can the offender cease the major part of his ritual offering.

In the terminal move of the interchange, the forgiven person conveys a sign of gratitude to those who have given him the indulgence of forgiveness.

The phases of the corrective process – challenge, offering, acceptance and thanks – provide a model for interpersonal ritual behavior, but a model that may be departed from in significant ways. For example, the offended parties may give the offender a chance to initiate the offering on his own before a challenge is made and before they ratify the offence as an incident. This is a common courtesy, extended on the assumption that the recipient will introduce a self-challenge. Further, when the offended persons accept the corrective offering, the offender may suspect that this has been grudgingly done from tact, and so he may volunteer additional corrective offerings, not allowing the matter to rest until he has received a second or third acceptance of his repeated apology. Or the offended persons may tactfully take over the role of the offender and volunteer excuses for him that will, perforce, be acceptable to the offended persons.

An important departure from the standard corrective cycle occurs when a challenged offender patently refuses to heed the warning and continues with his offending behavior, instead of setting the activity to rights. This move shifts the play back to the challengers. If they countenance the refusal to meet their demands, then it will be plain that their challenge was a bluff and that the bluff has been called. This is an untenable position; a face for themselves cannot be derived from it, and they are left to bluster. To avoid this fate, some classic moves are open to them. For instance, they can resort to tactless, violent retaliation, destroying either themselves or the person who had refused to heed their warning. Or they can withdraw from the undertaking in a visible huff – righteously indignant, outraged, but confident of ultimate vindication. Both tacks provide a way of denying the offender his status as an interactant, and hence denying the reality of the offensive judgement he has made. Both strategies are ways of salvaging face, but for all concerned the costs are usually high. It is partly to forestall such scenes that an offender is usually quick to offer apologies; he does not want the affronted persons to trap themselves into the obligation to resort to desperate measures.

It is plain that emotions play a part in these cycles of response, as when anguish is expressed because of what one has done to another's face, or anger because of what has been done to one's own. I want to stress that these emotions function as moves, and fit so precisely into the logic of the ritual game that it would seem difficult to understand them without it.[15] In fact, spontaneously expressed feelings are likely to fit into the formal pattern of the ritual interchange more elegantly than consciously designed ones.

Making points – the aggressive use of face-work

Every face-saving practice which is allowed to neutralize a particular threat opens up the possibility that the threat will be wilfully introduced for what can be safely gained by it. If a person knows that his modesty will be answered by others' praise of him, he can fish for compliments. If his own appraisal of self will be checked against incidental events, then he can arrange for favorable incidental events to appear. If others are prepared to overlook an affront to them and act forbearantly, or to accept apologies, then he can rely on this as a basis for safely offending them. He can attempt by sudden withdrawal to force the others into a ritually unsatisfactory state, leaving them to flounder in an interchange that cannot

15. Even when a child demands something and is refused, he is likely to cry and sulk not as an irrational expression of frustration but as a ritual move, conveying that he already has a face to lose and that its loss is not to be permitted lightly. Sympathetic parents may even allow for such display, seeing in these crude strategies the beginnings of a social self.

readily be completed. Finally, at some expense to himself, he can arrange for the others to hurt his feelings, thus forcing them to feel guilt, remorse and sustained ritual disequilibrium.[16]

When a person treats face-work not as something he need be prepared to perform, but rather as something that others can be counted on to perform or to accept, then an encounter or an undertaking becomes less a scene of mutual considerateness than an arena in which a contest or match is held. The purpose of the game is to preserve everyone's line from an inexcusable contradiction, while scoring as many points as possible against one's adversaries and making as many gains as possible for oneself. An audience to the struggle is almost a necessity. The general method is for the person to introduce favorable facts about himself and unfavorable facts about the others in such a way that the only reply the others will be able to think up will be one that terminates the interchange in a grumble, a meager excuse, a face-saving I-can-take-a-joke laugh, or an empty stereotyped comeback of the *Oh yeah?* or *That's what you think* variety. The losers in such cases will have to cut their losses, tacitly grant the loss of a point, and attempt to do better in the next interchange. Points made by allusion to social-class status are sometimes called snubs; those made by allusions to moral respectability are sometimes called digs; in either case one deals with a capacity at what is sometimes called 'bitchiness'.

In aggressive interchanges the winner not only succeeds in introducing information favorable to himself and unfavorable to the others, but also demonstrates that as interactant he can handle himself better than his adversaries. Evidence of this capacity is often more important than all the other information the person conveys in the interchange, so that the introduction of a 'crack' in verbal interaction tends to imply that the initiator is better at footwork than those who must suffer his remarks. However, if they succeed in making a successful parry of the thrust and then a successful riposte, the instigator of the play must not only face the disparagement with which the others have answered him but also accept the fact that his assumption of superiority in footwork has proven false. He is made to look foolish; he loses face. Hence it is always a gamble to 'make a remark'. The tables can be turned and the aggressor can lose more than he could have gained had his move won the point. Successful ripostes or comebacks in our society are sometimes called squelches or toppers; theoretically it would be possible for a squelch to be squelched, a topper to be topped, and a riposte to be parried with a counterriposte,

16. The strategy of maneuvring another into a position where he cannot right the harm he has done is very commonly employed but nowhere with such devotion to the ritual model of conduct as in revengeful suicide. See, for example, Jeffreys (1952).

but except in staged interchanges this third level of successful action seems rare.[17]

The choice of appropriate face-work

When an incident occurs, the person whose face is threatened may attempt to reinstate the ritual order by means of one kind of strategy, while the other participants may desire or expect a practice of a different type to be employed. When, for example, a minor mishap occurs, momentarily revealing a person in wrong face or out of face, the others are often more willing and able to act blind to the discrepancy than is the threatened person himself. Often they would prefer him to exercise poise,[18] while he feels that he cannot afford to overlook what has happened to his face and so becomes apologetic and shamefaced, if he is the creator of the incident, or destructively assertive, if the others are responsible for it.[19] Yet on the other hand, a person may manifest poise when the others feel that he ought to have broken down into embarrassed apology – that he is taking undue advantage of their helpfulness by his attempts to brazen it out. Sometimes a person may himself be undecided as to which practice to employ, leaving the others in the embarrassing position of not knowing which tack they are going to have to follow. Thus when a person makes a slight *gaffe*, he and the others may become embarrassed not because of inability to handle

17. In board and card games the player regularly takes into consideration the possible responses of his adversaries to a play that he is about to make, and even considers the possibility that his adversaries will know that he is taking such precautions. Conversational play is by comparison surprisingly impulsive; people regularly make remarks about others present without carefully designing their remarks to prevent a successful comeback. Similarly, while feinting and sandbagging are theoretical possibilities during talk, they seem to be little exploited.

18. Folklore imputes a great deal of poise to the upper classes. If there is truth in this belief it may lie in the fact that the upper-class person tends to find himself in encounters in which he outranks the other participants in ways additional to class. The ranking participant is often somewhat independent of the good opinion of the others and finds it practical to be arrogant, sticking to a face regardless of whether the encounter supports it. On the other hand, those who are in the power of a fellow-participant tend to be very much concerned with the valuation he makes of them or witnesses being made of them, and so find it difficult to maintain a slightly wrong face without becoming embarrassed and apologetic. It may be added that people who lack awareness of the symbolism in minor events may keep cool in difficult situations, showing poise that they do not really possess.

19. Thus, in our society, when a person feels that others expect him to measure up to approved standards of cleanliness, tidiness, fairness, hospitality, generosity, affluence and so on, or when he sees himself as someone who ought to maintain such standards, he may burden an encounter with extended apologies for his failings, while all along the other participants do not care about the standard, or do not believe the person is really lacking in it, or are convinced that he is lacking in it and see the apology itself as a vain effort at self-elevation.

such difficulties, but because for a moment no one knows whether the offender is going to act blind to the incident, or give it joking recognition, or employ some other face-saving practice.

Cooperation in face-work

When a face has been threatened, face-work must be done, but whether this is initiated and primarily carried through by the person whose face is threatened, or by the offender, or by a mere witness,[20] is often of secondary importance. Lack of effort on the part of one person induces compensative effort from others; a contribution by one person relieves the others of the task. In fact, there are many minor incidents in which the offender and the offended simultaneously attempt to initiate an apology.[21] Resolution of the situation to everyone's apparent satisfaction is the first requirement; correct apportionment of blame is typically a secondary consideration. Hence terms such as tact and *savoir-faire* fail to distinguish whether it is the person's own face that his diplomacy saves or the face of the others. Similarly, terms such as *gaffe* and *faux pas* fail to specify whether it is the actor's own face he has threatened or the face of other participants. And it is understandable that if one person finds he is powerless to save his own face, the others seem especially bound to protect him. For example, in polite society, a handshake that perhaps should not have been extended becomes one that cannot be declined. Thus one accounts for the *noblesse oblige* through which those of high status are expected to curb their power of embarrassing their lessers,[22] as well as the fact that the handicapped often accept courtesies that they can manage better without.

20. Thus one function of seconds in actual duels, as well as in figurative ones, is to provide an excuse for not fighting that both contestants can afford to accept.

21. See, for instance Toby (1952): 'With adults there is less likelihood for essentially trivial issues to produce conflict. The automatic apology of two strangers who accidentally collide on a busy street illustrates the integrative function of etiquette. In effect, each of the parties to the collision says, "I don't know whether I am responsible for this situation, but *if* I am, you have a right to be angry with me, a right that I pray you will not exercise." By defining the situation as one in which both parties must abase themselves, society enables each to keep his self-respect. Each may feel in his heart of hearts, "Why can't that stupid ass watch where he's going?" But overtly *each plays the role of the guilty party* whether he feels he has been miscast or not' (p. 325).

22. Regardless of the person's relative social position, in one sense he has power over the other participants and they must rely upon his considerateness. When the others act toward him in some way, they presume upon a social relationship to him, since one of the things expressed by interaction is the relationship of the interactants. Thus they compromise themselves, for they place him in a position to discredit the claims they express as to his attitude toward them. Hence in response to claimed social relationships every person, of high estate or low, will be expected to exercise *noblesse oblige* and refrain from exploiting the compromised position of the others.

Since social relationships are defined partly in terms of voluntary mutual aid, refusal

Since each participant in an undertaking is concerned, albeit for differing reasons, with saving his own face and the face of the others, then tacit cooperation will naturally arise so that the participants together can attain their shared but differently motivated objectives.

One common type of tacit cooperation in face-saving is the tact exerted in regard to face-work itself. The person not only defends his own face and protects the face of the others, but also acts so as to make it possible and even easy for the others to employ face-work for themselves and him. He helps them to help themselves and him. Social etiquette, for example, warns men against asking for New Year's Eve dates too early in the season, lest the girl find it difficult to provide a gentle excuse for refusing. This second-order tact can be further illustrated by the widespread practice of negative-attribute etiquette. The person who has an unapparent negatively valued attribute often finds it expedient to begin an encounter with an unobtrusive admission of his failing, especially with persons who are uninformed about him. The others are thus warned in advance against making disparaging remarks about his kind of person and are saved from the contradiction of acting in a friendly fashion to a person toward whom they are unwittingly being hostile. This strategy also prevents the others from automatically making assumptions about him which place him in a false position and saves him from painful forbearance or embarrassing remonstrances.

Tact in regard to face-work often relies for its operation on a tacit agreement to do business through the language of hint – the language of innuendo, ambiguities, well-placed pauses, carefully worded jokes, and so on.[23] The rule regarding this unofficial kind of communication is that the sender ought not to act as if he had officially conveyed the message he has hinted at, while the recipients have the right and the obligation to act as if they have not officially received the message contained in the hint. Hinted communication, then, is deniable communication; it need not be

---

of a request for assistance becomes a delicate matter, potentially destructive of the asker's face. Holcombe (1895) provides a Chinese instance: 'Much of the falsehood to which the Chinese as a nation are said to be addicted is a result of the demands of etiquette. A plain, frank "no" is the height of discourtesy. Refusal or denial of any sort must be softened and toned down into an expression of regretted inability. Unwillingness to grant a favor is never shown. In place of it there is seen a chastened feeling of sorrow that unavoidable but quite imaginary circumstances render it wholly impossible. Centuries of practice in this form of evasion have made the Chinese matchlessly fertile in the invention and development of excuses. It is rare, indeed, that one is caught at a loss for a bit of artfully embroidered fiction with which to hide an unwelcome truth' (pp. 274–5).

23. Useful comments on some of the structural roles played by unofficial communication can be found in a discussion of irony and banter in Burns (1943).

faced up to. It provides a means by which the person can be warned that his current line or the current situation is leading to loss of face, without this warning itself becoming an incident.

Another form of tacit cooperation, and one that seems to be much used in many societies, is reciprocal self-denial. Often the person does not have a clear idea of what would be a just or acceptable apportionment of judgements during the occasion, and so he voluntary deprives or depreciates himself while indulging and complimenting the others, in both cases carrying the judgements safely past what is likely to be just. The favorable judgements about himself he allows to come from the others; the unfavorable judgements of himself are his own contributions. This 'after you, Alphonse' technique works, of course, because in depriving himself he can reliably anticipate that the others will compliment or indulge him. Whatever allocation of favors is eventually established, all participants are first given a chance to show that they are not bound or constrained by their own desires and expectations, that they have a properly modest view of themselves, and that they can be counted upon to support the ritual code. Negative bargaining, through which each participant tries to make the terms of trade more favorable to the other side, is another instance; as a form of exchange perhaps it is more widespread than the economist's kind.

A person's performance of face-work, extended by his tacit agreement to help others perform theirs, represents his willingness to abide by the ground rules of social interaction. Here is the hallmark of his socialization as an interactant. If he and the others were not socialized in this way, interaction in most societies and most situations would be a much more hazardous thing for feelings and faces. The person would find it impractical to be oriented to symbolically conveyed appraisals of social worth, or to be possessed of feelings – that is, it would be impractical for him to be a ritually delicate object. And as I shall suggest, if the person were not a ritually delicate object, occasions of talk could not be organized in the way they usually are. It is no wonder that trouble is caused by a person who cannot be relied upon to play the face-saving game.

The ritual roles of the self

So far I have implicitly been using a double definition of self: the self as an image pieced together from the expressive implications of the full flow of events in an undertaking; and the self as a kind of player in a ritual game who copes honorably or dishonorably, diplomatically or undiplomatically, with the judgemental contingencies of the situation. A double mandate is involved. As sacred objects, men are subject to slights and profanation; hence as players of the ritual game they have had to lead themselves into duels, and wait for a round of shots to go wide of the mark before embracing their opponents. Here is an echo of the distinction between the value of a hand drawn at cards and the capacity of the person who plays it. This distinction must be kept in mind, even though it appears that once a person has gotten a reputation for good or bad play this reputation may become part of the face he must later play at maintaining.

Once the two roles of the self have been separated, one can look to the ritual code implicit in face-work to learn how the two roles are related. When a person is responsible for introducing a threat to another's face, he apparently has a right, within limits, to wriggle out of the difficulty by means of self-abasement. When performed voluntarily these indignities do not seem to profane his own image. It is as if he had the right of insulation and could castigate himself *qua* actor without injuring himself *qua* object of ultimate worth. By token of the same insulation he can belittle himself and modestly underplay his positive qualities, with the understanding that no one will take his statements as a fair representation of his sacred self. On the other hand, if he is forced against his will to treat himself in these ways, his face, his pride and his honor will be seriously threatened. Thus, in terms of the ritual code, the person seems to have a special licence to accept mistreatment at his own hands that he does not have the right to accept from others. Perhaps this is a safe arrangement because he is not likely to carry this licence too far, whereas the others, were they given this privilege, might be more likely to abuse it.

Further, within limits the person has a right to forgive other participants for affronts to his sacred image. He can forbearantly overlook minor slurs upon his face, and in regard to somewhat greater injuries he is the one person who is in a position to accept apologies on behalf of his sacred self. This is a relatively safe prerogative for the person to have in regard to himself, for it is one that is exercised in the interests of the others or of the undertaking. Interestingly enough, when the person commits a *gaffe* against himself, it is not he who has the licence to forgive the event; only the others have that prerogative, and it is a safe prerogative for them to have because they can exercise it only in his interests or in the interests of the undertaking. One finds, then, a system of checks and balances by which each participant tends to be given the right to handle only those matters which he will have little motivation for mishandling. In short, the rights and obligations of an interactant are designed to prevent him from abusing his role as an object of sacred value.

Spoken interaction

Most of what has been said so far applies to encounters of both an immediate and mediated kind, although in the latter the interaction is likely to be more attenuated, with each participant's line being gleaned from such things as written statements and work records. During direct personal contacts, however, unique informational conditions prevail and the significance of face becomes especially clear. The human tendency to use signs and symbols means that evidence of social worth and of mutual evaluations will be conveyed by very minor things, and these things will be witnessed, as will the fact that they have been witnessed. An unguarded glance, a momentary change in tone of voice, an ecological position taken or not taken, can drench a talk with judgemental significance. Therefore, just as there is no occasion of talk in which improper impressions could not intentionally or unintentionally arise, so there is no occasion of talk so trivial as not to require each participant to show serious concern with the way in which he handles himself and the others present. Ritual factors which are present in mediated contacts are here present in an extreme form.

In any society, whenever the physical possibility of spoken interaction arises, it seems that a system of practices, conventions, and procedural rules comes into play which functions as a means of guiding and organizing the flow of messages. An understanding will prevail as to when and where it will be permissible to initiate talk, among whom, and by means of what topics of conversation. A set of significant gestures is employed to initiate a spate of communication and as a means for the persons concerned to accredit each other as legitimate participants.[24] When this process of reciprocal ratification occurs, the persons so ratified are in what might be called a *state of talk* – that is, they have declared themselves officially open to one another for purposes of spoken communication and guarantee together to maintain a flow of words. A set of significant gestures is also employed by which one or more new participants can officially join the talk, by which one or more accredited participants can officially withdraw, and by which the state of talk can be terminated.

A single focus of thought and visual attention, and a single flow of

24. The meaning of this status can be appreciated by looking at the kinds of unlegitimated or unratified participation that can occur in spoken interaction. A person may overhear others unbeknownst to them; he can overhear them when they know this to be the case and when they choose either to act as if he were not overhearing them or to signal to him informally that they know he is overhearing them. In all of these cases, the outsider is officially held at bay as someone who is not formally participating in the occasion. Ritual codes, of course, require a ratified participant to be treated quite differently from an unratified one. Thus, for example, only a certain amount of insult from a ratified participant can be ignored without this avoidance practice causing loss of face to the insulted persons; after a point they must challenge the offender and demand redress. However, in many societies apparently, many kinds of verbal abuse from unratified participants can be ignored, without this failure to challenge constituting a loss of face.

talk, tends to be maintained and to be legitimated as officially representative of the encounter. The concerted and official visual attention of the participants tends to be transferred smoothly by means of formal or informal clearance cues, by which the current speaker signals that he is about to relinquish the floor and the prospective speaker signals a desire to be given the floor. An understanding will prevail as to how long and how frequently each participant is to hold the floor. The recipients convey to the speaker, by appropriate gestures, that they are according him their attention. Participants restrict their involvement in matters external to the encounter and observe a limit to involvement in any one message of the encounter, in this way ensuring that they will be able to follow along whatever direction the topic of conversation takes them. Interruptions and lulls are regulated so as not to disrupt the flow of messages. Messages that are not part of the officially accredited flow are modulated so as not to interfere seriously with the accredited messages. Nearby persons who are not participants visibly desist in some way from exploiting their communication position and also modify their own communication, if any, so as not to provide difficult interference. A particular ethos or emotional atmosphere is allowed to prevail. A polite accord is typically maintained, and participants who may be in real disagreement with one another give temporary lip service to views that bring them into agreement on matters of fact and principle. Rules are followed for smoothing out the transition, if any, from one topic of conversation to another.[25]

These rules of talk pertain not to spoken interaction considered as an ongoing process, but to *an* occasion of talk or episode of interaction as a naturally bounded unit. This unit consists of the total activity that occurs during the time that a given set of participants have accredited one another for talk and maintain a single moving focus of attention.[26]

The conventions regarding the structure of occasions of talk represent an effective solution to the problem of organizing a flow of spoken messages. In attempting to discover how it is that these conventions are maintained in force as guides to action, one finds evidence to suggest a functional relationship between the structure of the self and the structure of spoken interaction.

The socialized interactant comes to handle spoken interaction as he would any other kind, as something that must be pursued with ritual care. By automatically appealing to face, he knows how to conduct himself in

25. For a further treatment of the structure of spoken interaction see Goffman (1953, part 4).

26. I mean to include formal talks where rules of procedure are explicitly prescribed and officially enforced, and where only certain categories of participants may be allowed to hold the floor – as well as chats and sociable talks where rules are not explicit and the role of speaker passes back and forth among the participants.

E. Goffman 339

regard to talk. By repeatedly and automatically asking himself the question, 'If I do or do not act in this way, will I or others lose face?' he decides at each moment, consciously or unconsciously, how to behave. For example, entrance into an occasion of spoken interaction may be taken as a symbol of intimacy or legitimate purpose, and so the person must, to save his face, desist from entering into talk with a given set of others unless his circumstances justify what is expressed about him by his entrance. Once approached for talk, he must accede to the others in order to save their face. Once engaged in conversation, he must demand only the amount of attention that is an appropriate expression of his relative social worth. Undue lulls come to be potential signs of having nothing in common or of being insufficiently self-possessed to create something to say, and hence must be avoided. Similarly, interruptions and inattentiveness may convey disrespect and must be avoided unless the implied disrespect is an accepted part of the relationship. A surface of agreement must be maintained by means of discretion and white lies, so that the assumption of mutual approval will not be discredited. Withdrawal must be handled so that it will not convey an improper evaluation.[27] The person must restrain his emotional involvement so as not to present an image of someone with no self-control or dignity who does not rise above his feelings.

The relation between the self and spoken interaction is further displayed when one examines the ritual interchange. In a conversational encounter, interaction tends to proceed in spurts, an interchange at a time, and the flow of information and business is parcelled out into these relatively closed ritual units.[28] The lull between interchanges tends to be greater than the lull between turns at talking in an interchange, and there tends to be a less meaningful relationship between two sequential interchanges than between two sequential speeches in an interchange.

This structural aspect of talk arises from the fact that when a person volunteers a statement or message, however trivial or commonplace, he commits himself and those he addresses, and in a sense places everyone present in jeopardy. By saying something, the speaker opens himself up to the possibility that the intended recipients will affront him by not listening

27. Among people who have had some experience in interacting with one another, conversational encounters are often terminated in such a way as to give the appearance that all participants have independently hit upon the same moment to withdraw. The disbandment is general, and no one may be conscious of the exchange of cues that has been required to make such a happy simultaneity of action possible. Each participant is thus saved from the compromising position of showing readiness to spend further time with someone who is not as ready to spend time with him.

28. The empirical discreteness of the interchange unit is sometimes obscured when the same person who provides the terminating turn at talking in one interchange initiates the first turn at talking in the next. However, the analytical utility of the interchange as a unit remains.

or will think him forward, foolish or offensive in what he has said. And should he meet with such a reception, he will find himself committed to the necessity of taking face-saving action against them. Furthermore, by saying something the speaker opens his intended recipients up to the possibility that the message will be self-approving, presumptuous, demanding, insulting and generally an affront to them or to their conception of him, so that they will find themselves obliged to take action against him in defence of the ritual code. And should the speaker praise the recipients, they will be obliged to make suitable denials, showing that they do not hold too favorable an opinion of themselves and are not so eager to secure indulgences as to endanger their reliability and flexibility as interactants.

Thus when one person volunteers a message, thereby contributing what might easily be a threat to the ritual equilibrium, someone else present is obliged to show that the message has been received and that its content is acceptable to all concerned or can be acceptably countered. This acknowledging reply, of course, may contain a tactful rejection of the original communication, along with a request for modification. In such cases, several exchanges of messages may be required before the interchange is terminated on the basis of modified lines. The interchange comes to a close when it is possible to allow it to do so – that is, when everyone present has signified that he has been ritually appeased to a degree satisfactory to him.[29] A momentary lull between interchanges is possible, for it comes at a time when it will not be taken as a sign of something untoward.

In general, then, a person determines how he ought to conduct himself during an occasion of talk by testing the potentially symbolic meaning of his acts against the self-images that are being sustained. In doing this, however, he incidentally subjects his behavior to the expressive order that prevails and contributes to the orderly flow of messages. His aim is to save face; his effect is to save the situation. From the point of view of saving face, then, it is a good thing that spoken interaction has the conventional organization given it; from the point of view of sustaining an orderly flow of spoken messages, it is a good thing that the self has the ritual structure given it.

I do not mean, however, to claim that another kind of person related to another kind of message organization would not do as well. More important, I do not claim that the present system is without weaknesses or

29. The occurrence of the interchange unit is an empirical fact. In addition to the ritual explanation for it, others may be suggested. For example, when the person makes a statement and receives a reply at once, this provides him with a way of learning that his statement has been received and correctly received. Such 'metacommunication' would be necessary on functional grounds even were it unnecessary on ritual ones.

drawbacks; these must be expected, for everywhere in social life a mechanism or functional relation which solves one set of problems necessarily creates a set of potential difficulties and abuses all its own. For example, a characteristic problem in the ritual organization of personal contacts is that while a person can save his face by quarrelling or by indignantly withdrawing from the encounter, he does this at the cost of the interaction. Furthermore, the person's attachment to face gives others something to aim at; they can not only make an effort to wound him unofficially, but may even make an official attempt utterly to destroy his face. Also, fear over possible loss of his face often prevents the person from initiating contacts in which important information can be transmitted and important relationships re-established; he may be led to seek the safety of solitude rather than the danger of social encounters. He may do this even though others feel that he is motivated by 'false pride' – a pride which suggests that the ritual code is getting the better of those whose conduct is regulated by it. Further, the 'after you, Alphonse' complex can make the termination of an interchange difficult. So, too, where each participant feels that he must sacrifice a little more than has been sacrificed for him, a kind of vicious indulgence cycle may occur – much like the hostility cycle that can lead to open quarrels – with each person receiving things he does not want and giving in return things he would rather keep. Again, when people are on formal terms, much energy may be spent in ensuring that events do not occur which might effectively carry an improper expression. And on the other hand, when a set of persons are on familiar terms and feel that they need not stand on ceremony with one another, then inattentiveness and interruptions are likely to become rife, and talk may degenerate into a happy babble of disorganized sound.

The ritual code itself requires a delicate balance, and can be easily upset by anyone who upholds it too eagerly or not eagerly enough, in terms of the standards and expectations of his group. Too little perceptiveness, too little *savoir-faire*, too little pride and considerateness, and the person ceases to be someone who can be trusted to take a hint about himself or give a hint that will save others embarrassment. Such a person comes to be a real threat to society; there is nothing much that can be done with him, and often he gets his way. Too much perceptiveness or too much pride, and the person becomes someone who is thin-skinned, who must be treated with kid gloves, requiring more care on the part of others than he may be worth to them. Too much *savoir-faire* or too much considerateness, and he becomes someone who is too socialized, who leaves the others with the feeling that they do not know how they really stand with him, nor what they should do to make an effective long-term adjustment to him.

In spite of these inherent 'pathologies' in the organization of talk, the functional fitness between the socialized person and spoken interaction is a viable and practical one. The person's orientation to face, especially his own, is the point of leverage that the ritual order has in regard to him; yet a promise to take ritual care of his face is built into the very structure of talk.

Face and social relationships

When a person begins a mediated or immediate encounter, he already stands in some kind of social relationship to the others concerned, and expects to stand in a given relationship to them after the particular encounter ends. This, of course, is one of the ways in which social contacts are geared into the wider society. Much of the activity occurring during an encounter can be understood as an effort on everyone's part to get through the occasion and all the unanticipated and unintentional events that can cast participants in an undesirable light, without disrupting the relationships of the participants. And if relationships are in the process of change, the object will be to bring the encounter to a satisfactory close without altering the expected course of development. This perspective nicely accounts, for example, for the little ceremonies of greeting and farewell which occur when people begin a conversational encounter or depart from one. Greetings provide a way of showing that a relationship is still what it was at the termination of the previous coparticipation, and, typically, that this relationship involves sufficient suppression of hostility for the participants temporarily to drop their guards and talk. Farewells sum up the effect of the encounter upon the relationship and show what the participants may expect of one another when they next meet. The enthusiasm of greetings compensates for the weakening of the relationship caused by the absence just terminated, while the enthusiasm of farewells compensates the relationship for the harm that is about to be done to it by separation.[30]

It seems to be a characteristic obligation of many social relationships that each of the members guarantees to support a given face for the

30. Greetings, of course, serve to clarify and fix the roles that the participants will take during the occasion of talk and to commit participants to these roles, while farewells provide a way of unambiguously terminating the encounter. Greetings and farewells may also be used to state, and apologize for, extenuating circumstances – in the case of greetings for circumstances that have kept the participants from interacting until now, and in the case of farewells for circumstances that prevent the participants from continuing their display of solidarity. These apologies allow the impression to be maintained that the participants are more warmly related socially than may be the case. This positive stress, in turn, assures that they will act more ready to enter into contacts than they perhaps really feel inclined to do, thus guaranteeing that diffuse channels for potential communication will be kept open in the society.

other members in given situations. To prevent disruption of these relationships, it is therefore necessary for each member to avoid destroying the other's face. At the same time, it is often the person's social relationship with others that leads him to participate in certain encounters with them, where incidentally he will be dependent upon them for supporting his face. Furthermore, in many relationships, the members come to share a face, so that in the presence of third parties an improper act on the part of one member becomes a source of acute embarrassment to the other members. A social relationship, then, can be seen as a way in which the person is more than ordinarily forced to trust his self-image and face to the tact and good conduct of others.

The nature of the ritual order

The ritual order seems to be organized basically on accommodative lines. so that the imagery used in thinking about other types of social order is not quite suitable for it. For the other types of social order a kind of schoolboy model seems to be employed: if a person wishes to sustain a particular image of himself and trust his feelings to it, he must work hard for the credits that will buy this self-enhancement for him; should he try to obtain ends by improper means, by cheating or theft, he will be punished, disqualified from the race, or at least made to start all over again from the beginning. This is the imagery of a hard, dull game. In fact, society and the individual join in one that is easier on both of them, yet one that has dangers of its own.

Whatever his position in society, the person insulates himself by blindnesses, half-truths, illusions and rationalizations. He makes an 'adjustment' by convincing himself, with the tactful support of his intimate circle, that he is what he wants to be and that he would not do to gain his ends what the others have done to gain theirs. And as for society, if the person is willing to be subject to informal social control – if he is willing to find out from hints and glances and tactful cues what his place is, and keep it – then there will be no objection to his furnishing this place at his own discretion, with all the comfort, elegance and nobility that his wit can muster for him. To protect this shelter he does not have to work hard, or join a group, or compete with anybody; he need only be careful about the expressed judgements he places himself in a position to witness. Some situations and acts and persons will have to be avoided; others, less threatening, must not be pressed too far. Social life is an uncluttered, orderly thing because the person voluntarily stays away from the places and topics and times where he is not wanted and where he might be disparaged for going. He cooperates to save his face, finding that there is much to be gained from venturing nothing.

Facts are of the schoolboy's world – they can be altered by diligent effort but they cannot be avoided. But what the person protects and defends and invests his feelings in is an idea about himself, and ideas are vulnerable not to facts and things but to communications. Communications belong to a less punitive scheme than do facts, for communications can be by-passed, withdrawn from, disbelieved, conveniently misunderstood, and tactfully conveyed. And even should the person misbehave and break the truce he has made with society, punishment need not be the consequence. If the offence is one that the offended persons can let go by without losing too much face, then they are likely to act forbearantly, telling themselves that they will get even with the offender in another way at another time, even though such an occasion may never arise and might not be exploited if it did. If the offence is great, the offended persons may withdraw from the encounter, or from future similar ones, allowing their withdrawal to be reinforced by the awe they may feel toward someone who breaks the ritual code. Or they may have the offender withdrawn, so that no further communication can occur. But since the offender can salvage a good deal of face from such operations, withdrawal is often not so much an informal punishment for an offence as it is merely a means of terminating it. Perhaps the main principle of the ritual order is not justice but face, and what any offender receives is not what he deserves but what will sustain for the moment the line to which he has committed himself, and through this the line to which he has committed the interaction.

Throughout this paper it has been implied that underneath their differences in culture, people everywhere are the same. If persons have a universal human nature, they themselves are not to be looked to for an explanation of it. One must look rather to the fact that societies everywhere, if they are to be societies, must mobilize their members as self-regulating participants in social encounters. One way of mobilizing the individual for this purpose is through ritual; he is taught to be perceptive, to have feelings attached to self and a self expressed through face, to have pride, honor and dignity, to have considerateness, to have tact and a certain amount of poise. These are some of the elements of behavior which must be built into the person if practical use is to be made of him as an interactant, and it is these elements that are referred to in part when one speaks of universal human nature.

Universal human nature is not a very human thing. By acquiring it, the person becomes a kind of construct, built up not from inner psychic propensities but from moral rules that are impressed upon him from without. These rules, when followed, determine the evaluation he will make of himself and of his fellow-participants in the encounter, the distribution of his feelings, and the kinds of practices he will employ to maintain a specified and obligatory kind of ritual equilibrium. The general capacity to be bound by moral rules may well belong to the individual, but the particular set of rules which transforms him into a human being derives from requirements established in the ritual organization of social encounters. And if a particular person or group or society seems to have a unique character all its own, it is because its standard set of human-nature elements is pitched and combined in a particular way. Instead of much pride, there may be little. Instead of abiding by the rules, there may be much effort to break them safely. But if an encounter or undertaking is to be sustained as a viable system of interaction organized on ritual principles, then these variations must be held within certain bounds and nicely counterbalanced by corresponding modifications in some of the other rules and understandings. Similarly, the human nature of a particular set of persons may be specially designed for the special kind of undertakings in which they participate, but still each of these persons must have within him something of the balance of characteristics required of a usable participant in any ritually organized system of social activity.

References

BURNS, T. (1943), 'Friends, enemies, and the polite fiction', *Amer. Sociol. Rev.*, vol. 18, pp. 654–62.

CHAPPLE, E. D. (1940), 'Measuring human relations', *Genet. Psychol. Monogr.*, vol. 22, pp. 3–147.

DALE, H. E. (1941), *The Higher Civil Service of Great Britain*, Oxford University Press.

GOFFMAN, E. (1953), 'Communication conduct in an island community', unpublished doctoral dissertation, Department of Sociology, University of Chicago.

HOLCOMBE, C. (1895), *The Real Chinaman*, Dodd, Mead.

HORSFALL, A. B., and ARENSBERG, C. A. (1949), 'Teamwork and productivity in a shoe factory', *Hum. Org.*, vol. 8, pp. 13–25.

HSIEN CHIN HU (1944), 'The Chinese concept of "face"', *Amer. Anthrop.*, vol. 46, pp. 45–64.

JEFFREYS, M. D. W. (1952), 'Samsonic suicide, or suicide of revenge among Africans', *Afr. Stud.*, vol. 11, pp. 118–22.

JOHNSON, C. (1943), *Patterns of Negro Segregation*, Harper & Row.

LATOURETTE, K. S. (1942), *The Chinese: Their History and Culture*, Macmillan.

MACGOWAN, J. (1912), *Men and Manners of Modern China*, Allen & Unwin.

MAUSS, M. (1954), *The Gift*, I. Cunnison (tr.), Cohen & West.

MEAD, M. (1934), 'Kinship in the Admiralty Islands', *Anthrop. Pap. Amer. Mus. nat. Hist.*, vol. 34, pp. 183–358.

SMITH, A. H. (1894), *Chinese Characteristics*, Fleming H. Revell Company.

TOBY, J. (1952), 'Some variables in role conflict analysis', *Social Forces*, vol. 30, pp. 323–37.

WOLFF, K. H. (tr. & ed.) (1950), *The Sociology of Georg Simmel*, Free Press.

YANG, M. C. (1945), *A Chinese Village*, Columbia University Press.

18 E. Goffman

Alienation from Interaction

E. Goffman, 'Alienation from interaction', *Human Relations*, vol. 10, 1957
pp. 47–60.

Introduction

When the individual in our Anglo-American society engages in a conversational encounter with others he may become spontaneously involved
in it. He can become unthinkingly and impulsively immersed in the talk
and carried away by it, oblivious to other things, including himself.
Whether his involvement is intense and not easily disrupted, or meager
and easily distracted, the topic of talk can form the main focus of his
cognitive attention and the current talker can form the main focus of his
visual attention. The binding and hypnotic effect of such involvement is
illustrated by the fact that while thus involved the individual can simultaneously engage in other goal-directed activities (chewing gum, smoking,
finding a comfortable sitting position, performing repetitive tasks, etc.)
yet manage such side-involvements in an abstracted, fugue-like fashion so
as not to be distracted from his main focus of attention by them.

The individual, like an infant or an animal, can of course become spontaneously involved in unsociable solitary tasks. When this occurs the task
takes on at once a weight and a lightness, affording the performer a firm
sense of reality. As a main focus of attention talk is unique, howevei, for
talk creates for the participant a world and a reality that has other participants in it. Conjoint spontaneous involvement is a *unio mystico*, a
socialized trance. We must also see that a conversation has a life of its own
and makes demands on its own behalf. It is a little social system with its
own boundary-maintaining tendencies; it is a little patch of commitment
and loyalty with its own heroes[1] and its own villains.

Taking conjoint spontaneous involvement as a point of reference, I
want to discuss how this involvement can fail to occur and the consequence

[1]. One of its heroes is the wit who can introduce references to wider, important matters in a way that is ineffably suited to the current moment of talk. Since the witticism
will never again be as telling, a sacrifice has been offered up to the conversation, and
respect paid to its unique reality by an act which shows how thoroughly the actor is
alive to the interaction.

of this failure. I want to consider the ways in which the individual can become alienated from a conversational encounter, the uneasiness that arises with this, and the consequence of this alienation and uneasiness upon the interaction. Since alienation can occur in regard to any imaginable talk, we may be able to learn from it something about the generic properties of spoken interaction.

Involvement obligations

When individuals are in one another's immediate presence, a multitude of words, gestures, acts and minor events become available, whether desired or not, through which one who is present can intentionally or unintentionally symbolize his character and his attitudes. In our society a system of etiquette obtains that enjoins the individual to handle these expressive events fittingly, projecting through them a proper image of himself, an appropriate respect for the others present, and a suitable regard for the setting. When the individual intentionally or unintentionally breaks a rule of etiquette, others present may mobilize themselves to restore the ceremonial order, somewhat as they do when other types of social order are transgressed.

Through the ceremonial order that is maintained by a system of etiquette, the capacity of the individual to be carried away by a talk becomes socialized, taking on a burden of ritual value and social function. Choice of main focus of attention, choice of side-involvements and of intensity of involvement, become hedged in with social constraints, so that some allocations of attention become socially proper and other allocations improper.

There are many occasions when the individual participant in a conversations finds that he and the others are locked together by involvement obligations with respect to it. He comes to feel it is defined as appropriate (and hence either desirable in itself or prudent) to give his main focus of attention to the talk, and to become spontaneously involved in it, while at the same time he feels that each of the other participants has the same obligation. Due to the ceremonial order in which his actions are embedded, he may find that any alternate allocation of involvement on his part will be taken as a discourtesy and cast an uncalled-for reflection upon the others, the setting, or himself. And he will find that his offence has been committed in the very presence of those who are offended by it. Those who break the rules of interaction commit their crimes in jail.

The task of becoming spontaneously involved in something, when it is a duty to oneself or others to do so, is a ticklish thing, as we all know from experience with dull chores or threatening ones. The individual's actions must happen to satisfy his involvement obligations, but in a certain sense he cannot act *in order* to satisfy these obligations, for such an effort would require him to shift his attention from the topic of conversation to the problem of being spontaneously involved in it. Here in a component of non-rational impulsiveness – not only tolerated but actually demanded – we find an important way in which the interactional order differs from other kinds of social order.

The individual's obligation to maintain spontaneous involvement in the conversation and the difficulty of doing so place him in a delicate position. He is rescued by his co-participants, who control their own actions so that he will not be forced from appropriate involvement. But the moment he is rescued he will have to rescue someone else, and so his job as interactant is only complicated the more. Here, then, is one of the fundamental aspects of social control in conversation: the individual must not only maintain proper involvement himself but also act so as to ensure that others will maintain theirs. This is what the individual owes the others in their capacity as interactants, regardless of what is owed them in whatever other capacities they participate, and it is this obligation that tells us that, whatever social role the individual plays during a conversational encounter, he will in addition have to fill the role of interactant.

The individual will have approved and unapproved reasons for fulfilling his obligation *qua* interactant, but in all cases to do so he must be able rapidly and delicately to take the role of the others and sense the qualifications their situation ought to bring to his conduct if they are not to be brought up short by it. He must be sympathetically aware of the kinds of things in which the others present can become spontaneously and properly involved, and then attempt to modulate his expression of attitudes, feelings and opinions according to the company.

Thus, as Adam Smith argued in his *Theory of the Moral Sentiments*, the individual must phrase his own concerns and feelings and interests in such a way as to make these maximally usable by the others as a source of appropriate involvement; and this major obligation of the individual *qua* interactant is balanced by his right to expect that others present will make some effort to stir up their sympathies and place them at his command. These two tendencies, that of the speaker to scale down his expressions and that of the listeners to scale up their interests, each in the light of the other's capacities and demands, form the bridge that people build to one another, allowing them to meet for a moment of talk in a communion of reciprocally sustained involvement. It is this spark, not the more obvious kinds of love, that lights up the world.

The forms of alienation

If we take conjoint spontaneous involvement in a topic of conversation as a point of reference, we shall find that alienation from it is common indeed. Conjoint involvement appears to be a fragile thing, with standard points of weakness and decay, a precariously unsteady state that is likely at any time to lead the individual into some form of alienation. Since we are dealing with obligatory involvement, forms of alienation will constitute misbehavior of a kind that can be called 'misinvolvement'. Some of the standard forms of alienative misinvolvement may be considered now.

External preoccupation

The individual may neglect the prescribed focus of attention and give his main concern to something that is unconnected with what is being talked about at the time and even unconnected with the other persons present, at least in their capacity as fellow-participants. The object of the individual's preoccupation may be one that he ought to have ceased considering upon entering the interaction, or one that is to be appropriately considered only later in the encounter or after the encounter has terminated. The preoccupation may also take the form of furtive by-play between the individual and one or two other participants. The individual may even be preoccupied with a vague standard of work-activity, which he cannot maintain because of his obligation to participate in the interaction.

The offensiveness of the individual's preoccupation varies according to the kind of excuse the others feel he has for it. At one extreme there is preoccupation that is felt to be quite voluntary, the offender giving the impression that he could easily give his attention to the conversation but is wilfully refusing to do so. At the other extreme there is 'involuntary' preoccupation, a consequence of the offender's understandably deep involvement in vital matters outside the interaction.

Individuals who could excusably withdraw involvement from a conversation often remain loyal and decline to do so. Through this they show a nice respect for fellow-participants and affirm the moral rules that transform socially responsible people into people who are interactively responsible as well. It is of course through such rules, and through such reaffirming gestures, that society is made safe for the little worlds sustained in face-to-face encounters. No culture, in fact, seems to be without exemplary tales for illustrating the dignity and weight that might be given to these passing realities; everywhere we find enshrined a Drake who gallantly finishes some kind of game before going out to battle some kind of Armada, and everywhere an outlaw who is engagingly civil to those he robs and to those who later hang him for it.[2]

2. Yet different strata in the same society can be unequally concerned that members learn to project themselves into encounters; the tendency to keep conversations alive and lively may be a way in which some strata, not necessarily adjacent, are characteristically different from others.

Self-consciousness

At the cost of his involvement in the prescribed focus of attention, the individual may focus his attention more than he ought upon himself – himself as someone who is faring well or badly, as someone calling forth a desirable or undesirable response from others. It is possible, of course, for the individual to dwell upon himself as a topic of conversation – to be self-centered in this way – and yet not to be self-conscious. Self-consciousness for the individual does not, it seems, result from his deep interest in the topic of conversation, which may happen to be himself, but rather from his giving attention to himself as an interactant at a time when he ought to be free to involve himself in the content of the conversation.

A general statement about sources of self-consciousness ought to be added. During interaction the individual is often accorded by others and by impersonal events in the situation an image and appraisal of self that is at least temporarily acceptable to him. He is then free to turn his attention to matters less close to home. When this definition of self is threatened, the individual typically withdraws attention from the interaction in a hurried effort to correct for the incident that has occurred. If the incident threatens to raise his standing in the interaction, his flight into self-consciousness may be a way of rejoicing; if the incident threatens to lower his standing and damage or discredit his self-image in some way, then flight into self-consciousness may be a way of protecting the self and licking its wounds. As a source of self-consciousness, threat of loss seems more common and important than threat of gain.

Whatever the cause of self-consciousness, we are all familiar with the vacillation of action and the flusterings through which self-consciousness is expressed; we are all familiar with the phenomenon of embarrassment.

Self-consciousness can be thought of as a kind of preoccupation with matters internal to the interactive social system, and as such has received more common-sense consideration than other kinds of internal preoccupation. In fact we do not have common-sense words to refer to these other kinds of improper involvement. Two forms of these I shall refer to as 'interaction-consciousness' and 'other-consciousness' to emphasize a similarity to self-consciousness.

Interaction-consciousness

A participant in talk may become consciously concerned to an improper degree with the way in which the interaction, *qua* interaction, is proceeding, instead of becoming spontaneously involved in the official topic of conversation. Since interaction-consciousness is not as famous as self-consciousness, some sources of it may be cited by way of illustration.

A common source of interaction-consciousness is related to the special responsibility that an individual may have for the interaction 'going well', i.e. calling forth the proper kind of involvement from those present. Thus, at a small social gathering the hostess may be expected to join in with her guests and become spontaneously involved in the conversation they are maintaining, and yet at the same time if the occasion does not go well she, more than others, will be held responsible for the failure. In consequence, she sometimes becomes so much concerned with the social machinery of the occasion and with how the evening is going as a whole that she finds it impossible to give herself up to her own party.

Another common source of interaction-consciousness may be mentioned. Once individuals enter a conversation they are obliged to continue it until they have the kind of basis for withdrawing that will neutralize the potentially offensive implications of taking leave of others. While engaged in the interaction it will be necessary for them to have subjects at hand to talk about that fit the occasion and yet provide content enough to keep the talk going; in other words, safe supplies are needed.[3] What we call 'small talk' serves this purpose. When individuals use up their small talk, they find themselves officially lodged in a state of talk but with nothing to talk about; interaction-consciousness experienced as a 'painful silence' is the typical consequence.

Other-consciousness

During interaction, the individual may become distracted by another participant as an object of attention – exactly as in the case of self-consciousness he can become distracted by concern over himself.[4]

If the individual finds that whenever he is in the conversational presence of specific others they cause him to be overly conscious of them at the expense of the prescribed involvement in the topic of conversation, then they may acquire the reputation in his eyes of being faulty interactants, especially if he feels he is not alone in the trouble he has with them. He is then likely to impute certain characteristics to those who are thus perceived, doing so in order to explain and account for the distraction they cause him. It will be useful to our understanding of interaction to list a few of the attributes imputed in this way.

By the terms 'affectation' and 'insincerity' the individual tends to identify those who seem to feign through gestures what they expect him to accept as an uncontrived expressive overflow of their behavior. Affectation, as Cooley suggests,

3. The problem of safe supplies is further considered in Goffman (1953, ch. 15).
4. Other-consciousness is briefly but explicitly considered in Baldwin (1902, pp. 213–214).

. . . exists when the passion to influence others seems to overbalance the established character and give it an obvious twist or pose (1922, p. 196).

Thus there are persons who in the simplest conversation do not seem to forget themselves, and enter frankly and disinterestedly into the subject, but are felt to be always preoccupied with the thought of the impression they are making, imagining praise or depreciation, and usually posing a little to avoid the one or gain the other (1922, p. 215).

Affected individuals seem chiefly concerned with controlling the evaluation an observer will make of them, and seem partly taken in by their own pose; insincere individuals seem chiefly concerned with controlling the impression the observer will form of their attitude toward certain things or persons, especially toward him, and seem not to be taken in by their own pose. It may be added that while those who are felt to be self-conscious give the impression of being overly concerned with what will happen or has happened to them, those who are felt to be insincere or affected give the impression that they are overly concerned with what they can achieve in what is to follow and are willing to put on an act in order to achieve it. When the individual senses that others are insincere or affected he tends to feel they have taken unfair advantage of their communication position to promote their own interests; he feels they have broken the ground rules of interaction. His hostility to their unfair play leads him to focus his attention upon them and their misdemeanor at the price of his own involvement in the conversation.

In considering the attributes imputed to those who cause another to be conscious of them, we must give importance to the factor of immodesty. On analytical grounds over-modesty should equally count as a source of other-consciousness, but, empirically, immodesty seems much the more important of the two. What the individual takes to be immodesty in others may present itself in many forms: immodest individuals may seem to praise themselves verbally; they may talk about themselves and their activity in a way that assumes greater interest in and familiarity with their personal life than the individual actually possesses; they may speak more frequently and at greater length than the individual feels is fitting; they may take a more prominent 'ecological' position than he thinks they warrant, etc.

One interesting source of other-consciousness is to be found in the phenomenon of 'over-involvement'. During any conversation, standards are established as to how much the individual is to allow himself to be carried away by the talk, how thoroughly he is to permit himself to be caught up in it. He will be obliged to prevent himself from becoming so swollen with feelings and a readiness to act that he threatens the bounds regarding affect that have been established for him in the interaction. He will be obliged to express a margin of disinvolvement, although of course this margin will differ in extent according to the socially recognized importance of the occasion and his official role in it. When the individual does become over-involved in the topic of conversation, and gives others the impression that he does not have a necessary measure of self-control over his feelings and actions, when, in short, the interactive world becomes too real for him, then the others are likely to be drawn from involvement in the talk to an involvement in the talker. What is one man's over-eagerness will become another's alienation. In any case we are to see that over-involvement has the effect of momentarily incapacitating the individual as an interactant; others have to adjust to his state while he becomes incapable of adjusting to theirs. Interestingly enough, when the impulse of the over-involved individual has ebbed a little, he may come to sense his impropriety and become self-conscious, illustrating again the fact that the alienative effect the individual has on others is usually one he cannot escape having upon himself. Regardless of this, we must see that a readiness to become over-involved is a form of tyranny practised by children, *prima donnas*, and lords of all kinds, who momentarily put their own feelings above the moral rules that ought to have made society safe for interaction.

A final source of other-consciousness may be mentioned. If the individual is to become involved in a topic of conversation, then, as a listener, he will have to give his aural and usually his visual attention to the source of communication, that is, to the speaker, and especially to the speaker's voice and face. (This physical requirement is underlined by social rules that often define inattention to the speaker as an affront to him.) If the speaker's communication apparatus itself conveys additional information all during the time that transmission is occurring, then the listener is likely to be distracted by competing sources of stimuli, becoming over-aware of the speaker at the expense of what is being said. The sources of this distraction are well known: the speaker may be very ugly or very beautiful; he may have a speech defect such as a lisp or a stutter; he may have inadequate familiarity with the language, dialect or jargon that the listeners expect to hear; he may have a slight facial peculiarity, such as a hare lip, eye twitch, crossed or wall eyes; he may have temporary communication difficulties such as a stiff neck, a hoarse voice, etc. Apparently the closer the defect is to the communication equipment upon which the listener must focus his attention, the smaller the defect need be to throw the listener off balance. (It should be added that in so far as a speaker is required to direct his attention to his listener and yet not be overly conscious of him, defects in the appearance of the listener can cause the speaker to be uneasy.) These minor defects in the apparatus of communication tend to shut off the afflicted individual from the stream of daily contacts, transforming him into a faulty interactant, either in his own eyes or in the eyes of others.

In concluding this discussion of sources of alienating distraction, I should like to state an obvious caution. When the individual senses that others are unsuitably involved, it will always be relative to the standards of his group that he will sense the others have behaved improperly. Similarly an individual who would cause certain others to be unduly conscious of him because of his apparent insincerity, affectation or immodesty would pass unnoticed in a subculture where conversational discipline was less strict. Hence, when members of different groups interact with one another, it is quite likely that at least one of the participants will be distracted from spontaneous involvement in the topic of conversation because of what appears to him to be unsuitable behavior on the part of the others.[5] It is to these differences in expressive customs that we ought to look first in trying to account for the improper behavior of those with whom we happen to be participating and not try, initially at least, to find some source of blame within the personalities of the offenders.

On the repercussive character of involvement offences

I have suggested that disenchantment with an interaction may take the form of preoccupation, self-consciousness, other-consciousness and interaction-consciousness. These forms of alienation have been separated for purposes of identification. In actual conversation, when one kind occurs the others will not be far behind.

When the individual senses that he or other participants are failing to allocate their involvement according to standards that he approves, and in consequence that they are conveying an improper attitude toward the interaction and the participants, then his sentiments are likely to be roused by the impropriety – much as they would be were any other obligations of the ceremonial order broken. But matters do not stop here. The witnessing of an offence against involvement obligations, as against other ceremonial obligations, causes the witness to turn his attention from the conversation at hand to the offence that has occurred during it. If the individual feels responsible for the offence that has occurred, he is likely to be led to feel shamefully self-conscious. If others seem responsible for

5. For example, in social intercourse among traditional Shetlanders, the pronoun *I* tends to be little used; its greater use by individuals from the mainland of Great Britain, and especially its relatively frequent use by Americans, leads the Shetlander to feel that that non-Shetlandic people are immodest and gross. Shetlandic tact, it might be added, frequently prevents non-islanders from learning that their manner causes Shetlanders to be uneasy.

the offence, then he is likely to be led to feel indignantly other-conscious in regard to them. But to be self-conscious or other-conscious is in itself an offence against involvement obligations. The mere witnessing of an involvement offence, let alone its punishment, can cause a crime against the interaction, the victim of the first crime himself being made a criminal. Thus, during spoken interaction, when one individual is stricken with uneasiness, others often come down with the disease.

A note of qualification should be added. The individual may become misinvolved and yet neither he nor others may become aware that this is the case, let alone become improperly involved because of this awareness. He commits a latent offence that only awaits someone's perception of it to make it manifest. When others come to see that he is misinvolved, and convey the fact of this judgement to him, he may become self-consciously flustered in consequence, as he may also do when he discovers this fact for himself. Thus an individual may 'come to' from a brown study and embarrassingly find himself in the midst of an interaction but patently alienated from it.

The affectation of involvement

When a conversation fails to capture the spontaneous involvement of an individual who is obliged to participate in it, he is likely to contrive an appearance of being really involved. This he must do to save the feelings of the other participants and their good opinion of him, regardless of his motives for wanting to effect this saving. In doing so he has a damping effect upon the repercussive consequences of misinvolvement, insuring that while he may be disaffected his disaffection will not contaminate others. At the same time, however, he drives a wedge between himself and the world that could become real for him. And the gap that is created in this way he fills with that special kind of uneasiness that is characteristically found during conversation; the kind of uneasiness that occurs when involvement obligations can neither be laid aside nor spontaneously realized; the kind that occurs when the individual is separated from the reality of interaction, yet at a time when interaction is all around him.

As a form of contrivance, affected involvement will be differently judged according to the motive the alienated individual has for contriving it. Some shows of involvement are felt to be cynical because the individual seems to be interested ultimately not in the feelings of the others but rather in what can be gained by deluding the others into a belief that they have captured his attention. He gives the impression that he is occupied with the talk but proves to be really occupied with the task of giving this impression.

On the other hand, if the alienated individual is genuinely concerned with the feelings of the others, as important matters in their own right, then any act that protects these feelings may be considered a form of tact and approved on this ground.

It should be noted that often the show of involvement given by the tactful interactant is not as good a show as he is capable of giving. Some power that is almost beyond him will force him to demonstrate to others and to himself that this kind of interaction with these participants is not the sort of thing that can capture his attention; someone must see that he is perhaps above or beyond it. Here we find a form of insubordination carried on by those who may not really be in a position to rebel.

The ways of not quite concealing tactfully concealed misinvolvement constitute, then, the symptoms of boredom. Some symptoms of boredom suggest that the individual will make no effort to terminate the encounter or his official participation in it but that he will no longer give as much to it. The initiation of side-involvements, such as leafing through a magazine or lighting a cigarette, are instances. Other symptoms of boredom suggest that the individual is about to terminate official participation and function as a tactful warning of this.[6]

To manifest signs of boredom is an inconsiderate thing. But in a certain way he who does so assures the others that he is not affecting something that is not felt; they at least know where they stand with him. To suppress these signs completely is suspect, for this prevents others from obtaining the benefit of feedback cues that might tell them what the situation really is. Thus, while there is one obligation to affect involvement, there is another one inducing the individual not to affect it too well. It is an interesting fact that when the self of the boring individual is deeply committed to the proceedings, as it may be, for example, during leave-takings and avowals of affection, then the bored individual is likely to feel a strong compunction to conceal signs of alienation and thoroughly affect involvement. It is thus at the most poignant and crucial moments of life that the individual is often forced to be the most contriving; these, too, will be the times when the boring individual will be in greatest need of candor from others and least able to bear receiving it.

I have suggested that a show of involvement may be affected by cynical participants and by tactful ones; the same show may also be affected by those who feel self-consciously embarrassed. They may even add to their production by affecting signs of boredom. A condition that casts doubt upon the individual himself is thus exchanged, he hopes, for one that casts doubt upon the others. There is a psychological doctrine that carries this

6. There is in fact a small literature in 'applied human relations' detailing ways in which the superordinate can imply that an interview is over, allowing the actual leave-taking to be initiated, in a face-saving way, by the other.

observation one step further and argues that when the individual is himself convinced that he is bored, he may be trying to conceal from himself that he is actually embarrassed.[7]

Conversational encounters in which participants feel obligated to maintain spontaneous involvement and yet cannot manage to do so are ones in which they feel uneasy, and ones in which they may well generate uneasiness in others. The individual recognizes that certain situations will produce this alienation in him and others, and that other situations are quite unlikely to do so. He recognizes that certain individuals are faulty interactants because they are never ready to become spontaneously involved in social encounters and he will have folk-terms such as 'cold fish', 'kill-joy', 'drag', 'wet blanket' to refer to these refractory participants. Those who fail to support conversations with their social betters he may call *gauche*; while those who disdain involvement with their inferiors he may call snobs; in either case condemning these persons for putting rank before interaction. As previously suggested, the individual will also know some persons who are faulty because their manner and social attributes make it difficult for others to become properly involved. It is apparent, too, that in any interaction a role-function develops, that of ensuring that everyone becomes and remains spontaneously involved. This sparking function may be fulfilled by different participants at different times in the interaction. Should one participant fail to help keep the interaction going, other participants will have to do his share of work. An individual may acquire a reputation for this kind of labor, creating gratitude or resentment as one who is always the life of the encounter.

Generalizing the framework
The context of involvement obligations

One limitation we have set ourselves is to deal with situations where all those present to one another are officially obliged to maintain themselves as participants in conversation and to maintain spontaneous involvement in the conversation. This is a frequent enough condition to serve as a reference point, but there is no need to be ultimately bound by it. Involvement obligations are in fact defined in terms of the total context in which the individual finds himself. Thus there will be some situations where the main involvement of those present is supposed to be invested in a physical task; conversation, if carried on at all, will have to be treated as a side-involvement to be picked up or dropped, depending on the current demands of the task at hand. There will be other situations where the role

7. For psychoanalytic version of this theme see Greenson (n.d.) and Fenichel (1953). Some interesting observations on the cult of boredom and the place of this cult in the world of adolescence can be found in Salinger (1951).

and status of a particular participant will be nicely expressed by his right to treat a conversation in a cavalier fashion, participating in it or not, depending on his inclination at the moment. A father sometimes has this right regarding the mealtime conversation maintained by lesser members of the family, while they do not.

I should like to cite another way in which the individual may accept a different allocation of involvement for himself from that expected of others. In the teasing that the young receive from the old, or in the interrogations that employees receive from employers, loss of composure on the subordinate's part may be accepted by the superordinate as an expected and proper part of the involvement pattern. At such times the subordinate may feel he would like to be spontaneously involved in the talk but is in too much of a panic to do so, while the superordinate may feel that for him the appropriate focus of attention, and one he can sustain with comfort, is not the actual talk but the wider situation created by the humorous plight of the inferior as he struggles in the conversation.[8] In fact, if the subordinate shows composure on these occasions, the superior may feel affronted and embarrassed. Similarly there will be occasions when we feel an individual ought, out of respect for the difficulties he is in, to be preoccupied or over-involved. This misinvolvement may somewhat disrupt the interaction, but perfect poise on his part might so scandalize those present as to disrupt the interaction even more. Thus while it is true that sometimes an individual will be thought an interaction hero if he remains involved in a conversation under difficult conditions, at other times such loyalty will be thought foolhardy.

Differential obligations regarding the same spoken interaction may be seen most clearly in large-scale interactions, such as public speeches, where we are likely to find specialization and segregation of involvement roles, with a division between full participants, who are expected to talk or listen, and non-participating specialists, whose job is to move unobtrusively about and look after some of the mechanics of the occasion. Examples of these non-participants are domestics, ushers, doormen, stenographers and microphone men. The special alignment these officials have to the interaction is their particular right and obligation; it is accepted openly by them and for them, and they would in fact cause uneasiness were they to become manifestly involved in the content of the talk. They show respect for the occasion by treating it as a side-involvement.

8. The plight of the self-conscious person is in fact so good a stimulus for calling forth spontaneous involvement on the part of those who witness it, that during conversations where there may be difficulty in capturing the involvement of those present, individuals may take turns both at committing minor infractions against propriety and at becoming embarrassed, thus ensuring involvement. Hence the paradox that if all the rules of correct social behaviour are exactly followed, the interaction may become flaccid, stale and flat.

Participants, themselves, in large-scale interaction can have a licence in regard to involvement that could not be afforded them in two- or three-person talk, perhaps because the more participants there are to sustain the proceedings, the less dependent the occasion will be on any one participant. In any case, we often find in large-scale interaction that it is permissible for a few participants to enter for a moment into by-plays and side-discussions, providing they modulate their voice and manner to show respect for the official proceedings. In fact, a participant may even leave the room for a moment and do this in such a way as to convey the impression that his main focus of attention is still held by the talk, even though his body is not present. On such occasions, main involvement and side-involvements may become fictions maintained officially in form while alternate involvement patterns are actually maintained in practice.

Pseudo-conversations

We have so far restricted our attention to interactions that have as their constituent communicative acts the turns at talking taken by participants. We can extend our view and consider conversation-like interactions in which the token exchanged is not speeches but stylized gestures, as in the interchange of non-verbal greetings,[9] or moves of some kind, as in card games. These unspoken yet conversation-like interactions seem to be similar, structurally, to spoken interaction, except that the capacities that must be mobilized in order to carry on such interaction seem to have more to do with muscular control of limbs than in the case of spoken interaction.

Unfocused interaction

I have suggested that speech-, gesture- and game-interactions are characterized by a single official focus of cognitive and visual attention that all full-fledged participants help to sustain. (The focus of visual attention may move, of course, from one participant to another as one speaker gives up his speaking-role and returns to the role of listener.) With this focused kind of interaction we must contrast the unfocused kind, where individuals

9. The following is an instance of psychiatrist–patient interaction that is verbal on one side only: '. . . in the course of an analysis of a very disturbed schizophrenic with depressive features the patient hid herself within her only garment, a blanket, so that only the eyebrow showed; nothing daunted I continued the conversation from where we left off last time and noted changes in that eloquent but only visible member, which changes – a frown, scowl, surprise, a flicker of amusement, a softening of that curve – indicated the changes in her mood and thought. My surmises proved correct for when next she displayed her face and used her voice she corroborated the general trend of my guesses as to what had gone on in her mind. That session was no verbal *interchange* – it might even be called an eyebrow analysis – but there was an endeavor to verbalize, to conceptualize and make concrete "in the here and now" what was occurring concurrently in her mind' (Rickman, 1950, p. 189).

in one another's visual and aural range go on about their respective business unconnected by a shared focus of attention. Street behavior and conduct at a large social party are instances.

When we examine unfocused interactions we find that involvement obligations are defined not in relation to a conjoint focus of cognitive and visual attention but in relation to a role that can be suggested by the phrase 'decorous individual non-interferingly going about his proper business'. Once we shift to this point of reference, however, we find that all the kinds of misinvolvement that occur during focused interaction also occur during unfocused interaction, though sometimes under a different name. Just as an adolescent may become self-consciously uneasy when talking to his teacher, so, in walking into a full classroom, he may feel that he is being critically observed and that his way of walking, which he feels is stiff and wooden, reveals his social anxiety. Just as we can have preoccupied persons in conversational interaction, so in unfocused interaction we can have 'absent-minded' participants, who by their posture, facial expression, and physical movements suggest that they are momentarily 'away', that they have momentarily let fall the expressive costume that individuals are expected to wear whenever they are in the immediate presence of others. And, of course, boredom, too, can occur during unfocused interaction, as we may observe in almost any queue of individuals waiting to buy a ticket. And just as agencies such as alcohol and marijuana may be employed to transform a conversation into something that is not embarrassing or boring, so these may function to put individuals at ease in the wider scene provided by unfocused interaction. Just as a witticism may do honor to the conversational moment, so the wearing of new or special clothing, the serving of rare or costly food, and the use of perishable flowers can draw attention to the unique value of a wider social occasion. Clearly, then, there are ways in which the perspective employed in this paper can be used for studying unfocused interaction.

We must not, however, expect the similarity between the two kinds of interaction to be too complete. For example, it appears that individuals are more frequently unself-conscious in their capacity as participants in unfocused interaction than they are as participants in focused interaction, especially focused interaction of the spoken kind. In fact, in spoken interaction, spontaneous 'normal' involvement seems to be the exception and alienation of some kind the statistical rule. This is understandable. On the one hand, participants are required to be spontaneously carried away by the topic of conversation; on the other hand, they are obliged to control themselves so that they will always be ready to stay within the role of communicator and stay alive to the touchy issues that might cause the others to become ill at ease. On the one hand they are obliged to adhere to all applicable rules of conduct, on the other they are obliged to take enough liberties to ensure a minimum level of involving excitement. These obligations seem to be in opposition to each other, requiring a balance of conduct that is so delicate and precarious that alienation and uneasiness for someone in the interaction are the typical result. Unfocused interaction does not seem to require the same delicacy of adjustment.

Conclusion

Many social encounters of the conversational type seem to share a fundamental requirement: the spontaneous involvement of the participants in an official focus of attention must be called forth and sustained. When this requirement exists and is fulfilled, the interaction 'comes off' or is euphoric as an interaction. When the encounter fails to capture the attention of the participants, but does not release them from the obligation of involving themselves in it, then persons present are likely to feel uneasy; for them the interaction fails to come off. A person who chronically makes himself or others uneasy in conversation and perpetually kills encounters is a faulty interactant; he is likely to have such a baleful effect upon the social life around him that he may just as well be called a faulty person.

Of any individual, then, it will be significant to know whether his status and manner tend to hinder the maintenance of spontaneous involvement in the interaction, or to help it along. It should be noted that this information pertains to the individual in his capacity as interactant, and that, regardless of the other capacities in which he may be active at the time, the role of interactant is something he will be obliged to maintain.

Social encounters differ a great deal in the importance that participants give to them but, whether crucial or picayune, all encounters represent occasions when the individual can become spontaneously involved in the proceedings and derive from this a firm sense of reality. And this kind of feeling is not a trivial thing, regardless of the package in which it comes. When an incident occurs and spontaneous involvement is threatened, then reality is threatened. Unless the disturbance is checked, unless the interactants regain their proper involvement, the illusion of reality will be shattered, the minute social system that is brought into being with each encounter will be disorganized, and the participants will feel unruled, unreal and anomic.

Aside from the sense of reality it offers, a particular encounter may be of little consequence, yet we must see that the rules of conduct that oblige individuals to be able and ready to give themselves up to such moments are of transcendent importance. Men who are held by these rules are held ready for spoken interaction, and spoken interaction between many kinds of people on many kinds of occasion is necessary if society's work is to be done.

The sense of reality that has been discussed in this paper takes its form in opposition to modes of alienation, to states like preoccupation, self-consciousness and boredom. In turn, these modes of disengagement are to be understood by reference to the central issue of spontaneous involvement. When we have seen the way in which a spoken encounter can succeed or fail in bringing its participants to it, and have seen that unfocused interaction can be looked at in the same way, we have a lead to follow in the understanding of other kinds of commitments – the individual's occupational career, his political involvements, his family membership – for there will be a sense in which these wider matters consist in recurrent occasions of focused and unfocused interaction. By looking at the ways in which the individual can be thrown out of step with the sociable moment, perhaps we can learn something about the way in which he can become alienated from things that take much more of his time.

References

BALDWIN, J. (1902), *Social and Ethical Interpretations in Mental Development*, London.

COOLEY, C. H. (1922), *Human Nature and the Social Order*, Scribners.

FENICHEL, O. (1953), 'The psychology of boredom', in *The Collected Papers of Otto Fenichel* (first series), Norton.

GOFFMAN, E. (1953), 'Communication conduct in an island community', unpublished doctoral dissertation, Department of Sociology, University of Chicago.

GREENSON, R., 'On boredom', *J. Amer. psychoanal. Assoc.*, vol. 1, pp. 7–21.

RICKMAN, J. (1950), 'The role and future of psychotherapy within psychiatry', *J. ment. Sci.*, vol. 96, pp. 181–9.

SALINGER, J. D. (1951), *The Catcher in the Rye*, Little, Brown; Hamish Hamilton.

19 R. F. Bales

How People Interact in Conferences

R. F. Bales, 'How people interact in conferences', *Scientific American*, March 1955, pp. 3–7. Reprinted with permission. Copyright © 1955 by Scientific American Inc. All rights reserved.

Social interaction is made up largely of the talking that people do when they get together. Talk is an elusive object of study, in spite of the fact that a good deal of it exists. It is also a rather sensitive subject. Even a friend might find it hard to put up with a dissection of the following kind: 'I was just noticing how much you talk. In the last ten minutes I noticed that you made a total of 114 remarks, while I made a total of 86. According to my count you gave about twice as many opinions as facts. Although I agreed with you fifteen times and didn't disagree at all, I noticed that you stammered once and blushed twice.'

I first began to develop a systematic procedure for analysing social interaction when I became interested in trying to account for the success of Alcoholics Anonymous in helping apparently hopeless drinkers to stop drinking. Although I attended meetings and talked with many members, I did not feel free to ask all the questions I wished. Consequently I fell back on observation and began to develop crude methods for recording who did what, who spoke to whom, and how. Eventually even this quiet occupation began to appear sinister and the effort was abandoned. But by this time my fascination with the process of social interaction had developed to the point of no return. I decided that I must pursue my studies in the more favorable conditions of a laboratory.

A number of laboratories for the study of social interaction within small groups and organizations have been started in the last ten years – in hospitals, clinics, special research centers and military installations. The studies and experiments I shall describe were conducted in one of the earliest of these laboratories, established in 1947 at Harvard University.

The laboratory consists of a large, well-lighted room for the group under study and an adjoining room for observers, who listen and watch from behind windows with one-way vision. The subjects are told at the beginning that the room has been constructed for the special purpose of studying group discussion, that a complete sound recording will be made and that there are observers behind the one-way mirrors. The purpose of the separation is not to deceive the subjects but to minimize interaction between them and the observing team.

After much research we developed a standardized task from which significant generalizations could be drawn. A group of persons (ranging from two to seven in number) is asked to discuss a complex human relations problem of the sort typically faced by an administrator. Each member of the group first reads a five-page presentation of facts about the case to be discussed, but each is left uncertain as to whether he has been given exactly the same range of facts as the others in the group. The members are not introduced to one another or coached in any way; they must develop their own organization and procedure. They are to consider the facts and report to an administrator, as if they were his staff, their joint conclusions concerning the problem and what should be done about it. They are allowed forty minutes for the discussion. The group is observed for four such sessions.

On the other side of the one-way screen the observers systematically record every step of the interaction, not omitting such items as nods and frowns. Each observer has a small machine with a moving paper tape on which he writes in code a description of every act – an act being defined

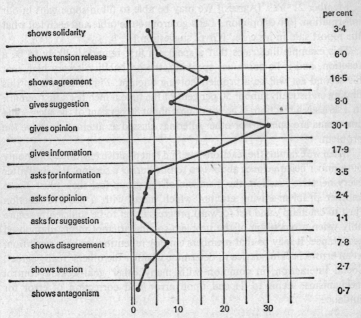

per cent

shows solidarity	3·4
shows tension release	6·0
shows agreement	16·5
gives suggestion	8·0
gives opinion	30·1
gives information	17·9
asks for information	3·5
asks for opinion	2·4
asks for suggestion	1·1
shows disagreement	7·8
shows tension	2·7
shows antagonism	0·7

Figure 1 Types of acts in social interaction may be classed in four main categories: positive reactions, problem-solving attempts, questions and negative reactions. The averages for ninety-six group sessions show that 56 per cent of the acts fall into the problem-solving category.

essentially as a single statement, question or gesture. Acts ordinarily occur at the rate of fifteen to twenty per minute. The recorded information on each includes identification of the person speaking and the person spoken to and classification of the act according to pre-determined categories. There are twelve categories, covering positive and negative reactions, questions and attempts to solve the problem by the offering of information, opinion or suggestions (see Figure 1).

As this table shows, on the average about half (56 per cent) of the acts during a group session fall into the categories of problem-solving attempts; the remaining 44 per cent are distributed among positive reactions, negative reactions and questions. In other words, the process tends to be two-sided, with the reactions acting as a more or less constant feedback on the acceptability of the problem-solving attempts. The following is a typical example of the pattern of interchange:

Member 1: 'I wonder if we have the same facts about the problem? [Asks for opinion.] Perhaps we should take some time in the beginning to find out.' [Gives suggestion.]

Member 2: 'Yes. [Agrees.] We may be able to fill in some gaps in our information. [Gives opinion.] Let's go around the table and each tell what the report said in his case.' [Gives suggestion.]

This example illustrates that a speaker's first remark is likely to be a reaction, and if he continues speaking, the probability is very high that his second act will be a problem-solving attempt. Figure 2 sums up this finding statistically: about 50 per cent of the time a member's first remark in a series is a reaction; if he continues, about 80 per cent of the succeeding comments are opinions or other offerings classed as attempts to solve the problem.

When we examine the reactions, we find that positive reactions commonly outnumber negative ones about two to one during a session. It is as if after every negative reaction, the members of the group feel they must make another problem-solving attempt which meets with a positive reaction 'just to catch up', and net forward progress is felt to be sufficiently secure only when a repetition of the problem-solving attempt meets unopposed acceptance. It may be that members employ repetition, or near repetition, as an error-checking device to determine whether the others 'really agree'. Social interaction, in common with many other goal-seeking control mechanisms, seems to depend upon error and correction of error for guidance.

The process of attempting to arrive at a group decision through discussion is in many ways very like the operation of a large-scale communication and control system such as an air-defence network. I recently compared the

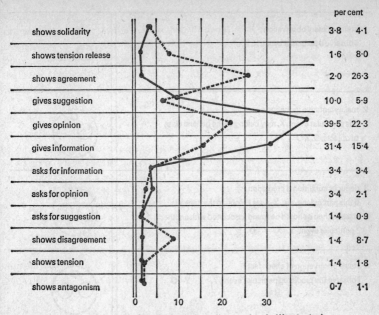

	per cent	
shows solidarity	3·8	4·1
shows tension release	1·6	8·0
shows agreement	2·0	26·3
gives suggestion	10·0	5·9
gives opinion	39·5	22·3
gives information	31·4	15·4
asks for information	3·4	3·4
asks for opinion	3·4	2·1
asks for suggestion	1·4	0·9
shows disagreement	1·4	8·7
shows tension	1·4	1·8
shows antagonism	0·7	1·1

Figure 2 Pattern of action of individuals in a discussion is illustrated statistically. When a member takes the floor, his first remark (*broken curve*) is likely to be a reaction to the preceding speaker. His next remarks (*black curve*) tend to be problem-solving attempts.

two processes in collaboration with John Kennedy of the Systems Research Laboratory at the Rand Corporation.

In the military case there are three functions to be performed: surveillance of the air by radar, identification of planes as friendly or unknown and direction of fighters sent out to intercept unknown planes. These are something like the three problems confronting our groups in the standard interaction task: assembling the given information on the case, evaluating it and proceeding toward a solution as the goal. Now the stepwise operations involved in the air-defence system may be tolerably well described as an interlocking series of seven types of information-processing operations (see Figure 3). Here x stands for the path of a plane tracked by radar, and O represents the class of objects unknown. If no known flight plan of a friendly plane coincides with x – a fact represented by the symbol y – then x must belong to the class O. Since there is a general rule, W, that all unknown planes are to be intercepted, the conclusion is that a specific order, w, should be given to intercept x.

Such a decision, involving many groups and interlocking processes, is

1 states primary observation: I observe a particular event, X. X	
2 makes tentative induction: this particular event, X, may belong to the general class of objects, O. X O	
3 deduces conditional prediction: If this particular event, X, does belong to the general class O, then it should be found associated with another particular event, Y. X Y O	
4 states observation of check fact: I observe the predicted particular event, Y. X Y O	
5 Identifies object as member of a class: I therefore identify X–Y as an object which is a member of the predicted general class of objects, O. O X Y	
6 states major premise relating classes of objects: All members of the general class of objects L, should be treated by ways of the general class, W. O X Y W	
7 Proposes specific action: This particular object, X–Y, should therefore be treated in a particular way, W. O X Y W W	

Figure 3 Process in reaching a group decision is analogous to the operation of a large-scale communication and control system such as the air-defence network. The steps consist of observing an object or event, comparing it with several possible identifications, considering the associated facts and, once its nature is understood, taking the appropriate action.

obviously a very complicated affair, socially as well as technically. The job of the decision-making organization is essentially to build and maintain through means of communication and evaluation a sufficiently complex and commonly accepted symbolic structure to guide or control the stages of behavior of all the operating units. Effective decision making is basically a continuous process of building and maintaining a structure of cultural objects which in their totality constitute the common culture of the organization affected.

The seven types of acts, or stages, just described are very general: they apply quite as well to the interaction of five experimental subjects in the laboratory group, trying to decide in forty minutes what the administrator in their case should do about his problem, as to the large-scale operations of an air-defence network. Not all of the elements in the process are primarily logical in character. They involve elements of perception, memory, association and perhaps inductive insight. All sorts of motivational and evaluative pressures affect the process. The steps make sense not as a formally perfect chain of logic, but rather as a set of symbol transformations which help to guide, although in an imperfect way, a process of decision-making behavior. Error checking is an integral part of this fallible process.

The reason for calling attention to the seven-step structure of the process is that it may help to explain the unequal ratios of suggestions, opinions and information offered in the problem-solving attempts of the groups in our tests. As the first table shows, of every seven problem-solving attempts, on the average four are opinions, two are offers of information and one is a suggestion. It seems significant that in the idealized seven-step outline of the air-defence operation two steps have the interaction form of giving information, four intermediate steps have the interaction form of giving opinion and only one step, the final one, has the form of giving a suggesttion.

From the transcription of a group discussion it is often possible to reconstruct complete seven-step chains leading to agreement on specific points and the final conclusion. In a general way there is even a tendency for the steps to proceed in a regular order in time. During a session the rates of giving information tend to be highest in the first third of the meeting and to decline in the next two thirds (see Figure 4). Rates of giving opinion are usually highest in the middle portion of the meeting. Rates of giving suggestion are generally low in the early period and reach their high point in the last third of the meeting.

Rates of both positive and negative reactions tend to rise from the first third of the meeting to the last third. These increases may be connected mainly with social and emotional problems of the group process itself. The

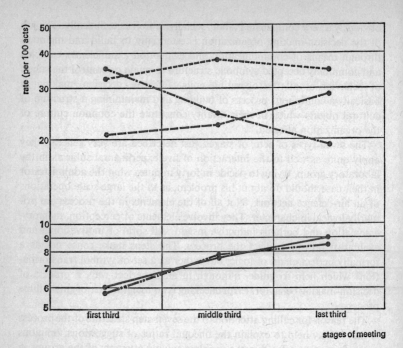

first third   middle third   last third

stages of meeting

○----------○ opinion
○----------○ information
○----------○ positive reactions
○----------○ suggestion
○----------○ negative reactions

Figure 4 Group progress toward a decision is characterized by a change in the frequency of different types of social acts, as the meeting wears on. Information-giving decreases while suggestions and positive and negative reactions increase

ratio of negative to positive reactions tends to be higher in response to suggestions than in response to factual statements. The decision point is a critical bottleneck in the process. Once the decision point has been passed, however, the rates of negative reaction usually fall off and the rates of positive reaction rise sharply. Joking and laughter, indicating solidarity and tension release, become more frequent. With the problems of the task and common values stabilized for the time being by the decision, the interaction process apparently turns to restabilizing the emotional states of the individuals and their social relations to one another.

There is a good deal of evidence that the process of social interaction, like other processes involving feedback, tends to fall into oscillation as it 'hunts' around a hypothetical steady state. Over a small time span the action tends to alternate every few acts between the problem-solving attempts of one person and the social-emotional reaction of some other. But this rapid oscillation is not quite rapid enough to keep all elements of the process in perfect balance. There is a drift toward inequality of a participation, which in time has cumulative effects on the social relationships of the members. The reason for this drift may be seen fairly easy. When a person has completed one act, the chances are a little better than even that he will continue for another act. After each succeeding act his probability of continuing drops, but never as far as if he simply flipped a coin at each point to determine whether to continue or to yield the floor. In fact, relatively speaking, he exceeds this chance probability by a larger and larger fraction with each succeeding act.

We have already noted that when a person continues several acts in succession the probability is very high that he is giving information, opinion or suggestion – in other words, specializing in problem-solving attempts. We may also infer from the seven-step theory of problem-solving attempts that the tendency to continue for several acts in succession is probably due in part to a felt need on the part of the speaker to provide inferences and check facts which will result in the acceptance of a more advanced step in the series, with an accepted suggestion as the goal.

This tendency toward inequality of participation over the short run has cumulative side effects on the social organization of the group. The man who gets his speech in first begins to build a reputation. Success in obtaining acceptance of problem-solving attempts seems to lead the successful person to do more of the same, with the result that eventually the members come to assume a rank order by task ability. In some groups the members reach a high degree of consensus on their ranking of 'who had the best ideas'. (The members are interviewed by questionnaire after each meeting.) Usually the persons so ranked also did the most talking and had higher than average rates of giving suggestions and opinion.

While one person becomes a specialist in advancing ideas, another is apt to be developing a specialization on the reactive side. The men most commonly rated 'best liked' typically have higher than average rates of showing tension release (mainly smiling and laughing) and showing agreement. It is not impossible for the man ranked at the top in ideas also to be best liked, but apparently it is difficult. In one set of experiments the top idea man had about an even chance of also being best liked at the end of the first meeting, but by the end of the fourth meeting his chances were only about one in 10. The best-liked man is usually second or third in the participation hierarchy.

The task specialist seems to 'lock onto' the person who is most responsive to what he is saying and address more remarks to him than to the others. In turn, the best-liked man talks more and agrees more with the top-ranking idea specialist than with any other member. The idea specialist and the best-liked man often form a mutually supporting pair. However, the best-liked man may attract the idea specialist even though they are not always in agreement. Indeed, in order for a person to become established in the minds of other members as a social-emotional specialist, it is probably more important that he be representative of their reactions, both positive and negative, than that he should ardently support everything the task specialist says. Apparently reactions that are emotionally gratifying to other members tend to be generalized by them into liking for the person who expresses the reactions.

Giving suggestions, necessary as it may be for accomplishment of the task, is more likely to arouse negative reactions than is giving information or opinions. This tends to put the task specialist in a vulnerable position. The group commonly develops a certain amount of negative feeling toward him. Not only is he likely to lose the status of being best liked, but he may lose his position as task leader unless he is sensitive to the problem and is well supported by other members. Even in a group which ends its first meeting with a high consensus on who has the best ideas, the second meeting is apt to see a challenge to his leadership, with a rise in rates of disagreement and antagonism and a precipitous drop in his popularity. But then, in a group where the original consensus was high, a peculiar thing seems to happen. Apparently as progress toward accomplishment of the task slows down, some members rally around the leader again and and his popularity tends to rise. By the third meeting the rates of disagreement and antagonism go down. The task leader may not retain all the liking that was transferred to him in his time of need, but the net effect of the hunting kind of oscillation that takes place is a tendency to maintain the original rank order of task ability.

In a group that starts with a low degree of consensus on who has the best ideas, the developments usually are more dismal. There tends to be a high turnover in the top ranks throughout the four meetings, with one would-be leader replacing another. In such a group the man ranked as having the best ideas is less apt to be best liked. Furthermore an additional specialist is likely to appear – a man who talks more than anybody else but is neither best liked nor most highly respected for his task ability.

It appears probable that whether the members will agree on who has the best ideas depends to a large degree on how well they agree on basic premises or norms – what we may call the 'common culture'. If such consensus is not present, at least implicitly, at the beginning, it may take a long time to build. While consensus on major values does not solve all the problems of arriving at a stable social organization, probably no stable organization is possible without this control factor. If it is lacking, the interaction process becomes primarily a means for the expression of individual emotional states.

Our studies have made clear that social stability is an extremely complex achievement: it takes time and patience to arrive at a common culture extensive enough and sensitive enough to regulate strong counter motives, to promote task accomplishment, to harmonize social relationships and to rejuvenate itself whenever the conditions demand. A clear recognition of the complexity of cultural control of behavior should encourage us to believe that interminable series of meetings around the conference table, international and otherwise, are perhaps worth while after all.

20 E. A. Schegloff

Sequencing in Conversational Openings[1]

E. A. Schegloff, 'Sequencing in conversational openings', *American Anthropologist*, vol. 70, 1968, pp. 1075–95.

An attempt is made to ascertain rules for the sequencing of a limited part of natural conversation and to determine some properties and empirical consequences of the operation of those rules. Two formulations of conversational openings are suggested and the properties 'non-terminality' and 'conditional relevance' are developed to explicate the operation of one of them and to suggest some of its interactional consequences. Some discussion is offered of the fit between the sequencing structure and the tasks of conversational openings.

My object in this paper is to show that the raw data of everyday conversational interaction can be subjected to rigorous analysis. To this end, I shall exhibit the outcome of one such analysis, confined to one limited aspect of conversation. The aspect is sequencing, in this case sequencing in two-party conversations, with attention directed to the opening of such conversations (although only one kind of opening is considered). The paper proceeds by suggesting a first formulation – referred to as a 'distribution rule' – to analyse materials drawn from telephone conversation. The first formulation is found deficient, and the search for a more adequate analysis leads to a second formulation not limited to telephone conversations alone, but able to deal with them, and subsuming the 'distribution rule' as a special case. Some properties of the second formulation – called 'summons-answer sequences' – are detailed, and consideration is given to the uses of the interactional mechanism that has been analysed.

This work may have relevance for anthropologists for several reasons.

1. This discussion is a shortened and modified version of chapters two and three of the author's Ph.D. dissertation (Schegloff, 1967). It is based on the analysis of tape-recorded phone calls to and from the complaint desk of a police department in a middle-sized Midwestern city. References to the 'data' in the text should be understood as references to this corpus of materials. Names have been changed to preserve anonymity; numbers preceding citations of data identify calls within the corpus. The Disaster Research Center, Department of Sociology, Ohio State University, provided this recorded material, which was obtained in connection with studies of organizational functioning under stress, especially disaster conditions.

First, there is a possible direct interest in the materials under investigation; second, the developing interest in the ethnography of communication, recently represented by a special number of this journal (Gumperz and Hymes, 1964); and third, what I take to be a prevailing interest of anthropologists in the possibility of direct analysis of the 'stuff of everyday life' so as to discover its orderly or methodical character.

I cannot say for what domain my analysis holds, but, as the references to settings other than the contemporary United States should indicate, I do not think the findings are limited to America today. Since cross-cultural variability and invariance are of abiding interest to anthropologists, information on this question will have to be sought from them. Whether this sort of analysis is possible or practical on materials from societies of which the analyst is not a member is also not clear, and again it may remain for anthropologists to supply the answer (see, for example, Moerman (in press)).

Introduction

I use 'conversation' in an inclusive way. I do not intend to restrict its reference to the 'civilized art of talk' or to 'cultured interchange' as in the usages of Oakeshott (1959) or Priestly (1926), to insist on its casual character thereby excluding service contacts (as in Landis and Burtt, 1924), or to require that it be sociable, joint action, identity related, etc. (as in Watson and Potter, 1962). 'Dialogue', while being a kind of conversation, has special implications derived from its use in Plato, psychiatric theorizing, Buber, and others, which limits its usefulness as a general term. I mean to include chats as well as service contacts, therapy sessions as well as asking for and getting the time of day, press conferences as well as exchanged whispers of 'sweet nothings'. I have used 'conversation' with this general reference in mind, occasionally borrowing the still more general term 'state of talk' from Erving Goffman.

It is an easily noticed fact about two-party conversations that their sequencing is alternating. That is to say, conversational sequence can be described by the formula $ababab$, where 'a' and 'b' are the parties to the conversation. (I am indebted to Sacks (in press) for suggesting the significance of this observation, and some of its implications.) The $abab$ formula is a specification, for two-party conversations, of the basic rule for conversation: *one party at a time*. The strength of this rule can be seen in the fact that in a multi-party setting (more precisely, where there are four or more), if more than one person is talking, it can be claimed not that the rule has been violated, but that more than one conversation is going on. Thus, Bales can write:

The conversation generally proceeded so that one person talked at a time, and all members in the particular group were attending the *same conversation*. In this sense, these groups might be said to have a 'single focus', that is, they did not involve a number of conversations proceeding at the same time (Bales *et al.*, 1951, p. 461).

When combined with an analytic conception of an utterance, the *abab* specification has a variety of other interesting consequences, such as allowing us to see how persons can come to say *X is silent*, when no person in the scene is talking. (For a psychiatric usage, see Bergler, 1938.)

The problem I wish to address is the following: the *abab* formula describes the sequencing of a two-party conversation already underway It does not provide for the allocation of the roles 'a' and 'b' (where 'a' is a first speaker and 'b' is a second speaker) between the two persons engaged in the conversation. Without such an allocation, no ready means is available for determining the first speaker of the convention. The *abab* sequence makes each successive turn sequentially dependent upon the previous one; it provides no resources when who the first speaker might be is treated problematically. I should like to examine the ways in which coordinated entry by two parties into an orderly sequence of conversational turns is managed. (This general area has been considered from a somewhat different perspective in Goffman, 1953, ch. 14; see also Goffman, 1965, pp. 88–95.)

Notice that I do not mean to identify a 'turn' necessarily with any syntactic or grammatical unit or combination of units, nor with any activity. In the former case, it should be clear that a turn may contain anything from a single *mm* (or less) to a string of complex sentences. In the latter, it is crucial to distinguish a single turn in which two activities are accomplished from two turns by the same party without an intervening turn of the other. An example of the latter occurs when a question must be repeated before it is heard or answered; an example of the former is the line following the inquiry *How are you, Oh I'm fine. How are you.* A 'turn', as I am using the term, is thus not the same as what Goffman refers to as a 'natural message', which he describes as the 'sign behavior of a sender during the whole period of time through which a focus of attention is continuously directed at him' (Goffman, 1953, p. 165). There are, of course, other views of the matter, such as using a period of silence or 'appreciable pause' to mark a boundary (as in Stephen and Mishler, 1952, p. 600, or Steinzor, 1949, p. 109). But unanalysed pauses and silences are ambiguous (theoretically) as to whether they mark the boundary of a unit, or are included in it (as the very term 'pause' suggests).

Telephone conversation: the distribution rule

A first rule of telephone conversation, which might be called a 'distribution rule for first utterances', is: *the answerer speaks first*. Whether the utterance be *hello, yeah, Macy's, shoe department, Dr Brown's office, Plaza 1–5000*, or whatever, it is the one who picks up the ringing phone who speaks it.

This rule seems to hold in spite of a gap in the informational resources of the answerer. While the caller knows both his own identity, and, typically, that of his intended interlocutor (whether a specific person or an organization is being phoned), the answerer, at least in most cases, knows only who he is and not specifically who the caller is. That is not to say that no basis for inference might exist, as, for example, that provided by time of day, the history of a relationship, agreed upon signalling arrangements, etc. To the question *whom are you calling?* a caller may give a definitive answer, but to the question *who's calling?* the answerer, before picking up the phone, can give only a speculative answer.

Without developing a full analysis here, the import of the gap in the answerer's information ought to be noted. If, in this society, persons uniformly used a single standardized item to open a conversation without respect to the identity of the other party or the relationship between the two, then the informational lack would have no apparent import, at least for the opening. This, however, is not the case. A variety of terms may be used to begin conversation and their propriety is geared to the identity, purposes and relationships of either or both parties. Intercom calls, for example, are typically answered by a *yeah* or *yes* while incoming outside calls are seldom answered in that way. (In citations of data in which the police receive the call, 'D' refers to the police 'dispatcher' and 'C' refers to the caller.):

#68
D: Yeah.
C: Tell 85 to take that crane in the west entrance. That's the only entrance that they can get in.
D: O.K. Will do.
C: Yeah.

#88
D: Yes.
C: Uh Officer Novelada.
D: Yes, speaking.
C: Why uh this is Sergeant —,
D: Yes Sergeant.
C: And uh I just talked to [etc.]

#123
D: Yeah.
C: If you can get a hold of car 83, go'm tell him to go to [etc.]

Full consideration of the problem that this answerer's information gap presents, and some solutions to it, requires reference to aspects of conversational openings other than sequencing, and cannot be adequately discussed here (see Schegloff, 1967, ch. 4).

It may help to gain insight into the working of the distribution rule to consider, speculatively, what might be involved in its violation, and the reader is invited to do so. (For the illumination of normal scenes produced by considering disruption of them, I am indebted to Harold Garfinkel; see Garfinkel, 1967.) One possible violation would involve the following: The distribution rule provides that the answerer normally talks first, immediately upon picking up the receiver. To violate the rule and attempt to have the other person treated as the one who was called, he would not talk, but would remain silent until the caller spoke first. Suppose after some time the caller says *Hello?* This might be heard as an attempt by the caller to check out the acoustic intactness of the connection. In doing so, the caller employs a lexical item, and perhaps an intonation, that is standardly used by called parties in answering their home phones. This would provide the violator (i.e. the answerer acting as a caller) with a resource. Given the identity of the lexical items used by persons to check out and to answer in this case, the violater may now treat the checking out *hello* as an answering *hello*. Continuing the role reversal, he would be required to offer a caller's first remark.

We may note that, without respect to the detailed substance of their remarks, it is a property of their respective utterances that the answerer typically says just *hello*, whereas the caller, if he says *hello*, typically then adds a continuation, e.g. *this is Harry*. Our hypothetical violator, in having to make a caller's first remark to achieve the role reversal, must then say *hello* with a continuation.

To be sure, a caller might say only *hello*, so as to invite the called person to recognize who is calling. This is a common attempt to establish or confirm the intimacy or familiarity of a relationship. To cite one instance from our data, in which a police complaint clerk calls his father:

#497

OTHER: Hello

POLICE: Hello

OTHER: Hello, the letter, you forgot that letter

POLICE: Yeah but listen to me, the — just blew up, [etc.]

The 'intimacy ploy', however, is available only to a 'genuine' caller, and not to the hypothetical violator under consideration. If the violator says it, the genuine caller might hear it as a correct answerer's first remark that was delayed. The attempted violation would thereupon be frustrated.

In saying *hello* with a continuation, however, the would-be violator would encounter trouble. While trying to behave as a caller, he does not have the information a genuine caller would have. In having to add to the *hello* to play the caller's part, the choice of an appropriate item depends on his knowing (as a genuine caller would know) to whom he is speaking. We may give three examples of what this bind might consist of:

1. One common addition to a caller's *hello* involves the use of a term of address, for example: Answerer: *Hello*?; Caller: *Hello, Bill*. Not knowing to whom he is speaking, the violator can obviously not employ such an addition.

2. Another frequent addition is some self-identification appended to the *hello*. Self-identification involves two parts: (a) a frame and (b) a term of identification. By 'frame' is meant such things as *this is —*, *my name is —*, or *I am —*.[2] Terms of identification include among others, first names, nicknames, or title plus last name. We may note that the choice both of appropriate frames and appropriate self-identification terms varies with the identity and relationship of the two parties. For example, the frame *My name is —* is normally used only in identifying oneself to a stranger. Similarly, whether one refers to oneself as Bill or Mr Smith depends upon the relationship between the two parties. Our imagined violator would not have the information requisite to making a choice with respect to either determination. Although these two examples are not exhaustive of the variety of caller's continuations, a great many calls proceed by use of one or more of them, and in each case a masquerading caller, not having the simple information a genuine caller would have, would have trouble in using such a continuation.

3. An alternative continuation for a caller, whether used in combination with one of the foregoing continuations or as the caller's next turn suggests another rule of opening conversations: the caller provides the first 'topic' of conversation. This rule would confront a violator with the problem of formulating a topic of conversation that could serve appropriately without respect to whom he is speaking. Whether there are such topics is unclear. A promising candidate as a general first topic might seem to be the ritual inquiry *How are you?* or some common variant thereof. This inquiry is usable for a very wide range of conversational others, but not for all conversational others. For example, telephone solicitors or callers from the Chamber of Commerce would not be typically greeted in this way. As formulated here, the rule 'The caller provides the first "topic"'

2. The latter framing item, *I am —* is not normally used on the telephone as the frame for a name, although it may be used in a next item, as when an organizational affiliation is offered to provide further identification. In face-to-face interaction, *This is —* is not typically used for self-identification but only for introducing a third party. *My name is —* is usable in both face-to-face and in telephone interactions.

is not nearly as general as the distribution rule. There are obvious occasions where it is not descriptive, as when the 'caller' is 'returning a call'. A formulation that would hold more generally might be 'The initiator of a contact provides the first topic.' But this alternative is no better in providing a continuation to *hello* that is usable for all conversational others. (It may be noted here that much of the analysis in this section will be superseded below.)

Other violations of the distribution rule are readily imaginable, and need not be enumerated here. My interest is chiefly in exploring the operation and constraints provided by the distribution rule, as well as the resources it provides for keeping track of the developing course of a conversation. I found, in attempting to imagine violations, that without the proper operation of the simple distribution rule, it was difficult to keep track of who was who, who the genuine caller and who the violator, the order of events, what remarks were proper for whom, etc. Although I have attempted to describe the hypothetical violation clearly, I fear, and trust, that the reader will have been sore-pressed to follow the 'play-by play' account and keep the 'players' straight. It may be noted, then, that not only does the distribution rule seem to be routinely followed in the actual practice of telephone conversationalists, but that it provides a format by which observers maintain a grasp of the developing activity.

Finally, consider as evidence of the binding character of the distribution rule the following personal anecdote recounted by a student. At one time, she began receiving obscene phone calls. She noted that the caller breathed heavily. She, therefore, began the practice of picking up the receiver without speaking. If she heard the heavy breathing, she would hang up. The point she wanted to make in relating this anecdote was that she encountered considerable irritation from her friends when it turned out that it was they calling and she had not made a first utterance upon picking up the receiver. She took this to be additional evidence for the correctness of the rule 'the answerer speaks first'. However, she has supplied an even more pointed demonstration than she intended. It is notable that she could avoid hearing the obscenities by avoiding making a first utterance; however obscene her caller might be, he would not talk until she had said *hello*, thereby obeying the requirements of the distribution rule.

A deviant case

The distribution rule discussed above holds for all but one of the roughly five-hundred phone conversations in the entire corpus of data. In the vast majority of these, the dispatcher, when calls were made to the police, or others, when calls were made by the police, spoke first. In several cases the tape recordings contained instances of simultaneous talk at the beginning of the interchange (often because the caller was still talking to the switchboard operator when the dispatcher 'came on the line'). In these cases, a resolution occurred by the callers withdrawing in favour of the called. That is, either the caller stopped and the dispatcher continued, or both stopped and the dispatcher went on.

#364

D: Police Desk.

C: First aiders with me.   } Simultaneous

D: Police Desk.

C: Hello?

D: Yes.

C: Uh this is [etc.]

#66

D: Police Desk.

C: (Simultaneously giving phone number in background to operator)

D: Hello

C: I am a pharmacist. I own [etc.]

#43

D: Police Desk.

C: Say, what's all the excitement ...   } Simultaneous

D: Police Desk?

C: Police Headquarters?

D: Yes.

C: What's all the excitement [etc.]

Simultaneous talk is of special interest because it is the converse of *abab*, which requires that only one party talk at a time. If simultaneous talk could be shown to be regularly resolved via the distribution rule, at the beginning of telephone conversations, then its status as a solution to the problem of coordinated entry would be more general. A fully adequate demonstration might involve giving somewhat stronger explication of the notion of one party's 'withdrawal', perhaps by reference to some utterance unit, e.g. a sentence, begun but not finished. (For this last point, I am indebted to Harvey Sacks.)

One case clearly does not fit the requirements of the distribution rule:

#9 (Police make call)

    Receiver is lifted, and there is a one second pause

POLICE: Hello.

OTHER: American Red Cross.

POLICE: Hello, this is Police Headquarters . . . er, Officer Stratton [etc.]

In this case the caller talks first, while the distribution would require that the first line be *American Red Cross*, the statement of the called party.

While indeed there is only one such violation in my data, its loneliness in the corpus is not sufficient warrant for not treating it seriously. Two alternatives are open. We might focus exclusively on this case and seek to develop an analysis particular to it that would account for its deviant sequencing. This would constitute an *ad hoc* attempt to save the distribution rule, using a technique commonly used in sociology – deviant case analysis. Alternately, we might re-examine the entire corpus of materials seeking to deepen our understanding of the opening sequencing. We might ask: Is this best treated as a deviant case, or would a deeper and more general formulation of the opening sequencing reveal properties of the initiation of talk that the distribution rule glosses over. Analysis of the case reveals that the distribution rule, while it holds in most cases, is in fact best understood as a derivative of more general rules. As we shall see, the additional sequencing rules, which this case forces us to examine, clarify properties of talk in non-telephone communication as well as in telephone communication. The rules discussed below do not make the distribution rule superfluous, but concern more finely grained aspects of the opening sequence. They require that we analyse aspects of the opening structure that the distribution rule does not handle. The distribution rule is but one, if indeed a most typical, specification of the formulation to follow, and the deviant case is another specification. As Michael Moerman has suggested, the distribution rule is no less a 'special case' for having many occurrences, nor the latter more so for having only one (in my corpus of materials). Not number of occurrences, but common subsumption under a more general formulation is what matters. It will be shown that, in broadening the fomulation of the opening sequence, a set of more interesting and formal properties of the opening sequencing structure are exposed.

Summons–answer sequences

Originally we spoke of two parties to a telephone interaction, a caller and an answerer. The distribution rule held that the answerer spoke first. One of the activities in the material under examination seems to be 'answering', and it is appropriate to ask what kind of answering activity is involved and what its properties are.

Let us consider for a moment what kinds of things are 'answered'. The most common item that is answered is a question, and a standardized exchange is question–answer. At first glance, however, it seems incorrect to regard the 'called' party as answering a question. What would be the question? A telephone ring does not intuitively seem to have that status. Other items that are answered include challenges, letters, roll calls and summonses. It seems that we could well regard the telephone ring as a summons. Let us consider the structure of summons–answer sequences.

It can be noted at the outset that a summons – often called an 'attention-getting device' – is not a telephone-specific occurrence. Other classes besides mechanical devices, such as telephone rings, include:

1. Terms of address (e.g. *John*? *Dr, Mr Jones*?, *waiter*,[3] etc.).
2. Courtesy phrases (e.g. *Pardon me*, when approaching a stranger to get his attention).
3. Physical devices (e.g. a tap on the shoulder, waves of a hand, raising of a hand by an audience member, etc.).

It is to be noted that a summons occurs as the first part of a two-part sequence. Just as there are various items that can be used as summonses, so are there various items that are appropriately used as answers, e.g. *Yes*?, *What*?, *Uh huh*?, turning of the eyes or of the body to face the beckoner, etc. Some typical summons–answer sequences are: telephone ring – *hello*; *Johnny?* – *yes*; *Excuse me* – *Yes*; *Bill?* – looks up.

The various items that may be used as summonses are also used in other ways. *Hello*, for example, may be used as a greeting; *Excuse me* may be used as an apology; a name may be used as a term of address only, not requiring an answer. How might we differentiate between the summons uses of such terms and other uses? Taking as an example items whose other use is as terms of address, it seems that the following are ways of differentiating their uses:

1. When addressing, the positioning of a term of address is restricted. It may occur at the beginning of an utterance (*Jim, where do you want to go?*), at the end of an utterance (*What do you think, Mary?*) or between clauses or phrases in an utterance (*Tell me, John, how's Bill?*). As summons items, however, terms of address are positionally free within an utterance. (This way of differentiating the usages has a 'one-way' character; that is, it

3. We may note here special classes of occupational titles. Most occupational titles cannot be used as terms of address or to summon persons of whom they are descriptive. So, for example, one would not introduce into a sentence as a term of address, nor seek to get attention via the term *secretary*. There is a small collection of occupational titles that can be used, under appropriate circumstances, as terms of address or to summon their possessors. For example, one may either address or summon by way of *Doctor, Rabbi, Officer, Nurse*, etc. There is a still smaller class of occupational titles which, while not usable as terms of address, are usable as summons items. For example, *cabby*, or *ice cream man*, etc. About this collection we may note that aside from their referential uses, e.g. *He is a cabby*, they seem to be used only as summons items.

is determinative only when an item occurs where terms of address [as non-summons items] cannot. When it occurs within the restrictions on placement of terms of address, it clearly is non-differentiating.) As a mere address term, an item cannot occur between a preposition and its object, but as a summons it may, as in the following telephone call from the data:

#398
c: Try to get out t' – Joe?
d: Yeah?
c: Try to get ahold of [etc.]

2. Summons items may have a distinctive rising terminal juncture, a raising of the voice pitch in a quasi-interrogative fashion.[4] This seems to be typically the case when a summons occurs after a sentence has already begun, as in the above datum. It need not be the case when the summons stands alone, as in *Jim*, when trying to attract Jim's attention.

3. A term of address is 'inserted' in an utterance. By that I mean that after the term of address is introduced, the utterance continues with no break in its grammatical continuity; e.g. *Tell me, Jim, what did you think of*. . . . When a summons occurs in the course of an utterance, it is followed by a 'recycling' to the beginning of the utterance. The utterance is begun again, as in the datum cited in point 1 above. Although in that datum the original utterance is altered when started again, alteration is not intrinsic to what is intended by the term 'recycling'.

It is an important feature of summonses and answers that, like questions and answers, they are sequentially used. This being so, the unit of our analysis is a sequence of summons and answer, which shall henceforth be abbreviated as 'SA' sequence. Question–answer sequences shall be referred to as 'QA'. We now turn to an examination of two major and several subsidiary properties of SA sequences.

Non-terminality of SA sequences

By non-terminality I mean that a completed SA sequence cannot properly stand as the final exchange of a conversation. It is a specific feature of SA sequences that they are preambles, preliminaries or prefaces to some further conversational or bodily activity. They are both done with that purpose, as signaling devices to further actions, and are heard as having that character. This is most readily noticed in that very common answer to a summons *What is it?* Non-terminality indicates that not only must

4. Bolinger (1958). We say, with Bolinger, 'quasi-interrogative' because there is in American English apparently no definitive interrogative intonation, such that anything so intoned is a question, or if not so intoned cannot be a question.

something follow, but that SA sequences are specifically preliminary to something that follows.

Is the continuation upon the completion of an SA sequence constrained in any way, e.g. in which party produces it? The very property of non-terminality is furnished by the obligation of the summoner to talk again upon the completion (by the summoned) of the SA sequence. It is he who has done the summoning and by making a summons incurs the obligation to talk again. With exceedingly rare exceptions, some of which will be noted below, the summoner fulfills this obligation and talks again. It is the fact of the routine fulfillment of the obligation to talk again that produces data in which every conversation beginning with an SA sequence does not terminate there.

It may be noted in passing that the structure of SA sequences is more constraining than the structure of QA sequences. It seems to be a property of many QA sequences that the asker of a question has the *right* to talk again, but not an obligation to do so.[5] SA sentences more forcefully constrain both contributors to them. One way to see the constraining character of non-terminality as a normative property of an SA sequence is by observing what regularly occurs when the summoner, for whatever reason, does not wish to engage in whatever activity the SA sequence he originated may have been preliminary to. Here we characteristically find some variant of the sequence: *Sam? Yeah? Oh, never mind.* Note that in the very attempt to appropriately withdraw from the obligation to continue after a completed SA sequence, an original summoner must in fact conform to it and not simply be silent. Even in telephone conversations between strangers, where maintaining the intactness of some relationship would not seem to be at issue, the obligation to continue talk upon an SA sequence has been observed to hold. For example, in calling an establishment to learn if it is open, that fact may sometimes be established positively when the ringing phone (summons) is lifted and *hello* or an establishment name is heard. Rather than hang up, having obtained the required information, many persons will continue with the self-evidently answered question *Are you still open?* (although note here the common tendency to append to it a more reasonable inquiry, one not rendered superfluous by the very act, as *How late are you open?* even though that might not, on the given occasion, be of interest). The limited rule 'the caller supplies the first topic' advanced earlier may be seen to be one partial application of the obligation of a summoner to talk again.

5. I am indebted to Harvey Sacks for the first part of this observation. Some questions may, to be sure, obligate their askers to talk again. The statement in the text may, therefore, reflect a stage in the analysis of questions where such questions have not yet been closely examined.

A property directly related to the non-terminality of SA sequences is their non-repeatability. Once a summons has been answered, the summoner may not begin another SA sequence. A contrast is suggested with QA sequences where a questioner, having a *right* to talk again after an answer is given, may fill his slot with another question. Although a questioner may sometimes be constrained against asking the same question again (e.g. in two-person interaction: A: *How are you?* B: *Fine.* A: *How are you?*), he may choose some question to fill the next slot. A summoner is not only barred from using the same summons again but from doing any more summoning (of the same 'other'). If, as occurs on occasion, a summoner does not hear the answer of the other, and repeats the summons, should the answerer hear both summonses he will treat the second one as over-insistent. This is most likely to occur in those situations where physical barriers make it difficult for the summoned person to indicate his having received the summons and having initiated a course of answering. Continued knocking on the door is often met with the complaint as the answerer is on his way, *I'm coming, I'm coming.* To sum up, the summoner's obligation to talk again cannot be satisfied by initiating another SA sequence to the same other. This does not mean, however, that one might not have, in a transcript of the opening of a conversation, two SA sequences back-to-back. As we shall shortly see, if the non-terminality property is not met, i.e. should the summoner not fulfill his obligation to talk again, the answerer of the first SA sequence may, in turn, start another with a summons of his own, as in the first line below (E has called M – the initial S):[6]

M: MacNamara (pause). Hello? (A#S)
E: Yeah uh John? (A . . .)
M: Yeah.
E: I uh just trying to do some uh intercom here in my own set up and get ahold of you at the same time.

We may further see the operation of the non-terminality property in a common misunderstanding of the use of a name. Names may serve, as suggested above, both as simple terms of address or as summoning terms of address. Should a name intendedly uttered as a simple term of address be heard as a summons, the hearer will expect a continuation while the speaker will not be prepared to give one. While not a particularly frequent occurrence, when found, it usually occurs in the following way: X uses Y's name, and in so doing waves. This is a typical way to perform a greet-

6. The datum is from a collection of calls to and from a public agency other than the one from which the bulk of the data are drawn. The first two SA sequences are indicated in parentheses.

ing, part of which is verbally accomplished and part of it gesturally accomplished. The lexical item perceived alone, i.e. where the gesture is not seen, may be heard as a summons, and one who hears it in this way will then answer it and await the activity to which it was expectably preliminary. The misinterpreted sender, like he who calls merely to find out information that the answer conveys, may feel obligated to say *I was just saying 'hello'*.

It is worth noting about such occurrences that misinterpreted persons can see how they were misinterpreted. Being able to see the kind of error involved rather than having to investigate its character, allows immediate correction. Such availability of the nature of an error may be quite important. One consequence may be the following. That the systematic ambiguity of the term (i.e. its use to do more than one activity – here 'summoning' and 'greeting') is available when invoked by the second party, suggests that the summoner can see how the error could be made; he can see its methodical character. Members may be able, then, not only to methodically detect which of two activities a term is being used for, but also to detect methodical errors in such determinations. The hope may, therefore, be warranted that investigators will be able to describe methods for differentiating 'term of address' usages from 'summons' usages, even if the three suggestions offered earlier prove wrong.

Non-terminality is an outcome of the obligation of the summoner to talk again. Corollary to that obligation is the obligation of the answerer, having answered the summons, to listen further. Just as the summoner, by virtue of his summons, obligates himself for further interaction, so the answerer, by virtue of his answer, commits himself to staying with the encounter. More will be said about this matter and some of its ramifications in the discussion of what I term the problem of 'availability'. For the present it may suffice to give an example of a common situation under which the power of this reciprocality makes itself felt. Compare, for example, two ways in which a mother may seek to call her child to dinner from a play area. One way would involve the use of his name as a term of address with the request that he return home, e.g. *Johnny, come home. It's time for dinner*. It is not an anomalous experience in this culture that such calls may elicit no response from the parties to whom they are directed. It may be claimed, upon complaint about this nonresponse, that the call was not heard. Contrast with this, however, a sequence in which the child is summoned prior to a statement of the summoner's intention. If the child answers the summons, he is stopped from ignoring what follows it, e.g. *Johnny? Yes? Come home for dinner*. Children may resist answering the summons, knowing what may follow it, and realizing that to answer the summons commits them to hearing what they do not want to hear. Although they may none the less not obey the commandment, claiming they have not heard, it is more difficult if they have answered the summons.

It is to be noted that the non-terminality of an SA sequence and the obligations that produce it are mutually oriented to by the parties to the interaction and may affect the very choice of an answer to the original summons. A prospective answerer of a summons is attuned to the obligation of the summoner to respect the non-terminality of the sequence (i.e. to continue the interaction, either by talk or bodily activity) once the answer is delivered. He is likewise attuned to his obligation, having answered, to be prepared to attend the summoner's obligated next behavior. Should he not be in a position to fulfill this listener's obligation, he may provide for that fact by answering the summons with a 'motion to defer', e.g. *John? Just a minute, I'll be right there.* Of course, such deferrals may, in fact, serve to cancel the interaction, as when a *just a minute* either intendedly or unwittingly exhausts the span of control of the summons. More will be said below about deferrals, and their appropriateness, in our consideration of the issue of availability to interact. (Compare Goffman, 1953, p. 197: 'sometimes the reply may contain an explicit request to hold off for a moment . . .' The present analysis is intended to explicate why this should be needed (its occurrence being independently establishable) by reference to the temporal organization of the opening sequence.)

We now turn to a consideration of another property of SA sequences, one that will allow us to examine not only the relationship between completed SA sequences and their sequels, but the internal structure of the sequences themselves.

Conditional relevance in SA sequences

The property of conditional relevance is formulated to address two problems. (The term and some elements of the idea of 'conditional relevance' were suggested by Sacks [in press].) The first of these is: How can we rigorously talk about two items as a sequenced pair of items, rather than as two separate units, one of which might happen to follow the other? The second problem is: How can we, in a sociologically meaningful and rigorous way, talk about the 'absence' of an item; numerous things are not present at any point in a conversation, yet only some have a relevance that would allow them to be seen as 'absent'. Some items are, so to speak, 'officially absent'. It is to address these problems that the notion of conditional relevance is introduced. By conditional relevance of one item on another we mean: given the first, the second is expectable; upon its occurrence it can be seen to be a second item to the first; upon its non-occurrence it can be seen to be officially absent – all this provided by the occurrence of the first item.

We may begin to explicate conditional relevance in SA sequences by employing it to clarify further some materials already discussed. The property of 'non-terminality' may be reformulated by saying that further talk is conditionally relevant on a completed SA sequence. In such a formulation we treat the SA sequence as a unit; it has the status of a first item in a sequence for which further talk becomes the second item, expectable upon the occurrence of the first. As noted, the specific focus of this expectation is upon the summoner who must supply the beginning of the further talk. Within this reformulation, if he fails to do so, that fact is officially noticeable and further talk is officially absent. It is by orienting to these facts that an answerer may find further talk coming fast upon him and, if unprepared to fulfill his obligation to attend to it, may seek to defer it by answering *Just a minute*, as was noted above.

My main interest in conditional relevance at this point does not, however, have to do with that of further talk upon a completed SA sequence, but with the internal workings of the sequence itself. Simply said, *A is conditionally relevant on the occurrence of S*.

We can see the conditional relevance of A on S most clearly in the following sort of circumstance. If one party issues an S and no A occurs, that provides the occasion for repetition of the S. That is to say, the non-occurrence of the A is seen by the summoner as its official absence and its official absence provides him with adequate grounds for repetition of the S. We say 'adequate grounds' in light of the rule, previously formulated, that the summoner may *not* repeat the S if the sequence has been completed. As long as the sequence is not completed, however, the S may be repeated.

Two qualifications must be introduced at this point, one dealing with the extendability of repetitions of S, the other with the temporal organization of those repetitions relative to the initial S. To take the second point first: In order to find that an A is absent, the summoner need not wait for posterity. In principle, unless some limitation is introduced, the occurrence of S might be the occasion for an indefinite waiting period at some point in which an A might occur. This is not the case. In noting this fact, a subsidiary property of the conditional relevance of A on S may be formulated – the property of immediate juxtaposition.

The following observations seem to hold: In QA sequences, if one asks a question, a considerable amount of silence may pass before the other speaks. None the less, if certain constraints on the content of his remarks (having to do with the relation of their substantive content to the substantive content of the question) are met, then the other's remark may be heard as an answer to the question. Secondly, even if the intervening time is filled not with silence but with talk, within certain constraints some later utterance may be heard as the answer to the question (e.g. X: *Have you seen Jim yet?* Y: *Oh is he in town?* X: *Yeah he got in yesterday.* Y: *No, I haven't seen him yet.*).

By contrast with this possible organization of QA sequences, the following may be noted about SA sequences. The conditional relevance of an A on an S must be satisfied within a constraint of *immediate juxtaposition*. That is to say, an item that may be used as an answer to a summons will not be heard to constitute an answer to a summons if it occurs separated from the summons. While this point may seem to imply that temporal ordering is involved, it is far from clear that 'time' or 'elapsed time' is the relevant matter. An alternative, suggested by Harvey Sacks, would make reference to 'nextness' plus some conception of 'pacing' or of units of activity of finer or coarser grain by reference to which 'nextness' would be located.

We may now note the relevance of this constraint to the formulation of the absence of an A. When we say that upon A's absence S may be repeated, we intend to note that A's absence may be found if its occurrence does not immediately follow an S. The phenomenon is encountered when examining occurrences in a series such as S-short pause-S-short pause, or *Dick* . . . no answer . . . *Dick* . . ., etc. In this mechanical age it may be of interest to note that the very construction and operation of the mechanical ring is built on these principles. If each ring of the phone be considered a summons, then the phone is built to ring, wait for an answer, if none occurs, to ring again, wait for an answer, ring again, etc. And indeed, some persons, polite even when interacting with a machine, will not interrupt a phone, but wait for the completion of a ring before picking up the receiver.

The other qualification concerning the repeatability of an S upon the official absence of an A concerns a *terminating rule*. It is empirically observable that Ss are not repeated without limitation, until an A is actually returned. There is, then, some terminating rule used by members of the society to limit the number of repetitions of an S. I cannot at this point give a firm formulation of such a terminating rule, except to note my impression that Ss are not strung out beyond three to five repetitions at the most. However, that some terminating rule is normally used by adult members of the society can be noted by observing their annoyance at the behavior of children who do not employ it. Despite the formulation in numerical terms, a similar reservation must be entered here as was entered with respect to time above. It is not likely that 'number' or 'counting' is the relevant matter. Aside from contextual circumstances (e.g. location), the requirement of 'immediate juxtaposition' discussed above may be related to the terminating rule(s). It may be by virtue of a telephone caller's assumption of the priority or 'nextness' of a response, given the ring of the phone, that the telephone company finds it necessary to use the phone book to advise callers to allow at least ten rings to permit prospective answerers time to maneuver their way to the phone.

One further observation may be made at this point about repetitions of S. 'Repetition' does not require that the same lexical item be repeated; rather, successive utterances are each drawn from the class of items that may be summonses, although the particular items that are used may change over some string of repetitions. For example, *Mommy . . . Mommy* may then shift to *Mom . . . Mom* or *Mother . . .*; *Jim* may shift to *Mr Smith*, or *Jim Smith* (as, for example, when trying to attract someone from the rear in a crowded setting). A ring of a doorbell may shift to a knock on the door, the mechanical ring of a phone is replaced by some lexical item, such as *hello* when the caller hears the receiver lifted and nothing is said (as with the deviant case introduced earlier to which I shall return later).

While I am unable to formulate a terminating rule for repetitions of S when no A occurs, it is clear that we have a terminating rule when an A does occur: *A terminates the sequence.* As noted, upon the completion of the SA sequence, the original summoner cannot summon again. The operation of this terminating rule, however, depends upon the clear recognition that an A has occurred. This recognition normally is untroubled. However, trouble sometimes occurs by virtue of the fact that some lexical items, e.g. *Hello*, may be used both as summonses and as answers. Under some circumstances it may be impossible to tell whether such a term has been used as summons or as answer. Thus, for example, when acoustic difficulties arise in a telephone connection, both parties may attempt to confirm their mutual availability to one another. Each one may then employ the term *Hello?* as a summons to the other. For each of them, however, it may be unclear whether what he hears in the earpiece is an answer to his check, or the other's summons for him to answer. One may, under such circumstances, hear a conversation in which a sequence of some length is constituted by nothing but alternatively and simultaneously offered *hellos*. Such 'verbal dodging' is typically resolved by the use, by one party, of an item on which a second is conditionally relevant, where that second is unambiguously a second part of a two-part sequence. Most typically this is a question, and the question *Can you hear me?* or one of its common lexical variants, regularly occurs.

We may note that the matters we have been discussing are involved in problems having to do with the coordinated character of social interaction, whether they be coordinated entry into a conversation, coordinated re-entry into an interrupted conversation, or the coordination of the activity in its course. In particular, we will shortly turn to a consideration of the bearing of S A sequences on coordinated entry.

The power of the conditional relevance of A on S is such that a variety of strong inferences can be made by persons on the basis of it, and we now turn to consider some of them. We may first note that not only does conditional relevance operate 'forwards', the occurrence of an S providing the expectability of an A, but it works in 'reverse' as well. If, after a period of conversational lapse, one person in a multi-person setting (and particularly when persons are not physically present, but within easily re-callable range) should produce an item that may function as an A to an S, such as *What?*, or *Yes?*, then another person in that environment may hear in that utterance that an unspoken summons was heard. He may then reply *I didn't call you.* (This, then, is another sort of circumstance in which we find an immediately graspable error, such as was remarked on earlier.) The connection between a summons and an answer provides both prospective and retrospective inferences.

A further inferential structure attached to the conditional relevance of A on S can lead us to see that this property has the status of what Durkheim (1950) intended by the term social fact; i.e. the property is both 'external' and 'constraining'. When we say that an answer is conditionally relevant upon a summons, it is to be understood that the behaviors referred to are not 'casual options' for the persons involved. A member of the society may not 'naïvely choose' not to answer a summons. The culture provides that a variety of 'strong inferences' can be drawn from the fact of the official absence of an answer, and any member who does not answer does so at the peril of one of those inferences being made.

(Terms such as 'casual option', 'naïvely choose' and 'strong inference' are used here in a fashion that may require explanation. Although not supplying a fully adequate explication, the following suggestion may be in order. By 'may not naïvely choose' is meant that the person summoned cannot deny that *some* inference may legitimately be made. If some *particular* inference is proposed, then in denying *it* the summoned offers a substitute, thereby conceding the legitimacy of *an* inference, though not perhaps of a *particular one*. If questioned as to the warrant for his inference, the summoner may refer to the absence of an answer, and this stands as an adequate warrant. A sequence constructed to exemplify these remarks might be:

SUMMONER: Are you mad at me?
SUMMONED: Why do you think that?
SUMMONER: You didn't answer when I called you.
SUMMONED: Oh. No, I didn't hear you.

Conversely, the following observed exchange may suggest what is intended by 'casual option' (or 'naïve choice')

WIFE: What are you thinking about?
HUSBAND: Who says I'm thinking?
WIFE: You're playing with your hair.
HUSBAND: That doesn't mean anything.

The activity 'playing with one's hair' is a 'casual option' (or 'naïve choice') in this interaction and, therefore, the claim can be made that no inference is warranted.)

What sorts of inferences are involved? A first inference is 'no answer – no person.' When a person dials a number on the telephone, if the receiver on the other end is not picked up, he may say as a matter of course *there is no one home*; he does not typically announce *they decided not to answer*. A person returning home seeking to find out if anyone else is already there may call out the name of his wife, for example, and upon not receiving an answer, may typically take it that she is not home or, while physically home, is not interactionally 'in play' (e.g. she may be asleep. The term is from Goffman, 1965). If one person sees another lying on a couch or a bed with eyes closed and calls their name and receives no answer, he takes it that that person is asleep or feigning sleep. He does not take it that the person is simply disregarding the summons. Or, to use a more classical dramatic example, when Tosca, thinking that her lover has been only apparently and not really executed, calls his name, she realizes by the absence of his answer that he is not only apparently dead but really so. She does not take it that he is merely continuing the masquerade.

It is this very structure of inferences that a summoner can make from the official absence of an answer that provides a resource for members of the society who seek to do a variety of insolent and quasi-insolent activities. The resource consists in this: the inference from official absence of an answer is the physical or interactional absence of the prospective answerer. Persons who want to engage in such activities as 'giving the cold shoulder', 'sulking', 'insulting', 'looking down their noses at', etc., may employ the fact that such inferences will be made from 'no answer' but will be controverted by their very physical presence and being interactionally in play (they are neither asleep nor unconscious). So, although members can, indeed, 'choose' not to answer a summons, they cannot do so naïvely; i.e. they know that if the inference of physical or interactional absence cannot be made, then some other inference will, e.g. they are cold shouldering, insulting, etc.

We may note what is a corollary of the inferential structure we have been describing. The very inferences that may be made from the fact of the official absence of an answer may then stand as accounts of the 'no answer'.

So, not only does one infer that 'no one is home', but, also 'no one is home' accounts for the fact of no answer. Not only may one see in the no answer that 'he is mad at me', but one can account for it by that fact. More generally then, we may say that the conditional relevance of A on S entails not only that the non-occurrence of A is its official absence, but also that that absence is 'accountable'. Furthermore, where an inference is readily available from the absence of an answer, that inference stands as its account.

However, where no ready inference is available, then no ready account is available and the search for one may be undertaken. Something of this sort would seem to be involved in an incident such as the following (field notes): A husband and wife are in an upstairs room when a knock on the door occurs; the wife goes to answer it; after several minutes the husband comes to the head of the stairs and calls the wife's name; there is no answer and the husband runs down the stairs. If the foregoing analysis is correct, we might say that he does so in search of that which would provide an account for the absence of the wife's answer. The point made here does not follow logically, but empirically. From the relationship of the availability of an inference to its use as an account, it does not logically follow that the absence of an inference entails the absence of an account and the legitimacy of a search. An account may not be needed even if absent. It happens, however, that that is so although not logically entailed.

We have now introduced as many of the features of conditional relevance as are required for our further discussion. While the discussion of conditional relevance in this section has focused on the relations between A and S, these features are intrinsic to conditional relevance generally, and apply as well to the relations between completed SA sequences, as a unit, and further talk. If a called person's first remark is treated as an answer to the phone ring's summons, it completes the SA sequence, and provides the proper occasion for talk by the caller. If the conditional relevance of further talk on a completed SA sequence is not satisfied, we find the same sequel as is found when an A is not returned to an S: repetition or chaining. In our data:

#86

D: Police Desk (pause). Police Desk (pause). Hello, police desk (longer pause). Hello. (A#AA#A)

C: Hello. (S)

D: Hello (pause). Police Desk? (A#A)

C: Pardon?

D: Do you want the Police Desk?

We turn now to a consideration of the problem of the availability to talk that provides the theoretical importance of SA sequences and opening sequences in general. In doing so we return to the concerns with the coordinated entry into an encounter, and the deviant case that required the reformulation of the distribution rule.

The availability to talk

After having formulated a simple description for the opening sequence of telephone calls, we encountered a deviant case that was not described by that formulation. Rather than developing a deviant case analysis we set out to try to deepen the formulation of the opening sequence so that it would encompass with equal ease the vast majority of cases already adequately described and the troublesome variant. It will be recalled that the datum that gave us trouble read as follows:

#9   Police make call – receiver is lifted and there is a one-second pause.
D: Hello.
OTHER: American Red Cross
D: [etc.]

In that piece, the caller made the first remark, whereas the distribution rule requires that the called party makes the first remark. The foregoing analysis provides for this occurrence as being as rule-governed a phenomenon as other interchanges are. Treating the ringing of the phone as a summons and recalling the conditional relevance of an answer on it, we find that after the receiver has been lifted, the expectation of an answer is operative. In this piece of data, what occurs after the receiver is picked up would have passed as a normal case of the distribution rule had it not been noted that it was the caller, not the called who uttered it. The SA formulation gives us the circumstances under which it is not unusual for that remark to be uttered by the caller: treating the ring of the phone (which the distribution rule disregards) as a summons to which no answer is returned. As was noted in our discussion of conditional relevance, A is conditioned upon the occurrence of an S and should it not occur it is officially absent and warrants a repetition of the S. Hearing, now, the *Hello* as such a repetition provides for its status as a second summons in such an occurrence. The structure of the datum thus is seen to be S, no answer, S, A.

Likewise, all the cases easily handled by the distribution rule are handled with equal ease by the SA formulation, so long as the telephone ring is regarded as a summons. Thus, the rule 'the called talks first' follows clearly from the conditional relevance of an A upon the occurrence of an S; and the less general rule, the 'caller provides the first topic', follows from the conditional relevance of further talk upon a completed SA sequence. The distribution rule's operation is incorporated within the structure of SA sequencing.

We will now discuss the work SA sequences do by elaborating some properties of the component summons and answer items. The remainder of the present discussion, on the availability to talk and the coordinated entry into the sequence, will be devoted to further explicating the opening interactional structure.

Many activities seem to require some minimum number of participants. For thinking or playing solitaire, only one is required; for dialogue, at least two; and, for 'eristic' dialogue, at least three.[7] When an activity has as one of its properties a requirement of a minimal number of parties, then the same behavior done without that 'quota' being met is subject to being seen as an instance of some other activity (with a different minimum requirement, perhaps), or as 'random' behavior casting doubt on the competence or normality of its performer. (This is so where the required number of parties is two or more; it would appear for any activity to get done, one party at least must be available.) Thus, one person playing the piano while another is present may be seen to be performing, while in the absence of another he may be seen to be practising. Persons finding themselves waving to no one in particular by mistake may have to provide for the sense of their hand movement as having been only the first part of a convoluted attempt to scratch their head.

Conversation, at least for adults in this society, seems to be an activity with a minimal requirement of two participants. This may be illustrated by the following observations.

Buses in Manhattan have as their last tier of seats one long bench. On one occasion two persons were observed sitting on this last bench next to one another but in no way indicating that they were, to use Goffman's term (1965, pp. 102–3), 'with each other'. Neither turned his head in the direction of the other and for a long period of time, neither spoke. At one

7. I touch here only tangentially on a larger area – what might be termed 'n-party properties and problems'. What is suggested by that term is that for activities with a common value for n (i.e. two-party activities, three-party activities, etc.), there may be, by virtue of that common feature, some common problems or properties. For example, two-party activities may share some problems of coordination, or some properties as compared to three-party activities. Alternatively, activities that have a minimum-number-of-parties requirement may have common properties as compared to those whose relevant parameter is a maximum number of participants. It is the latter possibility that is being touched on here.

On 'eristics', see Perelman (1963, p. 166): 'Were there any need for a clear sign enabling one to contrast the criterion of eristic dialogue with that of the other kinds, it would be found in the existence of a judge or arbitor charged with giving the casting vote between the antagonists, rather than in the intentions and procedures of the adversaries themselves. Because the purpose of the debate is to convince not the adversary but the judge; because the adversary does not need to be won over to be beaten; for this very reason the eristic dispute is of no great interest to the philosopher.'

point, one of them began speaking without, however, turning his head in the direction of the other. It was immediately observed that other passengers within whose visual range this 'couple' were located, scanned the back area of the bus to find to whom that talk was addressed. It turned out, of course, that the talk was addressed to the one the speaker was 'with'. What is of interest to us, however, is that the others present in the scene immediately undertook a search for a conversational other. On other occasions, however, similar in all respects but one to the preceding, a different sequel occurred. The dissimilarity was that the talker was not 'with' anyone and, when each observer scanned the environment for the conversational other, no candidate for that position, including each scanner himself, could be located. The observers then took it that the talker was 'talking to himself' and the passengers exchanged 'knowing glances'. The issue here could be seen to involve what Bales (1951, pp. 87–90) has called 'targeting', and, to be sure, that is what the persons in the scene appear to have been attending to. It is to be noted, however, that it is by reference to the character of conversation as a minimally two-party activity that the relevance of seeking the target is established in the first place. In this connection, it may be remarked that such phenomena as 'talking to the air' (Goffman, 1953, p. 159) or glossing one's behavior by 'talking to oneself', are best understood not as exceptions to the minimal two-party character of conversation, but as special ways of talking to others while not addressing them, of which other examples are given in Bales (1951, pp. 89–90).

On another occasion, two persons were observed walking toward one another on a college campus, each of them walking normally. Suddenly one of them began an extremely pronounced and angular walk in which the trunk of his body was exaggeratedly lowered with each step and raised with the next. The one encountering him took such a walk to be a communicative act and immediately turned around to search the environment for the recipient of the communication. In the background a girl was approaching. The two males continued on their respective paths and after some fifteen to twenty paces the one looked back again to see if, indeed, it was to the girl in the background that the gesture was directed.

We have said that conversation is a 'minimally two-party' activity. The initial problem of coordination in a two-party activity is the problem of availability; that is, a person who seeks to engage in an activity that requires the collaborative work of two parties must first establish, via some interactional procedure, that another party is available to collaborate. It is clear that a treatment of members' solutions to the problem of availability might, at the same time, stand as a description of how coordinated entry into an interactive course of action is accomplished.

Our task is to show that SA sequences are, indeed, germane to the problems both of availability and coordinated entry, and how they provide solutions to both these problems simultaneously.

We must show how the working and properties of SA sequences *establish* the availability of the two parties to a forthcoming two-party interaction (and, in the absence of a completed sequence, foreclose the possibility of the activity) and how they, furthermore, ensure that availability, both at the beginning and in the continuing course of the interaction. We noted before that the absence of an answer to a summons led strongly to the inference of the absence of a party or claimed the other's unavailability to interact. Conversely, the presence of an answer is taken to establish the availability of the answerer; his availability involves, as we have seen, his obligation to listen to the further talk that is conditionally relevant upon the completion of the sequence. In sum, the completion of a sequence establishes the mutual availability of the parties and allows the activity to continue, and failure to complete the sequence establishes or claims the unavailability of at least one of them and perhaps undercuts the possibility of furthering that course of action.

We may note, in qualification, that a distinction must be made between a party's 'presence' and his 'availability' to interact (as we shall later distinguish between his 'availability' to interact and his 'commitment' to do so). In our earlier discussion, we pointed out that the resource that members of the society draw upon in doing such activities as 'cold shouldering', 'insulting', 'sulking', etc., involves the joint observability of physical presence, social presence (that is, consciousness and awakeness) and the absence of an answer to a summons, indicating or claiming unavailability for interaction. For the insolent activity to be accomplished via such a contrast, obviously enough, requires the distinctness of the items so contrasted. Several additional illustrations may serve to extend the scope of our sense of this difference.

Those who can remember their adolescence may recall occurrences such as the following in their high schools. In the morning, quite often as a first piece of official business, the teacher would 'call the roll'. In that case, a student, when his name was called, would respond by answering *present* or by raising his hand. Neither party then expected that further interaction between them would occur. Mere presence was being established. If they went to a 'proper' high school they may have been required to respond to a teacher's calling of their name in a recitation period by jumping to their feet, and awaiting some further behavior by the teacher. In that situation, their presence already established, they were being summoned to be available for some interaction, typically some examination. Teachers who saw a student physically present but not attentive to the official environment might make that fact observable to the public there assembled by calling a student's name and allowing all to see that he did not answer by standing up and establishing his availability. In that way then, the properties of a summons–answer sequence could be employed not only to establish availability or unavailability but to proclaim it to all who could but see.

In telephone interactions, the lifting of a receiver without further ado serves to establish the presence of a person at the called number. It does not, however, establish the availability of that person for further conversation. Indeed, the deviant case that was introduced earlier presents precisely this set of circumstances, and was met by further summoning by the caller to elicit some demonstration of availability, i.e. some answering remark.[8] In this age, in which social critics complain about the replacement of men by machines, this small corner of the social world has not been uninvaded. It is possible, nowadays, to hear the phone you are calling picked up and hear a human voice answer, but nevertheless not be talking to a human. However small its measure of consolation, we may note that even machines such as the automatic answering device are constructed on social, and not only mechanical, principles. The machine's magnetic voice will not only answer the caller's ring but will also inform him when its ears will be available to receive his message, and warns him both to wait for the beep and confine his interests to fifteen seconds. Thereby both *abab* and the properties of SA sequences are preserved.

While the machine's answer to a summoning incoming call is specific-

8. Note that the French may answer the phone with a remark specifically orientated to their availability – *j'écoute*; while the British may respond to an interlocutor's failure to answer a summons or question by inquiring if the 'no answer – no person' inference is correct – *Are you there?* After this paper had been completed, Miss Gail Ziferstein brought to my attention the following datum (from another corpus of materials) that is relevant here and at other points in the analysis:

OPERATOR: Hello, Mister Lehrhoff?
LEHRHOFF: Mh hm ...
OPERATOR: Mister Savage is gon' pick ⎫
   up an' talk to ya.   ⎬ simultaneous
LEHRHOFF: Alright.   ⎭
[Fifty-two seconds intervening]
OPERATOR: Hello.
LEHRHOFF: Yes.
OPERATOR: Did Mistuh Savage ever pick up?
LEHRHOFF: If he did, he didn't say hello.
OPERATOR: Oh, o alright, smarty, ⎫
   just hold on.   ⎪
LEHRHOFF: heh! heh heh heh   ⎬ simultaneous
   heh heh heh   ⎪
OPERATOR: hhh!   ⎭

ally constructed to allow the delivery of the message by the summoner, and is mechanically constructed with a slot for its receipt, the fact that it is a machine gives callers more of an option either to answer or not than they have when the voice emanates from a larynx and not a loudspeaker. One thing that is specifically clear and differentiated between a human and mechanical answerer is that although both may provide a slot for the caller to talk again, the human answerer will then talk again himself whereas currently available machines will not. We have previously provided for the obligation of the answerer to listen to that talk, but we have not yet provided for the possibility that the answerer may then talk again, and it is to that we now turn.

One hitherto unnoticed and important fact about answers to summonses is that they routinely either are, or borrow some properties of, questions.[9] This is most obviously so in the case of *what?* but seems equally so of *yeah?*, and *yes?*, which three terms, together with glances of the eyes and bodily alignments, constitute the most frequently used answer items. The sheer status of these items as questions, and the particular kinds of questions that they are, allow us to deepen the previous analysis of the obligation of the summoner to talk again upon the completion of the sequence, the obligation of the answerer to listen, and what may follow the talk he listens to.

The obligation of the summoner to talk again is not merely a distinctive property of SA sequences. In many activities similar to the SA sequence, where, for example, someone's name may also be called the caller of it need not talk again to the person called. Such activities as indicating someone's 'turn to go', as in a discussion or game, share with 'signalling' by rings of the telephone the fact that they are prearranged or invoke some shared orders of priority and relevance. Such activities much more directly can be seen to be pure signaling devices and not summoning devices. That an activity starting, for example, with the enunciation of a name, is a summons, is provided by its assembly over its course. The obligation of the summoner to talk again is, therefore, not merely 'the obligation of a summoner to talk again'; it is the obligation of a member of the society to answer a question if he has been asked one. The activity of summoning, is, therefore, not intrinsic to any of the items that compose it; it is an assembled product whose efficacious properties are cooperatively

9. I am indebted here to David Sudnow. The notion of 'borrowing properties of questions' is a difficult one. How one might prove that some item, while not a question, borrowed some property of questions is not clear, in part because it is not clear how one would prove that some item was or was not a question. The discussion that follows may, therefore, be read as being limited to items that are, intuitively, 'clearly' questions, e.g. items that have 'interrogative intonation', or that are lexically question items (e.g. *what?*), deferring the issue of 'borrowing properties'.

yielded by the interactive work of both summoner and answerer. The signaling devices accomplish different outcomes. By not including questions as their second items, they do not constrain the utterers of their first items to talk again. Rather, they invoke prearrangements, priorities, and shared relevances as matters to which the addressed party must now direct his attention.

We now see that the summons is a particularly powerful way of generating a conversational interaction. We have seen that it requires, in a strong way, that an answer be returned to it. By 'in a strong way' we intend that the strong set of inferences we described before attend the absence of an answer, e.g. physical absence, social absence (being asleep or unconscious), or purposeful ignoring. Moreover, it seems to be the case that the answer returned to it has the character of a question. The consequence of this is two-fold: (a) that the summoner now has, by virtue of the question he has elicited, the obligation to produce an answer to it, and (b) the person who asked the question thereby assumes an obligation to listen to the talk he has obligated the other to produce. Thus, sheerly by virtue of this two-part sequence, two parties have been brought together; each has acted; each by his action has produced and assumed further obligations; each is then available; and a pair of roles has been invoked and aligned. To review these observations with specific reference to the two steps that are their locus:

SUMMONER: Bill? [A summons item; obligates other to answer under penalty of being found absent, insane, insolent, condescending, etc. Moreover, by virtue of orientation to properties of answer items, i.e. their character as questions, provides for user's future obligation to answer, and thereby to have another turn to talk. Thus, preliminary or prefatory character, establishing and ensuring availability of other to interact.]

SUMMONED: What? [Answers summons, thereby establishing availability to interact further. Ensures there will be further interaction by employing a question item, which demands further talk or activity by summoner.]

We may notice that in relating our observations to the first two steps of the sequence we have dealt not only with two steps but with the third as well. We may now show that the span of control of the first two items extends further still. Not only is it the case that a question demands an answer and thereby provides for the third slot to be filled by the summoner, but also one who asks a question, as we noted above, has the right to talk again. The consequence of this is that after the summoner has talked for the second time, this talk will have amounted to the answer to the answerer (of the summons), and the latter will have a right to take another turn. This provides for the possibility of four initial steps following from the use of a summons, which thus emerges as an extraordinarily powerful social item.[10] We have not yet exhausted its power.

We may note that the item the summons elicits in the second slot is not adequately described as merely 'a question'. It is a question of a very special sort. Its special characteristic may become observable by contrast with other kinds of questions. One not unusual type of question has the property that its asker knows the specific content of the answer that must be returned to it. So, for example, radio interviewers acquainted with the person they are interviewing and perhaps long and intimate friends of theirs, may none the less ask such a question as was heard posed to one musician by another who doubles as a disc jockey: *Tell me, Jim, how did you first break into music?* In a second type of question, while the asker does not know the specific content of the answer, he knows, if we may use a mathematical analogy, the general parameters that will describe it. So, for example, while the doctor in an initial interview may not know specifically what will be answered to his *What seems to be the trouble?* he very readily takes it that the answer will include references to some physical or psychic troubles.

The character of the question that is returned to a summons differs sharply from either of these. Its specific feature seems to be that the asker of *what?* may have little notion of what an accomplished answer may look like, both with respect to its substantive content and with respect to the amount of time that may be necessary for its delivery. This property – the specific ambiguity of what would constitute an answer – is clearly seen in the use that is often made of it by those persons in the society who may have restricted rights to talk. Thus, we may understand the elegance involved in

10. That conversational oaks may out of conversational acorns grow is a frequent theme in folklore. One version of such a story, starting from a somewhat different acorn, is the following:

On the express train to Lublin, a young man stopped at the seat of an obviously prosperous merchant.

'Can you tell me the time?' he said.

The merchant looked at him and replied: 'Go to hell!'

'What? Why, what's the matter with you! I ask you a civil question in a properly civil way, and you give me such an outrageous rude answer! What's the idea?'

The merchant looked at him, sighed wearily, and said, 'Very well. Sit down and I'll tell you. You ask me a question. I have to give you an answer, no? You start a conversation with me – about the weather, politics, business. One thing leads to another. It turns out you're a Jew – I'm a Jew. I live in Lublin – you're a stranger. Out of hospitality, I ask you to my home for dinner. You meet my daughter. She's a beautiful girl – you're a handsome young man. So you go out together a few times – and you fall in love. Finally you come to ask for my daughter's hand in marriage. So why go to all that trouble. Let me tell you right now, young man, I won't let my daughter marry anyone who doesn't even own a watch!!' ('To Save Time', in Ausubel, 1948, pp. 404–5)

a standardized way in which children often begin conversations with adults. A phrase such as *You know what, Mommy?*, inviting a *what?* as its return, allows the child to talk by virtue of the obligation thereby imposed upon him to answer a question while retaining a certain freedom in his response by virtue of the adult's inability to know in advance what would have been an adequate, complete, satisfactory or otherwise socially acceptable answer. (For these points I am indebted to Harvey Sacks.)

Such an open-ended question does not expand what can be said beyond the constraints of the categorical relationship of the parties. But as compared with other kinds of answers to summonses, it does not introduce additional constraints. Additional constraints may of course be introduced by modifications on *what?*, such as intonation or addition (e.g. *what now?*). (Other lexical items used as answers are [on the telephone] *hello* or some self-identification [e.g. *Macy's*]. For a discussion of the ways the latter items impose additional constraints, see Schegloff, 1967, ch. 4.)

In other words, there are constraints on the 'contents' of a speaker's remarks once a conversational course is entered into and some conversational 'line' is already present to be coordinated to. At the beginning of a conversation, however, no such 'line' is already present and the open-endedness of the answer that *what?* allows is a reflection of the fact and the requirement that if there is to be a conversation it must be about something. The fact of open-endedness, however, does not necessarily imply the absence of all constraint. How much constraint is to be put, or can be put, on the content of some opening substantive remark may depend strongly on the relationship of the parties to one another, and that includes not only their relationship as it may turn out to be formulated, but their relationship as it develops from moment to moment. While two parties who are about to be joined by an interaction medium, may later be properly categorized as father and son, for them, as the phone rings, and indeed when it is picked up and the *hello* is uttered, they may be strangers. Their relationship to one another may have to be 'discovered' while interactional work must precede the 'discovery'. Under such a circumstance, given that strangers have restricted rights to talk to one another and restricted topics about which they may talk, then a completely open-ended *what* may be a 'hazardous' opening for a phone conversation in which, at the moment of its utterance, the other may be a stranger. The consequences of such matters for the infrequence of answers such as *what* or *yes* on the phone, and for the alternatives that may be employed in their stead, are matters that cannot be gone into here.

To conclude the present discussion, it may be noted that provision is made by an SA sequence not only for the coordinated entry into a conversation but also for its continued orderliness. First, we may note, that in the very doing of the two items that constitute SA sequences, and in the two turns these items specifically provide for, the first two alternations of *abab* are produced and that sequence is established as a patterned rule for the interaction that follows.

In so far as the answerer of the summons does not use his right to talk again to introduce an extended utterance, the work of SA sequences may be seen to extend over a yet larger span of conversation. By 'not introducing an extended utterance', I mean that he simply employs one of what might be called the 'assent terms' of the society, such as *mmhmm* or *yes* or *yeah*, or *uh huh*. Under that circumstance the following may be the case: as the initial response to the summons establishes the answerer's availability and commits him to attend the next utterance of the summoner (that is, ensures his continued availability for the next remark), this obligation to listen and this insurance that he will, may be renewable. Each subsequent *uh huh* or *yes* then indicates the continuing availability of its speaker and recommits him to hear the utterance that may follow. Availability may, in this way, be 'chained', and, in fact, speakers with extended things to say may routinely leave slots open for the other to insert an *uh huh*, thereby recalling them to and recommitting them to the continuing course of the activity.[11]

It was remarked earlier that conversation is a 'minimally two-party' activity. That requirement is not satisfied by the mere copresence of two persons, one of whom is talking. It requires that there be both a 'speaker' and a 'hearer'. (That 'hearership' can be seen as a locus of rules, and a status whose incumbency is subject to demonstration, is suggested by some of Sacks's work.) To behave as a 'speaker' or as a 'hearer' when the other is not observably available is to subject oneself to a review of one's competence and 'normality'. Speakers without hearers can be seen to be 'talking to themselves'. Hearers without speakers 'hear voices'. (But cf. Hymes, 1964, on cultural variations in the definition of participants in speech events.) SA sequences establish and align the roles of speaker and hearer, providing a summoner with evidence of the availability or unavailability of a hearer, and a prospective hearer with notice of a prospective speaker. The sequence constitutes a coordinated entry into the activity, allowing each party occasion to demonstrate his coordination with the other, a coordination that may then be sustained by the parties demon-

11. It is as wry recognition of the operation and subversion of this mechanism that a standard joke of the society may be appreciated. In it, a tired husband returns from the office, sinks gratefully into his easy chair and opens the evening paper to the sports page. His nagging wife, however, wishes to unburden herself of the accumulated troubles of the day and begins an extended monologue. Routinely, she leaves a slot of silence and he dutifully inserts *Yes, dear*, until, dimly aware that all is not as it appears to be, she says, *Are you ignoring me?* and he replies *Yes, dear*.

strating continued speakership or hearership. It is by way of the status of items such as *uh huh* and *mmhmm* as demonstrations of continued, coordinated hearership that we may appreciate the fact that they are among the few items that can be spoken while another is speaking without being heard as 'an interruption'.

References

AUSUBEL, N. (ed.) (1948), *A Treasury of Jewish Folklore*, Crown.

BALES, R. F. (1951), *Interaction Process Analysis*, Addison-Wesley.

BALES, R. F., STRODTBECK, F. L., MILLS, T. M., and ROSEBOROUGH, M. E. (1951), 'Channels of communication in small group interaction', *Amer. Sociol. Rev.*, vol. 16, pp. 461–8.

BERGLER, E. (1938), 'On the resistance situation: the patient is silent', *Psychoanal. Rev.*, vol. 25, pp. 170–86.

BOLINGER, D. (1958), *Interrogative structures of American English*, University of Alabama Press.

DURKHEIM, E. (1950), *The Rules of Sociological Method*, S. A. Solovay and J. H. Mueller (trs.), G. E. G. Catlin (ed.), Free Press.

GARFINKEL, H. (1967), *Studies in Ethnomethodology*, Prentice-Hall.

GOFFMAN, E. (1953), 'Communication conduct in an island community', unpublished Ph.D. dissertation, Department of Sociology, University of Chicago.

GOFFMAN, E. (1965), *Behavior in Public Places*, Free Press.

GUMPERZ, J. J. and HYMES, D. (eds.) (1964), 'The ethnography of communication', *Amer. Anthrop.*, vol. 66, no. 6, part 2.

HYMES, D. (1964), 'Introduction', in J. J. Gumperz and D. Hymes (eds.), 'The ethnography of communication', *Amer. Anthrop.*, vol. 66, no. 6, part 2, pp. 1–34.

LANDIS, M. H. and BURTT, H. E. (1924), 'A study of conversations', *J. Comp. Psychol.*, vol. 4, pp 81–9.

MOERMAN, M. (in press), 'Analysis of the conversation', in D. Sudnow (ed.), *Studies in Interaction*, Free Press.

OAKESHOTT, M. (1959), *The Voice of Poetry in the Conversation of Mankind*, Bowers & Bowes.

PERELMAN, C. (1963), *The Idea of Justice and the Problem of Argument*, Routledge & Kegan Paul.

PRIESTLY, J. B. (1926), *Talking*, Harper & Row.

SACKS, H., 'The diagnosis of depression' (manuscript).

SACKS, H. (in press), 'The search for help: no one to turn to', in D. Sudnow (ed.), *Studies in Interaction*, Free Press.

SCHEGLOFF, E. A. (1967), 'The first five seconds: the order of conversational openings', unpublished Ph.D. dissertation, Department of Sociology, University of California, Berkeley.

STEINZOR, B. (1949), 'The development and evaluation of a measure of social interaction', *Hum. Relat.*, vol. 2, pp. 103–22, 319–47.

STEPHEN, F. F., and MISHLER, E. Y. (1952), 'The distribution of participation in small groups: an exponential approximation', *Amer. Sociol. Rev.*, vol. 17, pp. 598–608.

WATSON, J., and POTTER, R. (1962), 'An analytical unit for the study of interaction', *Hum. Relat.*, vol. 15, pp. 245–63.

Further Reading

M. Argyle, *The Psychology of Interpersonal Behaviour*, Penguin, 1967.

M. Argyle, *Social Interaction*, Methuen, 1969.

B. Bernstein, *Class, Codes and Control, Volume 1*, Routledge & Kegan Paul, 1971.

R. L. Birdwhistell, *Kinesics and Context*, University of Pennsylvania Press, 1970.

R. Brown, *Social Psychology*, Free Press; Collier-Macmillan, 1965.

D. Crystal, *Prosodic Systems and Intonation in English*, Cambridge University Press, 1969.

J. A. Fishman (ed.), *Readings in the Sociology of Language*, Mouton, 1968.

P. P. Giglioli (ed.), *Language and Social Context*, Penguin, 1972.

E. Goffman, *The Presentation of Self in Everyday Life*, Doubleday Anchor Books 1959; Allen Lane The Penguin Press, 1969.

E. Goffman, *Encounters*, Bobbs-Merrill, 1961.

E. Goffman, *Behavior in Public Places*, Free Press; Collier-Macmillan, 1963.

E. Goffman, *Stigma*, Prentice-Hall, 1963; Penguin, 1968.

E. Goffman, *Interaction Ritual*, Doubleday, 1967; Penguin, 1971.

E. Goffman, *Relations in Public*, Allen Lane The Penguin Press, 1971.

J. J. Gumperz and D. Hymes (eds.), *Directions in Sociolinguistics: The Ethnography of Communications*, Holt, Rinehart & Winston, 1972.

E. T. Hall, *The Silent Language*, Doubleday, 1959.

E. T. Hall, *The Hidden Dimension*, Doubleday, 1966; Bodley Head, 1969.

D. Hymes (ed.), *Language in Culture and Society*, Harper & Row, 1964.

W. Labov, *The Social Stratification of English in New York City*, Center for Applied Linguistics, 1966.

D. G. Mandelbaum (ed.), *Selected Writings of Edward Sapir in Language, Culture and Personality*, University of California Press, 1949.

R. E. Pittenger, C. F. Hockett and J. J. Danehy, *The First Five Minutes*, Martineau, 1960.

J. Ruesch and W. Kees, *Non-Verbal Communication*, University of California Press, 1956.

T. A. Sebeok, A. S. Hayes and M. C. Bates (eds.), *Approaches to Semiotics*, Mouton, 1964.

A. G. Smith (ed.), *Communication and Culture*, Holt, Rinehart & Winston, 1966.

R. Sommer, *Personal Space*, Prentice-Hall, 1969.

Acknowledgements

Permission to reproduce the Readings in this volume is acknowledged to the following sources:

1 Academic Press Inc.
2 *British Journal of Disorders of Communication*
3 University of Chicago Press
4 University of Pittsburgh Press
5 The MIT Press
6 American Psychological Association
7 Routledge & Kegan Paul Ltd and Harcourt Brace Jovanovich Inc.
8 The Journal Press
9 American Psychological Association
10 *British Journal of Disorders of Communication*
11 Duke University Press
12 *Psychiatry*
13 American Anthropological Association
14 Association for Research in Nervous & Mental Diseases
15 American Sociological Association
16 American Sociological Association
17 *Psychiatry*
18 Plenum Publishing Co. Ltd
19 Scientific American Inc.
20 American Anthrolopogical Association

Author Index

Subject Index

Abyssinians, 208
Act-rate, 32–3
Activity modifiers, 94–7
Address-terms, 101, 103–26, 128–45, 383–4, 387
Addressee, 103–26, 128–45
'Ademanes', 221–2
Aethiopic, 116
Affective information 37, 43, 53, 68–9, 72, 83, 97, 172–84, 201, 207–22, 242, 373 *see also* Emotive meaning
Affiliation, 39, 301–15
Afrikaans, 116, 117
Age, 97, 133, 155, 160, 162, 167, 170, 172–3, 196, 226, 256
Ainu, 208, 211
Alienation, 251, 317, 347–63
Amazonians, 210, 218
Andaman Islanders, 211
Anger, 68, 124, 181, 266
Anxiety, 34, 39, 47–8, 52, 181, 251, 304–5, 312
Approach-avoidance conflict, 47, 304–5
Arabic, 116, 247, 251, 260–61, 264–6, 276–7, 279, 287–8
'Area markers', 42
Argentinians, 221–2
Armenian, 276
Arousal, 39–40, 53, 197, 304, 314
Ashkenazim, 218
Autism, 28, 40, 53, 222, 235, 243
Aztec, 215

Bali, 219
Basuto, 213
Bengali, 208, 213
Biological physical information, 12–14, 153, 196–7, 199–200
Body movements 17, 19, 30, 41–4, 55, 65–6, 93–4, 99, 225–45, 384, 388 *see also* Gesture
Body orientation, 11, 13, 19, 25–30, 54, 66, 205, 225–45, 289, 99
Body semantics, 67 *see also* Posture
'Bookending', 238
Bororo, 220
Bushman, 216

Cheyenne, 215
Chindi, 268
Chinese, 213, 215–19, 252, 319, 321, 327, 335
Chukchee, 214
Cognitive information, 11, 13, 101 *see also* Referential meaning
Comanche, 215
'Complementarity', 240
Copper Eskimo, 210

Dakota, 69
Depression, 32, 53, 220, 222, 235
Distance, 25–7, 30, 247–71, 274–88, 292, 294–9, 301–15 *see also* Proximity
Djuka, 214
Dobuan, 210
Dutch, 276
Dyaks, 208
Dynamic features, 25, 30–44, 54

Effector processes, 22
Egyptian, 116
Elaborated code, 35
Embarrassment, 46–8, 213, 321, 324, 333, 344, 356–9, 361
Emotive meaning, 18, 69, 149 *see also* Affective information
Equilibrium, 24–5, 39, 228, 301, 304–6, 312–15, 341, 346
Eskimo, 214

Evil eye, 39
Exhibitionism, 47
Extralinguistic features, 12–14, 17, 153
Eye-contact, 11, 13–14, 25–7, 30, 37–44, 48, 55, 67, 205, 260, 281, 287, 289, 291, 294, 298–9, 301–15, 317 *see also* Gaze, Vision

'Face', 317, 319–46
Facial expression, 11–14, 19, 30, 39, 41–4, 53, 55, 67, 69, 84, 213–14, 286, 302
Fear, 68, 179
Feedback, 20, 48–50, 54, 277, 301, 314, 357, 366, 371
Fijians, 213
Focused interaction, 19, 25, 29, 360–62
Formality, 36
French, 77, 103, 104, 107, 110, 111, 113, 114, 115, 116, 117, 119, 120, 121, 124, 126, 249, 275–6
Friendly Islanders, 213

Games theory, 24
Gaze, 19, 37–44, 53, 260–61, 269, 302–3, 307–9, 312–13 *see also* Eye-contact, Vision
German, 103, 104, 107, 111, 113, 114, 117, 119, 126, 139, 276
Gesture, 11–13, 20, 46, 66–7, 73–5, 84, 93, 205, 207–22, 229, 286, 317, 339, 360, 366, 387, 397 *see also* Body movements
Greek, 116, 250–61, 276–7
Gujerati, 116, 117

Hununóo, 136
Hebrew, 116
Hesitancy, 21, 34, 40 *see also* Hesitation, Speech continuity
Hesitation, 36–7, 42, 302
Hindi, 116, 117, 219
Hottentot, 216
Hypomania, 235
Hysteria, 45, 52–3, 220, 235

Idiokinesic system, 94
Indexical information, 11–14, 17, 74, 101, 153, 189, 191, 196–202, 205, 317
Insecurity, 45
Intelligence, 24, 174
Interaction management, 12–14, 67, 205, 225–45, 301–15, 317, 374–405 *see also* Temporal structure of interaction
Interjections, 67, 69
Intimacy, 23, 27, 39, 101, 107, 132–44, 251, 264, 266, 283–5, 295, 297, 304–5, 307, 312–13, 378
Intonation, 12, 14, 31, 69, 76–8, 86, 89–90, 156, 174, 182, 220, 231, 248, 384, 400
Involvement, 20, 251, 281, 317, 347–63
Italian, 77, 103, 104, 105, 106, 107, 110, 111, 113, 114, 116, 117, 119, 124

Japanese, 36, 77, 92, 138, 210, 213–15, 217, 267, 279

Kachins, 218
Kaingang, 69
Kayan, 211
Kinemorphic, 93–5
Kines, 93–5
Kinesics, 17, 42–3, 66, 85, 88, 93–8, 230, 232, 236–7, 252, 254
Kinic, 94
Kiowa, 209, 212
Kissing, 211, 213–14, 216, 221
Korean, 215
Kru, 216
Kurds, 211

Larynx, 73–4, 190–93, 196, 199
Linguistic style, 30–31, 79–90, 87, 94, 266, 285
Latin, 105, 116, 119, 217
Loudness, 30, 35–6, 43, 156, 175, 192, 195, 253, 263–5, 270–71 *see also* Voice intensity, Voice level

Malayan, 214
Manchu, 214
Mania, 53, 220, 222, 235
Maori, 208, 213
Masai, 213
Maya, 213, 215
Medical state, 97, 196–7
Melanesian, 150, 210
Menomini, 214
Mental illness, 17, 48, 50, 52–5, 220
'Metacommunication', 341
Metalinguistic, 66
Microkinesic, 93
Middle English, 105
Moslem, 208
Motion qualifiers, 94–5

Navaho, 216, 260–61, 268
Neurosis, 34, 177, 222
Non-verbal features, 12–13, 64–5, 153, 172–3, 176, 178, 181–2, 229, 319, 360
Non-vocal features, 12–13, 205, 207–22, 225–45, 247–71, 274–88, 289–99, 301–15, 317

Old French, 105
Olfaction, 26, 30, 251, 253–4, 263–4, 268, 270–71, 278–9, 282, 284, 288, 299

Palaungs, 218
Papuan, 210
'Paracommunication', 287
Parakinesic, 93–7
Paralanguage, 13, 64–9, 85, 90, 182, 254
Paralinguistic features, 12–14, 17–18, 64–9, 89, 95, 182, 205, 287, 303
Paranoia, 45, 53–4, 220, 222, 235
Pawnee, 215
Personality, 71–81, 85–8, 90, 93–5, 97, 155–71, 173, 175–8, 184, 198–201, 237, 252
Phases of interaction, 14, 101, 227, 330
Phatic communion, 101, 151–2

Phonation type, 191–3 *see also* Register
Phonetic symbolisn, 79
Physical contact, 11, 13, 26, 29–30, 249–51, 253, 256–9, 269–71, 277–8, 282, 285, 287–8, 299
Pitch height, 91–2
Pitch range, 76, 156, 175, 177–8, 180, 190–92, 195 *see also* Tessitura
Plains Indian, 215, 217–18
'Points' 31, 41, 230–33, 244
Polynesian, 210, 214, 219
Portuguese, 105
'Positions', 31, 41, 230, 232, 234, 245
Posture, 11–14, 19, 25–7, 29–31, 41–3, 53–4, 65–7, 69, 205, 220, 225–45, 253–5, 270–71, 317, 322
Power-semantic, 105–7, 109, 114, 124
'Presentation', 31, 230, 234
Proxemic, 67, 247–71, 274–88
Proximity, 11, 13, 19, 27, 39, 67, 205, 239, 243, 247–71, 274–88, 304, 307, 313, 315 *see also* Distance
Psycholinguistics, 88, 94
Psychological information, 12–14, 71–81, 101, 153, 196–201, 205
Psychopathy, 52, 54
Psychosis, 236

Referential meaning, 18, 68–9, 78, 90, 93, 149, 152, 178, 383 *see also* Cognitive information
Register, 68 *see also* Phonation type
Restricted code, 35
Role, 12–13, 23, 29, 35, 45, 49, 97, 330, 334, 358, 360
Russians, 218, 279

Scalogram Analysis, 121
Schizophrenia, 34, 52–4, 177, 220, 243, 299, 309
Schlosberg's Oval, 43
Self-consciousness, 47, 251, 351–3, 361
Self-image, 19, 45–6, 319, 322, 341